# Oxford
# Crossword
# Dictionary

*Edited by*
Catherine Soanes

**OXFORD**
UNIVERSITY PRESS

# OXFORD
## UNIVERSITY PRESS

Great Clarendon Street, Oxford OX2 6DP

Oxford University Press is a department of the University of Oxford.
It furthers the University's objective of excellence in research, scholarship,
and education by publishing worldwide in

Oxford  New York

Auckland  Cape Town  Dar es Salaam  Hong Kong  Karachi
Kuala Lumpur  Madrid  Melbourne  Mexico City  Nairobi
New Delhi  Shanghai  Taipei  Toronto

With offices in

Argentina  Austria  Brazil  Chile  Czech Republic  France  Greece
Guatemala  Hungary  Italy  Japan  Poland  Portugal  Singapore
South Korea  Switzerland  Thailand  Turkey  Ukraine  Vietnam

Oxford is a registered trade mark of Oxford University Press
in the UK and in certain other countries

© Oxford University Press 2006

Database right Oxford University Press (maker)

British Library Cataloguing in Publication Data

Data available

Library of Congress Cataloging in Publication Data

Data available

Designed by George Hammond
Typeset by Alliance Interactive Technology
Printed in Great Britain by Clays Ltd.
Bungay, Suffolk

ISBN 0–19–280711–0   978–0–19–280711–3

1

# Contents

Foreword . . . . . . . . . . . . . . . . . . . . . .v

## SINGLE WORDS

Two letters . . . . . . . . . . . . . . . . . . . 1

Three letters . . . . . . . . . . . . . . . . . . 1

Four letters . . . . . . . . . . . . . . . . . . . 4

Five letters . . . . . . . . . . . . . . . . . . 13

Six letters . . . . . . . . . . . . . . . . . . . 28

Seven letters. . . . . . . . . . . . . . . . . 52

Eight letters. . . . . . . . . . . . . . . . . . 79

Nine letters . . . . . . . . . . . . . . . . . 111

Ten letters . . . . . . . . . . . . . . . . . . 140

Eleven letters . . . . . . . . . . . . . . . 163

Twelve letters . . . . . . . . . . . . . . . 183

Thirteen letters . . . . . . . . . . . . . . 197

## MULTIPLE WORDS

Two words. . . . . . . . . . . . . . . . . . 207

Three words . . . . . . . . . . . . . . . . . 285

Four words . . . . . . . . . . . . . . . . . . 319

Five words. . . . . . . . . . . . . . . . . . 338

Six words . . . . . . . . . . . . . . . . . . . 344

# Foreword

This brand-new edition of the *Oxford Crossword Dictionary* is aimed specifically at the millions of people who do quick crosswords for fun and who, from time to time, find themselves stuck, for example, for a eight-letter word beginning with 'a', fifth letter 'g'. With the dictionary to hand, it only takes a second to discover that the answer is almost certainly *almighty*.

The dictionary draws on the unique and vast language databases that are used to compile all Oxford's English dictionaries. This data has been edited down to the 64,000 entries in the *Oxford Crossword Dictionary* by keeping the words to the vocabulary of current everyday English, which is what you will find in the majority of quick crosswords in newspapers and puzzle magazines. As well as single words, this includes a huge selection of commonly used phrases, sayings, and proverbs, such as *as mad as a hatter* and *home is where the heart is*.

Technical terms and specialist jargon are also found here, but they are limited to words and phrases familiar to non-specialists, such as *neutron*, *download*, and *thyroid*. In the same way, a selection of well-known literary, historical, and old-fashioned terms have been included, such as *ague*, *kirtle*, and *coxcomb*, which remain crossword setters' favourites, even if they have long since passed out of everyday speech. You will also find an extensive selection of the names of famous people, places (such as cities, countries, rivers, and mountains), and historical events, and even personal names such as *Sophie* and *David*. Again the selection has been made with the needs of the typical crossword solver in mind.

In addition to the standard form of a word, the *Oxford Crossword Dictionary* gives accepted British alternative spellings (*guerrilla* as well as *guerilla*; *recognize* and *recognise*), plurals where they are irregular (for example, *bacteria*, *knives*), and irregular forms of verbs (*gave* as well as *give*).

For ease of use, this material has been arranged into two main sections. The first part is made up of single words (up to 13 letters long), divided by the number of letters and then arranged alphabetically. The second consists of phrases (from two to six words long, and up to 26 letters in all), organized first by the number of words in the phrase and next by the length of its first word, then alphabetically.

This dictionary is intended as a companion volume to the *Oxford Puzzle Solver*, which provides lists of words arranged by subject category. Together they make an invaluable tool in helping you with every kind of word puzzle.

Hugh Stephenson
Crossword Editor
*The Guardian*

# Single words

## 2 LETTERS

| | | | | | | | |
|---|---|---|---|---|---|---|---|
| aa | ba | 'em | if | me | oi | pi | up |
| ab | be | er | I'm | mi | OK | Po | Ur |
| ad | bi | ex | in | mo | om | qi | us |
| ah | bo | fa | Io | Mr | on | Ra | U2 |
| Al | by | Fo | is | Ms | oo | re | Vi |
| am | Di | go | it | mu | op | St | we |
| an | DJ | ha | Jo | my | or | so | ye |
| as | do | he | ka | né | ow | ta | yo |
| at | Dr | hi | ki | no | ox | te | |
| aw | Ed | ho | la | Ob | oy | to | |
| ax | ee | id | lo | of | Oz | uh | |
| ay | eh | I'd | ma | oh | pa | um | |

## 3 LETTERS

### A

| | | | |
|---|---|---|---|
| Abe | ail | Ann | ask |
| Abo | aim | ant | asp |
| ace | air | any | ass |
| act | aka | ape | ate |
| Ada | alb | apt | auk |
| add | ale | arc | Ava |
| ado | Alf | are | awe |
| aft | Ali | ark | awl |
| age | all | arm | awn |
| ago | alp | Arp | axe |
| aid | amp | art | aye |
| | Amy | Asa | Ayr |
| | and | ash | |

### B

| | | |
|---|---|---|
| | bed | bob | bum |
| | bee | bod | bun |
| baa | beg | bog | bur |
| bad | ben | boo | bus |
| bag | bet | bop | but |
| bah | bey | bot | buy |
| ban | bib | bow | bye |
| bap | bid | box | |
| bar | big | boy | |
| bat | bin | Boz | |
| Bax | bit | bra | |
| bay | biz | bud | |
| Bea | boa | bug | |

### C

| |
|---|
| cab |
| cad |
| cal |

cam
can
cap
car
cat
caw
cep
chi
cob
cod
Coe
cog
col
con
coo
cop
cos
cot
cow
cox
coy
coz
cry
cub
cud
cue
cum
cup
cur
cut
cwm

**D**

dab
dad
Dai
dam
dan
day
deb
Dee
Del
den
Des

dew
die
dig
dim
din
dip
dis
doc
doe
dog
doh
don
dot
dry
dub
dud
due
dug
dun
duo
dye

**E**

ear
eat
ebb
Eco
Edo
eel
e'er
egg
ego
Eid
eke
elf
Eli
elk
ell
elm
Ely
emu
end
Eos
era

ere
erg
Ern
err
Esq.
etc.
Eva
eve
ewe
eye

**F**

fab
fad
fag
fah
fan
far
fat
fax
Fay
Fed
fee
fen
Fès
few
fey
fez
fib
fie
fig
fin
fir
fit
fix
Flo
flu
fly
fob
foe
fog
fop
for
fox

fry
fug
fun
fur

**G**

gab
gad
gag
gal
gap
gas
gay
gee
gel
gem
gen
get
Gib
gig
gin
gip
git
gnu
Goa
gob
God
goo
got
gum
gun
Gus
gut
guv
guy
gym
gyp

**H**

hag
hah
haj
Hal

ham
Han
hap
hat
haw
hay
he'd
hem
hen
her
he's
hew
hex
hey
hie
him
hip
his
hit
hob
hod
hoe
hog
hon
hop
hot
how
hoy
hub
hue
hug
huh
hum
Hun
hut
Huw

**I**

Ian
ice
icy
Ida
ide
Ike

ilk
I'll
imp
ink
inn
ion
Ira
ire
irk
ism
it'd
its
I've
ivy

**J**

jab
jag
Jah
jam
Jan
jar
jaw
jay
Jed
Jem
Jen
jet
Jew
jib
jig
Jim
job
Joe
jog
Jon
jot
joy
jug
jus
jut

**K**

Kay
keg
ken
key
kid
kif
Kim
kin
kip
kit
koi
Kos
Kum
Kyd

**L**

lab
lac
lad
lag
lah
lam
lap
lat
law
lax
lay
lbw
lea
lee
leg
lei
Len
Leo
Les
let
leu
lev
Lew
Lex
ley
lib

lid
lie
lig
Lil
lip
lit
Liz
lob
log
loo
lop
lot
Lou
low
lox
lug
lux
lye
Lyn

**M**

mac
mad
Mae
man
map
mar
mat
maw
max
may
Med
Meg
Mel
men
met
mew
Mia
mic
mid
mil
Mir
mix
moa

| | | | | | | | |
|---|---|---|---|---|---|---|---|
| mob | Nye | pax | Qum | run | sol | tin | Vic |
| mod | Nyx | pay | | rut | son | tip | vid |
| mol | | pea | **R** | rye | sop | tit | vie |
| mom | **O** | pec | | | sot | tod | vim |
| moo | | pee | Rab | **S** | sou | toe | Vin |
| mop | oaf | peg | rad | | sow | tog | Viv |
| mow | oak | Pei | Rae | sac | soy | tom | viz. |
| Mrs | oar | pen | rag | sad | spa | ton | vow |
| mud | oat | pep | rai | sae | spy | too | |
| mug | obi | per | Raj | sag | Stu | top | **W** |
| mum | och | pet | ram | Sal | sty | tor | |
| | odd | pew | ran | Sam | sub | tot | wad |
| **N** | ode | pia | rap | San | sue | tow | wag |
| | o'er | pic | rat | sap | sum | toy | wan |
| nab | off | pie | raw | sat | sun | try | war |
| nag | oft | pig | ray | saw | sup | tub | was |
| Nam | ohm | pin | red | sax | Syd | tug | wat |
| nan | oik | pip | ref | say | | tum | wax |
| nap | oil | pit | Reg | sea | **T** | tun | way |
| Nat | old | pix | rem | Seb | | tup | web |
| nay | olé | plc | rep | sec | tab | tux | wed |
| neb | one | ply | rev | see | tad | two | wee |
| ned | Ono | pod | Rex | seq. | tag | | wen |
| née | opt | Poe | ria | set | tam | **U** | wet |
| net | orb | Pom | rib | sew | tan | | who |
| new | ore | poo | rid | sex | tap | ugh | why |
| Ney | our | pop | rig | she | tar | Ulm | wig |
| nib | out | pot | Rik | shy | tat | Una | win |
| Nik | ova | pox | rim | sib | tax | uni | wit |
| nil | owe | pro | Rio | sic | Tay | urn | wiz |
| Nin | owl | pry | rip | Sid | tea | use | woe |
| nip | own | pub | rob | sin | tec | Uzi | wok |
| nit | owt | pug | rod | sip | Ted | | won |
| nix | | pun | roe | sir | tee | **V** | woo |
| nob | **P** | pup | Ron | sis | Tel | | wot |
| nod | | pus | roo | sit | ten | vac | wow |
| Noh | pad | put | Ros | six | Tex | Val | wry |
| nor | pal | Pym | rot | ska | the | van | Wye |
| not | Pam | pyx | row | ski | tho | vas | |
| now | pan | | Roy | sky | thy | vat | **Y** |
| nth | pap | **Q** | rub | sly | tic | veg | |
| nub | par | | rue | sob | tie | vet | yak |
| nun | pat | Qom | rug | sod | tig | vex | yam |
| nut | paw | qua | rum | soh | Tim | via | yap |

| | | | | | |
|---|---|---|---|---|---|
| yaw | yew | **Z** | zip | | |
| yea | yin | | zit | | |
| yeh | yob | Zak | Zoë | | |
| yen | yon | zap | zoo | | |
| yes | you | Zen | | | |
| yet | yuk | | | | |

# 4 LETTERS

| **A** | airy | Amoy | arum | back | baud | bias |
|---|---|---|---|---|---|---|
| | ajar | Amun | asap | bade | bawl | bide |
| Abba | Ajax | Amur | Ashe | Baez | bead | bier |
| abbé | akee | anal | ashy | baht | beak | biff |
| Abby | akin | Andy | Asia | bail | beam | bike |
| abed | Alan | anew | Aten | bait | bean | Biko |
| Abel | alas | ankh | atom | bake | bear | bile |
| abet | Albi | Anna | Aton | Baku | beat | bilk |
| able | Alec | Anne | atop | bald | beau | Bill |
| ably | Aled | anon | aunt | bale | beck | bind |
| abut | Alex | ante | aura | Bali | Bede | Bing |
| acer | alga | anti | auto | balk | Beeb | bird |
| ache | Algy | anus | aver | ball | beef | biro |
| achy | Alix | Anya | avid | balm | been | birr |
| acid | ally | apex | Avon | band | beep | bite |
| acme | Alma | Apia | avow | bane | beer | blab |
| acne | alms | apse | away | bang | beet | blag |
| acre | aloe | Arab | awry | bani | Behn | blew |
| Adam | Alps | arak | axel | bank | bell | blin |
| Aden | also | Aral | axil | barb | belt | blip |
| adit | alto | Aran | axis | bard | bend | blob |
| adze | alum | arch | axle | bare | Benn | bloc |
| aeon | Alun | area | axon | barf | bent | blog |
| afar | amah | areg | Axum | Bari | Benz | blot |
| Afro | Amal | Ares | ayah | bark | Berg | blow |
| agar | amen | argh | Ayer | barm | berk | blub |
| aged | amid | Argo | | barn | berm | blue |
| agog | Amin | aria | **B** | Bart | Bern | Blum |
| Agra | amir | arid | | base | Bert | blur |
| ague | Amis | arms | Baal | bash | Bess | boar |
| ahoy | ammo | army | babe | bask | best | Boas |
| aide | amok | Arne | Babs | bass | beta | boat |
| Aids | Amon | Arno | baby | bate | Beth | bode |
| ain't | Amos | arty | Bach | bath | bevy | body |

| | | | | | | |
|---|---|---|---|---|---|---|
| Boer | Brie | Cain | chew | coir | crow | dash |
| boff | brig | cake | chez | coke | crud | data |
| bogy | brim | calf | chic | cola | crux | date |
| boho | brio | call | chin | cold | Cuba | daub |
| Bohr | Brit | calm | chip | cole | cube | Dave |
| boil | Brno | came | chit | Coll | cuff | Davy |
| bold | Bros | camp | chop | Colm | cull | dawn |
| bole | brow | Cana | chow | colt | cult | daze |
| boll | Brum | cane | chub | coma | curb | dead |
| bolt | brut | cant | chug | comb | curd | deaf |
| bomb | Bryn | cape | chum | come | cure | deal |
| bond | bubo | capo | ciao | Como | curl | dean |
| bone | buck | card | cine | cone | curt | dear |
| bonk | budo | care | cite | conk | Cush | debt |
| Bonn | buff | Carl | city | Conn | cusp | deck |
| bony | buhl | carp | clad | cony | cuss | deed |
| boob | bulb | cart | clam | cook | cute | deem |
| book | bulk | Cary | clan | cool | cyan | deep |
| boom | bull | case | clap | coop | cyme | deer |
| boon | bumf | cash | claw | coot | cyst | deft |
| boor | bump | cask | clay | cope | czar | defy |
| boot | bung | Cass | clef | Copt | | deli |
| bore | bunk | cast | Clem | copy | **D** | dell |
| Borg | buoy | Cath | Cleo | Cora | | demo |
| born | burn | Cato | clew | cord | dace | Dena |
| Bose | burp | caul | Clio | core | Dada | dene |
| bosh | burr | cava | clip | cork | Dadd | dent |
| boss | Burt | cave | clod | corm | dado | deny |
| both | bury | cavy | clog | corn | daft | derv |
| bout | bush | Cebu | clop | cosh | Dahl | desk |
| bowl | busk | cede | clot | cost | Dáil | Devi |
| boxy | bust | cedi | cloy | cosy | dais | Dewi |
| Boyd | busy | cell | club | cote | dale | dewy |
| bozo | Bute | Celt | clue | coup | Dali | dhal |
| brad | butt | cent | Cnut | cove | Dame | dhow |
| brae | buzz | Ceri | coal | cowl | damn | dial |
| brag | Byrd | cert | coat | crab | damp | Dias |
| bran | byre | Chad | coax | crag | Dana | dice |
| brat | byte | chap | coca | cram | Dane | Dick |
| braw | | char | cock | craw | Dani | Dido |
| bray | **C** | Chas | coda | cred | dank | diet |
| bred | | chat | code | Cree | dare | dike |
| Brel | Caen | chav | coif | crew | dark | Dili |
| Bret | cafe | chef | coil | crib | darn | dill |
| brew | cage | Cher | coin | crop | dart | dime |

| | | | | | | |
|---|---|---|---|---|---|---|
| Dina | doxy | earl | Eric | faro | flan | Fred |
| dine | doze | earn | Erie | fast | flap | free |
| ding | dozy | Earp | Erik | fate | flat | fret |
| dint | drab | ease | Erin | faun | flaw | Frey |
| Dion | drag | east | Erle | faux | flax | frog |
| Dior | dram | easy | Eros | fawn | flay | from |
| dire | drat | eave | Erse | Faye | flea | fuel |
| dirk | draw | Ebro | Erté | faze | flee | Fuji |
| dirt | dray | echo | Esau | fear | flew | full |
| disc | drew | echt | Esme | feat | flex | fume |
| dish | drey | ecru | espy | feed | flip | fund |
| disk | drip | Edam | etch | feel | flit | funk |
| diss | drop | Edda | Etna | feet | floe | furl |
| diva | drub | eddo | Etta | fell | flog | fury |
| dive | drug | eddy | euro | felt | flop | fuse |
| dock | drum | Eden | Evan | fend | flow | fuss |
| dodo | dual | edge | even | Fens | flue | fuzz |
| doer | duck | edgy | ever | fern | flux | |
| doff | duct | Edie | Evie | feta | foal | |
| doge | dude | edit | evil | fête | foam | **G** |
| Doha | duel | Edna | Ewan | feud | Foch | |
| dojo | duet | Edwy | Ewen | fiat | foci | Gabi |
| dole | duff | eely | ewer | fief | fogy | Gabo |
| doll | Dufy | efit | exam | fife | föhn | Gaby |
| dolt | duke | eggy | exit | Fifi | foil | Gaea |
| dome | dull | Eigg | Eyre | Fiji | fold | Gael |
| done | duly | Eire | Ezra | file | folk | gaff |
| dong | dumb | elan | | fill | fond | gaga |
| don't | dump | Elat | **F** | film | font | gage |
| doom | dune | Elba | | filo | food | Gaia |
| door | dung | Elbe | face | fils | fool | Gail |
| dope | dunk | Ella | fact | find | foot | gain |
| dopy | dupe | Elma | fade | fine | fora | gait |
| Dora | dusk | Elsa | fado | fink | ford | gala |
| Doré | dust | else | faff | Finn | fore | gale |
| dorm | duty | Emil | fail | fino | fork | gall |
| dory | dyad | emir | fain | fire | form | game |
| dose | Dyak | emit | fair | firm | fort | gamy |
| dosh | dyer | Emma | fake | fish | foul | gang |
| doss | dyke | Emmy | fall | fist | four | gaol |
| dote | dyne | Enid | fame | five | fowl | gape |
| Doug | | envy | fang | fizz | foxy | garb |
| dour | **E** | épée | fare | flab | Fran | Gary |
| dove | | epic | farl | flag | Frau | gash |
| down | each | ergo | farm | flak | fray | gasp |
| | | | | | | gate |

| | | | | | | |
|---|---|---|---|---|---|---|
| Gaul | glut | Guam | hash | hoar | hurl | Iowa |
| gave | Glyn | guff | hasp | hoax | hurt | Ipoh |
| gawk | gnat | gulf | hate | hobo | hush | Iran |
| gawp | gnaw | gull | haul | hock | husk | Iraq |
| Gaye | goad | gulp | have | hoer | huss | iris |
| gaze | goal | gunk | hawk | Hogg | Hutu | Irma |
| gear | goat | Gunn | Hawn | hoki | hymn | iron |
| geek | Gobi | gurn | haze | hold | hype | Isis |
| geld | goby | guru | hazy | hole | | Isla |
| gelt | goer | gush | head | Holi | **I** | isle |
| gene | goes | gust | heal | hols | | isn't |
| gent | gold | Gwen | heap | holt | Iain | itch |
| Geri | golf | Gwyn | hear | holy | iamb | item |
| germ | gone | gybe | heat | home | ibex | it'll |
| Getz | gong | gyre | hebe | homy | ibid. | Ivan |
| ghat | good | gyro | heck | hone | ibis | Ives |
| ghee | goof | | heed | honk | iced | Ivor |
| gibe | goon | **H** | heel | hood | icky | |
| Gide | gore | | heft | hoof | icon | **J** |
| gift | gory | hack | heir | hook | idea | |
| gild | gosh | haft | hell | hoop | idem | jack |
| gill | Goth | Hahn | helm | hoot | ides | jade |
| gilt | gout | Haig | help | hope | idle | jail |
| Gina | gown | hail | hemp | Hopi | idly | Jain |
| gird | Goya | hair | Hera | horn | idol | jake |
| girl | Gozo | haji | herb | hose | iffy | jamb |
| girn | grab | hajj | herd | host | Ifor | Jane |
| giro | Graf | haka | here | hour | Igor | jape |
| girt | gram | hake | hero | hove | ikat | Java |
| Gish | gran | hale | Herr | Howe | ikon | jazz |
| gist | gray | half | hers | howl | ilea | Jean |
| Gita | Graz | hall | Hess | hoya | ilex | jeep |
| gîte | Greg | halo | hewn | Huey | ilia | jeer |
| give | grew | Hals | hick | huff | Ilse | Jeff |
| Giza | grey | halt | hide | huge | imam | Jehu |
| glad | grid | hand | high | Hugh | Iman | jell |
| glam | grig | hang | hike | Hugo | impi | Jena |
| glee | grim | hank | hill | hula | Inca | jerk |
| glen | grin | Hans | hilt | hulk | inch | jess |
| glib | grip | hard | hind | hull | Inez | jest |
| glob | Gris | hare | hint | Hume | info | Jesu |
| glow | grit | hark | hire | hump | inky | jeté |
| glue | grog | harm | hiss | hung | into | jiao |
| glug | grow | harp | Hite | hunk | Iona | jibe |
| glum | grub | hart | hive | hunt | iota | jiff |

| | | | | | | |
|---|---|---|---|---|---|---|
| Jill | Kali | Klee | Laos | levy | live | luce |
| jilt | Kama | knee | Lapp | lewd | Livy | luck |
| jink | Kant | knew | Lara | Liam | Liza | Lucy |
| jinn | Kara | knit | lard | liar | load | ludo |
| jinx | Karl | knob | lari | lias | loaf | luff |
| jive | kart | knot | lark | lice | loam | luge |
| Joan | Kate | know | Lars | lick | loan | Luis |
| Jobs | Kath | Knox | lash | lido | lobe | Luke |
| jock | Katy | Knut | lass | lied | loch | lull |
| Jodi | kava | koan | last | lief | loci | Lulu |
| Jody | Kaye | Kobe | late | lien | lock | lump |
| Joel | Kean | kobo | lath | lieu | loco | lung |
| Joey | keck | kohl | lati | life | lode | lunk |
| John | keel | kola | laud | lift | Łódź | lure |
| join | keen | Komi | lava | like | loft | lurk |
| joke | keep | kook | lave | Lila | logo | lush |
| jolt | Keir | kora | lawn | Lili | loin | lust |
| Joni | kelp | kris | laze | lilo | Lois | lute |
| José | Kent | kudu | lazy | lilt | Loki | luxe |
| josh | kepi | kune | lead | lily | Lola | lwei |
| Joss | kept | Kurd | leaf | Lima | loll | Lyly |
| Jove | kerb | Kurt | Leah | limb | Lomé | Lynn |
| jowl | kerf | kyat | leak | lime | Lomu | lynx |
| Juan | Keri | kyle | lean | limn | lone | Lyra |
| Juba | Kern | | leap | limo | long | lyre |
| Jude | khan | **L** | Lear | limp | look | |
| Judi | khat | | Leda | limy | loom | **M** |
| judo | Khoi | lace | leek | Lina | loon | |
| Judy | kick | lack | leer | Lind | loop | ma'am |
| juju | Kidd | lacy | lees | line | loot | Maat |
| July | Kiel | lade | left | ling | lope | mace |
| jump | Kiev | lady | Lego | link | Lora | Mach |
| June | kill | lain | Leix | lino | lord | made |
| Jung | kiln | lair | Lela | lint | lore | magi |
| junk | kilo | lake | Lely | Linz | Lori | Maia |
| Juno | kilt | lakh | Lena | lion | lorn | maid |
| Jura | kind | lama | lend | lipa | lory | mail |
| jury | kine | lamb | lens | lira | lose | maim |
| just | king | lame | lent | lire | loss | main |
| Jute | kink | lamp | León | Lisa | lost | make |
| | kirk | Lana | less | Lise | loth | mako |
| **K** | kiss | land | lest | lisp | loud | male |
| | kite | lane | Leto | list | lour | Mali |
| kail | Kivu | Lang | let's | Lita | lout | mall |
| kale | kiwi | lank | Levi | lite | love | malt |

| | | | | | | |
|---|---|---|---|---|---|---|
| mama | mesa | mode | **N** | nick | oath | Oran |
| mane | mesh | mojo | | niff | oaty | orca |
| Mann | mess | moke | naan | nigh | Oban | orfe |
| Manu | meta | Mold | Naas | Nike | obey | Orff |
| Manx | mete | mole | nada | Nile | oboe | orgy |
| many | Metz | moll | naff | Nina | oche | oryx |
| Mara | mewl | Mona | Nagy | nine | odds | Oslo |
| marc | mews | monk | Naha | Nita | Oder | Otho |
| mare | meze | mono | naif | Niue | Odin | Otis |
| mark | mica | Mons | nail | Noah | Offa | Otto |
| marl | mice | mood | Nama | Noam | ogee | ouch |
| Mars | Mick | Moog | name | nock | ogle | Oudh |
| mart | midi | moon | nana | node | ogre | ours |
| Marx | mien | Moor | nape | Noel | Ohio | Ouse |
| Mary | miff | moot | Nara | noir | oick | oust |
| mash | mike | mope | nark | Nola | oily | ouzo |
| mask | mild | more | nary | Nome | oink | oval |
| mass | mile | Mori | Nash | Nona | okay | oven |
| mast | milk | morn | Nato | none | okra | over |
| mate | mill | mosh | nave | nook | Olaf | Ovid |
| math | milo | moss | navy | noon | Olav | ovum |
| matt | milt | most | Nazi | Nora | olde | Owen |
| Maud | mime | mote | Neal | nori | Olga | oxen |
| Maui | Mimi | moth | neap | norm | Oman | Oxus |
| maul | Mina | moue | near | nose | Omar | oyez |
| maxi | mind | move | neat | nosh | omen | Ozzy |
| Maya | mine | mown | neck | nosy | omit | |
| Mayo | Ming | much | need | note | Omsk | **P** |
| maze | mini | muck | neem | noun | once | |
| mead | mink | muff | neep | nous | only | paan |
| meal | mint | Muir | ne'er | nova | onto | paca |
| mean | minx | mule | Neil | nowt | onus | pace |
| meat | mire | mull | Nell | nude | onyx | pack |
| meek | Miró | muon | neon | nuke | Oona | pact |
| meet | miry | murk | nerd | null | oops | pacy |
| mega | miso | muse | Nero | numb | Oort | page |
| Meir | miss | mush | ness | nuts | ooze | paid |
| meld | mist | musk | nest | Nuuk | oozy | pail |
| melt | mite | muso | nett | | opal | pain |
| memo | mitt | muss | Neva | **O** | Opel | pair |
| mend | Moab | must | névé | | open | pale |
| menu | moan | mute | news | Oahu | Opie | pall |
| meow | moat | mutt | newt | Oaks | oppo | palm |
| mere | mobe | Myra | next | oaky | opus | palp |
| Merv | mock | myth | nice | oast | oral | pane |

**SINGLE WORD**

| | | | | | | |
|---|---|---|---|---|---|---|
| pang | Phil | polo | pulp | rand | Riga | rota |
| pant | phiz | poly | puma | rang | rile | rote |
| papa | phut | pomp | pump | rank | rill | Roth |
| para | Piaf | pond | Pune | rant | rime | roti |
| pare | pica | pong | punk | rape | rimu | roué |
| park | pick | pons | punt | rapt | rimy | rout |
| parr | Pict | pony | puny | rare | Rina | roux |
| part | pied | pooh | pupa | rash | rind | rove |
| pass | pier | pool | pure | rasp | ring | Roxy |
| past | pike | poop | puri | rate | rink | rube |
| pate | pile | poor | purl | rave | riot | ruby |
| path | pill | pope | purr | raze | ripe | ruck |
| paua | pimp | pore | push | razz | rise | rudd |
| Paul | pine | pork | puss | read | risk | rude |
| pave | ping | porn | putt | real | Rita | Rudi |
| pawl | pink | port | pyre | ream | rite | Rudy |
| pawn | pint | pose | | reap | rive | ruff |
| peak | pion | posh | **Q** | rear | road | Ruhr |
| peal | pipe | post | | reck | roam | ruin |
| pear | Pisa | posy | Qing | redo | roan | rule |
| peat | pith | pour | quad | reed | roar | rump |
| peck | Pitt | pout | quay | reef | robe | rune |
| peek | pity | poxy | quid | reek | rock | rung |
| peel | pixy | pram | quin | reel | rode | runt |
| peen | plan | prat | quip | rein | Roeg | ruse |
| peep | play | pray | quit | rely | roil | rush |
| peer | plea | prep | quiz | Rena | role | rusk |
| Pegu | pleb | prey | | rend | Rolf | Russ |
| pein | plié | prig | **R** | René | roll | rust |
| Pelé | plod | prim | | Reno | Roly | Ruth |
| pelf | plop | prod | race | rent | Rome | Ryan |
| pelt | plot | prom | rack | repp | romp | |
| Penn | ploy | prop | racy | rest | Rona | **S** |
| peon | plug | prow | Rafe | rhea | rood | |
| père | plum | Prue | raft | Rhum | roof | Saar |
| perk | plus | Ptah | raga | Rhys | rook | Saba |
| perm | pock | pube | rage | rial | room | sack |
| pert | poem | puce | raid | rice | root | Sade |
| Peru | poet | puck | rail | rich | rope | safe |
| perv | pogo | puff | rain | rick | ropy | saga |
| peso | poke | puja | raja | ride | Rory | sage |
| pest | poky | puke | rake | riel | Rosa | sago |
| Peta | pole | pula | raki | rife | rose | said |
| Pete | Polk | pule | Rama | riff | Ross | sail |
| phew | poll | pull | ramp | rift | rosy | sake |

| | | | | | | |
|---|---|---|---|---|---|---|
| Saki | semi | Sind | smut | spry | swab | taut |
| sale | send | sine | snag | spud | swag | taxi |
| Salk | sent | sing | snap | spue | swam | teak |
| salt | seqq. | sink | snip | spun | swan | teal |
| same | sera | Sion | snob | spur | swap | team |
| Sami | Serb | sire | snog | stab | swat | tear |
| sand | sere | Sita | snow | stag | sway | teat |
| sane | serf | site | snub | Stan | swig | tech |
| sang | Seth | Siva | snug | star | swim | teem |
| sank | sett | size | soak | stat | swop | teen |
| sans | sewn | skep | soap | stay | swot | Tees |
| Sara | sexy | skew | soar | stem | swum | tell |
| sari | shad | skid | soca | step | sync | temp |
| Sark | shag | skim | sock | stet | | tend |
| sash | shah | skin | soda | stew | **T** | tent |
| sate | sham | skip | sofa | stir | | term |
| sati | Shaw | skit | soft | stoa | tack | tern |
| Saul | Shaz | skua | soil | stop | taco | Tess |
| save | shed | Skye | sole | stow | tact | test |
| sawn | Shem | slab | soli | stub | Taft | text |
| scab | she's | slag | solo | stud | Ta'if | Thai |
| scad | shew | slam | soma | stun | tail | than |
| scam | Shia | slap | some | stye | taka | Thar |
| scan | shim | slat | song | Styx | take | that |
| scar | shin | Slav | soon | such | talc | thaw |
| scat | ship | slaw | soot | suck | tale | Thea |
| Scot | shoe | slay | sore | suds | tali | thee |
| scry | shoo | sled | sort | suet | talk | them |
| scud | shop | slew | souk | Suez | tall | then |
| scum | shot | slim | soul | Sufi | tame | Theo |
| scut | show | slip | soup | suit | tamp | thew |
| seal | shun | slit | sour | sulk | Tana | they |
| seam | shut | slob | sown | Sulu | tang | thin |
| Sean | Siam | sloe | spam | sumo | tank | this |
| sear | sick | slog | span | sump | tapa | Thom |
| seat | side | slop | spar | sung | tape | Thor |
| sect | sift | slot | spat | sunk | Tara | thou |
| seed | sigh | slow | spay | surd | tare | thru |
| seek | sign | slub | spec | sure | tarn | thud |
| seem | sika | slug | spew | surf | taro | thug |
| seen | Sikh | slum | Spey | Susa | tart | thus |
| seep | silk | slur | spin | suss | tash | tick |
| seer | sill | slut | spit | Susy | task | tide |
| self | silo | smog | spiv | Suva | Tate | tidy |
| sell | silt | smug | spot | Suzy | Tati | tied |

| | | | | | | |
|---|---|---|---|---|---|---|
| tier | tote | tyke | veil | wale | whey | woof |
| tiff | tour | Tyne | vein | walk | Whig | wool |
| tike | tout | type | veld | wall | whim | word |
| tile | town | typo | vend | Walt | whin | wore |
| till | trad | tyre | vent | wand | whip | work |
| tilt | tram | tyro | Vera | wane | whir | worm |
| time | trap | tzar | verb | want | whit | worn |
| Tina | tray | | Vere | ward | whiz | wort |
| tine | tree | **U** | vert | ware | whoa | wove |
| ting | trek | | very | warm | who'd | wrap |
| tint | Trev | udon | vest | warn | whom | wren |
| tiny | trim | ugly | veto | warp | whop | writ |
| tipi | trio | Uist | vial | wart | who's | wuss |
| tire | trip | ulna | vibe | wary | whup | Wynn |
| Tito | Trix | umma | vice | wash | wick | |
| tizz | trot | umph | Vick | wasp | wide | **X** |
| toad | trow | undo | Vico | watt | wife | |
| Toby | troy | unit | vide | wave | wild | Xian |
| Todd | true | Unix | view | wavy | wile | Xmas |
| toff | trug | unto | Vigo | waxy | Wilf | |
| tofu | tsar | upon | Vila | weak | will | **Y** |
| toga | tuba | Urdu | vile | weal | wilt | |
| Togo | tube | urea | vine | wean | wily | yack |
| toil | tuck | Urey | vino | wear | wimp | Yale |
| Tojo | tufa | urge | viol | Webb | wind | Yama |
| toke | tuff | Uruk | visa | weed | wine | yang |
| toll | tuft | used | Vita | week | wing | Yank |
| tomb | Tula | user | viva | weep | wink | yard |
| tome | Tull | Utah | void | weft | wino | yarn |
| tone | tump | | vole | Weil | wipe | yawl |
| tong | tuna | **V** | volt | weir | wire | yawn |
| Toni | tune | | vote | weld | wiry | yawp |
| Tony | Tupi | Vaal | | well | wise | yaws |
| took | turf | vain | **W** | welt | wish | yeah |
| tool | Turk | vale | | wend | wisp | year |
| toot | turn | vamp | Waal | went | wist | yell |
| tope | tush | vane | wade | wept | with | yelp |
| torc | tusk | vary | wadi | were | woad | yeti |
| tore | tutu | vasa | waft | west | woke | yoga |
| tori | Tuva | vase | wage | we've | wold | yogi |
| torn | twee | vast | waif | wham | wolf | yoke |
| tort | twig | veal | wail | whap | womb | yolk |
| Tory | twin | Veda | wain | what | wonk | yomp |
| tosh | twit | veer | wait | when | wont | yoni |
| toss | twoc | Vega | wake | whet | wood | yore |

| York  | yuck | **Z** | Zara | Zeno | zing | zonk |
|-------|------|-------|------|------|------|------|
| you'd | Yule |       | zeal | zero | Zion | zoom |
| your  | yurt | Zack  | zebu | zest | Zita | Zora |
| yowl  | Yves | Zane  | Zeke | Zeus | Zola | zouk |
| yuan  |      | zany  | Zena | zinc | zone | Zulu |

# **5 LETTERS**

| **A**  | acute | aggro | alert | amass | anion | Arden  |
|--------|-------|-------|-------|-------|-------|--------|
|        | adage | agile | Alexa | Amati | anise | areal  |
| Aalto  | Adair | aglet | Alfie | amaze | Anita | arena  |
| Aaron  | Adams | aglow | algae | amber | Anjou | aren't |
| aback  | adapt | Agnes | algal | ambit | ankle | arête  |
| abaft  | adder | agony | Algie | amble | annal | argon  |
| abase  | addle | agora | alias | Ambon | Annan | argos  |
| abash  | Adela | agree | alibi | amend | annex | argot  |
| abate  | Adele | ahead | Alice | amice | Annie | argue  |
| Abbas  | adept | Ahern | Alick | amide | annoy | Arian  |
| abbey  | adieu | Ahmad | alien | amigo | annul | Ariel  |
| Abbie  | adios | Ahmed | align | amine | anode | Aries  |
| abbot  | Adler | Aidan | alike | Amish | Anona | arise  |
| Abduh  | admin | Ailsa | Alina | amiss | Anton | Arles  |
| Abdul  | admit | Aimee | Aline | amity | anvil | Arlon  |
| abeam  | admix | aioli | alive | Amman | Anwar | armed  |
| abhor  | adobe | airer | alkyl | Ammon | Anzac | Arnie  |
| abide  | Adolf | Aisha | Allah | amnia | Anzus | aroha  |
| Abner  | adopt | aisle | Allan | among | aorta | aroma  |
| abode  | adore | aitch | allay | amour | Aosta | arose  |
| abort  | adorn | Ajman | Allen | ample | apace | Arran  |
| about  | adult | Akbar | alley | amply | apart | arras  |
| above  | aegis | Akkad | Allie | amuck | aphid | array  |
| Abram  | Aesop | Aksum | allot | amuse | Aphra | arrow  |
| Abuja  | affix | Alain | allow | Anaïs | appal | arson  |
| abuse  | afoot | Alamo | alloy | Andie | apple | Artie  |
| abyss  | afore | Alana | aloft | Andre | apply | artsy  |
| Accra  | afoul | alarm | alone | angel | April | Aruba  |
| achey  | after | Alban | along | anger | apron | Aryan  |
| acidy  | again | Albee | aloof | Angie | aptly | asana  |
| ackee  | agape | album | aloud | angle | Aqaba | Ascot  |
| acorn  | agate | Alden | alpha | angry | Araby | asdic  |
| acrid  | agave | alder | altar | angst | arbor | ashen  |
| Acton  | agent | Aldis | alter | Angus | Arbus | Asher  |
| actor  | Aggie | Aldus | Alvin | anime | Archy | Asian  |

| | | | | | | |
|---|---|---|---|---|---|---|
| aside | awoke | Basel | Belau | bidet | blind | booth |
| askew | axial | basic | belay | bifid | bling | booty |
| Askey | axiom | Basie | belch | bight | blini | booze |
| Asoka | Aztec | basil | Belém | bigot | blink | boozy |
| aspen | azure | basin | belie | Bihar | bliny | borax |
| aspic | | basis | Bella | bijou | bliss | bored |
| Assad | **B** | Basle | belle | biker | blitz | borer |
| Assam | | Basra | belly | bilge | bloat | boric |
| assay | babel | bassi | below | billy | Bloch | Boris |
| asset | Babur | basso | bench | bimbo | block | borne |
| aster | baccy | baste | bendy | bindi | bloke | boron |
| astir | bacon | batch | Benes | binge | blond | Bosch |
| Astor | baddy | bated | Benin | bingo | blood | bosky |
| Astra | Baden | Bates | Benji | biome | bloom | bosom |
| Aswan | Bader | bathe | Benny | biota | blown | bossy |
| atlas | badge | batik | beret | biped | blowy | bosun |
| atoll | badly | baton | Beria | birch | blues | botch |
| atone | bagel | batty | Berio | birth | bluey | Botha |
| atria | baggy | baulk | Berne | bison | bluff | bothy |
| attar | Baha'i | bawdy | Berny | bitch | blunt | Botox |
| Attic | Baird | bayou | Berra | biter | blurb | botty |
| Auden | bairn | beach | berry | bitty | blurt | bough |
| audit | baize | beady | Berta | bivvy | blush | boule |
| Audra | baker | beaky | berth | Bizet | board | Boult |
| auger | Bakst | beano | beryl | Bjorn | boast | bound |
| aught | baler | beard | beset | black | bobby | bourn |
| augur | bally | beast | besom | blade | bodge | bowel |
| aunty | balmy | beaux | Bessy | Blair | bogey | Bowen |
| aurae | balsa | bebop | betel | Blake | boggy | bower |
| aural | balti | Becky | Betsy | blame | bogie | Bowie |
| aurar | banal | beech | Bette | blanc | bogus | bowls |
| Auric | Banda | beefy | Betti | bland | Boise | boxer |
| avail | bandy | beery | Betty | blank | bolas | boyar |
| avast | banjo | befit | Beuys | blare | bolus | Boyce |
| avert | Banks | began | Bevan | blasé | bombe | Boyer |
| avian | banns | begat | bevel | blast | bonce | Boyle |
| avoid | Bantu | beget | Bevin | blaze | Bondi | brace |
| Avril | barge | begin | Bevis | bleak | bongo | bract |
| await | barmy | begot | bevvy | bleat | bonny | Braga |
| awake | baron | begum | bezel | bleed | bonus | Bragg |
| award | Barra | begun | bhaji | bleep | booby | Brahe |
| aware | barre | Behan | bhang | blend | Boole | braid |
| awash | Barry | beige | bhuna | bless | boomy | brain |
| Awdry | Barth | being | Bible | Bligh | Boone | brake |
| awful | basal | Bekaa | biddy | blimp | boost | brand |

| | | | | | | |
|---|---|---|---|---|---|---|
| brash | brunt | byway | caper | chain | chock | Clark |
| brass | brush | | Capet | chair | choir | clash |
| Braun | brute | **c** | capon | Chaka | choke | clasp |
| brave | Bryan | | Capra | chalk | choky | class |
| bravo | Bryce | Caaba | Capri | champ | chomp | Claud |
| brawl | buddy | cabal | carat | chant | chook | clean |
| brawn | budge | cabby | cardy | chaos | chops | clear |
| braze | buggy | caber | carer | chaps | chord | cleat |
| bread | bugle | cabin | caret | chard | chore | cleft |
| break | build | cable | Carey | charm | chose | clerk |
| bream | built | Cabot | cargo | charr | Chris | click |
| Breda | bulge | cacao | Carib | chart | chuck | cliff |
| breed | bulgy | cache | Carla | chary | chuff | Clift |
| Brent | bulky | cacti | Carlo | chase | chump | climb |
| Brest | bully | caddy | Carly | chasm | chunk | clime |
| Brett | bumph | cadet | Carné | cheap | churl | Cline |
| breve | bumpy | cadge | carob | cheat | churn | cling |
| Brian | bunce | Cadiz | carol | check | churr | clink |
| briar | bunch | cadre | carpi | cheek | chute | Clint |
| bribe | bunny | caeca | carry | cheep | chyle | Clive |
| brick | burgh | cagey | carve | cheer | chyme | cloak |
| bride | burin | Caine | Caryl | chert | Ciara | clock |
| brief | burka | cairn | Carys | chess | cider | clomp |
| brier | Burke | Cairo | Casey | chest | cigar | clone |
| brill | burly | Cajun | caste | chewy | cilia | clonk |
| brine | Burma | cakey | catch | Chiba | cinch | close |
| bring | Burns | Caleb | cater | chick | Cindy | cloth |
| brink | burnt | Calum | Cathy | chide | circa | cloud |
| briny | burqa | calve | catty | chief | Circe | clout |
| brisk | Burra | calyx | caulk | child | cirri | clove |
| Britt | burro | camel | cause | Chile | cisco | clown |
| broad | burst | cameo | Cavan | chill | cissy | cluck |
| brock | busby | campy | caver | chime | civet | clump |
| broil | bushy | Camus | cavil | chimp | civic | clung |
| broke | busty | canal | cease | china | civil | clunk |
| Bronx | butch | candy | Cecil | chine | civvy | Clwyd |
| brood | butte | caned | cedar | ching | clack | Clyde |
| brook | butty | caner | Celia | chink | clade | coach |
| broom | butyl | canna | cello | chino | claim | coast |
| broth | buxom | canny | Ceram | Chios | Clair | coati |
| brown | buyer | canoe | Ceres | chirp | clamp | cobra |
| Bruce | buzzy | canon | Cerys | chirr | clang | cocci |
| bruit | bwana | canto | Ceuta | chive | clank | cocky |
| brume | Byatt | caped | chafe | chivy | Clara | cocoa |
| Bruno | Byron | Capek | chaff | Chloe | Clare | coder |

| | | | | | | |
|---|---|---|---|---|---|---|
| codex | count | crimp | cyder | debur | Devil | dizzy |
| Cohen | coupe | crisp | Cymru | debut | Devon | djinn |
| coign | court | croak | cynic | Debby | Dewar | dodge |
| coley | coven | Croat | Cyril | decal | Dewey | dodgy |
| colic | cover | Croce | Cyrus | decay | Dhaka | Dodie |
| Colin | covet | croci | Czech | decor | dhobi | doggo |
| colon | covey | crock | | decoy | dhoti | doggy |
| Colum | cower | croft | **D** | decry | Diana | dogma |
| comae | Cowes | Crome | | defer | Diane | doily |
| combe | coyly | crone | Dacca | Defoe | diary | doing |
| combo | coypu | crony | dacha | Degas | dicey | Dolby |
| comet | cozen | crook | daddy | deice | dicky | Dolin |
| comfy | crack | croon | daffy | deify | dicta | dolly |
| comic | craft | cross | daily | deign | didn't | dolma |
| comma | craic | croup | dairy | deism | Diego | domed |
| Comte | Craig | crowd | daisy | deist | Digby | Donal |
| Conan | crake | crown | Dakar | deity | digit | donga |
| conch | cramp | crude | dally | dekko | Dijon | Donna |
| condo | crane | cruel | Damon | delay | Dilys | Donne |
| coney | crank | cruet | Danae | delft | dimer | Donny |
| conga | crape | crumb | dance | Delhi | dimly | donor |
| Congo | craps | cruse | dandy | Delia | Dinah | doomy |
| Conor | crash | crush | Danny | Delos | dinar | dopey |
| Conwy | crass | crust | Dante | delta | diner | Doric |
| cooee | crate | crypt | Darby | delve | dingo | Doris |
| Cooke | crave | Cuban | Darcy | demob | dingy | dosha |
| coomb | crawl | cubby | Dario | demon | dinky | dotty |
| coopt | craze | cubic | Daryl | demur | diode | doubt |
| copal | crazy | cubit | datum | denar | Dione | dough |
| Copán | creak | cumin | daube | Dench | dippy | Douro |
| coper | cream | cupid | daunt | denim | Dirac | douse |
| copra | Crécy | curer | Davao | Denis | dirge | Dover |
| copse | credo | Curia | David | Denny | dirty | dowdy |
| coral | creed | curie | Davis | dense | disco | dowel |
| corer | creek | curio | davit | Denys | dishy | dower |
| Corfu | creel | curly | Davos | depot | ditch | downy |
| corgi | creep | curry | Dayak | depth | ditsy | dowry |
| corny | crêpe | curse | Dayan | derby | ditto | dowse |
| Corot | crept | curve | dealt | Derek | ditty | doyen |
| corps | cress | curvy | death | Derry | ditzy | dozen |
| Cosmo | crest | cushy | debag | Deryk | divan | Draco |
| Costa | Crete | cuvée | debar | desex | diver | draft |
| couch | Crewe | Cuzco | debit | deter | divot | drain |
| cough | crick | cycad | Debra | detox | divvy | drake |
| could | crime | cycle | debug | deuce | Dixie | drama |

| | | | | | | |
|---|---|---|---|---|---|---|
| drank | dunny | eider | Emile | ester | faith | Fidel |
| drape | duple | Eiger | Emily | Ethan | faker | field |
| drawl | Duras | eight | Emlyn | Ethel | fakir | fiend |
| drawn | Dürer | Eilat | Emmie | ether | Faldo | fiery |
| dread | Durey | eject | emote | ethic | Falla | fifth |
| dream | Durga | Elain | empty | Ethne | false | fifty |
| dreck | dusky | eland | Emrys | ethos | famed | fight |
| dregs | dusty | elate | enact | ethyl | fancy | filch |
| dress | Dutch | elbow | endow | Ettie | Fanny | filly |
| drier | duvet | elder | endue | étude | farad | filmy |
| drift | dwarf | Eldon | enema | Euler | Farah | filth |
| drill | dweeb | elect | enemy | evade | farce | final |
| drily | dwell | elegy | enjoy | Evans | Farsi | finch |
| drink | dwelt | Elena | Ennis | evens | fatal | finis |
| drive | Dyfed | elfin | ennui | event | Fates | Fiona |
| droid | dying | Elgar | Enoch | Evert | fatso | fiord |
| droll | dykey | Elgin | enrol | every | fatty | first |
| drone | Dylan | Elgon | Ensor | evict | fatwa | firth |
| drool | | Elias | ensue | Evita | fault | fishy |
| droop | **E** | elide | enter | evoke | fauna | fitly |
| dross | | Eliot | entry | exact | Fauré | fiver |
| drove | eager | Elise | envoy | exalt | Faust | fives |
| drown | eagle | elite | epoch | excel | Fauve | fixed |
| Druid | Eamon | Eliza | epoxy | exert | fayre | fixer |
| drunk | early | Ellen | Eppie | exile | feart | fizzy |
| drupe | earth | Ellie | Epsom | exist | feast | fjord |
| dryad | easel | Ellis | equal | expat | feign | flack |
| dryer | eaten | Elmer | equip | expel | feint | flail |
| dryly | eater | elope | erase | extol | Felix | flair |
| Duane | ebony | Elroy | Erato | extra | felon | flake |
| Dubai | ebook | Elsie | erect | exude | femur | flaky |
| ducal | éclat | Elton | ergot | exult | fence | flame |
| ducat | Eddie | elude | erica | eyrie | fenny | flank |
| duchy | Edgar | elven | Erich | eyrir | feral | flare |
| ducky | edger | elver | Erika | | Fermi | flash |
| Dufay | edict | Elvie | Ernie | **F** | ferny | flask |
| dully | edify | Elvin | Ernst | | ferry | fleck |
| dulse | Edina | Elvis | erode | fable | fetal | fleet |
| Dumas | Edith | Elwyn | Errol | facet | fetch | flesh |
| dumbo | Edwin | email | error | facia | fetid | Fleur |
| dummy | Edwyn | embed | erupt | faddy | fetor | flick |
| dumps | eerie | ember | esker | fader | fetus | flier |
| dumpy | Effie | emcee | essay | faery | fever | fling |
| dunce | egret | emend | Essen | faint | fibre | flint |
| Dunne | Egypt | emery | Essex | fairy | fichu | flirt |

| | | | | | | |
|---|---|---|---|---|---|---|
| float | forum | furze | gawky | glare | Gotha | grope |
| flock | found | fussy | Gayle | glary | Gouda | gross |
| flood | fount | fusty | gazer | glass | gouge | grosz |
| floor | foxed | futon | Gazza | glaze | Gould | group |
| flora | foyer | fuzzy | gecko | glazy | gourd | grout |
| floss | frail | | geeky | gleam | gouty | grove |
| flour | frame | **G** | geese | glean | Gowon | growl |
| flout | franc | | Gehry | glebe | grace | grown |
| flown | Frank | gabby | gelid | Glenn | grade | gruel |
| Floyd | Franz | gable | Gemma | glide | graft | gruff |
| fluff | fraud | Gabon | Genet | glint | Grail | grump |
| fluid | freak | Gabor | genie | glitz | grain | grunt |
| fluke | Freda | gaffe | genii | gloat | grand | guano |
| fluky | Frege | gaily | Genoa | globe | grant | guard |
| flume | fresh | Gaius | genre | gloom | grape | guava |
| flump | Freud | Galba | genus | gloop | graph | guess |
| flung | Freya | Galen | geode | glory | grasp | guest |
| flunk | friar | Galle | Geoff | gloss | grass | guide |
| flush | fried | Gamay | Gerda | glove | grate | Guido |
| flute | frill | gamer | Gerry | Gluck | grave | guild |
| fluty | Frink | gamey | gesso | gluey | gravy | guile |
| flyer | frisk | gamma | Getty | glyph | graze | guilt |
| Flynn | Frith | gammy | Ghana | gnash | great | guise |
| foamy | frizz | Gamow | Ghent | gnome | grebe | Gulag |
| focal | frock | gamut | ghost | goaty | greed | gulch |
| focus | Fromm | Gance | ghoul | Gobbi | Greek | gules |
| foehn | frond | ganja | giant | godet | green | gully |
| fogey | front | Gansu | Gibbs | godly | Greer | gumbo |
| foggy | frost | gappy | giddy | gofer | greet | gummy |
| foist | froth | Garbo | Gigli | Gogol | Greta | gunge |
| folio | frown | Garda | gigot | going | grief | gungy |
| folks | froze | Garry | Gilda | Golda | Grieg | guppy |
| folky | fruit | Garth | Giles | golem | grill | Gupta |
| folly | frump | gassy | gilet | golly | grime | gushy |
| Fonda | fryer | gated | Ginny | gonad | Grimm | gusto |
| foody | Fuchs | Gates | gipsy | goner | grimy | gusty |
| footy | fudge | Gaudí | girly | goody | grind | gutsy |
| foray | fugal | gaudy | girth | gooey | griot | Gwent |
| force | fuggy | gauge | given | goofy | gripe | Gyles |
| forex | fugue | gaunt | giver | gooly | grist | gypsy |
| forge | fully | gauss | gizmo | goose | grits | |
| forgo | fungi | gauze | glacé | Gordy | groan | **H** |
| forte | funky | gauzy | glade | gorge | groat | |
| forth | funny | gavel | gland | Gorky | groin | habit |
| forty | furry | Gavin | glans | gorse | groom | háček |

| | | | | | | |
|---|---|---|---|---|---|---|
| Hades | Hawke | hiker | horst | **I** | inner | Janis |
| hadn't | Hawks | Hilda | horsy | | input | Janus |
| Hagar | Haydn | hilly | Horta | iambi | inset | japan |
| Hague | Hayek | Hindi | Horus | Ibiza | inter | Jared |
| Haifa | Hayes | Hindu | Hosea | Ibsen | Inuit | Jarry |
| haiku | hazel | hinge | hosta | Iceni | inure | Jason |
| hairy | heady | hinny | hotel | ichor | Ionic | jaunt |
| Haiti | heart | hippo | hotly | icily | Iqbal | Javan |
| hajji | heath | hippy | hound | icing | Iraqi | Javed |
| halal | heave | Hiram | houri | Idaho | irate | Jayne |
| haler | heavy | hirer | house | ideal | Irene | jazzy |
| Haley | Hedda | Hirst | hovel | ident | Irgun | jeans |
| Hallé | hedge | hitch | hover | idiom | Irish | jehad |
| hallo | hefty | hives | howdy | idiot | irony | jello |
| halon | Hegel | hoard | Howel | idler | Irvin | jelly |
| halva | Heidi | hoary | Hoxha | Idris | Irwin | Jemma |
| halve | Heine | Hobbs | Hoyle | idyll | Isaac | jemmy |
| Hamas | Heinz | hobby | hubby | igloo | Islam | Jenna |
| hammy | heist | Hoffa | huffy | ileum | Islay | Jenny |
| handy | Hejaz | Hogan | hullo | iliac | islet | Jerba |
| Hanks | Hekla | hoick | human | Iliad | issue | Jerez |
| hanky | Helen | hoist | humid | ilium | Italy | jerky |
| Hanoi | Helga | hokey | humph | image | itchy | jerry |
| happy | helix | hokum | humpy | imago | ivied | Jesse |
| haram | hello | holey | humus | imbed | ivory | jessy |
| hardy | helot | holly | Hunan | imbue | Ixion | Jesus |
| harem | Henan | Holst | hunch | impel | Izaak | jetty |
| harpy | hence | Homer | hunky | imply | Izmir | jewel |
| harry | henge | homey | Huron | Imran | Izmit | Jewry |
| harsh | henna | homie | hurry | inane | | jiffy |
| Harte | Henri | Honan | Husák | inapt | **J** | jiggy |
| Harun | Henry | Honda | husky | Incan | | jihad |
| Hasid | Henze | honey | hussy | incur | jabot | Jimmy |
| hasn't | herby | hongi | hutch | index | Jacky | Jinny |
| haste | Herod | Honor | huzza | India | Jacob | jiver |
| hasty | heron | hooch | hydra | indie | jaded | Jodie |
| hatch | hertz | hoody | hydro | Indra | Jaffa | Johns |
| hater | Herzl | hooey | hyena | Indus | jaggy | joint |
| Hatty | Hesse | Hooke | hymen | inept | James | joist |
| haulm | Hetty | hooky | Hymie | inert | Jamie | joker |
| haunt | Heyer | hoper | hyoid | infer | Jammu | jokey |
| Havel | Hicks | hoppy | hyper | ingot | jammy | jolly |
| haven | hijab | horde | hypha | Inigo | Janet | Jonah |
| haver | Hijaz | horny | hyrax | inlay | Janey | Jonas |
| havoc | Hijra | horse | Hywel | inlet | Janie | Jones |

| | | | | | | |
|---|---|---|---|---|---|---|
| Jonti | Kauai | knoll | lanky | Léger | Limón | loopy |
| Jools | kauri | known | Laois | leggy | Linda | loose |
| Josie | kayak | knurl | lapel | Lehár | Lindy | Lorca |
| joule | Kazan | koala | lapis | Leigh | linen | Lords |
| joust | kazoo | kofta | lapse | Leila | liner | Loren |
| jowly | Keats | kooky | larch | lemon | lingo | Lorin |
| Joyce | kebab | kopek | lardy | lemur | links | loris |
| Judah | Keble | Koran | large | Lendl | linty | Lorna |
| Judas | kecks | Korda | largo | Lenin | lipid | Lorne |
| judge | kedge | Korea | Larry | Lenny | Lippi | Lorre |
| juice | Keene | korma | larva | lento | lippy | lorry |
| juicy | Keith | kraal | laser | Leona | lisle | loser |
| julep | kelim | kraft | lassi | Leone | Liszt | lotto |
| Jules | Kelly | Krebs | lasso | leper | litas | Lotty |
| Julia | Kempe | krill | latch | lepta | lithe | lotus |
| Julie | kendo | krona | latex | Leroy | litre | lough |
| Julio | Kenny | krone | lathe | Lesli | liven | Louie |
| jumbo | Kenya | kroon | lathi | Lethe | liver | Louis |
| Jumna | Kerri | Krupp | Latin | Letty | livid | louse |
| jumpy | Kerry | kudos | latte | levee | Lizzy | lousy |
| junky | Kesey | kukri | Lauda | level | llama | Louth |
| junta | ketch | kulak | laugh | lever | Lloyd | lovat |
| juror | Kevin | Kursk | Laura | Lewes | loach | lover |
| | khaki | kurta | Lauri | Lewis | loamy | lower |
| **K** | Khmer | kurus | laver | Leyte | loath | lowly |
| | Khufu | Kylie | laxly | Lhasa | lobar | Lowry |
| Kaaba | kiddy | Kyoto | layer | liana | lobby | loyal |
| Kabul | kilim | Kyrie | Lazio | liane | lobed | Lucan |
| Kafka | Kings | | leach | Libby | local | Lucas |
| Kahlo | kinky | **L** | leafy | libel | Locke | Lucca |
| Kamal | kiosk | | leaky | Libra | locum | Lucia |
| Kandy | Kirby | Laban | leant | Libya | locus | lucid |
| Kansu | Kirov | label | leapt | licit | loden | Lucie |
| kapok | kitty | labia | learn | Liddy | lodge | lucky |
| kaput | Klein | Lacan | Leary | liege | loess | lucre |
| karat | Klimt | laden | lease | Liesl | lofty | ludic |
| Karen | klutz | ladle | leash | lifer | Logan | Luger |
| Karin | knack | lager | least | light | logic | Luigi |
| karma | knave | Lagos | leave | liken | login | Lully |
| Karol | knead | Laing | ledge | Likud | logon | lumen |
| Karoo | kneel | laird | leech | lilac | Loire | lumpy |
| Karsh | knell | lairy | Leeds | Lille | lolly | lunar |
| karst | knelt | laity | leery | limbo | loner | lunch |
| Kathy | knife | Laius | lefty | Limey | longe | Lundy |
| Katie | knock | lance | legal | limit | loons | lunge |

| | | | | | | |
|---|---|---|---|---|---|---|
| lungi | Mainz | Marne | Melba | minke | Morag | munch |
| lupin | Maire | Marni | melee | minor | moral | mural |
| lupus | maize | marra | melon | Minos | moray | Murat |
| lurch | major | marry | Melos | Minsk | morel | murky |
| lurex | maker | marsh | Menes | minty | mores | mushy |
| lurgy | Malay | Marta | Mensa | minus | Morna | music |
| lurid | Malin | Marti | mercy | minxy | moron | musky |
| lusty | Malle | Marty | merge | mirth | morph | musty |
| Luton | Malmö | Masai | merit | miser | Morse | muzak |
| luvvy | Malta | maser | merry | missy | Morty | muzzy |
| Luxor | mamba | mason | Meryl | misty | Mosel | Myles |
| Luzon | mambo | match | meson | Mitch | Moses | mynah |
| Lycra | Mamet | mater | messy | Mitla | mosey | Myrna |
| Lydia | Mamie | matey | metal | mitre | Moshe | Myron |
| Lyell | mamma | maths | meter | Mitzi | mossy | myrrh |
| lying | mammy | matin | meths | mixed | Mosul | |
| lymph | Mandy | matte | metre | mixer | motel | **N** |
| lynch | Manet | Matty | metro | mobey | motet | |
| Lynda | manga | matzo | Meuse | mocha | motif | nabob |
| Lynne | mange | Maude | mezzo | modal | motor | nacho |
| Lynzi | mango | Maura | Miami | model | motte | nacre |
| Lyons | mangy | mauve | miaow | modem | motto | Nader |
| lyric | mania | maven | Micah | moggy | mould | Nadia |
| | manic | Mavis | Micky | Mogul | moult | nadir |
| **M** | manky | maxim | micro | Moira | mound | naevi |
| | manly | Mayan | Midas | moire | mount | Nahum |
| Mabel | manna | maybe | midge | moist | mourn | naiad |
| Mable | Manny | Mayer | midon | molar | mouse | naira |
| Macao | manor | mayn't | midst | molly | mousy | naive |
| Macau | manse | mayor | might | molto | mouth | Najaf |
| macaw | manta | Mbeki | Milan | mommy | mover | naked |
| macho | Maori | mealy | milch | monad | movie | Namib |
| macro | maple | means | miler | Monck | mower | Namur |
| madam | marae | meant | Miles | Monet | Moyra | Nanak |
| Maddy | Marah | Meath | milky | money | Mucha | nance |
| Madge | Marat | meaty | Mills | monte | mucky | nancy |
| madly | March | Mecca | Milly | month | mucus | Nandi |
| Maeve | Marco | medal | Milne | monty | muddy | nanna |
| Mafia | Marcy | Medan | mimic | mooch | mufti | nanny |
| Magda | marge | Medea | mimsy | moody | muggy | Naomi |
| magic | Margo | media | mince | mooli | mulch | nappy |
| magma | Maria | medic | Minch | moony | mulga | nasal |
| magus | Marie | Médoc | miner | Moore | mummy | Nashe |
| Mahon | Mario | Megan | mingy | moose | mumps | nasty |
| Maine | Marks | Meggy | minim | moped | mumsy | natal |

| | | | | | | |
|---|---|---|---|---|---|---|
| natty | nifty | numen | Olmec | outré | panic | peaky |
| Nauru | Nigel | nurse | Olwen | ouzel | panne | pearl |
| naval | Niger | nutty | Olwyn | ovary | pansy | Pears |
| Navan | night | Nyasa | Omagh | ovate | panto | Peary |
| navel | Nikki | nylon | Omaha | overt | pants | peaty |
| navvy | Niles | Nyman | Omani | ovine | Paolo | pecan |
| nawab | nimbi | nymph | omega | ovoid | papal | pedal |
| Naxos | Nimby | Nyree | Onega | ovule | papaw | Pedro |
| neath | Nîmes | | onion | Owain | paper | peeve |
| Neddy | ninja | **O** | onset | Owens | pappy | Peggy |
| needy | ninny | | oomph | owing | Papua | Pemba |
| Negev | ninth | oaken | opera | owlet | parch | penal |
| Nehru | Niobe | oakum | Ophir | owner | Paris | pence |
| neigh | nippy | oasis | opine | oxbow | parka | penis |
| Neill | nitre | Oates | opium | Oxfam | parky | penne |
| nelly | Nixon | obeah | optic | oxide | Parma | penny |
| Nepal | Nkomo | obeli | orach | ozone | Paros | peony |
| Nepia | nobby | obese | oracy | Ozzie | parry | peppy |
| nerdy | Nobel | Obote | orate | | parse | Pepys |
| Nerva | noble | occur | orbit | **P** | party | perch |
| nerve | nobly | ocean | Orczy | | pasha | Percy |
| Nervi | nodal | ochre | order | Paarl | passé | Peres |
| nervy | noddy | octet | organ | Pablo | pasta | peril |
| Nerys | Noele | oculi | oriel | pacey | paste | perky |
| Nessa | noise | oddly | Orion | pacha | pasty | Perón |
| Nesta | noisy | Odets | Ormuz | Paddy | patch | perry |
| Netta | Nolan | Odile | orris | padre | paten | Perth |
| never | nomad | odium | Orson | Padua | pater | perve |
| Nevil | nonce | odour | Orton | paean | Pathé | pervy |
| Nevis | nonet | Ofcom | Osaka | pagan | patio | pesky |
| Newby | nooky | offal | Oscar | pager | Patna | pesto |
| newel | noose | offer | osier | Paine | Paton | petal |
| newly | Norah | Ofgas | Osler | paint | patsy | peter |
| Newry | Norma | Oftel | Ossie | paisa | Patti | Petra |
| newsy | Norse | often | Ostia | paise | patty | petty |
| nexus | north | Ofwat | Otago | Palau | Paula | phage |
| ngwee | nosey | Ogden | other | Palio | Pauli | phase |
| Niall | notch | ogler | otter | pally | pause | Phebe |
| NiCad | noted | Ohrid | Otway | Palma | pavan | phial |
| Nicam | novae | Oisin | ought | Palme | paver | phlox |
| niche | novel | okapi | Ouida | palmy | payee | phone |
| Nicky | Nuala | olden | ounce | palsy | payer | phono |
| Nicol | nubby | oldie | ousel | Panay | peace | phony |
| niece | Nubia | olive | outdo | panda | peach | photo |
| niffy | nudge | Ollie | outer | panel | Peake | phyla |

| | | | | | | |
|---|---|---|---|---|---|---|
| piani | Plato | pouch | pseud | quark | rainy | redly |
| piano | plaza | poult | psych | quart | raise | Redon |
| picky | plead | pound | pubes | quash | raita | redox |
| picot | pleat | pouty | pubic | queen | rajah | redux |
| piece | plink | power | pubis | queer | Rajiv | reedy |
| Piers | Pliny | Powys | pudgy | quell | raker | reeve |
| piety | plonk | Prado | puffy | quern | rally | refer |
| piezo | pluck | Praia | Pugin | query | Ralph | refit |
| piggy | plumb | prang | pukey | quest | Raman | regal |
| pigmy | plume | prank | pukka | queue | Rambo | Reich |
| pilaf | plump | prate | pulao | quick | ramen | reify |
| piles | plumy | prawn | pulpy | quiet | ramie | reign |
| pilot | plunk | preen | pulse | quiff | Ramon | reiki |
| pinch | plush | press | punch | quill | ranch | Reims |
| pinko | Pluto | Priam | Punic | quilt | randy | Reith |
| pinky | poach | price | punky | quire | range | rejig |
| pinna | podgy | prick | pupae | quirk | rangy | relax |
| pinny | podia | pride | pupal | quirt | Raoul | relay |
| Pinot | poesy | prime | pupil | quite | rapid | relic |
| pinto | point | primp | puppy | Quito | raspy | relit |
| pious | poise | prink | purée | quits | Rasta | remit |
| piper | poker | print | purge | quoin | ratio | remix |
| pipit | pokey | prion | purse | quoit | ratty | Remus |
| Pippa | polar | prior | Pusey | quota | ravel | renal |
| pique | polio | prise | pushy | quote | raven | Renée |
| piste | polka | prism | pussy | quoth | raver | renew |
| pitch | Polly | privy | Putin | Qur'an | rawly | Renie |
| pithy | polyp | prize | putti | qursh | rayon | repay |
| piton | ponce | probe | putto | | razor | repel |
| pitta | pongy | prole | putty | **R** | reach | reply |
| Pitti | pooch | promo | Pygmy | | react | repot |
| pivot | Poole | prone | pylon | Rabat | ready | reran |
| pixel | Poona | prong | Pyrex | rabbi | realm | rerun |
| pixie | poppa | proof | Pyxis | rabid | rearm | resat |
| pizza | poppy | prose | pzazz | Rabin | rebar | reset |
| place | popsy | Prost | | racer | rebec | resin |
| plaid | porch | prosy | **Q** | radar | rebel | resit |
| plain | porky | proud | | Radha | rebus | retch |
| plait | porno | prove | Qatar | radii | rebut | retie |
| plane | Porto | Provo | quack | radio | recap | retro |
| plank | poser | prowl | quaff | radon | recce | reuse |
| plant | posey | proxy | quail | rager | recta | revel |
| plash | posit | prude | quake | ragga | recto | revue |
| plate | posse | prune | qualm | raggy | recur | rheum |
| Plath | potty | psalm | Quant | Raine | reddy | Rhine |

| | | | | | | |
|---|---|---|---|---|---|---|
| rhino | rogue | rusty | sapid | scoot | serif | Sheol |
| Rhoda | Roily | rutty | Sapir | scope | serum | sherd |
| Rhona | Rollo | Ryder | sappy | score | serve | shift |
| Rhône | Rolls | | Sarah | scorn | seven | shine |
| rhyme | Rolph | **S** | saree | Scots | sever | shiny |
| ribby | Roman | | sarge | Scott | sewer | shire |
| ricer | Romeo | Saale | sarin | scour | sexed | shirk |
| ricin | rondo | Sabah | sarky | scout | sexer | Shirl |
| Ricki | Ronny | sable | Sarto | scowl | shack | shirr |
| Ricky | roomy | sabot | Sarum | scrag | shade | shirt |
| rider | roost | sabra | sassy | scram | shady | Shiva |
| ridge | ropey | sabre | Satan | scrap | shaft | Shoah |
| ridgy | Rosie | Sacha | satay | scree | Shaka | shoal |
| rifle | rosin | Sachs | Satie | screw | shake | shock |
| right | rösti | sacra | satin | scrim | shako | Shona |
| rigid | rotor | Sadat | satyr | scrip | shaky | shone |
| rigor | Rouen | sadhu | sauce | scrub | shale | shook |
| Rikki | rouge | Sadie | saucy | scrum | shall | shoot |
| Riley | rough | sadly | Saudi | scuba | shaly | shore |
| Rilke | round | Sagan | sauna | scuff | shame | shorn |
| rinse | rouse | saggy | sauté | scull | Shane | short |
| Rioja | roust | Sahel | saver | scurf | Shang | shout |
| ripen | route | sahib | savoy | scuzz | shank | shove |
| risen | rover | saint | savvy | seamy | shan't | shown |
| riser | rowan | Sakha | Saxon | sebum | shape | showy |
| risky | rowdy | salad | sayer | sedan | shard | shred |
| ritzy | rowel | Salam | scads | sedge | share | shrew |
| rival | rower | Salem | scald | sedum | shark | shrub |
| riven | royal | sally | scale | seedy | sharp | shrug |
| river | Royce | salon | scalp | segue | Shaun | shtum |
| rivet | ruble | Salop | scaly | Seine | shave | shuck |
| riyal | ruche | salsa | scamp | seize | shawl | shunt |
| roach | ruddy | salty | scant | Seles | shawm | shush |
| Roald | Rudra | salve | scare | Selma | Shawn | Shute |
| roast | Rufus | salvo | scarf | semen | sheaf | shyly |
| Robey | rugby | Samar | scarp | senna | shear | sibyl |
| robin | ruler | samba | Scart | señor | Sheba | sicko |
| robot | rumba | samey | scary | sense | sheen | sided |
| Robyn | rummy | Sammy | scene | Seoul | sheep | sidle |
| rocky | runic | Samoa | scent | sepal | sheer | Sidon |
| Roddy | runny | Samos | scion | sepia | sheet | siege |
| rodeo | runty | Sana'a | scoff | sepoy | sheik | Siena |
| Rodin | rupee | sandy | scold | septa | shelf | sieve |
| roger | rural | Santa | scone | Seram | shell | sight |
| Roget | rushy | Saône | scoop | serge | Shema | sigil |

| | | | | | | |
|---|---|---|---|---|---|---|
| Silas | sleet | sneer | Sousa | spoke | Stasi | stout |
| silky | slept | snick | souse | spoof | state | stove |
| silly | slice | snide | south | spook | stats | Stowe |
| silty | slick | sniff | sower | spool | stave | strap |
| Simla | slide | snipe | Soyuz | spoon | stead | straw |
| Simon | Sligo | snood | space | spoor | steak | stray |
| Sinai | slime | snook | spacy | spore | steal | strew |
| since | slimy | snoop | spade | sport | steam | stria |
| sinew | sling | snore | Spain | spout | steed | strip |
| singe | slink | snort | spank | sprat | steel | strop |
| sinus | sloop | snout | spare | spray | steep | strum |
| Sioux | slope | snowy | spark | spree | steer | strut |
| siren | slosh | snuck | spasm | sprig | stein | stuck |
| sisal | sloth | snuff | spate | sprit | stela | study |
| sissy | slump | Soane | spawn | sprog | stele | stuff |
| sitar | slung | soapy | speak | sprue | steno | stump |
| Sitka | slunk | Soave | spear | spume | stern | stung |
| sixth | slurp | sober | speck | spunk | Steve | stunk |
| sixty | slush | Sochi | specs | spurn | stick | stunt |
| skank | slyly | Soddy | speed | spurt | stiff | stupa |
| skate | smack | Sodom | Speer | squab | stile | Sturt |
| skeet | small | Sodor | Speke | squad | still | style |
| skein | smarm | Sofia | spell | squat | stilt | styli |
| skier | smart | softy | spelt | squib | sting | suave |
| skiff | smash | soggy | spend | squid | stink | sucre |
| skill | smear | solar | spent | stack | stint | Sudan |
| skimp | smell | solid | sperm | Stacy | stoat | Sudra |
| skink | smelt | Solly | spice | staff | stock | sudsy |
| skint | smile | Solon | spicy | stage | stoep | suede |
| skirl | smirk | Solti | spiel | stagy | stoic | suety |
| skirt | smite | solve | spike | staid | stoke | sugar |
| skive | smith | Somme | spiky | stain | stole | suite |
| skulk | smock | sonar | spill | stair | stoma | Sukey |
| skull | smoke | Sonia | spilt | stake | stomp | sulky |
| skunk | smoky | sonic | spine | stale | stone | Sulla |
| slack | smolt | Sonja | spiny | stalk | stony | sully |
| slain | smote | sonny | spire | stall | stook | sumac |
| slake | Smuts | Sonya | spite | stamp | stool | Sumba |
| slang | snack | sooth | Spitz | stand | stoop | Sumer |
| slant | snail | sooty | splat | stank | store | Sunil |
| slash | snake | soppy | splay | stare | stork | Sunna |
| slate | snaky | sorry | split | stark | storm | Sunni |
| slave | snare | sough | Spock | Starr | story | sunny |
| sleek | snarl | sound | Spode | start | stoup | sunup |
| sleep | sneak | soupy | spoil | stash | Stour | super |

| | | | | | | |
|---|---|---|---|---|---|---|
| Surat | Synge | Tariq | thali | Tilda | Tonia | trews |
| surge | synod | tarot | thane | tilde | tonic | triad |
| surly | synth | tarry | thank | tiler | tonne | trial |
| Surya | Syrah | tarsi | theft | Tilly | Tonya | tribe |
| Susah | Syria | tarty | their | tilth | tooth | trice |
| Susan | syrup | Tasso | theme | timer | topaz | trick |
| sushi | | taste | Thera | timid | toper | trier |
| Susie | **T** | tasty | there | Timmy | topic | trike |
| sutra | | tater | therm | Timor | topoi | trill |
| swain | tabby | tatty | these | Timur | topos | Trina |
| swami | tabla | Tatum | they'd | tinea | Topsy | tripe |
| swamp | table | taunt | thick | tinge | toque | trite |
| swank | taboo | taupe | thief | tinny | Torah | troll |
| Swapo | tabor | Taupo | thigh | tipsy | torch | Troon |
| sward | tache | tawny | thine | tired | torsi | troop |
| swarf | tacit | teach | thing | Tiree | torso | trope |
| swarm | tacky | teary | think | Tirol | torte | troth |
| swash | Taffy | tease | third | Tisha | Toruń | trout |
| swath | Tagus | teddy | thole | Tisza | torus | trove |
| Swazi | taiga | teens | thong | Titan | total | truce |
| swear | taint | teeny | Thora | titch | totem | truck |
| sweat | Tajik | teeth | thorn | tithe | totty | Trudi |
| Swede | taken | Tegan | those | title | touch | Trudy |
| sweep | taker | telex | Thoth | Titus | tough | truly |
| sweet | tally | telly | three | tizzy | Tours | trump |
| swell | talon | tempi | threw | toady | towel | trunk |
| swept | talus | tempo | thrip | toast | tower | Truro |
| swift | Tamar | tempt | throb | Tobit | toxic | truss |
| swill | Tambo | tench | throw | today | toxin | trust |
| swine | tamer | tenet | thrum | toddy | trace | truth |
| swing | Tamil | tenon | Thule | toile | track | tryst |
| swipe | Tammy | tenor | thumb | toils | tract | tubal |
| swirl | Tampa | tense | thump | Tokay | Tracy | tubby |
| swish | tanga | tenth | thyme | token | trade | tuber |
| Swiss | Tange | tepee | thymi | Tokyo | trail | Tudor |
| swizz | tango | tepid | tiara | tolar | train | tufty |
| swoon | tangy | Terri | Tiber | Tolly | trait | tulip |
| swoop | Tania | terry | Tibet | Tommy | tramp | tulle |
| sword | tansy | terse | tibia | Tomsk | trash | Tulsa |
| swore | Tanya | tesla | tidal | tonal | trawl | tumid |
| sworn | tapas | Tessa | tiger | tondi | tread | tummy |
| swung | taper | testa | tight | tondo | treat | tuner |
| Sybil | tapir | testy | Tigre | toner | trend | tunic |
| sylph | tardy | Texan | Tikal | Tonga | Trent | Tunis |
| synch | Tarim | Texas | tikka | tongs | tress | tunny |

| | | | | | | |
|---|---|---|---|---|---|---|
| turbo | unfit | Varro | viral | waltz | where | woman |
| Turin | unify | vatic | vireo | Wanda | which | women |
| Turku | union | vault | Virgo | wanly | whiff | wonky |
| turps | unite | vaunt | virus | wanna | while | Woods |
| tutee | unity | Vedic | Visby | Warne | whine | woody |
| tutor | unlit | vegan | visit | warty | whiny | wooer |
| Tutsi | unman | veiny | visor | washy | whirl | Woolf |
| tutti | unpin | velar | vista | wasn't | whirr | woosh |
| Tuzla | unsay | Velda | vital | waste | whisk | woozy |
| twain | unsex | veldt | Vitus | watch | whist | wordy |
| twang | untie | Velma | Vivia | water | white | world |
| tweak | until | venal | vivid | Watts | whizz | Worms |
| Tweed | unwed | Venda | vixen | Waugh | whole | wormy |
| tweet | unzip | venom | vizor | waver | whomp | worry |
| twerp | upend | venue | vocal | waxen | whoop | worse |
| twice | upper | Venus | vodka | waxer | Whorf | worst |
| twill | upset | Verdi | vogue | Wayne | whorl | worth |
| twine | urban | verge | voice | Weald | whose | Wotan |
| twirl | Uriah | Verna | voila | weary | Wicca | would |
| twist | urine | Verne | voile | weave | widen | wound |
| Tyler | usage | verse | Volga | weber | widow | woven |
| Tyrol | usher | verso | Volta | wedge | width | wowee |
| Tyson | usual | verve | vomit | weedy | wield | wrack |
| Tzara | usurp | Vesta | voter | weeny | Wigan | wrapt |
| | usury | vetch | vouch | weepy | Wight | wrath |
| **U** | uteri | vexed | vowel | weigh | Wilde | wreak |
| | utter | viand | vulva | Weill | Willa | wreck |
| udder | uvula | vicar | | weird | Wills | wrest |
| ukase | Uzbek | Vichy | **W** | welch | Willy | wring |
| ulama | | Vicki | | Wells | Wilma | wrist |
| ulcer | **V** | Vicky | wacko | welly | wimpy | write |
| ulema | | Vidal | wacky | Welsh | wince | wrong |
| ulnae | vacua | video | wader | Welty | winch | wrote |
| ulnar | Vaduz | vigil | wafer | wench | windy | wroth |
| Ulric | vague | Vigny | waged | Wendy | winey | wrung |
| ultra | Valda | Vijay | wager | Weser | wiper | wryly |
| Uluru | valet | Vikki | wagon | wetly | wired | Wuhan |
| umbel | valid | villa | waist | whack | wispy | Wyatt |
| umber | value | villi | waive | whale | witch | Wynne |
| umbra | valve | Vilma | Wajda | wharf | withy | |
| ummah | vampy | Vince | waken | wheal | witty | **X** |
| uncle | Vanda | Vinny | Waldo | wheat | Woden | |
| uncut | vapid | vinyl | Wales | wheel | wodge | xebec |
| under | Varah | viola | wally | whelk | woken | Xenia |
| undue | Varna | viper | Walsh | whelp | Wolfe | xenon |

| Xerox | yakka | yodel | yours | Yupik | Zappa | zilch |
| Xhosa | yappy | yogic | youth | yuppy | zappy | zingy |
| xylem | yearn | yokel | you've | Yusuf | zazen | zippy |
| | yeast | yolky | Ypres | | zebra | zitty |
| **Y** | Yeats | yonks | yucca | **Z** | Zeiss | zloty |
| | Yemen | you'll | yucky | | Zelda | zonal |
| yacht | yield | young | Yukon | Zaire | Zelma | zooid |
| yahoo | yobbo | you're | yummy | Zante | zesty | |

# 6 LETTERS

| **A** | acidly | Aeneas | agorot | Alicia | Amiens |
| | acquit | Aeneid | aikido | alight | amnion |
| Aachen | across | Aeolus | Aileen | Alison | amoeba |
| Aarhus | action | aerate | ailing | alkali | amoral |
| abacus | Actium | aerial | airily | alkane | amount |
| Abadan | active | aether | airing | alkene | ampere |
| abbess | actual | affair | airman | allege | Amtrak |
| abduct | acuity | affect | airmen | allele | amulet |
| abject | acumen | affirm | airway | Allies | anally |
| abjure | adagio | afford | aisled | allium | analog |
| ablaze | addict | affray | akimbo | allude | anchor |
| aboard | adduce | Afghan | Alanna | allure | Ancona |
| abound | adhere | afield | Alaric | Almaty | Andean |
| abrade | adieux | aflame | Alaska | almond | Andrea |
| abroad | adjoin | afloat | Albany | almost | Andrei |
| abrupt | adjure | afraid | albeit | Alonzo | Andrew |
| abseil | adjust | afresh | Albers | alpaca | Angela |
| absent | admire | Africa | Albert | Alpine | Angelo |
| absorb | Adolph | afters | albino | Alsace | Angers |
| absurd | Adonis | Agadir | Albion | Althea | angina |
| abuser | adorer | agaric | Alcock | Altman | Angkor |
| acacia | Adorno | Agassi | Alcott | alumni | angled |
| accede | Adrian | Agatha | alcove | always | angler |
| accent | adrift | ageing | Alcuin | Amalfi | Angola |
| accept | adroit | ageism | Aldiss | Amalia | angora |
| access | adsorb | ageist | Aldous | Amalie | angsty |
| accord | advent | agency | Aldrin | Amanda | animal |
| accost | adverb | agenda | Alecto | Amazon | animus |
| accrue | advert | aghast | Aleppo | ambush | Ankara |
| accuse | advice | Agnesi | Alexia | Amelia | anklet |
| Achebe | advise | Agneta | Alexis | amends | anneal |
| acidic | Aegean | agorae | Alfred | amidst | annexe |

| | | | | | |
|---|---|---|---|---|---|
| Annika | arcade | Artois | atrium | Azrael | Banjul |
| Annora | arcana | Arturo | attach | | banker |
| annual | arcane | Asante | attack | **B** | banner |
| anoint | arched | ascend | attain | | bantam |
| anomie | archer | ascent | attend | babble | banter |
| anorak | Archie | Ascham | attest | baboon | banyan |
| Anselm | archly | Asgard | Attica | Bacall | banzai |
| answer | Arctic | ashlar | Attila | backer | baobab |
| Anthea | ardent | Ashley | attire | backup | barbed |
| anthem | ardour | Ashoka | Attlee | baddie | barbel |
| anther | Arendt | ashore | attune | badger | barber |
| antics | areola | ashram | Atwood | Baffin | Barbie |
| antler | argent | Ashton | Aubrey | baffle | Barbra |
| Antony | argosy | Asimov | auburn | bagful | bardic |
| Antrim | arguer | aslant | Audrey | bagger | Bardot |
| Anubis | argyle | asleep | Augeas | bagman | barely |
| anyhow | Ariane | Asmara | augury | bagmen | bargee |
| anyone | aright | aspect | August | Bahutu | barite |
| anyway | arisen | aspire | auntie | Baikal | barium |
| aortic | Arlene | assail | aurora | bailey | barker |
| Apache | armada | assent | Aussie | bakery | barley |
| apathy | Armagh | assert | Austen | balboa | barman |
| aperçu | Armand | assess | Austin | Balcon | barmen |
| apiary | Armani | assign | auteur | Balder | barnet |
| apical | armful | Assisi | author | baldly | barney |
| apiece | armlet | assist | autism | baleen | Barnum |
| aplomb | armory | assize | autumn | Balkan | barony |
| apnoea | armour | assume | Avalon | ballad | barque |
| apogee | armpit | assure | avatar | ballet | barrel |
| Apollo | Arnhem | Astana | avenge | ballot | barren |
| appeal | arnica | astern | avenue | balsam | Barrie |
| appear | Arnold | asthma | Averil | Baltic | barrio |
| append | around | astral | averse | Balzac | barrow |
| applet | arouse | astray | aviary | Bamako | barter |
| appley | arrack | Astrid | avidly | bamboo | Bartók |
| Apulia | arrant | astute | avocet | Bamian | Barton |
| Aquila | arrear | asylum | avowal | Banaba | Baruch |
| Arabia | arrest | ataxia | awaken | banana | baryon |
| Arabic | arrive | Athena | aweigh | bandit | baryte |
| arable | arroyo | Athene | awhile | banger | basalt |
| Arafat | Artaud | Athens | awning | bangle | basher |
| Aragon | artery | atomic | awoken | Bangui | basket |
| Ararat | artful | atonal | Ayesha | banian | basque |
| Arawak | Arthur | Atreus | azalea | banish | basset |
| arbour | artist | atrial | Azania | banjax | baster |

| | | | | | |
|---|---|---|---|---|---|
| Bastet | befall | Besant | biotin | boater | boozer |
| Bastia | befell | beside | birder | Bobbie | bopper |
| bather | before | Bessie | birdie | bobbin | borage |
| bathos | beggar | bestir | Birgit | bobble | border |
| batman | begone | bestow | Biscay | bobbly | boreal |
| batmen | behalf | betake | bisect | bobcat | Borges |
| batten | behave | Bethan | bishop | bodega | Borgia |
| batter | behead | betide | bisque | bodger | boring |
| battle | behest | betony | Bissau | bodice | Borneo |
| bauble | behind | betook | bistro | bodily | borrow |
| Baucis | behold | betray | bitchy | bodkin | borsch |
| Bayern | behove | better | biting | Bodley | borzoi |
| Baykal | Beirut | bettor | bitmap | Bodrum | Bosnia |
| Baylis | Béjart | Beulah | bitten | boffin | bosomy |
| bazaar | beldam | bewail | bitter | Bogart | Boston |
| beacon | belfry | beware | Blaine | boggle | botany |
| beadle | Belial | Bewick | Blaise | Bogotá | Botham |
| beagle | belief | beyond | Blakey | boiler | bother |
| beaked | Belize | bhajia | blanch | boldly | bothie |
| beaker | Belloc | Bharat | blazer | bolero | bottle |
| Beamon | bellow | bhoona | blazon | bolete | bottom |
| beanie | belong | Bhopal | bleach | Boleyn | bouclé |
| bearer | Belsen | Bhutan | bleary | Bolger | boudin |
| beaten | belted | Bhutto | blench | bolshy | bought |
| beater | belter | Biafra | blenny | bolter | Boulez |
| Beaton | beluga | Bianca | blewit | Bolton | boulle |
| Beatty | bemoan | biceps | blight | Bombay | bounce |
| beauty | bemuse | bicker | blimey | bombed | bouncy |
| beaver | bender | bidder | blithe | bomber | bounty |
| becalm | Bengal | bigamy | Blixen | bonbon | bourne |
| became | benign | bigwig | blobby | bonded | bourse |
| Becker | Benita | bijoux | blokey | Bonita | bovine |
| beckon | Benito | bikini | blonde | bonito | Bowery |
| become | Bennet | Bilbao | bloody | bonnet | bowler |
| bedbug | benumb | billet | blotch | Bonney | Bowles |
| bedded | benzin | Billie | blotto | bonnie | bowman |
| bedeck | berate | billow | blouse | bonsai | bowmen |
| bedlam | Berber | binary | blower | bonzer | boxcar |
| bedpan | bereft | binder | blowsy | boodle | boxing |
| bedsit | Bergen | binger | blowzy | boogie | boyish |
| Beduin | Bering | biogas | bluesy | booker | Brahma |
| beeper | Berlin | bionic | bluish | bookie | Brahms |
| beetle | Bernie | biopic | blurry | booted | Braine |
| Beeton | Bertha | biopsy | Blyton | bootee | brainy |
| beezer | Bertie | biotic | boatel | bootie | braise |

| | | | | | |
|---|---|---|---|---|---|
| Bramah | Brooks | Burgos | cafard | Canova | Carter |
| branch | browny | burial | caftan | canter | carton |
| Brando | browse | burkha | cagily | canton | Caruso |
| Brandt | Bruges | burlap | Cagney | cantor | carvel |
| brandy | bruise | Burman | caiman | Canuck | carver |
| Braque | Brummy | burner | caique | Canute | Casals |
| brassy | brunch | Burney | cajole | canvas | casbah |
| brawny | Brunei | burrow | Calais | canyon | casein |
| brazen | Brunel | bursar | calash | capful | cashew |
| Brazil | brutal | Burton | Calder | caplin | casing |
| breach | Brutus | bushed | calico | Capone | casino |
| breast | bryony | bushel | caliph | Capote | casket |
| breath | bubble | busily | Callao | capper | Caspar |
| Brecht | bubbly | busker | Callas | captor | cassia |
| breech | buccal | buskin | caller | carafe | Cassie |
| breeze | Buchan | Busoni | callow | carbon | cassis |
| breezy | bucket | buster | Callum | carboy | caster |
| Bremen | buckle | bustle | callus | carder | castle |
| Brenda | Buddha | butane | calmly | cardie | castor |
| Breton | budget | butler | Calvin | Cardin | Castro |
| brewer | budgie | butter | camber | careen | casual |
| bridal | buffer | buttie | cambia | career | catchy |
| bridge | buffet | button | camera | caress | catgut |
| Bridie | bugler | buyout | camper | caries | Cathay |
| bridle | bullet | buzzer | campus | Carina | Cather |
| briefs | bumbag | bygone | Canaan | caring | cation |
| Briggs | bumble | byline | Canada | Carlos | catkin |
| bright | bummer | bypass | canapé | Carlow | catnap |
| Brigid | bumper | byplay | canard | Carmel | catnip |
| Brigit | bundle | byroad | canary | Carmen | Catrin |
| Briony | bungee | byword | cancan | Carnac | cattle |
| Briton | bungle | | cancel | carnal | caucus |
| broach | bunion | **C** | cancer | Carnap | caudal |
| Broads | bunker | | Cancún | Carola | caught |
| brogue | bunkum | cabbie | candid | Carole | causal |
| broken | Bunsen | cachet | candle | carpal | Cavafy |
| broker | Bunter | cackle | canine | carpel | caveat |
| brolly | Buñuel | cactus | canker | carper | Cavell |
| bronco | Bunyan | caddie | canned | carpet | cavern |
| Brontë | burble | caddis | canner | carpus | caviar |
| bronze | burbot | cadger | Cannes | carrel | caving |
| bronzy | burden | Cadmus | cannon | Carrie | cavity |
| brooch | bureau | caecal | cannot | carrot | cavort |
| broody | burger | caecum | canoer | Carson | Cavour |
| Brooke | burgle | Caesar | canopy | cartel | Cawley |

| | | | | | |
|---|---|---|---|---|---|
| Caxton | cheery | chubby | clique | coldly | copper |
| Cayley | cheese | chukka | cloaca | coleus | Coptic |
| cayman | cheesy | chummy | cloche | collar | copula |
| Cecile | Chenin | chunky | clompy | collie | corbel |
| Cecily | Cheops | church | closed | collop | Corday |
| Cedric | cheque | Ciaran | closet | colony | cordon |
| celery | Cherie | cicada | clothe | colour | corker |
| Celina | cherry | cicely | Clotho | column | Cormac |
| Celine | cherub | Cicero | cloudy | combat | cornea |
| cellar | Cheryl | cilium | Clough | comber | corner |
| Celtic | chesty | cinder | cloven | comedy | cornet |
| cement | chèvre | cinema | clover | comely | corona |
| censer | chewer | cipher | Clovis | comfit | corpse |
| censor | chichi | circle | clumpy | Comino | corpus |
| census | chicle | circus | clumsy | comity | corral |
| centas | chicly | cirque | clunky | commit | corrie |
| centre | chigoe | cirrus | clutch | common | corset |
| cereal | chilli | Cissie | coarse | compel | Cortes |
| cerise | chilly | cistus | cobalt | comply | cortex |
| cerium | chintz | citric | cobber | concur | Cortez |
| cervix | chippy | citron | cobble | condom | corymb |
| Cesare | Chirac | citrus | Cobden | condor | cosily |
| Ceylon | Chiron | civics | cobnut | confab | Cosimo |
| chador | chirpy | Claire | cobweb | confer | cosine |
| chafer | chisel | clammy | coccus | confit | cosmic |
| chaise | chitin | claque | coccyx | conger | cosmos |
| chakra | chiton | claret | Cochin | conker | cosset |
| chalet | chivvy | Clarke | cockle | Connie | costar |
| chalky | choccy | classy | cocoon | Connor | costly |
| chalot | choice | Claude | coddle | Conrad | Cotman |
| chance | choker | clause | codger | consul | cottar |
| chancy | chokey | clawed | codify | convex | cotter |
| Chanel | choler | clayey | coerce | convey | cotton |
| Chaney | choose | cleave | coeval | convoy | cougar |
| change | choosy | Cleese | coffee | Conway | coulis |
| Chania | Chopin | clench | coffer | cooker | county |
| chapel | choppy | clergy | coffin | cookie | couple |
| charge | choral | cleric | cogent | cooler | coupon |
| Charis | chorea | clever | cognac | coolly | course |
| Charon | chorus | cliché | cohere | coolth | cousin |
| chaser | chosen | client | cohort | coombe | covert |
| chaste | chough | climax | cohosh | cooper | coward |
| chatty | chrism | clinch | cohost | copeck | cowboy |
| cheeky | Christ | clingy | coital | copier | cowled |
| cheers | chrome | clinic | coitus | coping | cowpat |

| Cowper | cruise | Cuvier | Daniel | decant | denial |
|--------|--------|--------|--------|--------|--------|
| cowpox | crumbs | Cybele | Danish | Deccan | denier |
| cowrie | crumby | cyborg | Danton | deceit | Denise |
| coyote | crummy | cyclic | Danube | decent | Dennie |
| Crabbe | crunch | cygnet | Danzig | decide | Dennis |
| crabby | crusty | cymbal | Daphne | Decius | denote |
| Cracow | crutch | Cymric | dapper | deckle | dental |
| cradle | Cruyff | cypher | dapple | Declan | dentil |
| crafty | crying | Cyprus | Darfur | decode | denude |
| craggy | cubism | cystic | Darien | decree | Denver |
| crania | cubist | Czerny | daring | deduce | Denzil |
| cranky | cuboid |        | darken | deduct | depart |
| cranny | cuckoo | **D**  | darkly | deejay | depend |
| crater | cuddle |        | darned | deepen | depict |
| cravat | cuddly | dabble | Darrel | deeply | deploy |
| craven | cudgel | Dachau | Darren | deface | deport |
| crayon | Cuenca | dacoit | Darryl | defame | depose |
| creaky | cummin | dactyl | Darwin | defeat | depute |
| creamy | cumuli | daemon | dative | defect | deputy |
| crease | Cunard | Dafydd | datura | defend | derail |
| create | cupola | dagger | Daudet | defier | Derain |
| crèche | curacy | Dagmar | Davies | defile | deride |
| credal | curare | dahlia | Davina | define | derive |
| credit | curate | daikon | dawdle | deform | dermal |
| creepy | curdle | dainty | daybed | defray | dermis |
| Creole | curfew | Dakota | dazzle | deftly | Dermot |
| crêpey | Curial | dalasi | deacon | defuse | derris |
| Cretan | curium | Dallas | deaden | dégagé | Dervla |
| crewel | curler | Dalton | deadly | degree | Deryck |
| crikey | curlew | damage | deafen | deicer | descry |
| Crimea | cursed | damask | dealer | Dekker | desert |
| cringe | cursor | Damian | Deanna | delete | design |
| cripes | Curtis | Damien | Deanne | Delius | desire |
| crisis | curtly | damned | dearly | Delors | desist |
| crispy | curtsy | dampen | dearth | Delphi | despot |
| critic | curvet | damper | debark | Delroy | Dessau |
| croaky | cusped | damply | debase | delude | detach |
| crocus | cussed | damsel | debate | deluge | detail |
| Cronin | Custer | damson | Debbie | demand | detain |
| Cronus | custom | dancer | debris | demean | detect |
| Crosby | cutely | dander | debtor | demise | detest |
| crosse | cutesy | dandle | debunk | demist | detour |
| crotch | cutler | danger | deburr | demote | detune |
| crouch | cutlet | dangle | decade | demure | device |
| cruddy | cutter | dangly | decamp | dengue | devise |

| | | | | | |
|---|---|---|---|---|---|
| devoid | disarm | donjon | drippy | durbar | eerily |
| devoré | disbar | donkey | drivel | duress | efface |
| devote | discus | doodad | driven | Durham | effect |
| devour | dismal | doodah | driver | durian | effete |
| devout | dismay | doodle | drogue | during | effigy |
| dewlap | Disney | dopily | drolly | duster | effort |
| dexter | disown | dorado | drongo | Dustin | Egbert |
| dharma | dispel | Dorcas | droopy | Dvořák | Egmont |
| diadem | distal | Doreen | dropsy | Dwayne | egoism |
| Dianne | distil | Dorian | drover | Dwight | egoist |
| diaper | disuse | Dorita | drowse | dyadic | egress |
| diatom | dither | dormer | drowsy | dynamo | Eiffel |
| dibber | Divali | Dorrie | drudge | dynast | eighth |
| dibble | divers | dorsal | Dryden | | eights |
| dickey | divert | Dorset | dually | **E** | eighty |
| Dickie | divest | dosage | dubbin | | Eileen |
| Dickon | divide | dosser | Dubcek | Eadwig | Eirene |
| dictum | divine | dotage | Dublin | eaglet | either |
| diddle | Diwali | dotard | Duccio | Eakins | Elaine |
| Dieppe | Djerba | Dottie | ducker | Eamonn | elapse |
| diesel | doable | dottle | Dudley | earful | Elbert |
| dieter | docent | Douala | duenna | earner | Elbrus |
| differ | docile | double | duffel | Eartha | eldest |
| digest | docker | doubly | duffer | earthy | eleven |
| digger | docket | douche | duffle | earwax | elfish |
| diktat | doctor | Dougal | Dugald | earwig | elicit |
| dilate | dodder | doughy | Duggie | easily | Elijah |
| Dillon | doddle | Dougie | dugong | Easter | Elinor |
| dilute | dodgem | dourly | dugout | eatery | Elisha |
| dimity | dodger | dovish | duiker | Eccles | Elissa |
| dimmer | Dodoma | downer | dulcet | echoey | elixir |
| dimple | doesn't | dowser | Dulcie | echoic | Elliot |
| dimply | dogged | dozily | Dulles | eclair | Eloise |
| dimwit | Dogger | drably | Duluth | eczema | Éluard |
| dinghy | doggie | drachm | dumbly | Edberg | Elvira |
| dingle | dollar | dragon | dumdum | Edenic | elvish |
| dinkum | dollop | Dralon | dumper | edgily | embalm |
| dinner | dolmen | draper | Dunbar | edging | embark |
| Dionne | dolour | drawer | Duncan | edible | emblem |
| dioxin | domain | dreamt | Dundee | Edison | embody |
| dipole | domino | dreamy | dunlin | editor | emboli |
| dipper | Donald | dreary | Dunlop | Edmond | emboss |
| direct | donate | dredge | dupion | Edmund | embryo |
| dirham | Donets | drench | duplex | Edward | Emelyn |
| dirndl | dongle | dressy | Durban | Edwina | emerge |

| | | | | | |
|---|---|---|---|---|---|
| emetic | épater | eureka | **F** | Fawkes | fiesta |
| émigré | epical | Europa | | fealty | figure |
| Emilia | Epirus | Europe | Fabian | fecund | Fijian |
| empire | eponym | evader | Fabius | fedora | filial |
| employ | equate | Evadne | fabled | feeble | filing |
| Empson | equine | Evelyn | fabric | feebly | filler |
| enable | equity | evenly | facade | feeder | fillet |
| enamel | eraser | evilly | facial | feeler | fillip |
| encamp | erbium | evince | facile | feisty | filmic |
| encase | Erebus | evolve | facing | feline | filter |
| encash | Erevan | Evonne | factor | feller | filthy |
| encode | Erfurt | exceed | faecal | fellow | finale |
| encore | ermine | except | faeces | felony | finder |
| endear | Ernest | excess | Faenza | female | finely |
| ending | erotic | excise | faerie | femora | finery |
| endive | errand | excite | faggot | fencer | Fingal |
| endure | errant | excuse | fairly | fender | finger |
| energy | errata | exempt | fakery | Fenian | finial |
| enfold | ersatz | exequy | falcon | fennel | fining |
| engage | escape | Exeter | fallen | Fergal | finish |
| Engels | Escher | exeunt | fallow | Fergie | finite |
| engine | eschew | exhale | falter | Fergus | finito |
| engulf | escort | exhort | family | Fermat | Finlay |
| enigma | escrow | exhume | famine | ferret | Finney |
| enjoin | escudo | Exmoor | famous | ferric | Finola |
| enlist | Esdras | exodus | fandom | fervid | firkin |
| enmesh | Eskimo | exotic | fanged | fescue | firmly |
| enmity | Esmond | expand | Fangio | festal | fiscal |
| enough | España | expect | farmer | fester | fisher |
| enrage | esprit | expend | Farouk | fetish | fitful |
| enrapt | estate | expert | farrow | fetter | fitted |
| enrich | esteem | expire | fasces | fettle | fitter |
| ensign | Esther | expiry | fascia | feudal | fixate |
| ensure | etcher | export | fasten | fiancé | fixing |
| entail | ethane | expose | father | fiasco | fixity |
| entice | ethics | extant | fathom | fibber | fizzle |
| entire | ethnic | extend | Fatima | fibril | fizzog |
| entity | Euboea | extent | fatten | fibrin | flabby |
| entomb | euchre | extort | faucet | fibula | flagon |
| entrap | Euclid | exvoto | faulty | fickle | flambé |
| entrée | Eudora | eyeful | faunae | fiddle | flange |
| enwrap | Eugene | eyelet | faunal | fiddly | flappy |
| enzyme | eulogy | eyelid | Faunus | fidget | flashy |
| Eocene | Eunice | | favela | Fields | flatly |
| Eoghan | eunuch | | favour | fierce | flaunt |

Flavia
flaxen
fleadh
fledge
fleece
fleecy
flense
fleshy
flexor
flight
flimsy
flinch
flinty
flippy
flirty
flitch
floaty
floozy
floppy
florae
floral
Flores
floret
Florey
florid
florin
flossy
floury
flower
fluent
fluffy
flunky
flurry
flying
fo'c's'le
fodder
foetal
foetid
foetus
foible
Fokine
Fokker
folder
foliar
folkie

folksy
follow
foment
fondle
fondly
fondue
foodie
footer
footie
footle
forage
forbid
forcer
forego
forest
Forfar
forger
forget
forgot
forint
forked
formal
Forman
format
Formby
former
Fornax
fossil
foster
fought
foully
fourth
fowler
Fowles
foxily
foxing
fracas
framed
framer
Franca
France
Franck
Franco
Franny
frappé

Fraser
Frauen
Frazer
freaky
Freddy
freely
freeze
French
frenzy
fresco
Fresno
friary
Friday
fridge
Frieda
friend
frieze
Frigga
fright
frigid
frilly
fringe
fringy
frisée
frisky
frizzy
froggy
frolic
Fronde
frosty
frothy
frowsy
frowzy
frozen
frugal
fruity
frumpy
frypan
Fugard
führer
fulcra
fulfil
fuller
fulmar
fumble

funder
fungal
fungus
funnel
furore
furrow
Fuseli
fusion
futile
future
Fuzhou

**G**

Gabbie
gabble
gabbro
gabled
gadfly
gadget
Gaelic
Gaenor
gaffer
gaggle
gaiety
gainer
gaiter
galaxy
galena
galley
Gallic
gallon
gallop
galoot
galore
galosh
Galton
Galway
Gambia
gambit
gamble
gambol
gamely
gamete
gamine

gammon
gander
Gandhi
Ganesh
ganger
Ganges
gangly
gannet
gantry
garage
garble
Garcia
garçon
Gardai
garden
Gareth
gargle
garish
garlic
garner
garnet
garret
garter
Garvey
gasbag
gasify
gasket
gaslit
gasper
gasser
gateau
gather
gauche
gaucho
gauger
gavial
Gawain
gawker
gawper
gaydar
Gaynor
gazebo
gazump
Gdańsk
Gdynia

geezer
Gehrig
Geiger
geisha
Gemini
gender
genera
Geneva
genial
genius
genome
gentle
gently
gentry
George
Gerald
Gerard
gerbil
German
Gertie
gerund
Gerwyn
Gethin
gewgaw
geyser
ghetto
gibber
gibbet
gibbon
Gibran
Gibson
Gideon
giggle
giggly
gigolo
gilder
gillie
gimbal
gimlet
ginger
gingko
ginkgo
Giotto
girder
girdle

| | | | | | |
|---|---|---|---|---|---|
| girlie | golfer | greasy | guitar | halloo | hatred |
| Gisela | goodby | greave | Gujrat | hallow | hatter |
| gladly | goodie | Greece | Gullah | halter | Hattie |
| Gladys | goodly | greedy | gullet | halvah | hauler |
| glance | googly | Greene | gulley | Hameln | haunch |
| glassy | gopher | greedy | gunman | Hamish | Havana |
| Glenda | Gordon | Gregor | gunmen | hamlet | Havant |
| Glenis | Göreme | Gretel | gunnel | hammam | haven't |
| Glenys | gorger | Greuze | gunner | hammer | Hawaii |
| glibly | gorget | grieve | Gunter | Hamnet | hawker |
| glider | gorgio | grille | gurgle | hamper | hawser |
| Glinka | gorgon | grilse | Gurkha | Handel | haying |
| Glinys | gospel | grimly | gurney | handle | Hayley |
| glitch | gossip | Grinch | gusher | hangar | hazard |
| glitzy | Gotham | grisly | gusset | hanger | hazily |
| global | Gothic | gritty | Gussie | hanker | header |
| gloomy | gouger | groats | Gustaf | hankie | healer |
| gloopy | goujon | grocer | Gustav | Hannah | health |
| Gloria | Gounod | groggy | gutted | hansom | Heaney |
| glossy | govern | groove | gutter | happen | hearer |
| gloved | Gracie | groovy | guv'nor | haptic | hearse |
| glower | grader | groper | Guyana | Harare | Hearst |
| glumly | Graeme | grosze | guzzle | harass | hearth |
| glutei | Graham | groszy | Gwenda | harden | hearty |
| gluten | grainy | grotto | Gwilym | Hardie | heater |
| Glynis | gramme | grotty | Gwylim | hardly | heaven |
| gnarly | Grammy | grouch | gypsum | harken | heaver |
| gneiss | grange | ground | gyrate | Harlem | Hebrew |
| gnomic | Grania | grouse | | Harley | Hebron |
| gnosis | granny | grovel | **H** | harlot | Hecate |
| goalie | Granth | grower | | Harlow | heckle |
| goatee | grapey | growth | hacker | Harold | hectic |
| gobbet | grappa | groyne | hackle | Haroun | hector |
| gobble | Grasse | Grozny | Hadith | Harris | Hecuba |
| goblet | grassy | grubby | Hadlee | Harrod | hedger |
| goblin | grater | grudge | hadron | harrow | Hedley |
| Godard | gratin | grumpy | Haggai | Harvey | Hedwig |
| Godiva | gratis | grunge | haggis | Hashim | Hegira |
| godown | gravel | grungy | haggle | haslet | heifer |
| godson | graven | Gstaad | Hainan | Hassan | height |
| godwit | graver | Guardi | hairdo | Hassid | Hejira |
| Goethe | Graves | Gudrun | halala | hassle | Helena |
| goggle | gravid | guffaw | halide | hasten | Helene |
| goitre | grazer | Guiana | halier | hatful | Helios |
| golden | grease | guilty | Halley | Hathor | helium |

| | | | | | |
|---|---|---|---|---|---|
| Heller | Hobart | horsey | Huxley | impure | insect |
| helmet | Hobbes | hostel | huzzah | impute | insert |
| helper | hobbit | hotbed | hyaena | inborn | inside |
| Hendry | hobble | hotdog | hybrid | inbred | insist |
| hepcat | hobnob | hotpot | hymnal | incest | insole |
| herald | hockey | hourly | hyphae | incise | instep |
| herbal | hogger | Howard | hyphen | incite | instil |
| herbed | hogget | howdah | Hypnos | income | insult |
| Herbie | holder | howler | hyssop | incubi | insure |
| herder | holism | howzat | | indeed | intact |
| hereby | holler | hoyden | **I** | indent | intake |
| herein | hollow | Hubble | | Indian | intend |
| hereof | Holmes | hubbub | iambic | indict | intent |
| heresy | homage | hubcap | iambus | indigo | intern |
| hereto | homely | Hubert | Ianthe | Indira | intone |
| Herman | homily | hubris | Ibadan | indium | intuit |
| Hermes | homing | huddle | Iberia | indoor | invade |
| Hermia | hominy | Hudson | Ibizan | induce | invent |
| hermit | honcho | hugely | Icarus | induct | invert |
| hernia | honest | hugger | icebox | infamy | invest |
| heroic | honour | Hughes | icicle | infant | invite |
| heroin | Honshu | Hughie | iconic | infect | invoke |
| herpes | hooded | humane | idiocy | infest | inward |
| Herren | hoodie | Humber | ignite | infill | iodide |
| Herzog | hoodoo | humble | ignore | infirm | iodine |
| Hesiod | hoofed | humbly | Iguaçu | inflow | iodise |
| Hester | hoofer | humbug | iguana | influx | iodize |
| heyday | hookah | humeri | imager | inform | Ionian |
| hiatus | hooked | hummer | imbibe | infuse | ionise |
| hiccup | hooker | hummus | Imbros | ingest | ionize |
| hickey | hookey | humour | Imelda | Ingres | irenic |
| Hickok | hooped | hunger | immune | Ingrid | ironic |
| hidden | hoopla | hungry | immure | inhale | irrupt |
| hiding | hoopoe | hunker | Imogen | inhere | Irtysh |
| highly | hooray | hunter | impact | inject | Irvine |
| hijack | hootch | hurdle | impair | injure | Irving |
| Hilary | hooter | hurley | impala | injury | Isabel |
| hinder | Hoover | hurrah | impale | inland | Isaiah |
| hipped | hopper | hurray | impart | inmate | Ischia |
| hippie | Horace | hurtle | impede | inmost | Iseult |
| hither | Hormuz | Husain | impend | innate | Ishbel |
| Hitler | horned | hussar | impish | inning | Ishtar |
| hitter | hornet | hustle | import | inroad | island |
| hoarse | horrid | Huston | impose | inrush | Ismail |
| hoaxer | horror | Hutton | impugn | insane | isobar |

| | | | | | |
|---|---|---|---|---|---|
| Isobel | jejuna | Jolene | **K** | kernel | kopeck |
| Isolde | jejune | Jolson | | Kernow | Korbut |
| isomer | Jekyll | Jolyon | Kabila | Kerrie | Korean |
| Israel | Jemima | Jonson | kabuki | ketone | koruna |
| issuer | Jenner | Joplin | kaftan | kettle | kosher |
| isthmi | Jennie | Jordan | kagoul | Keynes | Kosovo |
| italic | jerboa | Jorvik | kahuna | keypad | kowtow |
| Ithaca | Jeremy | Joseph | kaiser | Khaled | kraken |
| itself | jerker | josher | kakapo | Khalid | Kraków |
| | jerkin | Joshua | kameez | Khalsa | kronor |
| **J** | Jerome | Josiah | Kanpur | kibosh | Kronos |
| | jersey | Josias | Kansas | kicker | kronur |
| jabber | jessie | jostle | kaolin | kiddie | krooni |
| jabiru | jester | jotter | Kapoor | kidnap | Kruger |
| jackal | Jesuit | jounce | karate | kidney | kümmel |
| jacket | Jethro | jovial | Kariba | Kieran | Kuwait |
| Jackie | jetsam | joyful | Karina | Kigali | kvetch |
| jacksy | Jewess | joyous | karmic | killer | kwacha |
| Jacobi | Jewish | joypad | Karnak | Kilroy | kwaito |
| Jacqui | Jibuti | Juárez | Karpov | kilted | kwanza |
| Jaffna | Jiddah | Jubran | Karroo | kilter | kybosh |
| jagged | jigger | Judaea | kasbah | kimchi | Kyushu |
| Jagger | jiggle | Judaic | Kaunda | kimono | |
| jaguar | jiggly | judder | Kaveri | kindle | |
| jailer | jigsaw | Judges | Keaton | kindly | **L** |
| Jaipur | jihadi | Judith | Keegan | kingly | |
| jalopy | jingle | juggle | Keeler | Kinsey | laager |
| Jancis | jingly | juicer | Keeley | kipper | labial |
| jangle | Jinnah | jujube | keenly | Kirkuk | labile |
| jangly | jitter | Julian | keeper | kirsch | labium |
| Janice | joanna | Juliet | Keller | Kirsty | labour |
| Janine | Joanne | Julius | Kellie | kirtle | lacing |
| Jansen | jobber | jumble | keloid | kismet | lackey |
| jargon | Joburg | jumper | kelpie | kisser | Laclos |
| Jarman | jockey | Juneau | kelson | kitbag | lactic |
| Jarrod | jocose | jungle | kelvin | kitsch | lacuna |
| Jarrow | jocund | jungly | Kemble | kitten | Ladakh |
| Jarvis | Joffre | junior | Kendal | klaxon | ladder |
| jasper | jogger | junket | Kendra | kludge | laddie |
| jaunty | joggle | junkie | kennel | klutzy | Ladino |
| Jeanie | Johnny | jurist | Kenton | knight | Ladoga |
| Jeanne | Johore | Justin | Kenyan | knobby | lagoon |
| Jeddah | joiner | justly | Kepler | knotty | Lahore |
| Jeeves | jojoba | Jutish | Kerala | Kodály | lamely |
| jehadi | Joleen | | kermes | Komodo | lament |
| | | | | | lamina |

| | | | | | |
|---|---|---|---|---|---|
| Lammas | laxity | Lerner | limply | lodger | Lugosi |
| lancer | layman | Lesage | linage | logger | Lukács |
| lancet | laymen | Lesbos | linden | loggia | lumbar |
| landau | La'youn | lesion | lineal | logjam | lumber |
| landed | layout | Lesley | linear | loiter | lumina |
| lander | lazily | Leslie | lingam | Lolita | lummox |
| Landor | leaded | lessee | linger | lollop | lumpen |
| langur | leaden | lessen | lining | Lombok | lunacy |
| Lantau | leader | lesser | linker | London | lupine |
| lapdog | league | lesson | linnet | lonely | lurker |
| lappet | leaker | lessor | lintel | Lonnie | Lusaka |
| laptop | Leakey | Lester | Lionel | loofah | lushly |
| larder | Leanne | lethal | lipase | looker | lustre |
| lardon | leaper | letter | lippie | lookup | Luther |
| lariat | learnt | Lettie | liquid | loosen | Lutuli |
| Larkin | leaven | Levant | liquor | looter | luvvie |
| larvae | leaver | levity | Lisbon | lopper | luxury |
| larval | Leavis | lewdly | lisper | loquat | Lyceum |
| larynx | Lebrun | Leyden | lissom | lordly | lychee |
| lassie | lecher | liable | listed | Loreen | Lyndon |
| Lassus | ledger | liaise | listen | Lorenz | Lytton |
| lastly | leeway | Lianne | Lister | lotion | |
| lately | leftie | libber | Liston | Lottie | |
| latent | legacy | libido | litany | louche | **M** |
| lather | legate | Libran | litchi | louden | |
| Latina | legato | Libyan | litmus | loudly | Maasai |
| Latino | legend | lichen | litter | Louisa | Mabuse |
| latish | legion | lidded | little | Louise | macron |
| Latium | legume | Liesel | Littré | lounge | macula |
| Latona | Leiden | Liffey | lively | louvre | macule |
| latter | Leilah | lifter | livery | lovage | Madame |
| Latvia | Lemmon | Ligeti | living | Lovell | madcap |
| Lauder | Lemnos | ligger | lizard | lovely | madden |
| Launce | lemony | lights | Lizzie | Lowell | madder |
| launch | Lemuel | lignin | Lloyd's | lowish | Maddie |
| laurel | lender | likely | loaded | Luanda | madman |
| Lauren | length | liking | loader | lubber | madmen |
| Laurie | Lennie | Lilian | loafer | Lübeck | madras |
| Lavina | Lennon | Lilith | loathe | lucent | Madrid |
| lavish | Lennox | Lillee | lobate | Lucian | Madura |
| lawful | Lenore | Lillie | locale | Lucien | maenad |
| lawman | Lenten | limber | locate | Lucius | Magadi |
| lawmen | lentil | limner | locker | Luella | Maggie |
| Lawrie | Leonie | limpet | locket | Lugano | maggot |
| lawyer | lepton | limpid | locust | lugger | maglev |
| | | | | | magnet |

| | | | | | |
|---|---|---|---|---|---|
| magnox | Mansel | maroon | meddle | mermen | minded |
| magnum | Manson | marque | mediae | Mersey | minder |
| Magnus | mantel | marrow | medial | Mervin | minger |
| magpie | mantis | Marsha | median | Mervyn | mingle |
| Magyar | mantle | marshy | Medici | mescal | Mingus |
| Mahler | mantra | marten | medico | Meshed | minima |
| Mahore | Mantua | Martha | medina | Mesmer | minion |
| mahout | manual | Martie | medium | Messrs | Minnie |
| maiden | Manuel | martin | medlar | meteor | minnow |
| mailer | manuka | Martyn | medley | method | Minoan |
| mainly | manure | martyr | medusa | methyl | Minton |
| Maisie | Maoism | marvel | meekly | métier | minuet |
| making | Maoist | Marvin | Meggie | metric | minute |
| Malabo | Maputo | Marvyn | Meghan | mettle | mirage |
| malady | Maquis | Masada | Mekele | Meucci | Miriam |
| Malaga | maraca | masala | Meknès | Mexico | mirror |
| Malawi | maraud | mascot | Mekong | miasma | miscue |
| Malaya | marble | Maseru | Melaka | Michel | misery |
| Malian | Marcel | masked | Mellon | mickey | misfit |
| Malibu | Marcia | masque | mellow | mickle | mishap |
| malice | Marcie | massif | melody | Micmac | mishit |
| malign | Marcus | Masson | Melvin | micron | mislay |
| mallee | Marduk | master | Melvyn | midair | missal |
| mallet | Margie | mastic | member | midday | missis |
| mallow | margin | matily | Memnon | midden | missus |
| Malory | Margot | matrix | memoir | middle | mister |
| mammae | Mariam | matron | memory | midget | misuse |
| mammal | Marian | matted | menace | midoff | mither |
| Mammon | Mariel | matter | Mendel | midrib | mitten |
| manage | Marika | Mattie | mender | midway | mizuna |
| Manama | marina | mature | menhir | mighty | mizzen |
| mañana | marine | matzoh | menial | mihrab | mizzle |
| Manaus | Marion | Maudie | meninx | mikado | moaner |
| Manchu | Marisa | Maundy | menses | milady | mobile |
| manège | Marita | maxima | mental | milage | Mobutu |
| manful | Marius | Maxine | mentor | mildew | mocker |
| manger | marked | Mayday | Mercia | mildly | Modena |
| mangle | marker | mayfly | Merckx | milieu | modern |
| maniac | market | mayhem | merely | miller | modest |
| Manila | markka | McEwan | merger | millet | modify |
| manioc | markup | meadow | Meriel | Millie | modish |
| Manley | Marley | meagre | merino | milord | module |
| manned | marlin | mealie | merlin | Milton | moduli |
| manner | marmot | meanly | Merlot | mimosa | moggie |
| manqué | Marnie | measly | merman | mincer | Moghul |

| | | | | | |
|---|---|---|---|---|---|
| mohair | Mosley | Murray | narrow | neural | Norris |
| Mohave | mosque | muscat | Narvik | neuron | Norway |
| Mohawk | Mossad | muscle | Naseby | neuter | nosily |
| moiety | Mostar | muscly | Nassau | Nevada | notary |
| Mojave | mostly | museum | Nasser | Nevers | notate |
| molest | mother | muskeg | Nathan | Newark | notice |
| Molise | motile | musket | nation | Newman | notify |
| mollie | motion | Muslim | native | newton | notion |
| Moloch | motive | muslin | Natron | niacin | nougat |
| molten | motley | mussel | natter | Niamey | nought |
| moment | Motown | muster | nature | nibble | Nouméa |
| Monaco | mottle | mustn't | naught | niblet | novena |
| Monday | mouldy | mutant | nausea | Nicaea | novice |
| Mongol | mouser | mutate | Navaho | nicely | nozzle |
| Monica | mousey | mutely | Navajo | nicety | nuance |
| monied | mousse | mutiny | Nazism | nickel | Nubian |
| monism | mouthy | mutter | nearby | nicker | nubile |
| monist | moving | mutton | nearly | Nicola | Nubuck |
| monkey | Mozart | mutual | neaten | Nicole | nuclei |
| monody | mucker | muumuu | neatly | niello | nudism |
| Monroe | muckle | muzzle | nebula | niggle | nudist |
| moolah | mucosa | myelin | Neckar | niggly | nudity |
| Moonie | mucous | myopia | nectar | nights | nugget |
| moppet | muddle | myopic | Neddie | nimble | number |
| moptop | muesli | myriad | needle | nimbly | numbly |
| morale | muffin | myrtle | needn't | nimbus | numina |
| morass | muffle | myself | negate | Nimrud | nuncio |
| morbid | Mugabe | Mysore | Negros | ninety | nutmeg |
| Moreau | mugger | mystic | Neisse | Ninian | nutria |
| Morgan | Mughal | mythic | Nellie | nipper | nutter |
| morgue | mukluk | | nelson | nipple | nuzzle |
| Morley | mulish | **N** | Nepali | Nippon | nympho |
| Mormon | mullah | | nephew | nitwit | |
| mornay | mullet | Nablus | Nereid | nobble | **O** |
| Moroni | Mumbai | Nadine | Nereus | nobody | |
| morose | mumble | naevus | Nerina | noddle | oafish |
| Morris | mummer | namely | Neruda | nodule | Oakley |
| morrow | Munich | Nansen | Nesbit | Noelle | obelus |
| morsel | muppet | Nantes | Nessie | noggin | Oberon |
| mortal | Murcia | napalm | nester | noodle | object |
| mortar | murder | napery | nestle | nookie | oblate |
| Morton | Muriel | Napier | Nestor | Nordic | oblige |
| mosaic | murmur | napkin | nether | Noreen | oblong |
| Moscow | Murnau | Naples | Nettie | normal | oboist |
| Moslem | Murphy | napper | nettle | Norman | O'Brien |

obsess
obtain
obtuse
O'Casey
occult
occupy
ocelot
o'clock
octane
octave
octavo
ocular
oculus
oddity
Odense
Odessa
Odette
odious
oedema
Oenone
oeuvre
Offaly
offcut
offend
office
offing
offish
offset
Ofsted
Ogaden
oilcan
Ojibwa
Oldham
oldish
Oliver
Olivia
omertà
onager
O'Neill
oniony
online
onrush
onside
onward
oodles

oolite
oolong
oompah
Oonagh
opaque
opener
openly
opiate
opioid
Oporto
oppose
oppugn
optics
optima
option
orache
oracle
orally
orange
orator
orchid
ordain
ordeal
ordure
Oregon
orgasm
Oriana
orient
origin
oriole
orison
Orissa
Orkney
ormolu
ornate
ornery
orphan
orrery
Ortega
Orwell
Osbert
Oshawa
Osiris
osmium
Osmond

osprey
Ossian
ossify
Ostend
ostler
Oswald
otiose
otitis
O'Toole
Ottawa
outage
outbid
outcry
outfit
outfox
outgas
outgun
outing
outlaw
outlay
outlet
output
outran
outrun
outset
outwit
overdo
overly
Oviedo
ovular
owlish
Oxford
oxtail
oxygen
oyster

# P

pablum
pacify
Pacino
packer
packet
Padang
paddle

padsaw
paella
paeony
Pagnol
pagoda
Pahang
pained
Paiute
pakora
palace
palais
palate
palely
paling
Pallas
pallet
pallid
pallor
Palmer
paltry
Pamela
pampas
pamper
Panaji
panama
pander
pandit
paneer
panini
panino
Panjim
pantry
panzer
papacy
papaya
papery
Papuan
papule
papyri
parade
Paraná
parcel
pardon
parent
parget

pariah
paring
parish
parity
Parker
parkin
parlay
parley
parody
parole
parrot
parsec
Parsee
parson
partly
Parton
pascal
Pashto
passer
passim
pastel
pastie
pastis
pastor
pastry
patchy
patent
pathos
patina
Patmos
patois
Patras
patrol
patron
patten
patter
Pattie
paunch
pauper
pavane
Pavese
paving
Pavlov
Pawnee
pawpaw

Paxton
payola
payout
peachy
peahen
peaked
peanut
pearly
pebble
pebbly
pectin
pedalo
pedant
peddle
pedlar
peeler
peeper
peewit
Peking
Pelham
pellet
pelmet
pelota
pelvic
pelvis
Penang
pencil
penile
penman
penmen
pennon
pensée
pentad
penury
people
Peoria
Pepita
peplum
pepper
pepsin
peptic
period
perish
permit
Perrin

| | | | | | |
|---|---|---|---|---|---|
| Persia | picket | plaice | policy | pouchy | protea |
| person | pickle | plaint | polish | pouffe | proton |
| pertly | pickup | planar | polite | pounce | Proust |
| peruke | picnic | Planck | polity | pourer | proven |
| peruse | piddle | planer | pollen | pouter | prover |
| Pesach | pidgin | planet | Pollux | powder | Prozac |
| peseta | pierce | plaque | pomade | Powell | pruner |
| pester | Pierre | plashy | pomelo | powwow | Psalms |
| pestle | piffle | plasma | pommel | Poznań | pseudo |
| Pétain | pigeon | platen | Pompey | Prague | psyche |
| petard | piglet | plater | pompom | praise | psycho |
| Petipa | pigsty | player | pompon | prance | public |
| petite | Pilate | pleach | poncey | Pravda | pucker |
| petrel | pilfer | please | poncho | praxis | puddle |
| Petrie | pillar | plebby | ponder | prayer | pueblo |
| petrol | pillow | pledge | poodle | preach | puffer |
| Petula | pimple | plenty | poorly | precis | puffin |
| pewter | pimply | plenum | pootle | prefab | puller |
| peyote | Pinang | pleura | popgun | prefer | pullet |
| phalli | pincer | plexus | poplar | prefix | pulley |
| Pharos | Pindar | pliant | poplin | prepay | pulpit |
| phatic | Pinero | pliers | popper | preppy | pulsar |
| phenol | pinion | plight | poppet | preset | pumice |
| phenyl | pinkie | plinky | popsie | presto | pummel |
| Philby | pinnae | plinth | porker | pretty | punchy |
| Philip | Pinter | plough | porous | Previn | pundit |
| phizog | pintle | plover | portal | prewar | punily |
| phlegm | Pinyin | plucky | porter | pricey | punish |
| phloem | piping | plummy | Portia | priest | Punjab |
| phobia | pippin | plunge | portly | primal | punkah |
| phobic | piquet | plural | poseur | primer | punnet |
| Phoebe | piracy | plushy | poshly | primly | punter |
| phoney | pirate | pocked | posset | Primus | pupate |
| phonic | Pisano | pocket | possum | prince | puppet |
| phooey | Pisces | podium | postal | priory | purdah |
| photon | pistil | poetic | poster | prison | purely |
| phrase | pistol | poetry | potage | prissy | purify |
| Phuket | piston | pogrom | potash | privet | purism |
| phyllo | pistou | pointy | potato | prober | purist |
| phylum | pitchy | Poirot | poteen | profit | purity |
| physic | Pitman | poisha | potent | prolix | purler |
| physio | pitted | poison | pother | prompt | purlin |
| Piaget | placer | Poland | potion | pronto | purple |
| piazza | placid | polder | potted | propel | purply |
| picker | plague | police | potter | proper | purser |

pursue
purvey
pusher
Puskas
putrid
putsch
puttee
putter
puzzle
pylori
pyrite
Pyrrho
Pythia
python

# Q

Qatari
qigong
quagga
quaint
Quaker
quango
quanta
quarry
quarto
quartz
quasar
quaver
queasy
Quebec
Queens
Queeny
quench
quiche
quince
quinsy
quinta
quirky
quiver
Qumran
quorum
qwerty

# R

Rabbie
rabbit
rabble
rabies
raceme
Rachel
racial
racily
Racine
racing
racism
racist
racket
racoon
radial
radian
radish
radium
radius
radome
Rafael
raffia
raffle
rafter
ragbag
ragged
raglan
ragout
ragtag
raider
Raipur
raiser
raisin
Rajput
rakish
Ralegh
Ramani
ramble
Rameau
ramify
rammer
Ramona
ramrod

Ramsay
Ramsey
rancid
random
ranger
ranker
rankle
ransom
ranter
Ranulf
rapier
rapine
rapist
rappel
rapper
raptly
raptor
Raquel
rarely
raring
rarity
rascal
rasher
Rashid
rashly
raster
ratbag
rather
ratify
rating
ration
rattan
ratted
rattle
rattly
raunch
ravage
ravine
raving
ravish
razzle
reader
Reagan
really
realty

reamer
reaper
reason
rebate
reboot
reborn
rebuff
rebuke
recall
recant
recast
recede
recent
recess
Recife
recipe
recite
reckon
recoil
record
recoup
rectal
rector
rectum
recuse
redact
redcap
redden
redeem
redial
redone
redraw
redrew
reduce
reeded
reefer
reface
refill
refine
reflex
reflux
reform
refuel
refuge
refund

refuse
refute
regain
regale
regard
regent
reggae
Reggie
regime
Regina
region
regret
regrew
regrow
regulo
rehash
reheat
reject
rejoin
relate
relent
relict
relief
relish
relive
reload
remade
remain
remake
remand
remark
remedy
remind
remiss
remora
remote
remove
rename
Renata
render
renege
Rennes
rennet
Renoir
renown

rental
renter
reopen
repair
repast
repeal
repeat
repent
repine
replay
report
repose
Repton
repute
reread
resale
rescue
reseal
resell
resent
reside
resign
resist
resize
resort
result
resume
retail
retain
retake
retard
retell
retina
retire
retook
retort
retune
return
retype
Reuben
revamp
reveal
revere
revers
revert

| | | | | | |
|---|---|---|---|---|---|
| review | rising | Rostov | Russel | salvia | Saxony |
| revile | risqué | rostra | russet | salwar | Sayers |
| revise | ritual | rotary | Russia | Salyut | saying |
| revive | Rivera | rotate | rustic | sambal | scabby |
| revoke | Riyadh | rotgut | rustle | samite | scalar |
| revolt | roadie | Rothko | Ruthie | Samoan | scally |
| reward | roamer | rotten | rutted | samosa | scampi |
| rewind | robber | rotter | Rwanda | sampan | scanty |
| rewire | Robbie | rotund | | sample | scarab |
| reword | Robert | rouble | **S** | Samson | scarce |
| rework | Robina | router | | Samuel | scared |
| Rheims | Robson | Rowena | Sabina | sandal | scatty |
| rheumy | robust | Roxana | Sabine | sander | scenic |
| Rhodes | rocker | Roxane | sachem | Sandie | schema |
| rhombi | rocket | rozzer | sachet | Sandra | scheme |
| Rhonda | rococo | rubati | sacral | sanely | schism |
| rhumba | rodent | rubato | sacred | Sanger | schist |
| rhymer | Rodger | rubber | sacrum | sanity | schlep |
| rhythm | Rodney | rubble | sadden | santim | school |
| Rialto | Rogers | rubbly | saddle | sapele | schtum |
| ribald | Rohmer | Rubens | sadism | sapper | Schulz |
| riband | Roisin | rubric | sadist | Sappho | schuss |
| ribbed | Roland | ruched | safari | sarape | scilla |
| ribbon | roller | ruckus | safely | sarnie | Scipio |
| riches | Romans | rudder | safety | sarong | sclera |
| Richie | Romany | rudely | sagely | sarsen | sconce |
| richly | romcom | rudery | Sahara | Sartre | scorch |
| rictal | Romish | Rudolf | Saigon | Saskia | scorer |
| rictus | Rommel | rueful | sailor | sashay | Scotch |
| ridden | Romney | ruffle | Saipan | satang | Scouse |
| riddle | Ronald | rufous | saithe | sateen | scrape |
| riding | Ronnie | rugged | salaam | satiny | scrawl |
| Ridley | roofer | rugger | salami | satire | scream |
| riffle | rookie | ruling | salary | satrap | screed |
| rigger | Rooney | rumble | saline | Saturn | screen |
| rigour | rootle | rumour | Salish | saucer | screwy |
| Rimini | rootsy | rumple | saliva | savage | scribe |
| ringer | ropily | rumpus | sallow | Savai'i | scrimp |
| rinser | rosary | runnel | Salman | savant | script |
| rioter | Roseau | runner | salmon | saving | scroll |
| ripely | rosily | runway | Salome | savory | scrota |
| ripper | Rosina | Runyon | saloon | savour | scruff |
| ripple | Rosita | Rupert | saluki | sawfly | scrump |
| ripply | Roslyn | rupiah | salute | sawyer | sculpt |
| ripsaw | roster | Ruskin | salver | saxist | scummy |

| | | | | | |
|---|---|---|---|---|---|
| scurfy | Seneca | shader | shindy | Sigurd | skidoo |
| scurry | senile | shadow | shiner | Sikkim | skiing |
| scurvy | senior | shaggy | Shinto | silage | skimpy |
| scuzzy | señora | shaken | shinty | silent | skinny |
| Scylla | sensei | shaker | Shiraz | silica | skiver |
| scythe | sensor | shalom | Shires | silken | skivvy |
| seabed | sentry | shaman | shirty | silver | Skopje |
| sealer | sepsis | Shamir | shiver | Silvia | Skylab |
| seaman | septal | shammy | shoddy | Simeon | skyway |
| seamen | septet | shamus | shogun | simian | slalom |
| seamer | septic | shandy | shorts | simile | slangy |
| Seamus | septum | Shania | shorty | simmer | slater |
| Seanad | sequel | Shansi | should | Simnel | slaver |
| seance | sequin | shanty | shovel | Simone | Slavic |
| search | serape | Shanxi | shower | simony | slayer |
| Searle | seraph | shaped | shrank | simoom | sleaze |
| season | Serbia | shaper | shrewd | simoon | sleazy |
| seaway | Serena | sharer | shriek | simper | sledge |
| secant | serene | sharia | shrike | simple | sleepy |
| secede | Sergei | Sharon | shrill | simply | sleety |
| second | Sergio | Shauna | shrimp | Sinbad | sleeve |
| secret | serial | shaven | shrine | Sinead | sleigh |
| sector | series | shaver | shrink | sinewy | sleuth |
| secure | sermon | shaykh | shrive | sinful | slicer |
| sedate | serous | shears | shroud | singer | slider |
| seduce | server | sheath | shrove | single | slight |
| Seeger | sesame | sheave | shrunk | singly | slinky |
| seeing | sestet | Sheena | shtick | sinker | slippy |
| seeker | settee | Sheene | shufti | sinner | slitty |
| seemly | setter | sheikh | Sicily | sinter | sliver |
| seethe | settle | Sheila | sicken | siphon | Sloane |
| seldom | Seumas | shekel | sickie | sipper | slobby |
| select | Seurat | shelly | sickle | Sirius | slogan |
| Selena | severe | Shelta | sickly | siskin | sloosh |
| Selene | Severn | shelve | siding | Sisley | sloppy |
| Selina | Sèvres | Shensi | Sidney | sister | sloshy |
| seller | sewage | Sherpa | sienna | sitcom | slouch |
| Selous | sexily | Sherri | sierra | sitter | slough |
| Selwyn | sexism | sherry | siesta | sizzle | Slovak |
| Semele | sexist | Sheryl | sifter | Skanda | sloven |
| Semite | sexpot | shield | Signac | skanky | slowly |
| Semtex | sextet | shifty | signal | skater | sludge |
| senate | sexton | Shiism | signer | skerry | sludgy |
| Sendak | sexual | Shiite | signet | sketch | sluice |
| sender | shabby | shimmy | signor | skewer | slummy |

| | | | | | |
|---|---|---|---|---|---|
| slurry | socket | spadix | sprout | Steele | stride |
| slushy | sodden | sparky | spruce | steely | strife |
| slutty | sodium | sparse | sprung | stelae | strike |
| smarmy | sodomy | Sparta | spunky | Stella | Strine |
| smeary | soffit | spathe | spurge | stench | string |
| smelly | soften | specie | sputum | steppe | stripe |
| Smersh | softie | speech | squall | stereo | stripy |
| smiley | softly | speedo | square | sterna | strive |
| smirch | soigné | speedy | squash | Sterne | strobe |
| smirky | soirée | Spence | squawk | sterol | strode |
| smithy | solace | spewer | squeak | Steven | stroke |
| smoggy | solder | sphere | squeal | Stevie | stroll |
| smoker | solely | sphinx | squill | sticky | strong |
| smokey | solemn | spider | squint | stifle | strove |
| smooch | Solent | spiffy | squire | stigma | struck |
| smooth | solidi | spigot | squirm | stingy | strung |
| smudge | solute | spinal | squirt | stinky | Struve |
| smudgy | solver | spinel | squish | stitch | Stuart |
| smugly | Somali | spinet | stable | stocky | Stubbs |
| smutty | sombre | spiral | stably | stodge | stubby |
| Smyrna | Somoza | spirit | Stacey | stodgy | stucco |
| snaggy | sonata | spivvy | stadia | stoker | studio |
| snakey | sonics | splash | Staffa | stolen | studly |
| snappy | sonnet | spleen | stagey | stolid | stuffy |
| snarly | Sonora | splice | Stalin | stoned | stumpy |
| snatch | Sontag | spliff | stalky | stoner | stupid |
| snazzy | soothe | spline | stamen | stooge | stupor |
| sneaky | Sophia | splint | stance | Stopes | sturdy |
| sneeze | Sophie | splosh | stanch | storey | styler |
| sneezy | sorbet | spoilt | stanza | stormy | stylus |
| snidey | sordid | spoken | staple | stotin | stymie |
| sniffy | sorely | sponge | starch | strafe | subdue |
| sniper | sorrel | spongy | Starck | strain | sublet |
| snippy | sorrow | spooky | starer | strait | submit |
| snitch | sorted | sporty | starry | strand | suborn |
| snivel | sorter | spotty | starve | strata | subset |
| snobby | sortie | spouse | stasis | strath | subtle |
| snooty | sought | sprain | States | streak | subtly |
| snooze | source | sprang | static | stream | suburb |
| snoozy | sourly | sprawl | statin | Streep | subway |
| snorer | Sousse | spread | statue | street | Suchou |
| snugly | soviet | spring | status | stress | Suchow |
| Sobers | Soweto | sprint | stayer | strewn | sucker |
| soccer | spacer | sprite | steady | striae | suckle |
| social | spacey | spritz | steamy | strict | sudden |

| | | | | | |
|---|---|---|---|---|---|
| sudoku | swatch | talent | tautly | tetrad | throat |
| suffer | swathe | talker | tavern | Teuton | throes |
| suffix | sweaty | talkie | tawdry | texter | throne |
| Sufism | Sweden | Tallis | taxing | Thalia | throng |
| sugary | swerve | tallow | taxman | Thames | throve |
| suitor | swingy | Talmud | taxmen | thanks | thrown |
| sullen | swirly | tamale | Taylor | thatch | thrush |
| sultan | swishy | Tamara | teacup | Thebes | thrust |
| sultry | switch | tamely | teapot | theirs | Thurso |
| sumach | swivel | tamper | teasel | theism | thwack |
| summer | swoosh | tampon | teaser | theist | thwart |
| summit | swotty | Tamsin | teazel | Thelma | thymic |
| summon | Sydney | tandem | teazle | Themis | thymol |
| sunbed | sylvan | tangle | techie | thence | thymus |
| sundae | Sylvia | tangly | techno | theory | tibiae |
| Sunday | Sylvie | Tanith | Teddie | there's | tibial |
| sunder | symbol | tanker | tedium | thesis | ticker |
| sundew | Symons | tanner | teensy | Thetis | ticket |
| sundry | syndic | tannic | teepee | they'll | tickle |
| Sunita | syntax | tannin | teeter | they're | tickly |
| sunken | synthy | tannoy | teethe | they've | tiddly |
| sunlit | syphon | tantra | Teflon | thieve | tidily |
| sunset | Syrian | Taoism | Tehran | Thimbu | tiepin |
| suntan | syrupy | Taoist | teller | thingy | tiered |
| superb | system | tapper | telnet | thinly | tiffin |
| supine | | tappet | tempeh | thirst | tights |
| supper | **T** | target | temper | thirty | Tigray |
| supple | | tariff | temple | Thisbe | Tigris |
| supply | tabard | tarmac | tenant | Thomas | tiling |
| surely | tablet | tarpon | tender | thorax | tiller |
| Sûreté | tackle | tarsal | tendon | thorny | tilter |
| surety | tactic | tarsus | tenner | Thorpe | timber |
| surfer | tagine | tartan | tennis | though | timbre |
| Surrey | Tagore | Tartar | tenpin | Thrace | timely |
| surtax | tahini | tartly | tenure | Thrale | timing |
| survey | Tahiti | Tarzan | Teresa | thrall | tinder |
| Sussex | tailor | Tasman | termly | thrash | tingle |
| suttee | Tainan | tassel | terror | thread | tingly |
| suture | taipan | taster | Tessie | threat | tinily |
| Suzhou | Taipei | tatami | testae | thresh | tinker |
| Suzman | Taiwan | tattle | tester | thrice | tinkle |
| svelte | tajine | tattoo | testis | thrift | tinkly |
| swampy | takahe | taught | tetchy | thrill | tinpot |
| Swanee | taking | Taurus | tether | thrips | tinsel |
| swanky | Talbot | tauten | Tethys | thrive | tipper |

| | | | | | |
|---|---|---|---|---|---|
| tippet | torpor | triode | Tupian | uglify | unlace |
| tipple | torque | triple | turban | ullage | unless |
| tiptoe | torrid | triply | turbid | Ulrica | unlike |
| tirade | torten | tripod | turbot | Ulrika | unload |
| Tirana | totter | tripos | tureen | ulster | unlock |
| Tiranë | toucan | trippy | turgid | umbrae | unmade |
| tisane | touché | Trisha | Turing | umbral | unmask |
| tissue | touchy | Triton | turkey | Umbria | unmoor |
| titbit | Toulon | triune | Turkic | umlaut | unpack |
| titchy | toupee | trivet | turner | umpire | unpaid |
| titfer | tourer | trivia | turnip | unable | unpick |
| Titian | tousle | Trixie | Turpin | unbend | unplug |
| titled | toward | troika | turret | unbent | unread |
| titter | townie | Trojan | turtle | unbolt | unreal |
| tittle | tracer | Tromsø | Tuscan | unborn | unreel |
| Tobago | Tracey | trophy | tusked | uncial | unrest |
| Tobias | trader | tropic | tusker | unclad | unripe |
| Tobruk | tragic | troppo | tussle | unclip | unroll |
| tocsin | Trajan | trough | Tuvalu | unclog | unruly |
| toddle | Tralee | troupe | tuxedo | uncoil | unsafe |
| toecap | trampy | trowel | twangy | uncool | unsaid |
| toerag | trance | Troyes | tweedy | uncork | unseal |
| toffee | tranny | truant | tweeze | uncurl | unseat |
| toggle | trashy | trudge | twelve | undies | unseen |
| toiler | trauma | Trudie | twenty | undone | unshed |
| toilet | travel | truism | twiggy | unduly | unship |
| Toledo | Travis | Truman | twilit | undyed | unsold |
| Toltec | treaty | trunks | twinge | unease | unsung |
| tomato | treble | trusty | twirly | uneasy | unsure |
| tomboy | trebly | trying | twisty | Unesco | untidy |
| tomcat | Trefor | tsetse | twitch | uneven | untold |
| tomtit | tremor | Tuareg | Tyburn | unfair | untrue |
| Tongan | trench | tubing | tycoon | unfold | unused |
| tongue | trendy | tubule | typhus | unfurl | unveil |
| Tonkin | trepan | tucker | typify | unhand | unwary |
| tonsil | Trevor | Tucson | typing | unhook | unwell |
| toothy | triage | tuffet | typist | unholy | unwind |
| tootle | tribal | tufted | tyrant | unhurt | unwise |
| tootsy | Tricia | tumble | Tyrone | Uniate | unworn |
| Topeka | tricky | tumour | | unique | unwrap |
| topper | tricot | tumuli | **U** | unisex | upbeat |
| topple | trifid | tumult | | unison | update |
| Torbay | trifle | tundra | Uffizi | united | Updike |
| torero | trilby | tunnel | Uganda | unjust | uphill |
| torpid | trimly | Tupelo | Ugarit | unkind | uphold |

upkeep
upland
uplift
uplink
upload
uppish
uppity
uprate
uproar
uproot
uprush
upshot
upside
upsize
uptake
uptime
uptown
upturn
upward
upwind
Urania
Uranus
urbane
urchin
ureter
urgent
urinal
ursine
Ursula
usable
useful
Usenet
usurer
uterus
utmost
Utopia
Utsire
Uttley
uvulae

**V**

vacant
vacate
vacuum

vagary
vagina
vainly
Vaisya
Valéry
valise
Valium
valley
Valois
valour
valuer
vandal
vanish
vanity
vapour
Varèse
varied
varlet
Varuna
Vasari
vassal
vastly
vector
veggie
veined
Velcro
veleta
vellum
velour
velvet
vendor
veneer
venery
venial
Venice
venous
verbal
Verdun
verger
Vergil
verify
verily
vérité
verity
vermin

vernal
Vernon
Verona
versed
versus
vertex
vessel
vestal
vestry
viable
viably
Viagra
victim
victor
vicuña
Vienna
viewer
vigour
Viking
vilely
vilify
villus
Vinnie
vinous
violet
violin
virago
Virgil
virgin
virile
virtue
visage
viscid
viscus
Vishnu
vision
visual
vivace
Vivian
Vivien
vivify
vizier
vizsla
Vltava
volley

volume
volute
voodoo
vortex
Vosges
Vostok
votary
votive
voyage
voyeur
Vulcan
vulgar
vulval

**W**

waddle
waffle
waffly
waggle
waggly
waggon
Wagner
wailer
waiter
waiver
Wałesa
walker
wallah
Waller
wallet
Wallis
wallop
wallow
walnut
walrus
Walter
Walton
wampum
wander
wangle
wanton
wapiti
warble
warden

warder
Warhol
warily
warmer
warmly
warmth
Warner
warren
Warsaw
wasabi
washer
waspie
waster
Waters
watery
Watson
wattle
Watusi
wavery
waylay
weaken
weakly
wealth
weapon
wearer
weasel
weaver
webbed
webcam
Webern
weblog
weekly
weeper
weepie
weevil
weight
Weimar
weirdo
welder
welkin
Welles
wellie
welter
weren't
Werner

Wesker
Wesley
Wessex
wether
Weyden
whacko
whacky
whaler
whammy
wheeze
wheezy
whence
wherry
whiffy
whilst
whimsy
whiner
whinge
whinny
whippy
whisky
Whitby
whiten
whitey
whizzy
wholly
whoops
whoosh
Wiccan
wicked
wicker
wicket
widdle
widely
widget
Widnes
Wiesel
wifely
wigeon
wiggle
wiggly
wigwam
Wilbur
Wilcox
Wilder

| | | | | | |
|---|---|---|---|---|---|
| wildly | Wisden | woolly | **Y** | yolked | zenana |
| wilful | wisdom | worker | | yonder | zenith |
| Wilkie | wisely | worsen | yacker | yorker | zephyr |
| Willie | witchy | worthy | Yahweh | Yoruba | zester |
| willow | withal | wowser | yakuza | Yorvik | zeugma |
| Wilmer | wither | wraith | yammer | Yossef | Zeuxis |
| Wilson | within | wrasse | Yamuna | Yunnan | Zhukov |
| wimple | witter | wreath | Yankee | yuppie | Zidane |
| winder | wizard | wrench | Yardie | Yvette | zigzag |
| window | wobble | wretch | yarrow | Yvonne | Zillah |
| winery | wobbly | wright | Yasmin | | Zimmer |
| winged | woeful | writer | yatter | **Z** | zinnia |
| winger | woggle | writhe | Yeager | | zipper |
| winker | Woking | Wyclif | yearly | Zagreb | zircon |
| winkle | Wolsey | Wystan | yeasty | Zambia | zither |
| winner | wombat | wyvern | Yehudi | zander | zodiac |
| Winnie | wonder | | yellow | Zandra | zombie |
| winnow | wonted | **X** | Yemeni | zanily | zounds |
| winter | wonton | | yeoman | Zanuck | Zurich |
| wintry | wooded | Xavier | yeomen | Zapata | zydeco |
| wiring | wooden | Xuzhou | yippee | zapper | zygote |
| Wirral | woofer | xylene | yogurt | zealot | |

# **7 LETTERS**

| **A** | abscond | Acheron | adapter | advance | agitate |
|---|---|---|---|---|---|
| | absence | Acheson | adaptor | adverse | Agnetha |
| abalone | absolve | achieve | addenda | advised | agonise |
| abandon | abstain | acidify | Addison | adviser | agonize |
| abdomen | abusive | acidity | address | aerated | agoroth |
| Abelard | abysmal | acolyte | Adeline | aerator | Agrippa |
| Aberfan | abyssal | aconite | adeptly | aerobic | aground |
| abettor | academe | acquire | adipose | aerosol | Agulhas |
| abiding | academy | acreage | adjourn | affable | aileron |
| Abidjan | accidie | acrobat | adjudge | affably | ailment |
| Abigail | acclaim | acronym | adjunct | afflict | aimless |
| ability | account | acrylic | admiral | affront | Ainsley |
| abolish | accrete | Actaeon | admirer | afghani | Ainslie |
| Abraham | accrual | actress | adoptee | African | Aintree |
| abreast | accuser | actuary | adopter | against | airbase |
| abridge | acerbic | actuate | adrenal | ageless | aircrew |
| Abruzzi | acetate | acutely | Adriana | agilely | airdrop |
| abscess | acetone | adamant | adulate | agility | airfare |

| | | | | | |
|---|---|---|---|---|---|
| airhead | alleged | amusing | anodize | aquatic | arsenal |
| airless | Allegra | amylase | anodyne | aquavit | arsenic |
| airlift | Allegri | anaemia | anomaly | aqueous | Artemis |
| airline | allegro | anaemic | anoraky | aquifer | article |
| airlock | Allende | anagram | another | Aquinas | artisan |
| airmail | allergy | Anaheim | Anouilh | Arabian | artiste |
| airplay | Allison | analogy | Anouska | arabica | artless |
| airport | almanac | analyse | antacid | Arabise | artwork |
| airship | Almería | analyst | Antalya | Arabism | arugula |
| airsick | almoner | Ananias | antenna | Arabist | ascetic |
| airside | almonry | anarchy | anthill | Arabize | ascribe |
| airtime | aloofly | Anatoly | Anthony | Arachne | aseptic |
| Aisling | Aloysia | anatomy | anthrax | Arafura | asexual |
| Aislinn | already | anchovy | Antibes | Aramaic | ashamed |
| Ajaccio | alright | ancient | antigen | Arapaho | Ashanti |
| Akihito | alumina | andante | Antigua | arbiter | Ashdown |
| akvavit | alumnus | andiron | Antioch | Arcadia | Ashmole |
| Alabama | Alvarez | Andorra | antique | arcanum | ashtray |
| Aladdin | alveoli | Andreas | Antoine | archaic | Asiatic |
| Alannah | alyssum | Andrews | Antonia | archery | asinine |
| Alarcón | amalgam | android | Antonio | archive | askance |
| Albania | amateur | anemone | antonym | archway | asphalt |
| Alberta | amatory | Aneurin | Antwerp | arcuate | aspirin |
| Alberti | amazing | angelic | anxiety | arduous | Asquith |
| Alberto | ambient | Angelou | anxious | areolae | assault |
| albumen | Ambrose | angelus | anybody | Ariadne | assegai |
| albumin | amenity | Anglian | Apelles | Arianna | assuage |
| alchemy | America | angling | aphasia | aridity | assured |
| alcohol | Amerind | Angolan | aphasic | Ariosto | Assyria |
| alcopop | Amharic | angrily | aphelia | Arizona | Astaire |
| Aldabra | amiable | anguish | aplenty | Armando | Astarte |
| alembic | amiably | angular | apology | armband | astilbe |
| alertly | ammeter | aniline | apostle | Armenia | astound |
| Alethea | ammonia | animate | apparel | armhole | astride |
| alfalfa | amnesia | animism | appease | armless | asunder |
| Alfonso | amnesty | animist | applaud | armload | Atacama |
| Alfreda | amoebae | anionic | applied | armlock | Atatürk |
| Algarve | amoebic | aniseed | appoint | armoire | atavism |
| algebra | amongst | Annabel | apprise | armoury | atelier |
| Algeria | amorous | annatto | approve | armrest | atheism |
| Algiers | amphora | annelid | apricot | arousal | atheist |
| Aligarh | amplify | Annette | apropos | arraign | athlete |
| alimony | ampoule | annuity | apsidal | arrange | athwart |
| aliquot | ampulla | annular | aptness | arrival | Atlanta |
| Allecto | amputee | anodise | aquaria | arrowed | atomise |

| | | | | |
|---|---|---|---|---|
| atomize | **B** | bambini | bastion | beeline | Bernice |
| atrophy | | bambino | Bateman | beeswax | Bernini |
| Atropos | Baalbek | banally | Bateson | beggary | berserk |
| attaché | Babbage | bandage | bathtub | begonia | Bertram |
| attempt | Babbitt | bandana | Batista | begorra | beseech |
| attract | babbler | bandbox | batiste | beguile | besides |
| Auberon | Babette | bandeau | batsman | beguine | besiege |
| auction | babyish | banding | batsmen | behaved | bespeak |
| audible | Babylon | bandsaw | battery | Behrens | bespoke |
| audibly | babysat | Bandung | battler | Behring | bestial |
| auditor | babysit | Bangkok | batwing | Beijing | betaken |
| Audubon | Bacchae | banking | Bauhaus | Belarus | Bethany |
| augment | Bacchus | banksia | bauxite | belated | bethink |
| Augusta | bachata | bannock | Bavaria | beldame | betimes |
| aurally | bacilli | banquet | bayonet | Belfast | betoken |
| aureate | backhoe | banshee | bazooka | Belgian | Bettina |
| Aurelia | backing | Banting | beadily | Belgium | between |
| aureole | backlog | baptise | beanbag | believe | betwixt |
| auricle | backlot | baptism | bearded | Belinda | Beverly |
| aurochs | Bactria | Baptist | bearing | bellboy | bewitch |
| aurorae | badness | baptize | bearish | bellhop | bezique |
| auspice | Bagehot | Barbara | beastie | Bellini | bhangra |
| austere | baggage | Barbary | beastly | bellows | bibelot |
| austral | Baghdad | barbell | beatbox | beloved | bicycle |
| Austria | bagpipe | Barbour | beatify | beltway | bidding |
| autarky | Bahamas | Barbuda | beatnik | Benares | bifocal |
| autocue | Bahrain | Barents | Beatrix | Bendigo | Bigfeet |
| autopsy | bailiff | bargain | Beattie | beneath | Bigfoot |
| avarice | baklava | barista | because | benefit | biggish |
| Avebury | Bakunin | barking | Beckett | Benelux | bigness |
| avenger | balafon | barmaid | Beckham | Bengali | bigoted |
| average | balance | Barnaby | bedding | benison | bigotry |
| aviator | Balaton | Barnard | Bedelia | Bennett | bilious |
| avidity | balcony | baronet | bedevil | Bentham | billing |
| Avignon | balding | baroque | Bedford | Bentley | billion |
| avocado | baldish | barrack | bedhead | benzene | billowy |
| awesome | Baldwin | barrage | bedizen | benzine | bindery |
| awfully | baleful | Barrett | Bedouin | Beowulf | binding |
| awkward | Balfour | barrier | bedpost | bequest | biochip |
| axially | ballade | barring | bedrock | Bergman | biocide |
| axolotl | Ballard | Barthes | bedroom | Bergson | biofuel |
| Azikiwe | ballast | barytes | bedsore | Berkoff | biology |
| azimuth | ballboy | bashful | bedtime | Berlioz | biomass |
| | balloon | bassist | Beecham | Bermuda | bipedal |
| | baloney | bassoon | beehive | Bernard | biplane |

| | | | | | |
|---|---|---|---|---|---|
| bipolar | blogger | bombast | bracing | brioche | bugloss |
| birding | blokish | Bonaire | bracken | briquet | builder |
| biretta | Blondin | bonanza | bracket | brisket | Bukhara |
| biriani | bloomer | bondage | bradawl | briskly | Bukhoro |
| biryani | blooper | bonfire | Bradley | bristle | bulbous |
| biscuit | blossom | bonkers | Bradman | bristly | bulimia |
| Bishkek | blotchy | Bonnard | Brahman | Bristol | bulimic |
| bismuth | blotter | bookend | Brahmin | Britain | bulldog |
| bittern | blouson | booking | Braille | British | bullion |
| bitumen | blowfly | bookish | braless | Britten | bullish |
| bivalve | blowout | booklet | bramble | brittle | bullock |
| bivouac | blubber | Boolean | Bramley | broaden | bulrush |
| bizarre | bludger | boonies | Branagh | broadly | bulwark |
| blabber | blueish | boorish | Brandon | brocade | bumpkin |
| blacken | bluffer | booster | Branson | Brocken | bungler |
| blackly | Blunden | bootleg | Branwen | Brodsky | bunting |
| bladder | blunder | boracic | brashly | broiler | buoyant |
| blagger | bluntly | boredom | bravado | broking | Burbage |
| Blanche | blusher | Bormann | bravely | bromide | Burbank |
| blandly | bluster | Bornean | bravery | bromine | burdock |
| blanket | boarder | Borodin | bravura | bronchi | bureaux |
| blankly | boaster | borough | brawler | Bronwen | burette |
| blarney | boating | borscht | brazier | Bronwyn | burgeon |
| blasted | boatman | borstal | breaded | brothel | burgess |
| blaster | boatmen | Bosnian | breadth | brother | burgher |
| blatant | bobsled | bossily | breaker | brought | burglar |
| blather | bobtail | Boswell | breathe | Brouwer | Burkina |
| blazing | bodhrán | botanic | breathy | brownie | Burmese |
| bleakly | Bogarde | botcher | breccia | browser | Burnett |
| bleeder | bogyman | Botoxed | breeder | Brubeck | burning |
| bleeper | bogymen | Boucher | Bregenz | Bruegel | burnish |
| blemish | Bohemia | boudoir | Brendan | bruiser | burnous |
| blender | bohrium | boulder | Brescia | Brummie | burnout |
| Blériot | boiling | bouncer | Bresson | brushed | burrito |
| blessed | Bokassa | bounden | brevity | brusque | bursary |
| Blighty | Bokhara | bounder | brewery | brutish | Burundi |
| blinder | boletus | bouquet | bribery | bubonic | bushido |
| blindly | bolivar | bourbon | Bridges | buckler | bushily |
| blinker | Bolivia | bourrée | Bridget | buckram | bushing |
| blister | bollard | bowline | briefly | bucolic | Bushman |
| blither | Bologna | bowling | brigade | budding | Bushmen |
| bloated | bolshie | boycott | brigand | buffalo | busload |
| bloater | bolster | boyhood | brimful | buffoon | bustard |
| blocker | Bolzano | Brabant | brindle | bugaboo | bustier |
| Blodwen | bombard | Brabham | bringer | bugbear | butcher |

**C**

| | | | | | |
|---|---|---|---|---|---|
| buttery | calumny | caption | cascade | cellist | charged |
| buttock | Calvary | captive | cascara | Celsius | charger |
| buzzard | Calvino | capture | cashier | censure | chariot |
| byeline | calypso | caracal | Caspian | centaur | charity |
| Byronic | calzone | Caracas | Cassatt | centavo | Charles |
| | calzoni | caracul | cassava | centime | Charley |
| | cambium | Caradoc | Cassini | centimo | Charlie |
| | cambric | Caradog | Cassius | central | charmed |
| Caballé | Camelot | caramel | cassock | century | charmer |
| cabaret | Cameron | caravan | Castile | ceramic | charpoy |
| cabbage | Camilla | caravel | casting | cerebra | charter |
| cabinet | Camille | caraway | casuist | certain | Chassid |
| caboose | Camorra | carbide | Catalan | certify | chassis |
| cachaca | campery | carbine | catalpa | cession | chasten |
| cacique | camphor | carcase | Catania | cesspit | chateau |
| cadaver | campion | carcass | catarrh | ceviche | chattel |
| Cadbury | canasta | cardiac | catcall | Cézanne | chatter |
| caddish | Candace | Cardiff | catcher | Chablis | Chaucer |
| cadence | candela | cardoon | caterer | Chabrol | cheapen |
| cadenza | Candice | careful | catfish | chaddar | cheaply |
| cadmium | candida | caribou | cathode | Chadian | Chechen |
| caducei | candour | carious | catlike | Chagall | checked |
| caesium | Canetti | carjack | catmint | chagrin | checker |
| caesura | cannery | Carleen | Catrina | Chaldea | Cheddar |
| cagoule | cannily | Carlene | catseye | chalice | cheerio |
| cahoots | Canning | Carling | catsuit | challah | cheetah |
| caisson | cannula | Carlton | cattery | challis | Cheever |
| Caitlin | canonic | Carlyle | cattily | chaloth | Chekhov |
| calcify | canonry | Carmela | catwalk | chamber | Chelsea |
| calcine | cantata | carmine | caustic | chamfer | chemise |
| calcite | canteen | carnage | caution | chamois | chemist |
| calcium | Cantona | Carolyn | Cauvery | chancel | Chennai |
| calculi | canvass | carotid | cavalry | chancer | chequer |
| caldera | capable | carouse | caveman | chancre | cherish |
| caldron | capably | carport | cavemen | changer | cheroot |
| caleche | capelin | Carrara | caviare | channel | chervil |
| calends | caperer | carrier | cayenne | chanter | Chester |
| Calgary | capital | carrion | Cecilia | chantry | cheviot |
| calibre | capitol | Carroll | cedilla | chaotic | chevron |
| Calicut | caprice | carroty | ceilidh | chaplet | Chianti |
| caliper | caprine | carsick | ceiling | Chaplin | Chiapas |
| calling | capsize | Cartier | Celebes | Chapman | Chicago |
| callous | capstan | cartoon | celesta | chapter | chicane |
| caloric | capsule | carvery | celeste | charade | Chicano |
| calorie | captain | carving | Cellini | Charcot | chicken |

| | | | | | |
|---|---|---|---|---|---|
| chicory | cichlid | Clonmel | colitis | Compton | consort |
| chidden | ciliary | closely | collage | compute | consult |
| chiefly | cindery | closure | collate | comrade | consume |
| chiffon | circlet | clothes | collect | Conakry | contact |
| Chifley | circlip | clubber | colleen | concave | contain |
| chigger | circuit | cluster | college | conceal | contend |
| chignon | cistern | clutter | collide | concede | content |
| Chilean | citadel | coaming | collier | conceit | contest |
| chiller | citizen | coarsen | Collins | concept | context |
| chillum | citrusy | coastal | colloid | concern | contort |
| chimera | cittern | coaster | collude | concert | contour |
| chimney | civilly | coating | colobus | concise | control |
| Chinese | clamber | coaxial | cologne | concoct | contuse |
| Chinook | clamour | Cobbett | Colombo | concord | convect |
| chintzy | clamper | cobbled | colonel | concuss | convene |
| chinwag | clanger | cobbler | colonic | condemn | convent |
| chipper | clapper | cocaine | colossi | condign | convert |
| chippie | Clapton | cochlea | coltish | condole | convict |
| Chirico | Clarice | Cochran | Columba | condone | convoke |
| chirrup | clarify | cockade | combine | conduce | cookery |
| chitter | clarion | cockily | combust | conduct | Cookson |
| chloral | clarity | cockney | comedic | conduit | coolant |
| cholera | classic | cockpit | comfily | confect | coolish |
| Chomsky | clatter | coconut | comfort | confess | copilot |
| chopper | Claudia | cocotte | comfrey | confide | copious |
| chorale | clausal | Cocteau | comical | confine | Copland |
| chordal | cleaner | codeine | command | confirm | coppery |
| chorine | cleanly | codfish | commend | conform | coppice |
| chorizo | cleanse | codicil | comment | confuse | Coppola |
| chortle | clearly | codling | commode | confute | copycat |
| chowder | cleated | coequal | commune | congeal | copyist |
| Chrissy | cleaver | Coetzee | commute | conical | coracle |
| Christa | clement | coexist | Comoros | conifer | Coralie |
| Christy | clerkly | coffret | compact | conjoin | cordate |
| chromed | clichéd | cogency | company | conjure | cordial |
| chronic | climate | cognate | compare | connect | cording |
| chucker | climber | cohabit | compass | Connery | cordite |
| chuckle | clinker | Coimbra | compère | connive | Cordoba |
| chuddar | Clinton | coinage | compete | Connors | Cordova |
| chuffed | clipped | Colbert | compile | connote | Corelli |
| chunder | clipper | Colchis | complex | conquer | Corinna |
| Chunnel | cliquey | Colditz | comport | consent | Corinne |
| chunter | cloacae | Coleman | compose | consign | Corinth |
| churchy | clobber | Colette | compost | consist | corkage |
| chutney | Clodagh | colicky | compote | console | corking |

| | | | | | |
|---|---|---|---|---|---|
| corncob | cowlick | crochet | cumulus | Dadaist | decibel |
| corneal | cowling | Croesus | cunning | Dahomey | decided |
| cornice | cowpoke | crofter | cupcake | Daimler | decider |
| Cornish | cowslip | crooked | curable | damning | decimal |
| corolla | coxcomb | crooner | curaçao | Dampier | decking |
| coronae | coxless | cropper | curator | dampish | declaim |
| coronal | coyness | croquet | curette | dancing | declare |
| coroner | Cozumel | crosier | curious | Danelaw | decline |
| coronet | crabbed | crossly | curling | dangler | decoder |
| corpora | crabber | crouton | Curragh | daphnia | decorum |
| correct | cracked | crowbar | currant | Daphnis | decrypt |
| corrida | cracker | crozier | current | Dapsang | default |
| corrode | crackle | crucial | cursive | darkish | defence |
| corrupt | crackly | crucify | cursory | Darlene | defiant |
| corsage | crafter | crudely | curtail | darling | deficit |
| corsair | crammer | crudity | curtain | darning | defiler |
| Corsica | cramped | cruelly | Curtiss | Darnley | deflate |
| cortège | crampon | cruelty | curtsey | Darrell | deflect |
| Corunna | Cranach | cruiser | Cushing | dashiki | defraud |
| corvine | cranial | crumble | cushion | dashing | defrock |
| Cossack | cranium | crumbly | custard | datable | defrost |
| costing | Cranmer | crumpet | custody | Daumier | defunct |
| costume | crassly | crumple | customs | dauphin | deglaze |
| coterie | Crassus | crunchy | cutaway | Davinia | degrade |
| cottage | craving | crupper | cutback | dawdler | dehisce |
| cottony | crawler | crusade | cuticle | Dawkins | Deirdre |
| cougher | crazily | crusher | cutlass | daypack | deistic |
| couldn't | creamer | crybaby | cutlery | daytime | Delbert |
| coulomb | creator | cryonic | cutting | dazedly | Delfont |
| coulter | creedal | cryptic | Cwmbran | dazzler | Delibes |
| council | creeper | crystal | cyanide | deadpan | delight |
| counsel | cremate | cubical | cyclist | deanery | Delilah |
| counter | Cremona | cubicle | cyclone | deathly | delimit |
| country | crevice | cuckold | Cyclops | debacle | deliver |
| coupler | cricket | Cudlipp | cynical | debater | Delores |
| couplet | crimper | cuirass | Cynthia | Deborah | Delphic |
| courage | crimson | cuisine | cypress | debouch | deltoid |
| Courbet | crinkle | culotte | Cyprian | Debrett | demerge |
| courier | crinkly | culprit | Cypriot | debrief | demerit |
| courser | Crippen | cultish | czarina | Debussy | demesne |
| courtly | cripple | cultist | | decagon | Demeter |
| couture | Crispin | culture | **D** | decapod | demigod |
| cowbell | crisply | culvert | | decease | demisec |
| Cowdrey | critter | Cumbria | dabbler | deceive | demonic |
| cowherd | Croatia | cumquat | Dadaism | decency | demotic |

Dempsey
denarii
Deneuve
Denholm
denizen
Denmark
densely
density
dentate
dentine
dentist
denture
deplete
deplore
deposit
deprave
depress
deprive
derange
derrick
Derrida
dervish
descale
descant
descend
descent
deserts
deserve
Desiree
deskill
desktop
Desmond
despair
despise
despite
despoil
dessert
destine
destiny
destroy
détente
detract
detrain
Detroit
devalue

develop
deviant
deviate
devilry
devious
deviser
devolve
devoted
devotee
dewdrop
dhansak
dhurrie
diagram
dialect
dialler
diamond
diarist
Diarmid
dickens
dictate
diction
Diderot
dieback
diehard
dietary
diffuse
digital
dignify
dignity
digraph
digress
dilator
dilemma
diluter
dimness
dinette
dingbat
dingily
diocese
dioptre
diorama
diorite
dioxide
diploid
diploma

dipolar
diptych
dirtily
disable
disavow
disband
discard
discern
discoid
discord
discuss
disdain
disease
disgust
dishrag
dislike
dismast
dismiss
disobey
display
disport
dispose
dispute
disrobe
disrupt
dissect
dissent
distaff
distant
distend
distort
disturb
disused
dithery
diurnal
diverge
diverse
divider
diviner
divisor
divorce
divulge
dizzily
Dnieper
doddery

dogfish
doggone
dogwood
doleful
Dolores
dolphin
doltish
Domingo
Dominic
donator
Donegal
donnish
Donovan
doodler
doorman
doormat
doormen
doorway
Doppler
Dorinda
dormant
dormice
Dorothy
dossier
dottily
doubler
doublet
doubter
doughty
Douglas
dovecot
dowager
dowdily
Dowding
dozenth
Drabble
drachma
Dracula
draftee
drafter
draggle
dragnet
dragoon
drainer
drapery

drastic
dratted
draught
drawing
dreaded
dreamer
dredger
Dreiser
Dresden
dresser
Dreyfus
dribble
dribbly
driblet
drifter
driller
drinker
driving
drizzle
drizzly
droplet
dropout
dropper
droshky
drought
drugget
Druidic
drumlin
drummer
drunken
dryness
drysuit
dualism
dualist
duality
dubiety
dubious
dubnium
Duchamp
duchess
ductile
ducting
dudgeon
dukedom
dullard

Dundalk
Dunedin
dungeon
Dunkirk
dunnock
Dunstan
duodena
duopoly
durable
durably
durance
Durrell
duskily
dustbin
dustily
dustman
dustmen
dustpan
dutiful
dweller
dwindle
dynamic
dynasty

# E

eagerly
earache
eardrum
Earhart
earhole
earldom
earmark
earmuff
earnest
earplug
earring
earshot
earthen
earthly
easeful
eastern
easting
Eastman
eatable

ebonite
echelon
echidna
eclipse
ecology
economy
ecotour
ecstasy
Ecuador
edifice
edition
editrix
educate
Edwards
effendi
egghead
egotism
egotist
Ehrlich
eidetic
eirenic
ejector
elastic
elastin
elation
elderly
Eleanor
elector
Electra
elegant
elegiac
element
elevate
elision
elitism
elitist
ellipse
Elspeth
elusive
Elysian
Elysium
emailer
emanate
Emanuel
embargo

embassy
embolic
embolus
embrace
embroil
Emeline
emerald
Emerson
eminent
emirate
emitter
emotion
emotive
empanel
empathy
emperor
empiric
emporia
empower
empress
emptily
emulate
enabler
enactor
enamour
enchant
enclave
enclose
encoder
encomia
encrust
encrypt
endemic
endgame
endless
endmost
endorse
endways
endwise
enemata
enforce
engaged
England
English
engorge

engrave
engross
enhance
enlarge
enliven
ennoble
enquire
enquiry
enslave
ensnare
Entebbe
entente
enteric
enthral
enthuse
entitle
entrain
entrant
entreat
entropy
entrust
entwine
envelop
envious
environ
enzymic
Ephesus
Ephraim
epicene
epicure
epigone
epigoni
epigram
episode
epistle
epitaph
epithet
epitome
epochal
epoxide
Epstein
equable
equably
equally
equator

equerry
equinox
Erasmus
erasure
erectly
erector
eremite
Ericson
Eritrea
erosion
erosive
erotica
erratic
erratum
erudite
Esbjerg
escapee
escaper
escheat
Esfahan
esparto
espouse
esquire
essence
Estella
Estelle
Estonia
Estoril
estuary
etailer
etching
eternal
ethanol
etheric
ethical
Etruria
Eugenia
eugenic
Eugénie
euphony
Eurasia
Euratom
Europop
Eusebio
Eustace

Euterpe
evacuee
Evander
evasion
evasive
Evelina
Eveline
evening
eventer
Everard
Everest
evident
exactly
exalted
examine
example
excerpt
excited
exclaim
exclude
excreta
excrete
execute
exegete
exhaust
exhibit
exigent
exotica
expanse
expense
expiate
explain
explode
exploit
explore
exposer
expound
express
expunge
extinct
extract
extreme
extrude
eyeball
eyebrow

eyelash
eyesore
eyewash
Eysenck
Ezekiel

# F

Fabergé
faction
factoid
factory
factual
faculty
faddish
faddism
faddist
faggoty
faience
failing
failure
faintly
Fairfax
fairing
fairish
fairway
fajitas
falafel
Falange
Falkirk
fallacy
fallout
falsely
falsify
falsity
fanatic
fancier
fancily
fanfare
fantail
fantasy
fanzine
Faraday
faraway
farceur

| | | | | | |
|---|---|---|---|---|---|
| farming | Ferrara | fireman | flogger | foppish | foxtrot |
| Farnese | Ferrari | firemen | flokati | forager | fractal |
| Faroese | ferrety | firstly | Florian | foramen | fragile |
| farrago | Ferrier | Fischer | Florida | forayer | frailty |
| Farrell | ferrous | fishery | florist | forbade | Frances |
| farrier | ferrule | fisheye | floruit | forbear | Francie |
| fasciae | fertile | fishing | Flossie | forbore | Francis |
| fascism | fervent | fishnet | flotsam | forceps | Frankie |
| fascist | fervour | fissile | flounce | forearm | frankly |
| fashion | festive | fission | flouncy | foreign | Frannie |
| Fastnet | festoon | fissure | flowery | foreleg | frantic |
| fatally | fetcher | fistful | fluency | foreman | Frasier |
| fateful | fetlock | fistula | fluidly | foremen | fraught |
| fathead | fevered | fitment | flummox | foreran | Frazier |
| fatigue | Feydeau | fitness | flunkey | forerun | frazzle |
| fatness | Feynman | fitting | flusher | foresaw | freckle |
| fattish | fibroid | Fitzroy | fluster | foresee | freckly |
| fatuity | fibrous | fixable | fluting | forever | Freddie |
| fatuous | fibulae | fixedly | flutist | forfeit | Fredric |
| Faustus | fiction | fixture | flutter | forgave | freebie |
| fauvism | fictive | flaccid | fluvial | forgery | freedom |
| fauvist | fiddler | flagged | flyable | forgive | freeman |
| fearful | fidgety | flaming | flyaway | forgone | freemen |
| Feargal | fiefdom | flanged | flyleaf | forlorn | freesia |
| Feargus | fielder | flanker | flyover | Formica | freeway |
| feather | fierily | flannel | focally | Formosa | freezer |
| feature | fifteen | flapper | focuser | formula | freight |
| febrile | fifthly | flasher | foghorn | forsake | Frelimo |
| federal | fighter | flatbed | foliage | forsook | Frenchy |
| feeling | figment | flatlet | foliate | Forster | freshen |
| felafel | figural | flatten | folkish | Forsyth | fresher |
| Felicia | filbert | flatter | fondant | Fortean | freshet |
| fellies | filling | flavour | fondler | Forties | freshly |
| Fellini | Filofax | Flaxman | Fonteyn | fortify | fretful |
| felloes | finagle | fleapit | fontina | fortune | fretsaw |
| felspar | finally | Fleming | Foochow | forward | friable |
| felucca | finance | Flemish | foolery | forwent | Friedan |
| femoral | finding | fleshly | foolish | Fosbury | frigate |
| fencing | finesse | flexion | footage | fossick | frilled |
| Fenella | finicky | flicker | footing | fossil | frisbee |
| fenland | Finland | flighty | footman | foulard | Frisian |
| ferment | Finnish | flipper | footmen | founder | frisson |
| fermion | firearm | flitter | footpad | foundry | fritter |
| fermium | firedog | floater | footsie | Fourier | frizzle |
| fernery | firefly | Flodden | foppery | fowling | Froebel |

| | | | | | |
|---|---|---|---|---|---|
| froglet | Galicia | gearbox | gigabit | gnocchi | grammar |
| frogman | Galilee | gearing | giggler | gnomish | grampus |
| frogmen | Galileo | geekdom | Gilbert | Gnostic | Gramsci |
| frontal | gallant | Gehenna | gilding | goateed | Granada |
| frosted | galleon | gelatin | Gillian | goatish | granary |
| frowsty | gallery | gelding | gimmick | Göbbels | grandad |
| fuchsia | galling | Gemayel | Ginette | gobbler | grandee |
| fuddled | gallium | gemsbok | gingery | Goddard | grandly |
| fuehrer | gallows | general | gingham | goddess | grandma |
| Fuentes | galumph | generic | ginseng | godetia | grandpa |
| fulcrum | Galvani | genesis | giraffe | Godfrey | granita |
| fulness | Gambian | genetic | girlish | Godhead | granite |
| fulsome | gambler | genital | Gironde | godhood | grannie |
| fumbler | gamboge | genomic | Giselle | godless | granola |
| Funchal | gamelan | genteel | Gissing | godlike | granted |
| funding | Ganesha | gentian | gizzard | godsend | grantee |
| funeral | ganglia | Gentile | glacial | Godunov | grantor |
| funfair | gangway | genuine | glacier | Goering | granule |
| fungoid | garbage | geodesy | gladden | Golding | graphic |
| funkily | garbler | geology | glamour | Goldwyn | grapnel |
| funnily | Gardner | Geordie | Glasgow | Goliath | grapple |
| furious | garland | Georgia | glasses | gonadal | grasper |
| furlong | garment | Georgie | glazier | gondola | gratify |
| furnace | garnish | Geraint | glazing | goodbye | gratiné |
| furnish | Garonne | gerbera | gleaner | goodish | grating |
| furrier | garotte | germane | gleeful | Goodman | gravely |
| further | Garrick | Germany | gliding | goofily | gravity |
| furtive | Gascony | Gerrard | glimmer | Gorbals | gravlax |
| fusible | gaseous | Gervais | glimpse | Górecki | gravure |
| fussily | Gaskell | Gervase | glisten | gorilla | graylag |
| fusspot | gastric | gestalt | glister | goshawk | grazier |
| fustian | gateaux | Gestapo | glitter | gosling | grazing |
| fuzzily | gateway | gestate | gloater | gossipy | greaser |
| | Gatling | gesture | globose | Gotland | greatly |
| | Gatwick | getaway | globule | gouache | Greaves |
| | gaudily | gharial | glorify | goulash | Grecian |
| **G** | Gauguin | ghastly | glottal | gourami | greeter |
| | Gaulish | gherkin | glottis | gourmet | Gregory |
| gabbler | gauntly | ghillie | glowing | grabber | gremlin |
| Gabriel | Gauteng | ghostly | glucose | gradual | Grenada |
| Gaddafi | gavotte | Gibbons | gluteal | grafter | grenade |
| Gagarin | gawkily | gibbous | gluteus | Grafton | Grendel |
| gainful | gayness | giblets | glutton | Grahame | Gresham |
| gainsay | gazelle | giddily | Glyndwr | grained | greyish |
| Galahad | gazette | Gielgud | gnarled | Grainne | greylag |
| Galatea | | | | | |
| Galatia | | | | | |

| | | | | | |
|---|---|---|---|---|---|
| griddle | Gujarat | Haitink | hardpan | hayloft | heparin |
| griever | gumboil | Hakluyt | hardtop | hayrick | hepatic |
| griffin | gumboot | halberd | Hardwar | hayseed | Hepburn |
| griffon | gumdrop | halbert | harelip | haywire | herbage |
| grimace | gumshoe | halcyon | haricot | Hazlitt | herbert |
| Grimsby | gunboat | Haldane | harissa | headily | heretic |
| grinder | gunfire | halfway | Harlech | heading | Hermann |
| gripper | Gunnell | halfwit | harmful | headman | herniae |
| gristle | gunnery | halibut | harmony | headmen | heroine |
| gristly | gunplay | Halifax | harness | headset | heroism |
| gritter | gunship | hallway | harpist | headway | heronry |
| grizzle | gunshot | halogen | harpoon | healthy | Herrick |
| grizzly | Gunther | halting | harrier | hearing | herring |
| groaner | gunwale | halyard | Harriet | hearken | Herriot |
| grocery | gurnard | Hamburg | harshen | hearsay | herself |
| grockle | gushing | Hamelin | harshly | hearten | hessian |
| grommet | Gustave | Hammett | Hartley | heathen | hexagon |
| Gromyko | Guthrie | hammock | Harvard | heather | hiccupy |
| grooved | gutless | Hamnett | harvest | heating | hickory |
| groover | guzzler | Hampton | Harwich | heavily | hidalgo |
| Gropius | Gwalior | hamster | Haryana | heaving | hideous |
| grossly | Gwynedd | Hancock | hashish | Hebraic | hideout |
| grouchy | Gwyneth | handbag | Hasidic | Hebrews | highway |
| grouper | gymnast | handful | Hasidim | heckler | Hillary |
| groupie | gymslip | handgun | hassium | hectare | hillock |
| growbag | gyrator | handily | hassock | hedging | hilltop |
| growler | | handler | hastily | heedful | Himmler |
| grubber | **H** | handout | hatband | heftily | himself |
| gruffly | | handset | hatchet | heinous | Hinault |
| grumble | Haarlem | hangdog | hateful | heiress | hipness |
| grunter | habitat | hanging | hatless | helical | hipster |
| Gruyère | habitué | hangman | hauberk | Helicon | hirsute |
| gryphon | hackery | hangmen | haughty | helipad | history |
| guanaco | hackney | Hanover | haulage | hellcat | hitcher |
| guarana | hacksaw | Hansard | haulier | Hellene | Hittite |
| Guarani | haddock | Hanuman | haunted | hellish | hoarder |
| guarded | Hadrian | ha'pence | haunter | Hellman | hoarily |
| gubbins | hafnium | ha'penny | hautboy | Héloïse | hoarsen |
| gudgeon | hagfish | hapless | hauteur | helpful | Hobbema |
| guerdon | haggard | haploid | Hawking | helping | hobbler |
| guesser | haggler | ha'p'orth | Hawkins | hemline | hobnail |
| Guevara | haircut | happily | hawkish | hemlock | Hockney |
| Guignol | hairnet | harbour | Hawkyns | henbane | Hodgkin |
| guilder | hairpin | Harding | Haworth | Hendrix | hoedown |
| guipure | Haitian | hardish | haycock | henpeck | Hoffman |

| | | | | | |
|---|---|---|---|---|---|
| Hogarth | hotshot | Ibrahim | impress | inhaler | Ipswich |
| hogback | Hotspur | iceberg | imprint | inherit | Iranian |
| hoggish | Houdini | Iceland | improve | inhibit | irately |
| hogwash | housing | iciness | impulse | inhuman | Ireland |
| hogweed | Housman | iconify | inanely | initial | iridium |
| hoister | Houston | Ictinus | inanity | injured | irksome |
| Hokusai | hoverer | ideally | inaptly | Inkatha | Irkutsk |
| Holbein | howbeit | idiotic | inboard | inkling | ironing |
| holdall | however | idolise | inbound | inkwell | ironise |
| holding | howling | idolize | inbreed | innards | ironist |
| holiday | huffily | idyllic | inbuilt | innings | ironize |
| Holland | hulking | igneous | incense | inquest | Isadora |
| holmium | humanly | igniter | incisor | inquire | Isfahan |
| holster | humdrum | ignoble | inciter | inquiry | Ishmael |
| homburg | humeral | ignobly | incline | inshore | Islamic |
| homeboy | humerus | ikebana | include | insider | isolate |
| Homeric | humidly | illegal | incomer | insight | isotope |
| hominid | humidor | illicit | incubus | insipid | Ispahan |
| homonym | hummock | illness | indexer | inspect | Israeli |
| honesty | hundred | Illyria | Indiana | inspire | Israfel |
| honeyed | Hungary | imagery | indoors | install | isthmus |
| Honiara | hunkers | imagine | indrawn | instant | Italian |
| Honoria | hunting | imagism | inducer | instead | itemise |
| hoodlum | hurdler | imagist | indulge | instill | itemize |
| Hooghly | hurling | imamate | ineptly | insular | iterate |
| hopeful | Hurston | imbiber | inertia | insulin | Ivorian |
| Hopkins | hurtful | Imhotep | inertly | insurer | Iyengar |
| hopsack | husband | imitate | inexact | integer | |
| Horatio | huskily | immense | infancy | intense | **J** |
| Hordern | Hussein | immerse | infanta | interim | |
| horizon | Husserl | immoral | infarct | interne | Jacinta |
| hormone | hustler | impaler | inferno | introit | jackass |
| Hornung | Huygens | impanel | infidel | intrude | jackdaw |
| horrify | hydrant | impasse | infield | invader | Jacklin |
| hosanna | hydrate | impasto | inflame | invalid | jackpot |
| hosiery | hydride | impeach | inflate | inveigh | Jackson |
| hospice | hydrous | imperil | inflect | inverse | Jacques |
| hostage | hygiene | impetus | inflict | invitee | jacuzzi |
| hostess | hymnody | impiety | infuser | inviter | jadeite |
| hostile | hypoxia | impinge | ingénue | invoice | Jainism |
| hostler | hypoxic | impious | ingoing | involve | Jakarta |
| hotfoot | | implant | ingrate | inwards | Jamaica |
| hothead | **I** | implode | ingress | Ionesco | Janácek |
| hotline | | implore | ingrown | ioniser | Janette |
| hotness | Iberian | impound | inhabit | ionizer | janitor |

January
Japheth
jasmine
javelin
jawbone
jawline
jaywalk
jealous
Jeannie
Jeffery
Jeffrey
Jehovah
jejunum
jellaba
Jenifer
Jenkins
Jericho
jerkily
Jessica
jetboat
jetfoil
Jewison
Jezebel
Jillian
jingler
jittery
Joachim
Joaquim
Joaquin
jobbery
jobless
Jocasta
Jocelyn
jocular
Jodhpur
jogtrot
Johanna
Johnnie
Johnson
joinery
jointer
jointly
jollily
jollity
jonquil

Josepha
Josette
jotting
journal
journey
jouster
joyless
joyride
Juanita
jubilee
Judaise
Judaism
Judaist
Judaize
juddery
juggler
jugular
juicily
jukebox
Juliana
jumbuck
jumpily
Jungian
juniper
Jupiter
justice
justify
Justina
Justine
Jutland
Juvenal

**K**

Kabbala
Kaddish
Kaifeng
kalends
Kalinin
Kampala
kampong
Kantian
Karachi
Karajan
karakul

karaoke
Karbala
Karelia
Karloff
karstic
karting
Kashmir
Kathryn
Katrina
Katrine
katydid
kayaker
Keating
keelson
keeping
Kellogg
Kennedy
Kenneth
keratin
Kerouac
kestrel
Keswick
ketchup
keyhole
keynote
keyword
khanate
kibbutz
kicking
kiddush
Kilauea
Kildare
killing
killjoy
kiloton
kindred
kinesis
kinetic
kinfolk
kingcup
kingdom
kingpin
kinkily
kinship
kinsman

kinsmen
Kintyre
Kipling
Kirsten
kitchen
kitschy
knacker
knavery
knavish
kneecap
kneeler
Knesset
knitter
knobbed
knobble
knobbly
knocker
Knossos
knowing
knuckle
knurled
Kolkata
kolkhoz
kopecks
Koranic
Kosovan
Kosovar
Kosygin
Kowloon
kremlin
lamprey
Krishna
Kristen
Kristin
krypton
Kubrick
kumquat
Kundera
Kurdish
Kuwaiti

**L**

labiate
Lachlan
lacking

Laconia
laconic
lacquer
lactate
lactose
lacunae
laddish
ladette
ladybug
laggard
lagging
laicise
laicism
laicize
Lakonia
Lakshmi
Lalique
Lamarck
lambada
lambast
lambent
Lambert
Lambeth
lambing
lamella
laminae
laminar
lamplit
lampoon
lamprey
Lanchow
landing
Landsat
Langley
Langton
Langtry
languid
languor
laniard
lanolin
Lansing
lantern
lanyard
Laocoon
Laotian

Lapland
lapwing
Laraine
Laramie
larceny
largely
largess
largish
Larissa
Larwood
lasagne
Lascaux
lashing
lasting
latency
lateral
Lateran
Latimer
latrine
lattice
Latvian
laugher
launder
laundry
Laureen
Laverne
Lavinia
lawless
lawsuit
laxness
Layamon
layette
Lazarus
Leacock
leading
leafage
leaflet
leakage
Leander
leaning
learned
learner
leather
Lebanon
lechery

| | | | | | |
|---|---|---|---|---|---|
| lectern | leveret | liqueur | lounger | Luthuli | mailing |
| lecture | lexical | liquify | Lourdes | Lutyens | mailman |
| leeward | lexicon | Lisbeth | lousily | Lydgate | mailmen |
| leftish | liaison | Lisburn | loutish | lyncher | majesty |
| leftism | liberal | Lisette | louvred | Lynette | Majorca |
| leftist | Liberia | lissome | lovable | Lyotard | malacca |
| legally | liberty | listing | lovably | lyrical | Malachi |
| legatee | library | literal | lowbrow | | Malachy |
| Leghorn | licence | lithely | lowland | **M** | malaise |
| legible | license | lithium | lowlife | | Malamud |
| legibly | Liddell | litotes | lowness | macabre | Mälaren |
| legless | lidless | liturgy | loyally | macadam | malaria |
| legroom | Lifford | Livonia | loyalty | macaque | Malayan |
| legwork | lighten | Livorno | lozenge | Macbeth | Malcolm |
| Leibniz | lighter | Lizanne | lucency | Macedon | malefic |
| Leipzig | lightly | Lizbeth | Lucerne | machete | mallard |
| leisure | lignite | loading | Lucette | machine | Mallory |
| Leitrim | Liguria | lobelia | Luciana | Maclean | malmsey |
| lemming | likable | lobster | lucidly | macramé | Malraux |
| Lenclos | Lillian | locally | Lucifer | maculae | Maltese |
| lengthy | Limburg | Locarno | Lucille | macumba | Malthus |
| lenient | limeade | locator | Lucinda | madding | maltose |
| lensman | liminal | lockjaw | luckily | Madeira | Malvina |
| lensmen | limiter | locknut | Lucknow | Madison | mammary |
| Leonard | Limoges | lockout | Luddism | madness | mammoth |
| leonine | Limpopo | lodging | Luddite | Madonna | manacle |
| Leonora | Linacre | loftily | Ludovic | Madurai | manager |
| leopard | Lincoln | logbook | luggage | maestri | Managua |
| Leopold | linctus | logging | lughole | maestro | manatee |
| leotard | lindane | logical | lugworm | Mafiosi | mandala |
| Lepanto | Lindsay | Lombard | lullaby | Mafioso | mandate |
| Lepidus | Lindsey | longbow | lumbago | magenta | Mandela |
| leprosy | lineage | longing | Lumière | Maghreb | mandrel |
| leprous | Lineker | longish | lumpily | Maghrib | Manfred |
| Lerwick | Linette | lookout | lumpish | magical | mangold |
| lesbian | lingual | loosely | lunatic | magmata | manhole |
| Lesotho | linkage | Loraine | luncher | magnate | manhood |
| Lesseps | linkman | Lorelei | lunette | magneto | manhunt |
| Lessing | linkmen | Lorentz | lungful | magnify | manikin |
| Leticia | linocut | Lorenzo | lurcher | Mahalia | Manilla |
| Letitia | linseed | Loretta | luridly | mahatma | Manipur |
| Lettice | lionise | Lorient | lustful | Mahfouz | mankind |
| letting | lionize | Lothian | lustily | Mahican | Manning |
| lettuce | lipless | lottery | lustred | mailbag | mannish |
| levelly | liquefy | Louella | luthier | mailbox | mansard |

| | | | | | |
|---|---|---|---|---|---|
| Mansart | mascara | measure | message | minaret | mitosis |
| Mansell | Mashhad | Medawar | messiah | mindful | mixture |
| mansion | Masonic | meddler | messily | Mindoro | Mizoram |
| mantrap | masonry | mediate | Messina | mindset | mobster |
| Manuela | massage | medical | mestizo | mineral | mockery |
| manumit | masseur | medulla | Meteora | Minerva | mockney |
| Manzoni | Massine | medusae | methane | minging | modally |
| marabou | massive | meerkat | metical | minibar | modesty |
| marbled | mastery | meeting | metonym | minibus | modicum |
| Marburg | mastiff | Megaera | Mexican | minicab | modiste |
| Marceau | mastoid | megaton | Michael | minicam | modular |
| marcher | matador | Megiddo | Michele | minimal | modulus |
| Marconi | matelot | meiosis | microbe | minimum | Mohegan |
| Marcuse | Matilda | meiotic | Mideast | minivan | Mohican |
| Marengo | matinee | Meirion | Midgard | Minorca | moisten |
| Marilyn | Matisse | Meissen | midland | minster | moistly |
| marimba | Matthau | Meitner | midlife | Miocene | Moldova |
| mariner | Matthew | melange | midriff | Mirabel | Molière |
| Marissa | mattify | Melania | midship | miracle | mollify |
| marital | matting | Melanie | midterm | Miranda | mollusc |
| Maritsa | mattock | melanin | midweek | miscall | Molotov |
| Marjory | maudlin | Melilla | Midwest | miscast | Mombasa |
| marking | Maugham | Melinda | midwife | misdeed | momenta |
| Markova | maunder | Melissa | mightn't | misdial | monarch |
| Marlene | Maureen | melodic | migrant | miserly | moneyed |
| Marlowe | Mauriac | Melodie | migrate | misfire | mongrel |
| Marmite | Maurice | Melvina | Mikhail | mishear | moniker |
| marquee | mawkish | memento | Mikonos | Mishima | Monique |
| Márquez | maxilla | Memphis | Mildred | mislead | monitor |
| marquis | maximal | Mencius | mileage | misname | monkish |
| married | maximum | Mencken | Miletus | misread | monocle |
| Marryat | Maxwell | Mendoza | milfoil | misrule | monomer |
| Marsala | Mayfair | menfolk | Milhaud | missile | monsoon |
| marshal | mayoral | menisci | milieux | missing | monster |
| Marsyas | Mayotte | menorah | militia | mission | montage |
| martial | maypole | Menorca | milkily | missive | Montana |
| Martian | Mazarin | menthol | milkman | misstep | montane |
| Martina | mazurka | mention | milkmen | mistake | monthly |
| Martine | Mazzini | Menuhin | milksop | mistily | moodily |
| Martini | Mbabane | Menzies | Millais | mistime | moonlit |
| Marvell | McEnroe | Mercury | Millett | mistook | moorhen |
| Marxism | McLuhan | merguez | million | mistral | mooring |
| Marxist | meander | Merilyn | mimesis | Mitchum | Moorish |
| Masaryk | meaning | mermaid | mimetic | Mitford | moraine |
| Masbate | measles | merrily | mimicry | Mithras | morally |

| | | | | | |
|---|---|---|---|---|---|
| Moravia | Mururoa | nascent | niblick | notably | obscene |
| mordant | Muscovy | Nasmyth | Nichola | notelet | obscure |
| Mordred | musical | nastily | Nicolas | notepad | observe |
| moreish | muskrat | Natalia | Nicosia | nothing | obtrude |
| morello | mustang | Natalie | Nielsen | nourish | obverse |
| Morisot | mustard | Natasha | niftily | novella | obviate |
| morning | mutable | nattily | Nigeria | Novello | obvious |
| Morocco | mutagen | natural | niggard | novelty | ocarina |
| moronic | muzzily | naughty | nightie | Novotný | occiput |
| Morpeth | myalgia | nautili | nightly | nowhere | Occitan |
| morphia | myalgic | navarin | Nikolai | noxious | occlude |
| mortice | Myanmar | Navarre | Nilotic | nuclear | Oceania |
| mortify | mycelia | Ndebele | Nilsson | nucleon | Oceanic |
| mortise | Mycenae | nebulae | Ninette | nucleus | Oceanus |
| Moseley | myeloid | nebular | Nineveh | nullify | octagon |
| Moselle | myeloma | necklet | ninthly | nullity | Octavia |
| moulder | Myfanwy | necktie | niobium | Numbers | October |
| Mountie | Mykonos | needful | nippily | numeral | octopus |
| mourner | mystery | neglect | nirvana | numeric | octuple |
| movable | mystify | neither | niterie | Numidia | oculist |
| Mubarak | | nemesia | nitrate | Nunavik | oddball |
| mucosae | **N** | nemesis | nitride | Nunavut | oddment |
| mudbank | | Nennius | nitrify | nunnery | oddness |
| mudbath | | neonate | nitrite | nuptial | odorant |
| mudflap | Nabokov | neoNazi | nitrous | Nureyev | odorous |
| mudflat | nacelle | Neptune | Nkrumah | nursery | odyssey |
| muezzin | Nahuatl | nerdish | noctule | nursing | Oedipal |
| muffler | Naipaul | Nerissa | nodular | nurture | Oedipus |
| muggins | Nairobi | nervily | noirish | nutcase | oestrus |
| mugshot | naively | nervous | noisily | Nyerere | offbeat |
| mugwort | naiveté | netball | noisome | nymphal | offence |
| Muldoon | naivety | netsuke | nomadic | nymphet | offhand |
| Mülheim | nakedly | netting | nominal | | officer |
| mullein | Namibia | network | nominee | **O** | offline |
| mullion | Nanette | neurone | nonagon | | offload |
| mummery | Nanjing | neutral | noonday | Oakland | offside |
| mummify | nankeen | neutron | Norbert | oarsman | ogreish |
| mundane | Nanking | Neville | Norfolk | oarsmen | oilseed |
| Munster | nanobot | newborn | Noriega | oatcake | oilskin |
| muntjac | naphtha | Newgate | Norwich | oatmeal | Okayama |
| Murdoch | Narayan | newness | nosebag | Obadiah | O'Keeffe |
| Murillo | Narmada | Newport | nosegay | obelisk | Okinawa |
| murkily | narrate | newsman | nostril | obesity | oldness |
| murrain | narthex | newsmen | nostrum | oblique | oldster |
| Murtagh | narwhal | Niagara | notable | obloquy | Olivier |

| | | | | | |
|---|---|---|---|---|---|
| oloroso | ordinal | outpace | **P** | pantile | patcher |
| Olympia | oregano | outplay | | papally | patella |
| Olympic | Orestes | outpost | pabulum | Papeete | pathway |
| Olympus | Øresund | outrage | Pacific | papilla | patient |
| ominous | organic | outrank | package | papoose | Patmore |
| omnibus | organza | outsell | packing | paprika | Patrick |
| onanism | orifice | outside | padding | papyrus | patriot |
| onanist | origami | outsize | paddler | parable | Pattaya |
| Onassis | Orinoco | outsole | paddock | parador | pattern |
| oneiric | Orlando | outstay | padlock | paradox | paucity |
| oneness | Orleans | outvote | Padraig | paragon | Pauline |
| onerous | Orontes | outward | padrone | parapet | Pauling |
| oneself | orotund | outwith | pageant | parasol | paunchy |
| ongoing | Orpheus | outwork | pageboy | paratha | pavlova |
| onshore | ortolan | ovarian | Pahlavi | parboil | payable |
| onstage | Orvieto | ovation | painful | parfait | payback |
| Ontario | Orville | overact | painter | parkway | payload |
| onwards | Osborne | overall | paisley | parlour | payment |
| oolitic | osmosis | overarm | paladin | parlous | payroll |
| opacity | osmotic | overate | palatal | Parnell | payslip |
| opaline | osseous | overawe | palaver | parodic | peacock |
| opening | Ossetia | overdue | palazzi | parolee | peafowl |
| operand | ossicle | overeat | palazzo | parotid | pearled |
| operate | ossuary | overlap | Palermo | parquet | Pearson |
| Ophelia | ostrich | overlay | palette | parsley | peasant |
| opinion | Ottilie | overlie | palfrey | parsnip | peccary |
| opossum | Ottoman | overman | Palissy | Parsons | peckish |
| opposer | oughtn't | overmen | palmate | partake | peddler |
| oppress | ourself | overpay | palmier | Parthia | peerage |
| optical | outback | overran | palmist | partial | peeress |
| optimal | outcast | overrun | palmtop | parting | peevish |
| optimum | outcome | oversaw | Palmyra | partner | Pegasus |
| opulent | outcrop | oversee | Palomar | partook | pelagic |
| oralism | outdone | oversew | palpate | Parvati | pelican |
| oralist | outdoor | overtax | panacea | parvenu | pelisse |
| orality | outface | overtly | panache | paschal | peloton |
| orangey | outfall | overtop | pancake | passage | penalty |
| oration | outflow | overuse | Pandora | passata | penance |
| oratory | outgrew | oviduct | panicky | passing | pendant |
| Orbison | outgrow | ovulate | panicle | passion | pendent |
| orbital | outlast | oxidant | Panjabi | passive | pending |
| orbiter | outlier | oxidise | pannier | pastern | penguin |
| Orcagna | outline | oxidize | panoply | Pasteur | pennant |
| orchard | outlive | Oxonian | panther | pastime | pension |
| orderly | outlook | | panties | pasture | pensive |

| | | | | | |
|---|---|---|---|---|---|
| peppery | phalanx | pillory | plaster | politic | Poulenc |
| peptide | phallic | pillowy | plastic | pollack | poultry |
| percale | phallus | Pilsner | Plataea | pollard | pounder |
| percher | phantom | pimento | plateau | pollock | poussin |
| percuss | pharaoh | pimpled | platoon | pollute | poverty |
| Perdita | pharynx | pinball | platter | polygon | powdery |
| perfect | Phidias | pinhead | plaudit | polymer | praetor |
| perfidy | Phillip | pinhole | Plautus | Pompeii | prairie |
| perform | philtre | pinkish | playboy | pompous | praline |
| perfume | Phineas | pinnace | playful | poniard | prattle |
| perfuse | phlegmy | pinnate | playpen | pontiff | preachy |
| pergola | Phoebus | Pinsent | pleader | pontoon | precast |
| perhaps | phoenix | pintail | pleased | popadom | precede |
| peridot | phoneme | pioneer | plectra | popcorn | precept |
| perigee | phonics | piously | plenary | popular | precess |
| periwig | phrasal | pipette | pleurae | porcine | precise |
| perjure | Phrygia | piquant | pleural | porcini | precook |
| perjury | Phyllis | Piraeus | pleuron | Porsche | predate |
| perkily | physics | piranha | pliable | Porsena | predawn |
| perlite | pianism | piratic | pliancy | portage | predict |
| Permian | pianist | pirogue | plodder | portend | preempt |
| permute | pianola | Piscean | plosive | portent | preface |
| perplex | piastre | piscina | plotter | portico | prefect |
| Perseus | pibroch | piscine | Plovdiv | portion | preheat |
| Persian | picador | pissoir | plugger | portray | prelate |
| persist | Picardy | pitapat | plumage | possess | prelude |
| persona | Picasso | pitcher | plumber | postage | premier |
| perspex | piccolo | piteous | plummet | postbag | premise |
| pertain | pickaxe | pitfall | plunder | postbox | premiss |
| perturb | picture | pithead | plunger | postern | premium |
| Perugia | piebald | pithily | pluvial | posting | prepack |
| perusal | piercer | pitiful | plywood | postman | prepare |
| peruser | Pierrot | pivotal | poacher | postmen | preplan |
| pervade | piggery | Pizarro | pochard | posture | preppie |
| pervert | piggish | pizzazz | podcast | postwar | prepuce |
| pessary | Piggott | placard | poetess | potable | prequel |
| petiole | pigment | placate | poetics | potager | presage |
| petrify | pigskin | placebo | pointed | potency | present |
| pettily | pigtail | placing | pointer | pothole | preside |
| pettish | pikelet | placket | Poitier | Potomac | Presley |
| petunia | Pilates | plainly | Polaris | Potsdam | presser |
| Pevsner | pilgrim | planner | poleaxe | potshot | Preston |
| pfennig | pillage | planter | polecat | pottage | presume |
| Phaedra | pillbox | plasmic | polemic | pottery | pretend |
| phaeton | pillion | Plassey | polenta | pouched | pretext |

pretzel
prevail
prevent
preview
priapic
Priapus
pricker
prickle
prickly
primacy
primary
primate
primula
printer
privacy
private
privily
probate
probity
problem
proceed
process
proctor
procure
prodigy
produce
product
profane
profess
proffer
profile
Profumo
profuse
progeny
program
project
prolong
promise
promote
pronoun
propane
prophet
propose
prosaic
prosody

prosper
protean
protect
protégé
protein
protest
Proteus
protium
proudly
proverb
provide
proviso
provoke
provost
prowess
prowler
prudent
prudery
prudish
Prussia
psalter
psychic
Ptolemy
puberty
publish
Puccini
puckish
pudding
pudenda
puerile
puffery
Pullman
pulsate
pumpkin
puncher
pungent
Punjabi
punkish
punster
Purcell
Puritan
purlieu
purloin
purport
purpose

pursuer
pursuit
purview
Pushkin
pustule
putrefy
Puttnam
puzzler
pyjamas
pyloric
pylorus
Pynchon
pyramid
Pyramus
pyretic
pyrexia
pyrites
pyrrhic
Pyrrhus

# Q

Qabalah
Qaddafi
quaffer
qualify
quality
quantum
quarrel
quarter
quartet
quassia
quavery
Quechua
Queenie
queenly
queerly
Quentin
quester
quetzal
quibble
quicken
quickie
quickly
quieten

quietly
quietus
quilter
quinine
quinone
quintal
quintet
Quintin
quitter
quivery
quondam
quorate

# R

rabbity
rabidly
raccoon
Rachael
rackets
rackety
Rackham
racquet
raddled
radiant
radiate
radical
radicle
Raeburn
Rafaela
raffish
Raffles
rafting
raggedy
ragtime
ragwort
railcar
railing
railway
raiment
rainbow
Rainier
raisiny
Raleigh
Ramadan

Rambert
rambler
ramekin
rampage
rampant
rampart
rancher
rancour
Rangoon
ranking
ransack
Ransome
Raphael
rapidly
rapport
rapture
rarebit
ratable
ratafia
ratchet
ratline
rattler
raucous
raunchy
Ravenna
ravioli
rawhide
rawness
Raymond
Raymund
reactor
readily
reading
reagent
realign
realise
realism
realist
reality
realize
realtor
Rebecca
Rebekah
rebirth
rebound

rebrand
rebuild
rebuilt
receipt
receive
recheck
recital
reciter
reclaim
recline
recluse
recount
recover
recruit
rectify
rectory
recycle
redcoat
Redding
reddish
Redford
redhead
redline
redneck
redness
redoubt
redound
redraft
redrawn
redress
reducer
redwing
redwood
referee
refined
refiner
reflate
reflect
refocus
refract
refrain
refresh
refugee
refusal
refuser

| | | | | | |
|---|---|---|---|---|---|
| regalia | repress | retouch | righter | Rolland | routine |
| regally | reprint | retrace | rightly | rolling | rowboat |
| regatta | reprise | retract | rigidly | rollmop | rowdily |
| regency | reproof | retrain | Rimbaud | romaine | Rowland |
| regimen | reprove | retread | rimless | romance | Rowling |
| regnant | reptile | retreat | ringgit | Romania | rowlock |
| regrade | repulse | retrial | ringing | Romanov | Roxanna |
| regress | request | retsina | ringlet | Romberg | Roxanne |
| regroup | requiem | reunify | riotous | rompers | royally |
| regrown | require | reunion | ripcord | Romulus | royalty |
| regular | requite | reunite | riposte | Ronaldo | Royston |
| rehouse | reredos | Reuters | ripping | rondeau | rubbery |
| reissue | rescind | revalue | ripstop | röntgen | rubbing |
| rejoice | rescuer | revelry | risible | roofing | rubbish |
| relapse | reserve | revenge | risibly | rooftop | rubella |
| related | reshape | revenue | riskily | rookery | Rubicon |
| relater | residua | reverie | risotto | rooster | ruching |
| release | residue | reverse | rissole | rorqual | ruction |
| reliant | reskill | reviser | rivalry | rosacea | Rudolph |
| relieve | Resnais | revisit | riveter | Rosalie | ruffian |
| relight | resolve | revival | riviera | Rosalyn | rufiyaa |
| remains | resound | reviver | rivulet | Rosanna | ruinous |
| remarry | respect | revolve | roadway | Rosanne | Rumania |
| rematch | respell | rewrite | roaming | roseate | rumbler |
| remixer | respelt | rewrote | roaring | rosebud | rummage |
| remnant | respire | Reynard | roaster | Roselyn | runaway |
| remodel | respite | Rhenish | robbery | Rosetta | Runcorn |
| remorse | respond | rhenium | Robbins | rosette | rundown |
| remould | respray | rhizome | Roberta | Rossini | running |
| remount | restart | rhodium | Roberts | Rostand | rupture |
| removal | restate | rhombus | Robeson | Rostock | rurally |
| remover | restful | Rhondda | robotic | rostrum | Rushdie |
| Renault | restive | rhubarb | Robsart | Roswell | Russell |
| Rendell | restock | ribbing | robusta | rotator | russety |
| renewal | restore | ribcage | Rockall | Rotorua | Russian |
| renewer | restyle | Ricardo | rockery | rotunda | rustily |
| rentier | retaken | Richard | Roddick | Rouault | rustler |
| reoccur | rethink | Richler | Rodgers | roughen | Rutland |
| reorder | retinae | rickets | Rodrigo | roughly | Rwandan |
| repaint | retinal | rickety | roebuck | roulade | |
| replace | retinol | ricotta | Roedean | rounded | **S** |
| replant | retinue | riddler | roguery | roundel | |
| replete | retired | Riemann | roguish | rounder | sabbath |
| replica | retiree | rifling | roister | roundly | Sabrina |
| replier | retitle | rigging | Rolfing | rousing | sackbut |

| | | | | | |
|---|---|---|---|---|---|
| sackful | sarcoma | sceptic | scupper | sensory | Shankly |
| sacking | sardine | sceptre | Scutari | sensual | Shannon |
| saddler | Sargent | schemer | scutter | seppuku | shapely |
| sadness | sarkily | scherzi | scuttle | sequela | Sharjah |
| saffron | sashimi | scherzo | Scythia | sequoia | sharpen |
| Saharan | Sassoon | Schiele | seabird | Serbian | sharper |
| saintly | satanic | schlepp | Seaborg | serfdom | sharply |
| Saladin | satchel | Schlick | seafood | Sergius | Sharron |
| Salamis | Satchmo | schlock | seagull | serious | shatter |
| Salazar | satiate | schloss | seakale | serpent | Shavian |
| Salerno | satiety | schmuck | sealant | serried | shaving |
| Salford | satiric | scholar | seaport | servant | Shavuot |
| salient | satisfy | sciatic | seasick | servery | shawled |
| Salieri | satsuma | science | seaside | service | Shawnee |
| Sallust | satyric | scissor | seating | servile | shearer |
| salsify | saucily | sclerae | Seattle | serving | sheathe |
| saltily | saunter | scoffer | seaward | sessile | shebang |
| salting | saurian | scooter | seaweed | session | shebeen |
| saltire | sausage | Scorpio | seceder | setback | shedder |
| salvage | savanna | Scottie | seclude | setting | sheerly |
| Samaria | saveloy | scourer | secrecy | settler | Sheilah |
| sambuca | saviour | scourge | secrete | settlor | Shelagh |
| samovar | savoury | Scouser | section | seventh | Sheldon |
| Samoyed | sawdust | scraggy | secular | seventy | shellac |
| sampler | sawfish | scraper | seducer | several | shelled |
| Sampras | sawmill | scrapie | seedbed | Severus | Shelley |
| samurai | sayable | scrappy | seedily | seviche | shelter |
| sanctum | scabies | scratch | seeming | Seville | shelver |
| Sanctus | scalene | scrawny | seepage | sexless | shelves |
| sandbag | scallop | screech | segment | sextant | sherbet |
| sandbar | scalpel | scribal | Segovia | Seymour | sheriff |
| sandboy | scalper | scriber | seismic | Shaanxi | Sherman |
| sandfly | scammer | Scrooge | seizure | Shabaka | shiatsu |
| sandman | scamper | scrotal | Sekhmet | shackle | shifter |
| sandpit | scandal | scrotum | selfish | shading | Shikoku |
| sangria | scanner | scrubby | Selkirk | shadowy | Shilton |
| sapient | scantly | scruffy | Sellers | shagged | shimmer |
| sapling | scapula | scrummy | seltzer | shakily | shindig |
| Sapphic | scarfed | scrumpy | selvage | shallot | shingle |
| Sapporo | scarify | scrunch | seminal | shallow | shingly |
| sapwood | scarily | scruple | seminar | shalwar | shinily |
| Saqqara | scarlet | scuffle | Semitic | shamble | shiplap |
| Saracen | scarper | sculler | senator | shampoo | Shipley |
| Sarawak | scatter | scumbag | Senegal | Shankar | shipper |
| sarcasm | scenery | scumble | sensate | shanked | shirker |

| | | | | | |
|---|---|---|---|---|---|
| Shirley | sighter | skilled | slubbed | snuffly | Southey |
| shirted | Sigmund | skillet | slugger | snuggle | Soutine |
| shivery | signage | skimmer | slumber | soaking | soybean |
| shocker | signify | skinful | slummer | soapbox | Soyinka |
| shoebox | signing | Skinner | slyness | soberly | sozzled |
| shooter | signora | skipper | smacker | society | spacial |
| shopper | Sikhism | skitter | smarten | sockeye | spammer |
| shoring | silence | skittle | smartly | socking | spandex |
| shorten | Silenus | skulker | smashed | softish | spangle |
| shortie | Silesia | skydive | smasher | soggily | spangly |
| shortly | silicon | skylark | smeller | soignée | spaniel |
| shotgun | silkily | skyline | smelter | sojourn | Spanish |
| showbiz | Silvana | skywalk | Smetana | solaria | spanner |
| showery | silvery | skyward | smidgen | soldier | sparely |
| showily | Simenon | slacken | smidgin | solicit | sparing |
| showing | similar | slacker | smirker | solidly | sparkle |
| showman | simplex | slackly | smitten | solidus | sparkly |
| showmen | Simplon | slammer | smokily | soloist | sparrow |
| shrilly | Simpson | slander | smoochy | Solomon | Spartan |
| shrivel | Sinatra | slapper | smoothe | soluble | Spassky |
| shriven | sincere | slashed | smother | solvent | spastic |
| shrubby | Sindbad | slasher | smuggle | Somalia | spatial |
| shudder | singlet | slather | snaffle | somatic | spatter |
| shuffle | Sinhala | slatted | snapper | someday | spatula |
| shunter | sinuous | slavery | sneaker | somehow | spawner |
| shutter | Siobhan | slavish | sneezer | someone | speaker |
| shuttle | sirloin | sleekly | snicker | soonish | special |
| Shylock | sirocco | sleeper | snidely | soother | species |
| shyness | sitting | sleeved | sniffer | sophism | specify |
| shyster | situate | sleight | sniffle | sophist | speckle |
| Siamese | Sitwell | slender | sniffly | soppily | Spector |
| Siberia | sixfold | slicker | snifter | sopping | spectra |
| sibling | sixteen | slickly | snigger | soprano | spectre |
| Sichuan | sizable | slimmer | snippet | Sopwith | specula |
| sickbay | sizeism | slinger | snooker | sorcery | speeder |
| sickbed | sizeist | slipper | snooper | sorghum | speller |
| Sickert | sizzler | slipway | snoozer | sottish | Spencer |
| Siddons | sjambok | slither | snorkel | soufflé | spender |
| sidebar | skating | Sloaney | snorter | soukous | Spenser |
| sidecar | Skelton | slobber | snouted | soulful | spicily |
| sideman | sketchy | slogger | Snowdon | sounder | spicule |
| sidemen | skiable | sloshed | snowman | soundly | spidery |
| siemens | skidpan | slotted | snowmen | soupçon | spikily |
| sievert | skiffle | slouchy | snuffer | soursop | spiller |
| sighted | skilful | Slovene | snuffle | soutane | spinach |

| | | | | | |
|---|---|---|---|---|---|
| spindle | squidgy | Steiner | streaky | subvert | surlily |
| spindly | squiffy | stellar | stretch | subzero | surmise |
| spinner | squinty | stencil | strewth | succeed | surname |
| spinney | squirmy | Stephen | striker | success | surpass |
| Spinoza | squishy | stepson | stringy | succour | surplus |
| spiraea | stabber | sterile | striped | succubi | surreal |
| spitter | stacker | sternly | striven | succumb | Surtees |
| spittle | stadium | sternum | striver | sucrose | Surtsey |
| splashy | staffer | steroid | stroker | suction | survive |
| splenic | stagger | Stetson | stroppy | Sudbury | Susanna |
| splicer | stagily | Stettin | strudel | suffice | Susanne |
| splodge | staging | Stevens | stubble | Suffolk | suspect |
| splotch | stainer | steward | stubbly | suffuse | suspend |
| splurge | stalely | Stewart | student | suggest | sustain |
| spoiler | stalker | sticker | stumble | suicide | Suzanna |
| Spokane | stamina | stiffen | stunner | Sukarno | Suzanne |
| Spoleto | stammer | stiffly | stupefy | sulkily | Suzette |
| spondee | stamper | stilted | stushie | sulphur | swaddle |
| sponger | standby | Stilton | stutter | sultana | swagger |
| sponsor | standee | stimuli | Stygian | Sumatra | swagman |
| spoofer | Stanley | stinger | stylise | summary | swagmen |
| sporran | stapler | stinker | stylish | summery | Swahili |
| sporter | starchy | stipend | stylist | summons | swallow |
| spotlit | stardom | stipple | stylize | sunbeam | Swansea |
| spotted | starkly | stirrer | styptic | sunbelt | Swanson |
| spotter | starlet | stirrup | styrene | sunburn | swarthy |
| spousal | starlit | stoical | suasion | sundial | swearer |
| spouted | starter | stollen | suavely | sundown | sweated |
| spouter | startle | stomach | suavity | sunfish | sweater |
| sprayer | stately | stomata | subaqua | sunlamp | Swedish |
| springy | statice | stonily | subdued | sunless | sweeper |
| sputnik | statics | stonker | subedit | sunrise | sweeten |
| sputter | station | stopgap | subfusc | sunroof | sweetie |
| spyhole | statism | stopper | subhead | sunspot | sweetly |
| spyware | statist | storage | subject | support | swelter |
| squalid | stature | storied | sublime | suppose | swiftly |
| squally | statute | stormer | subplot | supreme | swimmer |
| squalor | staunch | stoutly | subside | supremo | swindle |
| squarer | stealer | stowage | subsidy | surcoat | Swindon |
| squashy | stealth | strange | subsist | surface | swinger |
| squeaky | steamer | strappy | subsoil | surfeit | swinish |
| squeeze | steepen | stratal | subsume | surfing | Swithin |
| squeezy | steeple | stratum | subtend | surgeon | swollen |
| squelch | steeply | stratus | subtext | surgery | syllabi |
| squidge | steerer | Strauss | subunit | Surinam | symptom |

synapse
syncope
synergy
synodal
synonym
syringe
systole

# T

Tabasco
Tabitha
tableau
tabloid
tabular
tacitly
Tacitus
tackler
tactful
tactile
tadpole
Tadzhik
taffeta
Tagalog
takeout
Taleban
Taliban
Talitha
tallboy
Tallinn
tallish
tallowy
taloned
tamarin
tambour
Tammany
Tampere
Tampico
tanager
Tanagra
Tancred
tandoor
tangent
Tangier
tankard

tankful
tankini
tannery
tantric
tantrum
tapioca
taproom
taproot
Taranto
tardily
tarnish
Tarquin
tarsier
tartare
Tartary
tartlet
tastily
Tatiana
tatters
tattily
tatting
tattler
taunter
Taunton
Taurean
Tavener
taverna
taxable
taxicab
taxiway
Tayside
Tbilisi
teacake
teacher
tearful
tearing
teatime
technic
tedious
teenage
Teheran
Telford
telling
Telstar
tempera

tempest
Templar
tempter
tempura
tenable
tenancy
tendril
tenfold
Teniers
Tenniel
tensely
tensile
tension
tenthly
tenuous
tepidly
tequila
terbium
Terence
termini
termite
ternary
terpene
terrace
terrain
terrier
terrify
terrine
terroir
tersely
tessera
testate
testify
testily
tetanic
tetanus
textile
textual
texture
thalami
theatre
theorem
therapy
thereat
thereby

therein
thereof
thereon
Theresa
Thérèse
thereto
thermal
thermic
Thermos
Theseus
Thespis
thiamin
thicken
thicket
thickly
thimble
Thimphu
thinker
thinner
thirdly
thirsty
thistle
thither
Thomson
Thoreau
thorium
thought
thready
thrifty
thriven
throaty
through
thrower
thulium
thumper
thunder
Thurber
thyroid
thyself
Tianjin
Tibetan
ticking
tickler
tidally
tiddler

tidings
Tiepolo
Tiffany
tighten
tightly
tigress
Tijuana
tilapia
Tilburg
Tilbury
tillage
timbale
timbrel
timidly
Timothy
timpani
tinfoil
tinnily
Tippett
tippler
tipsily
tipster
tiredly
tissuey
Titania
titanic
titmice
titrate
titular
toaster
toastie
tobacco
toccata
toddler
toehold
toeless
toenail
Tokelau
Tolkien
Tolstoy
toluene
tombola
tonally
tonight
tonnage

tonneau
tonsure
toolbar
toolbox
toothed
tootsie
topcoat
topiary
topical
topknot
topless
topmast
topmost
toponym
topping
topsail
topside
topsoil
topspin
torment
tornado
Toronto
torpedo
Torquay
Torquil
torrent
torsion
Tortola
torture
Toryism
totally
totemic
tottery
toughen
tourism
tourist
Tournai
tourney
towable
towards
towline
towpath
toylike
Toynbee
toytown

| | | | | | |
|---|---|---|---|---|---|
| Trabzon | Trianon | trucker | twirler | uncared | unlined |
| tracery | tribune | truckle | twister | uncivil | unlived |
| trachea | tribute | Trudeau | twitchy | unclasp | unloose |
| tracing | triceps | Trueman | twitter | unclean | unloved |
| tracker | tricker | truffle | twofold | unclear | unlucky |
| tractor | trickle | trumpet | twosome | uncouth | unmanly |
| traduce | tricksy | trundle | Tyddewi | uncover | unmixed |
| traffic | tricorn | trustee | tympana | uncross | unmoved |
| tragedy | trident | tsarina | tympani | unction | unnamed |
| trailer | Trieste | tsarist | Tyndale | uncured | unnerve |
| trainee | trifler | tsunami | Tynwald | undated | unpaved |
| trainer | trigger | tubular | typeset | undergo | unquiet |
| traipse | trilogy | Tuesday | typhoid | undoing | unravel |
| traitor | trimmer | tugboat | typhoon | undress | unready |
| tramcar | trinity | tuition | typical | undying | unscrew |
| trammel | trinket | tumbler | tyranny | unearth | unshorn |
| tramper | triplet | tumbrel | tzarina | uneaten | unsling |
| trample | triplex | tumbril | | unequal | unslung |
| tramway | Tripoli | tumulus | **U** | unfazed | unsound |
| tranche | tripper | tunable | | unfixed | unspool |
| trannie | Tripura | tundish | Uccello | unfrock | unstick |
| transit | trireme | tuneful | ufology | unfroze | unstuck |
| transom | trisect | Tunisia | Ugandan | unfunny | untamed |
| trapeze | trishaw | Tupolev | ukelele | unglued | untried |
| trapper | trismus | turbine | Ukraine | ungodly | untruth |
| travail | Tristan | Turkana | ukulele | unguent | untwist |
| travois | tritely | Turkish | Ulanova | unhappy | unusual |
| trawler | tritium | turmoil | ulcered | unheard | unwaged |
| treacle | triumph | turning | ululate | unhinge | unwound |
| treacly | trivial | turnkey | Ulysses | unhoped | upbraid |
| treadle | trochee | turnout | umbrage | unhorse | upfield |
| treason | trodden | Tuscany | umpteen | unicorn | upfront |
| treater | Troilus | Tussaud | unaided | unifier | upgrade |
| treetop | troller | tussock | unalike | uniform | upheave |
| trefoil | trolley | tussore | unarmed | unitard | Uppsala |
| trekker | trollop | twaddle | unasked | unitary | upraise |
| trellis | trooper | tweaker | unaware | unitise | upright |
| tremble | tropism | tweeter | unblock | unitive | upriver |
| trembly | Trotsky | twelfth | unbosom | unitize | upscale |
| tremolo | trotter | twiddle | unbound | unkempt | upstage |
| Trenton | trouble | twiddly | unbowed | unknown | upstart |
| trestle | trounce | twigged | unbuild | unladen | upstate |
| Trevino | trouper | twinkle | unbuilt | unlatch | upsurge |
| triable | trouser | twinkly | unburnt | unlearn | upswept |
| triadic | truancy | twinset | uncanny | unleash | upswing |

| | | | | | |
|---|---|---|---|---|---|
| uptempo | valence | verruca | visibly | Walkman | waxwork |
| uptight | valency | Versace | visitor | Walkmen | waybill |
| uptrend | Valerie | versify | visored | walkout | waymark |
| upwards | valiant | version | Vistula | walkway | wayside |
| Uranian | validly | vertigo | vitally | wallaby | wayward |
| uranium | vamoose | vervain | vitamin | Wallace | Wealden |
| urethra | vampire | vesicle | vitiate | walling | wealthy |
| urgency | vampish | vespers | Vitoria | Walloon | wearily |
| urinary | Vandyke | vestige | vitrify | Walpole | weather |
| urinate | Vanessa | veteran | vitrine | Walsall | webbing |
| urology | vanilla | vetiver | vitriol | waltzer | webcast |
| Uruguay | vantage | viaduct | Vivaldi | wangler | website |
| useable | Vanuatu | viatica | vivaria | wannabe | Webster |
| useless | vapidly | vibrant | Viviana | wanting | Weddell |
| Ushuaia | vaquero | vibrate | vividly | Warbeck | wedding |
| Üsküdar | variant | vibrato | Viyella | warbler | wedlock |
| Ustinov | variety | Vicente | vocalic | Warburg | weekday |
| usually | various | Vicenza | vocally | warfare | weekend |
| usurper | varmint | viceroy | vocoder | warhead | weepily |
| Utamaro | varnish | vicious | voguish | warlike | Wegener |
| utensil | varsity | vicomte | volcano | warlock | weighty |
| uterine | Vatican | victory | voltage | warlord | weirdly |
| utilise | Vaughan | victual | voltaic | warning | welcome |
| utility | vaulter | Vietnam | voluble | warpath | welfare |
| utilize | vegetal | Vignola | volubly | warrant | western |
| utopian | vehicle | village | voucher | warrior | westing |
| Utrecht | veining | villain | Vouvray | warship | wetland |
| Utrillo | velours | villein | voyager | warthog | wetness |
| utterer | velouté | villous | Vulgate | wartime | wetsuit |
| utterly | velvety | Vilnius | vulpine | Warwick | Wexford |
| uxorial | Venetia | Vincent | vulture | washbag | whacked |
| | venison | vinegar | | washing | whaling |
| **V** | ventral | vintage | **W** | washout | Wharton |
| | venture | vintner | | washtub | whatnot |
| vacancy | Venturi | violate | wackily | waspish | whatsit |
| vaccine | veranda | violent | wadding | wassail | wheaten |
| vacuity | verbena | violist | waffler | wastage | wheedle |
| vacuole | verbose | virally | waggish | wastrel | wheeler |
| vacuous | verdant | Virchow | waggler | watcher | wheelie |
| vaginae | verdict | Virgoan | wagoner | Watford | whereas |
| vaginal | verdure | virtual | wagtail | wattage | whereat |
| vagrant | verismo | viscera | waifish | Watteau | whereby |
| vaguely | Vermeer | viscose | Waikato | wavelet | wherein |
| Vaishya | Vermont | viscous | Waikiki | waverer | whereof |
| valance | vernier | visible | wakeful | waxwing | whereon |

| | | | | |
|---|---|---|---|---|
| whereto | Wichita | wishful | worldly | Wynford |
| whether | Wicklow | wistful | wormery | Wyoming |
| whicker | widgeon | withers | worrier | |
| whiffle | widower | without | worship | |
| whimper | wielder | witless | worsted | |
| whimsey | wigging | witness | wouldn't | Xenakis |
| whinger | wiggler | wittily | wouldst | Yangtze |
| whipper | Wilbert | witting | wrangle | Yaoundé |
| whippet | wildcat | wizened | wrapper | yardage |
| whipsaw | Wilfred | wobbler | wreathe | yardarm |
| whisker | Wilfrid | wolfish | wrecked | yardman |
| whiskey | Wilkins | wolfram | wrecker | yardmen |
| whisper | Willard | Wolfson | Wrecsam | yashmak |
| whistle | William | womanly | wrestle | yellowy |
| whitely | willies | wonkily | Wrexham | Yeltsin |
| whither | willing | woodcut | wriggle | Yenisei |
| whiting | willowy | Woodrow | wriggly | Yerevan |
| whitish | wimpish | woollen | wringer | Yiddish |
| Whitlam | windbag | Woolley | wrinkle | yielder |
| whitlow | windily | Woomera | wrinkly | yobbery |
| Whitman | winding | woozily | writing | yobbish |
| Whitney | Windsor | wordily | written | yoghurt |
| Whitsun | Winfrey | wording | Wrocław | Yolanda |
| whittle | winless | workday | wrongly | Yorkist |
| whoever | winning | working | wrought | yttrium |
| whoopee | winsome | workman | wryneck | Yucatán |
| whopper | Winston | workmen | wryness | yuppify |
| whorish | wintery | workout | Wyndham | |
| whorled | wiretap | worktop | Wynette | |

## X–Y

## Z

| |
|---|
| Zachary |
| Zairean |
| Zairian |
| Zambezi |
| Zambian |
| zarapes |
| Zatopek |
| Zealand |
| zealous |
| Zebulon |
| Zebulun |
| Zeeland |
| Zenobia |
| Zermatt |
| zestful |
| zillion |
| Zionism |
| Zionist |
| Zoffany |
| zombify |
| zoology |
| Zuleika |
| Zwingli |
| zygotic |

# 8 LETTERS

## A

| | | | |
|---|---|---|---|
| | Abertawe | abortion | absently | academia |
| | abetment | abortive | absinthe | academic |
| aardvark | abeyance | Abrahams | absolute | acanthus |
| abattoir | abjectly | abrasion | absorber | Acapulco |
| abdicate | Abkhazia | abrasive | abstract | acceptor |
| abductee | ablation | abrogate | abstruse | accident |
| abductor | ablative | abruptly | absurdly | accolade |
| Abdullah | ablution | abscissa | abundant | accoutre |
| Aberdeen | abnegate | abseiler | abutilon | accredit |
| aberrant | abnormal | absentee | abutment | accuracy |

| | | | | |
|---|---|---|---|---|
| accurate | adorable | alacrity | almanack | Anacreon |
| accursed | adorably | alarmism | almighty | analogue |
| accustom | Adrianne | alarmist | alopecia | analysis |
| acerbity | Adriatic | Alasdair | Aloysius | analytic |
| achiever | Adrienne | Alastair | alphabet | anaphora |
| Achilles | adultery | Albacete | Alphonse | anarchic |
| acoustic | advanced | albacore | Alphonso | anathema |
| acquaint | advisory | Albanian | alpinist | Anatolia |
| acquirer | advocaat | albinism | Alsatian | ancestor |
| acrimony | advocacy | Albinoni | Altamira | ancestry |
| acrostic | advocate | Alcatraz | although | Anchises |
| actinide | aeration | Alcestis | altitude | Andersen |
| actinium | aerobics | aldehyde | altruism | Anderson |
| activate | aerofoil | alderman | altruist | Andorran |
| actively | aesthete | aldermen | alveolar | Andretti |
| activism | affected | Alderney | alveolus | androgen |
| activist | affinity | aleatory | amaranth | Andropov |
| activity | affluent | alehouse | amaretti | anecdote |
| actorish | aflutter | Alekhine | amaretto | aneurism |
| actressy | aftersun | Alentejo | Amazonia | aneurysm |
| actually | agitator | alfresco | ambiance | angelica |
| actuator | agitprop | Algerian | ambience | Angelina |
| acupoint | agnostic | Algernon | ambition | Angeline |
| adaption | Agostini | Algonkin | ambrosia | Angharad |
| adaptive | agrarian | Alhambra | ambulant | Anglesey |
| addendum | Agricola | aliasing | amenable | Anglican |
| addicted | agrimony | Alicante | American | angstrom |
| addition | agronomy | alienate | amethyst | Anguilla |
| additive | airborne | Alistair | amicable | animated |
| Adelaide | airbrick | alkaline | amicably | animator |
| Adenauer | airbrush | alkaloid | ammonite | Annalisa |
| adenoids | aircraft | allegory | ammonium | annalist |
| adequacy | Airedale | alleluia | amnesiac | Annigoni |
| adequate | airfield | allergen | amniotic | annotate |
| adherent | airframe | allergic | amoeboid | announce |
| adhesion | airiness | alleyway | amortise | annoying |
| adhesive | airliner | alliance | amortize | annually |
| adjacent | airplane | Allister | amperage | anorexia |
| adjuster | airspace | allocate | amphorae | anorexic |
| adjutant | airspeed | allopath | ampullae | answerer |
| adjuvant | airstrip | allspice | amputate | anteater |
| admonish | airtight | allusion | Amritsar | antedate |
| Adolphus | airwaves | allusive | Amundsen | antelope |
| adoption | airwoman | alluvial | anabolic | antennae |
| adoptive | airwomen | alluvium | anaconda | anterior |

anteroom
anthemic
antibody
antidote
Antigone
Antiguan
antihero
antimony
antinomy
antiphon
antisera
Antonina
anything
anywhere
Aotearoa
aperient
aperitif
aperture
aphelion
aphorism
apiarist
Apollyon
apologia
apoplexy
apostasy
apostate
apparent
appeaser
appendix
appetite
applause
Appleton
appliqué
apposite
appraise
approach
approval
aptitude
Apuleius
aqualung
aquanaut
Aquarian
aquarist
aquarium
Aquarius

aquatint
aqueduct
aquiline
Arabella
arachnid
Araminta
arboreal
arboreta
Arcadian
arcading
arcanely
archaism
archduke
archival
archness
Ardennes
ardently
arguable
arguably
argument
Arkansas
Armagnac
armament
armature
armchair
Armenian
armorial
armoured
armourer
aromatic
arpeggio
arquebus
arranger
arrogant
arrogate
arsenide
arsonist
artefact
arterial
artfully
artifice
artiness
artistic
artistry
asbestos

ascender
Ashcroft
Ashgabat
Ashkelon
Ashqelon
ashtanga
asperity
asphodel
asphyxia
aspirant
aspirate
assassin
assemble
assembly
assessor
assorted
assuming
Assyrian
astatine
asterisk
asteroid
astonish
Asturias
astutely
Asunción
Atalanta
Athenian
athletic
Atkinson
Atlantic
Atlantis
atomiser
atomizer
atrocity
atropine
attached
attacker
attendee
attender
attitude
attorney
atypical
aubretia
Auckland
audacity

audience
audition
auditory
Auerbach
Augsburg
Augustan
Augustin
Augustus
Aurelian
Aurelius
Austrian
autarchy
autarkic
autistic
Autobahn
autocrat
autodial
autogiro
autogyro
automata
automate
autonomy
autumnal
Auvergne
Averroës
aversion
aversive
aviation
Avicenna
avionics
Avogadro
Ayrshire
Ayurveda

# B

babushka
babyhood
baccarat
bacchant
bachelor
bacillus
backache
backbeat
backbone

backchat
backcomb
backdate
backdrop
backfire
backhand
backlash
backless
backlist
backpack
backside
backspin
backward
backwash
backyard
bacteria
badinage
badlands
Baedeker
bagpiper
baguette
Bahamian
Bahraini
Baikonur
Bakelite
Bakewell
balancer
baldness
Balinese
balladry
Ballarat
ballcock
balletic
ballgirl
ballpark
ballroom
ballyhoo
balsamic
baluster
banality
bandanna
bandeaux
banditry
banditti
banister

| | | | | |
|---|---|---|---|---|
| banjoist | batterer | Belmopan | biblical | Blenheim |
| bankable | bavarois | bendable | bibulous | blessing |
| Bankhead | bayberry | Benedict | bicuspid | blighter |
| banknote | Baykonur | benefice | biddable | blimpish |
| bankroll | Bayreuth | Benenden | biennial | blinding |
| bankrupt | beanpole | Benetton | bigamist | blinking |
| barathea | bearable | Benghazi | bigamous | blissful |
| Barbados | bearably | Benguela | bilberry | blithely |
| barbaric | bearskin | benignly | billfold | blizzard |
| barbecue | beatable | Beninese | billhook | blockade |
| barberry | beatific | Benjamin | billycan | blockage |
| barbican | Beatrice | bentwood | bimbette | blokeish |
| barbless | Beaufort | bequeath | bindweed | bloodily |
| bareback | Beaumont | berberis | binnacle | bloomers |
| bareboat | beautify | Berenice | binomial | blooming |
| barefoot | béchamel | bergamot | biomorph | blowfish |
| bareness | Beckmann | Bergerac | birdcage | blowhard |
| baritone | becoming | beriberi | birdlime | blowhole |
| Barnabas | bedazzle | Berkeley | birdseed | blowlamp |
| barnacle | bedlinen | Bermudan | birdsong | blowpipe |
| Barnardo | bedstead | Bernardo | Birgitta | blubbery |
| Barnsley | bedstraw | Bernhard | birthday | bludgeon |
| barnyard | Beeching | Berthold | birthing | bluebell |
| baroness | beefcake | Bertrand | biscuity | bluebird |
| baronial | Beerbohm | Besançon | bisector | blueness |
| barouche | beetroot | besieger | bisexual | bluesman |
| barrette | befallen | besmirch | Bismarck | bluesmen |
| basaltic | befriend | besotted | bitchily | blustery |
| baseball | befuddle | besought | bitingly | Boadicea |
| baseless | begetter | bespoken | bitterly | boastful |
| baseline | beggarly | Bessemer | bivalved | boathook |
| basement | beginner | bestiary | biweekly | boatload |
| baseness | begotten | bestowal | blackcap | boatyard |
| Basildon | begrudge | bestride | Blackett | Bodhgaya |
| basilica | behemoth | bestrode | blackfly | bodysuit |
| basilisk | beholden | besuited | blacking | bodysurf |
| basketry | beholder | Betjeman | blackish | bodywork |
| bassinet | belabour | betrayal | blackleg | Boethius |
| bastardy | Belgrade | betrayer | blackout | bogeyman |
| Bastille | believer | beverage | Blantyre | bogeymen |
| bathetic | belittle | Beverley | blatancy | Bohemian |
| bathrobe | Belitung | bewilder | bleacher | boldness |
| bathroom | Belizean | biannual | blearily | Bolivian |
| Bathurst | Belizian | Biarritz | bleeding | bondsman |
| battered | bellyful | biathlon | | bondsmen |

| | | | | |
|---|---|---|---|---|
| bonehead | braggart | Bruckner | butchery | camomile |
| boneless | brainbox | Brueghel | buttress | campaign |
| bonemeal | Bramante | bruising | buzzword | Campania |
| bonhomie | Bramwell | Brummell | | Campbell |
| Boniface | Brancusi | Bruneian | **C** | campfire |
| boniness | brandish | brunette | | campsite |
| bonneted | brassica | Brunhild | cabochon | camshaft |
| bookable | brattish | Brussels | cachexia | Canadian |
| bookcase | brazenly | brutally | cadenced | canaille |
| bookmark | breakage | Buchanan | caduceus | canalise |
| bookshop | breakout | buckaroo | Caerdydd | canalize |
| bookworm | breather | buckshee | Caergybi | Canaries |
| bootable | breeches | buckshot | Caesarea | Canberra |
| bootlace | breeding | buckskin | caffeine | candidly |
| bootless | breezily | Budapest | caginess | canister |
| Bordeaux | bresaola | Buddhism | Cagliari | cannabis |
| bordello | brethren | Buddhist | cajolery | cannibal |
| borehole | Breughel | buddleia | cakehole | cannulae |
| Bornholm | breviary | building | cakewalk | canoeist |
| Borodino | Brezhnev | Bukharin | calabash | canonise |
| borrower | brickbat | Bulawayo | Calabria | canonize |
| Bosporus | briefing | Bulganin | calamine | canoodle |
| Bosworth | brighten | Bulgaria | calamity | canticle |
| botanist | brightly | bulkhead | calculus | capacity |
| Bothwell | Brighton | bulldoze | Calcutta | capoeira |
| Botswana | Brigitta | bulletin | Caldwell | capsicum |
| botulism | Brigitte | bullfrog | calendar | capstone |
| Boudicca | brindled | bullhorn | calender | capsular |
| bouffant | Brisbane | bullring | calfskin | captious |
| bouillon | brisling | bullrush | Caligula | capturer |
| bouldery | Brittany | bullseye | calliope | Capuchin |
| Boulogne | Broadway | bunfight | calliper | capybara |
| Boulting | broccoli | bungalow | Callisto | carapace |
| bouncily | brochure | buoyancy | Calloway | carbolic |
| bouncing | brokenly | Burghley | callused | carbonic |
| boundary | bronchus | burglary | calmness | carbonyl |
| boutique | Bronzino | burgundy | Calvados | carboxyl |
| bouzouki | broodily | Burkinan | Camargue | cardamom |
| bovinely | Brooklyn | burrower | cambered | cardigan |
| bowsprit | Brookner | bursitis | Cambodia | cardinal |
| bracelet | brougham | Buryatia | Cambrian | carefree |
| brackish | brouhaha | bushbaby | Cambyses | careless |
| Bradbury | browbeat | business | camellia | careworn |
| Bradford | browning | busybody | Cameroon | carillon |
| Braganza | brownish | busyness | camisole | Carlisle |

| | | | | |
|---|---|---|---|---|
| Carlotta | catheter | Chambers | Cherwell | cinnabar |
| carnally | Cathleen | Chambéry | Cheshire | cinnamon |
| Carnegie | Catholic | chambray | chestnut | circular |
| carnival | Catilina | Chamonix | chewable | citation |
| Carolina | Catiline | champers | Cheyenne | citified |
| Caroline | cationic | champion | chickpea | citywide |
| caroller | Catriona | chancery | chiefdom | civilian |
| carotene | Catullus | chandler | childbed | civilise |
| carousal | Caucasia | chapatti | Childers | civility |
| carousel | Caucasus | chaplain | childish | civilize |
| carouser | caudally | Chappell | children | cladding |
| Carracci | cauldron | charcoal | chimaera | claimant |
| Carreras | causally | Charente | chinless | clammily |
| carriage | causeway | charisma | chipmunk | clangour |
| carrycot | cautious | Charissa | chipping | clannish |
| Carthage | Cavalier | Charlene | chirpily | clansman |
| Cartland | Cawnpore | Charlton | Chişinau | clansmen |
| caryatid | celeriac | Charmian | chivalry | claptrap |
| Casanova | celerity | charming | chlorate | Clarabel |
| casebook | celibacy | Chartism | chloride | Clarence |
| caseload | celibate | Chartist | chlorine | Claribel |
| casement | cellmate | Chartres | choirboy | Clarinda |
| casework | cellular | Chasidim | choleric | clarinet |
| cashback | cemetery | chastise | chorally | Clarissa |
| cashless | cenotaph | chastity | chordate | classify |
| cashmere | Cenozoic | chasuble | Chrétien | classily |
| cassette | centrism | chateaux | Chrissie | Claudine |
| castanet | centrist | chatline | christen | Claudius |
| castaway | cephalic | chattily | Christie | clavicle |
| castrate | Cerberus | Chauncey | Christly | claymore |
| castrati | cerebral | Chechnya | chromate | cleanser |
| castrato | cerebrum | checkers | chromite | clearing |
| Castries | ceremony | checkout | chromium | clearway |
| casually | Cerenkov | cheekily | Chrystal | cleavage |
| casualty | Ceridwen | cheerful | chthonic | clematis |
| catacomb | cerulean | cheerily | chunkily | Clemence |
| catalyse | cervical | cheesily | churlish | clemency |
| catalyst | cesspool | chemical | chutzpah | clerical |
| catamite | cetacean | Chemnitz | ciabatta | clerihew |
| catapult | Cetewayo | chenille | cicatrix | cleverly |
| cataract | chaconne | Chequers | cicerone | Clifford |
| catching | Chadwick | Cherelle | ciceroni | climatic |
| category | chainsaw | Cherokee | cimbalom | clincher |
| catenary | chairman | cherubic | cinchona | clinical |
| catfight | chairmen | cherubim | cineaste | clipping |

| | | | | |
|---|---|---|---|---|
| cliquish | collagen | conceive | convener | counting |
| clitoral | collapse | concerti | convenor | Couperin |
| clitoris | collator | concerto | converge | coupling |
| cloddish | colliery | Concetta | converse | courtesy |
| cloister | colloquy | conclave | conveyor | courtier |
| clothier | Colombia | conclude | convince | Courtney |
| clothing | colonial | Concorde | convulse | couscous |
| clownish | colonise | concrete | cookbook | cousinly |
| clubmoss | colonist | condense | cookware | Cousteau |
| clubroot | colonize | conferee | coolibah | covalent |
| clueless | colophon | confetti | Coolidge | covenant |
| clumsily | Colorado | confined | coolness | Coventry |
| coachman | colossal | conflate | cooption | coverage |
| coachmen | colossus | conflict | coparent | coverall |
| coalesce | coloured | confound | copulate | covering |
| coalface | Coltrane | confrère | copybook | coverlet |
| coarsely | Columbia | confront | coquetry | covertly |
| cobwebby | Columbus | confused | coquette | covetous |
| cochleae | columnar | congener | Cordelia | cowardly |
| cochlear | columned | congress | cordless | coxswain |
| cockaded | Comanche | Congreve | corduroy | crabbily |
| cockatoo | Comaneci | conjoint | Cornelia | crablike |
| cockcrow | comatose | conjugal | corniced | crabmeat |
| cockerel | combiner | conjurer | corniche | crabwise |
| cockeyed | comeback | conjuror | cornmeal | crackers |
| cocksure | comedian | Connacht | cornrows | cracking |
| cocktail | comedown | Connolly | Cornwall | cracknel |
| codpiece | cometary | conquest | coronary | crackpot |
| coenzyme | commando | conserve | corporal | craftily |
| coercion | commence | consider | corridor | crankily |
| coercive | commerce | consommé | corselet | crankpin |
| cogently | commoner | conspire | corseted | crashing |
| cogitate | commonly | constant | corsetry | cravenly |
| cognomen | communal | construe | Corsican | crawfish |
| cogwheel | commuter | consular | cortical | Crawford |
| coherent | compadre | consumer | corundum | crayfish |
| cohesion | compiler | contempt | corvette | creamery |
| cohesive | complain | continua | cosecant | creamily |
| coiffeur | complete | continue | cosiness | creatine |
| coiffure | compline | continuo | cosmetic | creation |
| coincide | composer | contract | cosmical | creative |
| colander | compound | contrary | Cotopaxi | creature |
| coldness | compress | contrast | cottager | credence |
| coleslaw | comprise | contrite | cottagey | credible |
| coliseum | computer | contrive | countess | credibly |

| | | | | |
|---|---|---|---|---|
| creditor | cumulate | Dalriada | December | demagogy |
| creepily | cupboard | Damascus | decently | demented |
| creosote | cupidity | damnable | deciding | dementia |
| crescent | curation | damnably | decimate | Demerara |
| Cressida | curative | Damocles | decipher | demerger |
| cretonne | Curitiba | dampener | decision | demersal |
| crevasse | curlicue | dampness | decisive | demijohn |
| cribbage | currency | dandruff | deckhand | demister |
| Crichton | curtness | dandyish | déclassé | democrat |
| criminal | customer | Daniella | declutch | demolish |
| Crispian | cuteness | Danielle | decorate | demoniac |
| criteria | Cuthbert | daringly | decorous | demonise |
| critical | cutpurse | darkling | decouple | demonize |
| critique | cutwater | darkness | decrease | demotion |
| Croatian | cyanogen | darkroom | decrepit | demurely |
| crockery | cyanosis | Dartmoor | Dedekind | demurral |
| Crockett | cyanotic | databank | dedicate | denarius |
| Cromarty | Cycladic | database | deepness | denature |
| cromlech | cyclamen | dateable | deerskin | dendrite |
| Crompton | cyclical | Daubigny | defecate | deniable |
| Cromwell | cyclonic | daughter | defector | denounce |
| cronyism | cylinder | daunting | defender | Denpasar |
| crossbar | Cynewulf | Dauphiné | deferral | dentally |
| crossbow | cynicism | daybreak | defiance | departed |
| crossing | cynosure | daydream | definite | depilate |
| crotchet | Cyrillic | daylight | deflator | depleter |
| croupier | cystitis | dazzling | deflower | deponent |
| crowfoot | cytology | deadbeat | deforest | deportee |
| crucible | | deadbolt | deftness | depraved |
| crucifix | **D** | deadhead | Deianira | deprived |
| crudités | | deadline | Deighton | deputise |
| crusader | dabchick | deadlock | dejected | deputize |
| cryonics | dactylic | deadness | Delaunay | derelict |
| cucumber | Daedalus | deafness | Delaware | derision |
| cufflink | daemonic | deathbed | delegacy | derisive |
| culinary | daffodil | debility | delegate | derisory |
| Culloden | Dagestan | debonair | deletion | derogate |
| culpable | Daguerre | Debrecen | delicacy | derrière |
| culpably | daintily | debugger | delicate | descaler |
| Culpeper | daiquiri | debunker | delirium | describe |
| cultivar | dairying | debutant | delivery | deselect |
| cultural | dairyman | decadent | Delphine | deserter |
| cultured | dairymen | decanter | delusion | designer |
| cumbrous | Dalglish | deceased | delusive | desirous |
| cummings | Dalmatia | deceiver | delusory | desolate |

| | | | | |
|---|---|---|---|---|
| despatch | dictator | disgorge | Dniester | dopiness |
| despiser | didactic | disgrace | Doberman | Dordogne |
| despotic | dietetic | disguise | docilely | dormancy |
| detached | Dietrich | disinter | docility | dormouse |
| detailed | diffract | diskette | dockland | Dorothea |
| detainee | diffuser | dislodge | dockside | dorsally |
| detainer | digerati | disloyal | dockyard | Dortmund |
| detector | digester | dismally | doctoral | dotterel |
| dethrone | digestif | dismount | doctrine | doubloon |
| detonate | digitise | disorder | document | doubtful |
| detoxify | digitize | dispatch | docusoap | doubting |
| detrital | dihedral | dispense | dodderer | doughnut |
| detritus | dilation | disperse | dogfight | dourness |
| deviance | dilatory | dispirit | doggedly | dovecote |
| deviancy | diligent | displace | doggerel | dovetail |
| devilish | dilution | disposal | doghouse | downbeat |
| devilled | dilutive | disposer | dogmatic | downcast |
| Devonian | DiMaggio | disproof | dogsbody | downfall |
| devotion | Dimbleby | disprove | dogwatch | downhill |
| devourer | diminish | disquiet | Doisneau | downland |
| devoutly | dimmable | Disraeli | doldrums | downlink |
| dewberry | dinosaur | dissolve | dolerite | download |
| Dewsbury | diocesan | dissuade | Dollfuss | downpipe |
| dextrose | Diogenes | distally | dolomite | downplay |
| dextrous | Dionysus | distance | dolorous | downpour |
| diabetes | dioptric | distaste | Domesday | downside |
| diabetic | diplomat | distinct | domestic | downsize |
| diabolic | dipstick | distract | domicile | downtown |
| diaconal | directly | distrain | dominant | downturn |
| diagnose | director | distrait | dominate | downward |
| diagonal | disabled | distress | domineer | downwind |
| dialogic | disabuse | district | Dominica | doxology |
| dialogue | disagree | distrust | Dominick | doziness |
| dialysis | disallow | disunity | dominion | drabness |
| diamanté | disarray | ditherer | Domitian | drachmae |
| diameter | disaster | diuretic | donation | dragoman |
| dianthus | disburse | dividend | doolally | dragomen |
| diapason | disciple | divinely | doomsday | dragster |
| Diarmuid | disclaim | divinity | doomster | drainage |
| diaspora | disclose | division | doorbell | dramatic |
| diastole | discount | divisive | doorknob | Drambuie |
| diatomic | discover | divorcee | doornail | draughts |
| diatonic | discreet | Djakarta | doorstep | draughty |
| diatribe | discrete | djellaba | doorstop | drawback |
| diazepam | diseased | Djibouti | dopamine | dreadful |

SINGLE WORD | 8 LETTERS | D–E

dreamily
drearily
dressage
dressing
dribbler
drippily
dripping
drivable
driveway
Drogheda
drollery
droopily
drowsily
drubbing
drudgery
druggist
Druidism
drumbeat
drumhead
drunkard
drystone
Dubliner
Dubonnet
Dubuffet
duckling
duckweed
duellist
Duisburg
dulcimer
dullness
dumbness
dumbshow
dumfound
Dumfries
dumpling
dungaree
dunghill
duodenal
duodenum
duologue
duration
Durkheim
Dushanbe
dustcart
Dutchman

Dutchmen
dutiable
Duvalier
dwarfish
dwarfism
dwelling
dyestuff
dynamics
dynamism
dynamite
dynastic
dyslexia
dyslexic
dystopia

# E

earnings
earphone
earpiece
earthily
easiness
easterly
eastward
Eastwood
Ebenezer
ebonised
ebonized
Eboracum
eclectic
ecliptic
economic
ecstatic
edentate
Edgehill
edgeways
edginess
edifying
editable
editress
Edmonton
educable
educator
eeriness
effetely

efficacy
effluent
effluvia
effusion
effusive
eggplant
eggshell
egoistic
egomania
Egyptian
Eichmann
eighteen
Einstein
ejection
elastane
eldorado
eldritch
Eleanora
election
elective
electric
electron
electrum
elegance
Eleonora
elephant
elevated
elevator
eleventh
elicitor
eligible
ellipsis
elliptic
elongate
eloquent
Elsinore
embalmer
embezzle
embitter
emblazon
embolden
embolism
embosser
emergent
emeritus

emigrant
emigrate
eminence
emissary
emission
Emmanuel
Emmeline
Emmental
emoticon
empanada
empathic
emphasis
emphatic
employee
employer
emporium
empyrean
emulator
emulsify
emulsion
encipher
encircle
encomium
encroach
encumber
endanger
endemism
endorser
endpaper
Endymion
energise
energize
enervate
enfeeble
enfilade
enforcer
engaging
engender
engineer
engraver
enhancer
enlarger
enlistee
enormity
enormous

enquirer
ensconce
ensemble
enshrine
enshroud
enslaver
entangle
enthrone
entirely
entirety
entr'acte
entrails
entrance
entreaty
entrench
entrepôt
entropic
entryism
entryist
enuresis
envelope
enviable
enviably
environs
envisage
envision
Eolithic
ephemera
epically
Epicurus
epidemic
epidural
epigraph
epilator
epilepsy
epilogue
epiphany
epiphyte
episodic
equalise
equality
equalize
equation
equipage
erasable

erectile
erection
eremitic
Ericsson
Eriksson
Eritrean
errantry
eruption
eruptive
escalate
escalope
escapade
escapism
escapist
eschewal
Escorial
esculent
esoteric
espalier
especial
espousal
espresso
essayist
estimate
Estonian
estrange
etcetera
eternity
Ethelred
ethereal
etherial
Ethernet
ethicist
Ethiopia
ethology
ethylene
Etruscan
eucalypt
eugenics
eulogise
eulogist
eulogize
euphoria
euphoric
Eurasian

Eurocrat
Euroland
European
europium
eurozone
Eurydice
Eusebius
Eustacia
evacuate
evaluate
evanesce
evenness
evensong
eventful
eventide
eventing
eventual
evermore
everyday
Everyman
everyone
eviction
evidence
evildoer
evilness
exacting
exaction
examinee
examiner
excavate
exchange
excision
exciting
excluder
excursus
execrate
executor
exegesis
exemplar
exercise
exertion
exigency
exiguous
existent
exocrine

exorcise
exorcism
exorcist
exorcize
expanded
expander
expedite
expellee
expertly
explicit
exploder
explorer
exponent
exporter
exposure
expresso
extender
extensor
exterior
external
extranet
exultant
eyeglass
eyeliner
eyepatch
eyepiece
eyeshade
eyesight

**F**

fabulist
fabulous
faceless
facelift
facially
facility
factious
factotum
Faeroese
fairness
faithful
falconer
falconry
fallback

fallible
falsetto
familial
familiar
famished
famously
fanciful
fandango
fanlight
fantasia
farcical
farewell
farmhand
farmland
farmyard
farouche
Farquhar
farriery
farthest
farthing
fastener
fastness
fatalism
fatalist
fatality
fatherly
Faulkner
Faustian
Faustina
fearless
fearsome
feasible
feasibly
feathery
February
feckless
federate
feedback
feistily
feldspar
felicity
feminine
feminise
feminism
feminist

feminize
Ferguson
Fernando
ferocity
Ferranti
ferreter
ferryman
ferrymen
fervency
fervidly
festival
fetching
feverfew
feverish
fibrosis
fibrotic
fiddling
fidelity
Fielding
fiendish
fiercely
fiftieth
figurine
filagree
filament
filename
filicide
filigree
Filioque
Filipino
Fillmore
filthily
filtrate
finagler
finalise
finalist
finality
finalize
findable
fineness
finisher
finitely
fireball
firebomb
fireclay

| | | | | |
|---|---|---|---|---|
| firedamp | fleshpot | foolscap | foretell | Frederic |
| fireside | Fletcher | football | forewarn | Fredrica |
| firewall | flexible | footfall | forewent | Fredrick |
| firewood | flexibly | foothill | forewing | Fredrika |
| firework | flimflam | foothold | foreword | freebase |
| firmness | flimsily | footless | forgiven | freeboot |
| firmware | Flinders | footling | formable | freeborn |
| fiscally | flintily | footmark | formalin | freehand |
| fishable | flippant | footnote | formally | freehold |
| fishbowl | flipping | footpath | formerly | freeload |
| fishcake | floodlit | footrest | formless | freeness |
| fishmeal | flooring | footsore | formulae | Freetown |
| fishtail | florally | footstep | forsaken | freezing |
| fishwife | Florence | footwear | forsooth | Freiburg |
| fistulae | floridly | footwell | forswear | Frenchie |
| fitfully | flotilla | footwork | forswore | frenetic |
| fivefold | flounced | foramina | forsworn | frenzied |
| fixation | flounder | forborne | Forteana | frequent |
| fixative | flourish | forceful | fortieth | frescoed |
| flagella | flowered | forcible | fortress | freshman |
| flagpole | fluently | forcibly | fortuity | freshmen |
| flagrant | fluidity | fordable | forwards | fretwork |
| flagship | flummery | forebear | fosterer | Freudian |
| flambeau | fluoride | forebode | Foucault | friction |
| flamenco | fluorine | forecast | foulness | Friedman |
| flamingo | fluorite | foredoom | fountain | friendly |
| Flanders | flurried | forefeet | fourfold | Friesian |
| flapjack | Flushing | forefoot | foursome | frighten |
| flashgun | fluttery | foregone | fourteen | frigidly |
| flashily | flyblown | forehand | fourthly | fringing |
| flashing | flypaper | forehead | foxglove | frippery |
| flatfish | flysheet | foreland | foxhound | frittata |
| flatline | flywheel | forelimb | foxiness | froideur |
| flatmate | focaccia | forelock | fraction | frontage |
| flatness | fogbound | foremast | fracture | frontier |
| flattery | fogeydom | foremost | fragment | frontman |
| flattish | fogeyish | forename | fragrant | frontmen |
| flatware | fogeyism | forenoon | Francine | frostily |
| flatworm | foldable | forensic | francium | frosting |
| Flaubert | foldaway | foreplay | Frankish | frothily |
| flautist | folderol | foresail | Franklin | fructify |
| flawless | folklore | foreseen | Frascati | fructose |
| flaxseed | follicle | foreskin | Fräulein | frugally |
| flection | follower | forester | freakily | fruitful |
| fleeting | fondness | forestry | freakish | fruition |

fruitlet
fugitive
Fujairah
fullback
fullness
fumarole
fumbling
fumigant
fumigate
Funafuti
function
funerary
funereal
furbelow
furlough
furthest
fuselage
fusilier
futilely
futility
Futurism
Futurist
futurity

# G

Gabonese
Gaborone
gadabout
gadgetry
gadzooks
gaitered
galactic
galangal
Galilean
galliard
Galloway
Galtieri
galvanic
gameness
gamesman
gamesmen
gamester
gaminess
Ganapati

gangland
gangling
ganglion
gangrene
gangster
Ganymede
gardener
gardenia
Garfield
gargoyle
garishly
garlicky
garrison
garrotte
Gascogne
gaslight
gasoline
gasworks
gatefold
gatepost
gatherer
gauchely
Gaullism
Gaullist
gauntlet
Gavaskar
gazpacho
gazumper
gelatine
Geminian
gemstone
gendarme
gendered
generate
generous
genetics
genially
genitive
genocide
genomics
genotype
gentrify
geodesic
geodetic
Geoffrey

geologic
geomancy
geometry
Georgian
Georgina
geranium
Germaine
Germanic
germinal
Geronimo
Gershwin
Gertrude
gestural
Ghanaian
Ghiberti
ghosting
ghoulish
giantess
gigabyte
gigaflop
gigantic
gigawatt
gimcrack
gimmicky
gingerly
Ginsberg
Giovanni
girlhood
Gisborne
Giuseppe
giveaway
gladioli
gladness
glancing
glasnost
glassful
glassily
glaucoma
glaucous
Glazunov
glibness
glissade
glittery
gloaming
globally

globular
globulin
gloomily
Gloriana
glorious
glossary
glossily
glovebox
gloxinia
gluttony
glycerol
glycogen
gnashers
goalless
goalpost
goatherd
goatskin
Gobelins
Gobineau
godchild
Godspeed
Goebbels
goitrous
goldenly
goldfish
Goldmark
Golgotha
Gollancz
golliwog
Gomorrah
Goncourt
Gondwana
goodness
goodwill
Goodwood
Goodyear
Goossens
Gordimer
gorgeous
goriness
gormless
gossamer
gossiper
gourmand
governor

graceful
gracious
gradient
graduand
graduate
graffiti
Grainger
Grampian
granddad
grandeur
grandson
granitic
granular
graphics
graphite
grappler
Grasmere
grasping
grateful
gratuity
gravelly
gravitas
grayling
greasily
greedily
greenery
greenfly
greenish
Greenock
greeting
Grenache
Grenfell
Grenoble
Gretchen
greyness
gridiron
gridlock
Grierson
grievous
Griffith
Grimaldi
grimness
Griselda
grittily
grizzled

| | | | | |
|---|---|---|---|---|
| groggily | Habsburg | hardcore | headwind | Hercules |
| groovily | hachured | hardener | headword | herdsman |
| grosbeak | hachures | hardness | hearable | herdsmen |
| grouping | hacienda | hardship | heartily | heredity |
| grudging | hacksawn | hardware | heatedly | Hereford |
| gruesome | Hailwood | hardwood | heathery | hereupon |
| grumbler | Haiphong | harebell | Heathrow | Hereward |
| grumpily | hairball | harlotry | heatwave | herewith |
| Guadiana | hairband | harmless | heavenly | heritage |
| guaiacum | hairgrip | harmonic | heavyset | hermetic |
| guardian | hairless | harridan | hedgehog | Hermione |
| Guarneri | hairline | Harrison | hedgerow | hermitic |
| Guericke | halfback | harrumph | hedonism | herniate |
| guerilla | hallmark | Hartford | hedonist | herpetic |
| Guernica | halloumi | Hartnell | heedless | Herschel |
| Guernsey | Hallowes | Hasidism | heelball | Hertford |
| guidance | Hamilcar | Hastings | Hegelian | hesitant |
| guileful | Hamilton | hatchery | hegemony | hesitate |
| guiltily | handball | hatchway | heighten | hexagram |
| Guinness | handbell | Hathaway | heirloom | Hezekiah |
| Gujarati | handbill | haunting | heirship | Hiawatha |
| Gujerati | handbook | Hawaiian | heliport | hibiscus |
| gullible | handcart | hawfinch | Hellenic | hiccough |
| gumption | handclap | hawthorn | hellfire | hideaway |
| gunfight | handcuff | haymaker | hellhole | hieratic |
| gunmetal | handhold | haystack | hellward | highball |
| gunpoint | handicap | Hayworth | helmeted | highbrow |
| gunsight | handmade | hazelnut | helmsman | highland |
| gunsmith | handmaid | haziness | helmsmen | highness |
| gurdwara | handover | headache | helpless | hightail |
| Gustavus | handrail | headachy | helpline | hijacker |
| guttural | handsome | headband | Helpmann | hilarity |
| Guyanese | handspan | headbutt | helpmate | hillocky |
| Gwynneth | handyman | headcase | helpmeet | hillside |
| gymkhana | handymen | headgear | Helsinki | hindlimb |
| gymnasia | Hangchow | headhunt | Helvetia | hindmost |
| gypsyish | hangnail | headlamp | henchman | Hinduise |
| gyration | hangover | headland | henchmen | Hinduism |
| gyratory | Hangzhou | headless | heptagon | Hinduize |
| | Hannibal | headline | Hepworth | hindwing |
| | Hanukkah | headlock | Hepzibah | hippyish |
| **H** | Hapsburg | headlong | Heracles | hireable |
| | harangue | headrest | heraldic | hireling |
| Habakkuk | harasser | headroom | heraldry | Hirohito |
| Habermas | hardback | headship | herbaria | Hispanic |
| habitual | | | | |

| | | | | |
|---|---|---|---|---|
| historic | hornpipe | humpback | imbecile | indenter |
| hitherto | horology | Humphrey | imitable | Indiaman |
| hoarding | Horowitz | humpless | imitator | Indiamen |
| hoarsely | horrible | hungrily | immanent | indicate |
| hobbyist | horribly | huntress | Immanuel | indigent |
| Hoffmann | horridly | huntsman | immature | indirect |
| Hogmanay | horrific | huntsmen | imminent | indolent |
| hogshead | horsebox | hustings | immobile | inductee |
| Hokkaido | horsefly | hyacinth | immodest | inductor |
| holiness | horseman | hydrogen | immolate | Indurain |
| holistic | horsemen | hydroxyl | immortal | industry |
| hollowly | Hortense | hygienic | immunise | inedible |
| Holocene | hosannah | hymeneal | immunity | inequity |
| hologram | hosepipe | hyoscine | immunize | inertial |
| Holstein | hospital | hypnosis | impacted | inexpert |
| Holyhead | hostelry | hypnotic | impactor | infamous |
| Holyoake | hotelier | hysteria | impeller | infantry |
| homegirl | hothouse | hysteric | imperial | inferior |
| homeland | hotplate | | impetigo | infernal |
| homeless | houseboy | **I** | impishly | infinite |
| homesick | housefly | | implicit | infinity |
| homespun | houseful | idealise | impolite | informal |
| homeward | houseman | idealism | importer | informed |
| homework | housemen | idealist | imposing | informer |
| homicide | hoverfly | idealize | imposter | infrared |
| homilist | howitzer | identify | impostor | infringe |
| hominoid | huckster | identity | impotent | infusion |
| homology | hugeness | ideogram | imprison | inguinal |
| Honduran | huggable | ideology | improper | inhalant |
| Honduras | Huguenot | idiolect | improver | inherent |
| Honecker | humanely | idleness | impudent | inhumane |
| Honegger | humanise | idolater | impunity | inimical |
| honestly | humanism | idolatry | impurity | iniquity |
| honeybee | humanist | Iglesias | inaction | initiate |
| honeydew | humanity | Ignatius | inactive | injector |
| honeypot | humanize | ignition | inasmuch | inkstand |
| Honolulu | humanoid | ignominy | inchoate | inlander |
| honorary | Humboldt | ignorant | incident | Inmarsat |
| hoodwink | humidify | Ikhnaton | incision | innately |
| hookworm | humidity | Illinois | incisive | innocent |
| hooligan | humility | illumine | incoming | innovate |
| hopeless | hummable | illusion | increase | innuendo |
| hormonal | hummocky | illusive | incubate | inputter |
| hornbeam | humorist | illusory | indebted | inquirer |
| hornbill | humorous | imaginer | indecent | insanely |

insanity
inscribe
insecure
inserter
insignia
insolent
insomnia
insomuch
inspired
inspirer
inspirit
instance
instinct
instruct
insulant
insulate
intaglio
intarsia
integral
Intelsat
intended
intender
intently
interact
intercom
intercut
interest
interior
intermix
internal
internee
Internet
Interpol
intersex
interval
interwar
intifada
intimacy
intimate
intranet
intrepid
intrigue
intruder
inundate
invasion

invasive
inveigle
inventor
inverter
investor
inviting
involute
involved
inwardly
Iolanthe
Iorwerth
Irangate
Irishman
Irishmen
ironclad
ironical
ironwork
Iroquois
irrigate
irritant
irritate
Isabella
Isabelle
Ishiguro
Islamise
Islamism
Islamist
Islamize
islander
isobaric
isolated
isolator
isomeric
isotherm
isotonic
isotopic
Issachar
Istanbul
Itanagar

**J**

jackaroo
jackboot
Jacobean

Jacobite
Jacobsen
jacquard
jaggedly
Jahangir
jailbait
jailbird
Jakobson
jalapeño
jalfrezi
jalousie
Jamaican
jamboree
Japanese
japonica
jaundice
jauntily
Javanese
jealousy
Jeanette
Jeannine
Jeffreys
Jellicoe
Jennifer
jeopardy
jeremiad
Jeremiah
Jeremias
Jermaine
jeroboam
jerrican
jerrycan
Jessamyn
jetliner
jettison
jewelled
jeweller
Jharkand
jihadist
jingoism
jingoist
jocosely
jocosity
jodhpurs
Johannes

Johnston
joinable
Jonathan
Jordaens
Joscelin
jovially
joyfully
joyously
joyrider
joystick
jubilant
judicial
Jugurtha
Julianne
julienne
Juliette
jumpable
jumpsuit
junction
juncture
Jungfrau
junglist
Jurassic
juristic
justness
juvenile

**K**

Kabbalah
kaffiyeh
Kairouan
Kalahari
Kalmykia
kamikaze
Kandahar
kangaroo
Kashmiri
Kasparov
Kathleen
Katowice
Kattegat
Kauffman
Kawasaki
kedgeree

keelboat
keelhaul
keenness
keepsake
keffiyeh
Keflavik
Kelantan
Keneally
Kentucky
Kenyatta
kerbside
kerchief
kerosene
kerosine
ketamine
keyboard
keypunch
keystone
Khartoum
Khoikhoi
Khomeini
kickback
kidology
Kilkenny
kilobyte
kilogram
kilovolt
kilowatt
Kimberly
Kinabalu
kindling
kindness
kinetics
kingship
Kingsley
Kingston
kinkajou
kinsfolk
Kinshasa
Kirchner
Kiribati
Kirkwall
kissable
Kitemark
Klansman

Klansmen
Klaproth
Klondike
Klosters
knapsack
knapweed
knickers
knightly
knitting
knitwear
knockout
knothole
knotweed
knowable
Koestler
kohlrabi
kolkhozy
Komsomol
Korchnoi
Kordofan
Kotzebue
Krakatoa
Kreisler
Krishnan
Kristina
Kristine
Kumamoto
Kurosawa
Kuşadasi
Kyrgyzia

# L

Laayoune
laboured
labourer
Labrador
laburnum
lacerate
lacewing
Lachesis
Lackland
lacrimal
lacrosse
lacrymal

ladleful
ladybird
ladylike
Ladyship
Laetitia
Lagrange
Lakeland
lakeside
lamasery
lambaste
lamellae
lamellar
lameness
laminate
lancelet
Lancelot
landfall
landfill
landform
landlady
landless
landline
landlord
landmark
landmine
Landseer
landside
landslip
landsman
landsmen
landward
Langland
language
languish
Laoighis
lapidary
larboard
largesse
larkspur
Larousse
Larraine
larrikin
lashings
latchkey
lateness

latently
laterite
Latinate
Latinise
Latinism
Latinist
Latinity
Latinize
latitude
latterly
latticed
laudable
laudably
laudanum
laughter
Laughton
launcher
Lauraine
Laurasia
laureate
Laurence
Lauretta
Lausanne
lavatory
lavender
lavishly
lawfully
lawgiver
lawmaker
Lawrence
lawyerly
laxative
layabout
laywoman
laywomen
laziness
leadenly
leafless
leanness
leapfrog
learning
leathern
leathery
leavings
Lebanese

lecithin
lecturer
leftmost
leftover
leftward
legalese
legalise
legalism
legalist
legality
legalize
legation
leggings
Leighton
Leinster
leisured
lemonade
lengthen
lenience
leniency
Leninism
Leninist
Leonardo
lethally
lethargy
leveller
leverage
levitate
lewdness
libation
Liberace
liberate
Liberian
libretti
libretto
licensee
licenser
lichened
lifebelt
lifeboat
lifebuoy
lifeless
lifelike
lifeline
lifelong

lifespan
lifetime
liftable
ligament
ligature
lighting
lightish
ligneous
Ligurian
likeable
likeably
likeness
likewise
Lilongwe
Limassol
limbless
limekiln
limerick
limewash
Limousin
limpidly
limpness
linchpin
lineally
linearly
linesman
linesmen
lingerer
lingerie
linguine
linguist
liniment
Linnaean
Linnaeus
linoleum
Lipchitz
lipgloss
liposome
lipsalve
lipstick
liquidly
listener
listeria
listless
literacy

literary
literate
literati
litigant
litigate
littoral
liveable
livelong
liveried
liverish
lividity
Llewelyn
lobbyist
lobotomy
localise
locality
localize
location
lockable
lockdown
locution
lodestar
logician
logistic
loiterer
lollipop
lollygag
Lombardy
Londoner
lonesome
longboat
Longford
longhand
longhorn
Longinus
longline
longship
longstop
longueur
longways
loophole
loosener
lopsided
lordship
lorikeet

Lorraine
Lothario
loudness
loveable
lovebird
Lovelace
loveless
Lovelock
lovelorn
lovesick
lovingly
lowlands
lowlight
loyalism
loyalist
lubberly
Lubianka
Lubyanka
lucidity
luckless
Lucretia
Lucrezia
lukewarm
luminary
luminous
lumpfish
luncheon
lungfish
lunkhead
luscious
lushness
lustrous
lutanist
lutenist
lutetium
Lutheran
lychgate
lycopene
lymphoma
lynchpin
Lynnette
lyrebird
lyricism
lyricist
Lysander

# M

macaroni
macaroon
Macassar
Macaulay
macerate
machismo
mackerel
MacNeice
Madelina
Madeline
madhouse
madrigal
madwoman
madwomen
Maecenas
Mafeking
magazine
Magdalen
Magellan
Maggiore
magician
magnesia
magnetic
magnolia
Magritte
maharaja
maharani
Mahaweli
Mahayana
mahogany
mailshot
mainland
mainmast
mainsail
mainstay
maintain
maiolica
Maitreya
majestic
majolica
Majorcan
majority
makeover

Malagasy
malaprop
malarial
malarkey
Malawian
Malaysia
maleness
Malenkov
Malevich
Malherbe
malignly
malinger
Mallarmé
Mallorca
Malpighi
maltreat
maltster
Mamoutzu
managing
Manasseh
Manawatu
Manchego
Mandalay
mandarin
mandible
mandolin
mandrake
mandrill
maneater
manfully
mangabey
mangrove
maniacal
manicure
manifest
manifold
Manitoba
mannered
mannerly
Mannheim
mannikin
manorial
manpower
Mantegna
mantilla

manually
maquette
Maradona
marathon
marauder
Marbella
marbling
Marcella
Marcelle
Marciano
Margaret
marginal
margrave
mariachi
Marianne
Marietta
Mariette
marigold
marinade
marinara
marinate
maritime
marjoram
Marjorie
markedly
marketer
marksman
marksmen
marmoset
Maronite
marquess
marquise
marriage
Marshall
martinet
Maryland
marzipan
Masaccio
Mascagni
massacre
masterly
masthead
mastitis
mastodon
Matabele

| | | | | |
|---|---|---|---|---|
| matchbox | megalith | metaphor | ministry | moderato |
| material | megapode | metazoan | Minorcan | modernly |
| materiel | megastar | meteoric | minority | modestly |
| maternal | megavolt | methanol | Minotaur | modifier |
| mateship | megawatt | methinks | minstrel | modishly |
| matronly | Megillah | methodic | minutely | modulate |
| Matthews | melamine | metonymy | minutiae | Mohammed |
| Matthias | melanoma | metrical | Mirabeau | moisture |
| mattress | Melchior | meunière | mirepoix | molasses |
| maturely | Meleager | Mexicali | mirthful | Moldavia |
| maturity | Melicent | Meyerhof | misapply | Moldovan |
| mausolea | melodeon | Micawber | miscarry | molecule |
| maverick | meltdown | Michaela | mischief | molehill |
| maxillae | Melville | Michelin | miscible | moleskin |
| maximise | membrane | Michelle | miscount | molester |
| maximize | memorial | Michigan | mishmash | momentum |
| Maynooth | memorise | microdot | misjudge | Monaghan |
| mayoress | memorize | midbrain | mismatch | monarchy |
| Mazatlán | memsahib | middling | misnomer | monastic |
| McAleese | Menander | midfield | misogyny | Mondrian |
| McCarthy | mendable | Midlands | misplace | monetary |
| McGuffin | Menelaus | midnight | misprint | monetise |
| McKinlay | meniscus | midpoint | misquote | monetize |
| McKinley | menswear | midships | Missouri | Mongolia |
| mealtime | mentally | mightily | misspell | mongoose |
| meanness | mephitic | migraine | misspelt | monicker |
| meantime | Mercator | mildewed | misspend | monkfish |
| measured | Mercedes | mildness | misspent | Monmouth |
| measurer | merchant | milepost | misstate | monobloc |
| meatball | merciful | militant | mistaken | monogamy |
| mechanic | Mercosur | military | mistreat | monoglot |
| Mechelen | Mercouri | militate | mistress | monogram |
| meconium | mercuric | milkmaid | mistrial | monohull |
| Medellín | Meredith | milliard | mistrust | monolith |
| medially | merengue | millibar | Mitchell | monopoly |
| mediator | meridian | Milligan | mitigate | monorail |
| medicate | meringue | milliner | mixology | monotone |
| medicine | meristem | millpond | mnemonic | monotony |
| medieval | mescalin | minatory | mobilise | monoxide |
| mediocre | Mesdames | Mindanao | mobility | Monrovia |
| meditate | mesmeric | mindless | mobilize | Monsieur |
| meekness | Mesozoic | minidisc | moccasin | Montagna |
| megabuck | mesquite | minimise | modality | Montague |
| megabyte | Messiaen | minimize | modeller | Montcalm |
| megaflop | metallic | minister | moderate | Monterey |

Montreal
Montreux
Montrose
monument
moonbeam
moonwalk
moorland
moquette
moralise
moralist
morality
moralize
Moravian
morbidly
Mordecai
moreover
moribund
Moroccan
morosely
morpheme
Morpheus
morphine
Morrison
mortally
mortgage
Mortimer
mortuary
Morwenna
mosquito
mothball
motherly
motility
motivate
motorise
motorist
motorize
motorman
motormen
motorway
moulding
mountain
mounting
mournful
mourning
moussaka

mouthful
moveable
movement
movingly
muchness
mucilage
muckrake
mudguard
Muhammad
mulberry
muleteer
Mulhacén
Mulhouse
Mulroney
multiple
multiply
munchies
muniment
munition
Muqdisho
murderer
Murmansk
Muscadet
muscatel
muscular
Museveni
mushroom
musician
musketry
musquash
Mustique
mutation
muteness
mutilate
mutineer
mutinous
mutually
mycelium
mycology
myriapod
myrmidon
mystical
mystique
mythical

**N**

nacreous
naffness
Nagaland
Nagasaki
nameless
namesake
Namibian
Naphtali
Napoleon
Narbonne
narcissi
narcosis
narcotic
narrator
narrowly
nasalise
nasalize
Nathalie
national
nativity
naturism
naturist
nauseate
nauseous
nautical
nautilus
Navarino
navigate
Naxçivan
Nazarene
Nazareth
N'Djamena
nearness
nearside
neatness
Nebraska
nebulise
nebulize
nebulous
neckband
necklace
neckline
necropsy

necrosis
necrotic
needless
negation
negative
negligee
Nehemiah
nematode
neonatal
neophyte
neoplasm
neoprene
Nepalese
nephrite
nepotism
nestling
neurally
neuritis
neuronal
neurosis
neurotic
neutrino
newbuild
Newcomen
newcomer
newscast
newsfeed
newspeak
newsreel
newsroom
newswire
niceness
Nicholas
Nicklaus
nickname
nicotine
Niemeyer
Niflheim
Nigerian
Nigerien
nightcap
nightjar
nihilism
nihilist
Nijinsky

Nijmegen
Nimbyism
ninepins
nineteen
ninjutsu
nitrogen
nobelium
nobility
nobleman
noblemen
nocturne
noisette
nomadism
nominate
nonsense
noontide
noontime
normally
Normandy
Norseman
Norsemen
northern
northing
noseband
nosedive
nosiness
notarial
notarise
notarize
notation
notebook
notional
novelise
novelist
novelize
November
Novgorod
nowadays
nubility
nucleate
Nuffield
nugatory
nuisance
numbness
numeracy

numerate
numerous
numinous
numskull
Nuneaton
nursling
nuthatch
nutrient
nutshell

# O

obduracy
obdurate
obedient
obituary
objector
oblation
obligate
obliging
oblivion
observer
obsidian
obsolete
obstacle
obstruct
obtusely
occasion
Occident
occupant
occupier
Oceanian
ochreous
O'Connell
octaroon
Octavian
Octavius
octopoid
octoroon
octuplet
odiously
odometer
odyssean
Odysseus
oenology

offender
offering
official
offprint
offshoot
offshore
offstage
O'Higgins
oilcloth
oilfield
oiliness
oilstone
ointment
Okavango
Oklahoma
Oldfield
oleander
oligarch
Olympiad
Olympian
Olympics
Omdurman
omelette
omission
omnivore
oncogene
oncology
oncoming
Ondaatje
onlooker
ontology
opaquely
openable
opencast
openness
openwork
operable
operatic
operator
opercula
operetta
ophidian
opponent
opposite
optician

optimise
optimism
optimist
optimize
optional
opulence
oracular
orangery
oratorio
Orcadian
ordinand
ordinary
ordinate
ordnance
organdie
organise
organism
organist
organize
orgasmic
oriental
original
ornament
ornately
orpiment
orthodox
orthotic
ostinati
ostinato
outboard
outbound
outbreak
outburst
outclass
outdated
outdoors
outfield
outflank
outgoing
outgrown
outhouse
outlawry
outlying
outmatch
outmoded

outreach
Outremer
outrider
outright
outshine
outshone
outsider
outsmart
outstrip
outwards
outweigh
overarch
overbite
overbook
overcame
overcast
overcoat
overcome
overcook
overdone
overdose
overdraw
overdrew
overfall
overfeed
overfill
overfish
overflow
overhand
overhang
overhaul
overhead
overhear
overheat
overhung
overhype
overkill
overlain
overland
overleaf
overload
overlock
overlong
overlook
overlord

overmuch
overpass
overplay
overrate
override
overripe
overrode
overrule
overseas
overseen
overseer
oversell
oversewn
overshoe
overshot
oversize
overstay
overstep
overtake
overtime
overtone
overtook
overture
overturn
overview
overwear
overwork
owlishly
Oxbridge
oxidiser
oxidizer
oxymoron
oxytocin

# P

pacifier
pacifism
pacifist
packable
packager
packsack
Paganini
paganism
paginate

| | | | | |
|---|---|---|---|---|
| Paignton | paralyse | patience | pensioni | pharmacy |
| painless | paralyze | Patricia | pentacle | pheasant |
| paintbox | paramour | Paulette | pentagon | phenolic |
| painting | paranoia | pavement | penumbra | Philemon |
| Pakistan | paranoid | pavilion | Penzance | Philippa |
| palatial | paraquat | pawnshop | perceive | Philippi |
| palatine | parasail | payphone | Perceval | Phillida |
| paleface | parasite | peaceful | Percival | Phillipa |
| paleness | pardoner | peacenik | Perelman | Phillips |
| Palenque | parental | peatland | perforce | Philomel |
| Palgrave | parhelia | pecorino | perfumer | phishing |
| palimony | parietal | pectoral | Pergamum | phonetic |
| palisade | Parisian | peculiar | perianth | phosgene |
| palladia | parkland | pedagogy | pericarp | phosphor |
| Palladio | parlance | pedaller | Pericles | photofit |
| palliate | Parmesan | pedantic | Périgord | photonic |
| palmetto | parodist | pedantry | perilous | Phrygian |
| palomino | paroxysm | pederast | perineal | phthisis |
| palpable | Parsifal | pedestal | perineum | Phyllida |
| palpably | partaken | pedicure | periodic | physalis |
| pamphlet | parterre | pedigree | perisher | physical |
| Pamplona | particle | pediment | perjurer | physique |
| pancetta | partisan | peduncle | permeate | picayune |
| pancreas | Pasadena | peekaboo | peroxide | Pickford |
| pandanus | pashmina | peelable | Perpetua | pickings |
| pandemic | Pasiphaë | peelings | Perrault | piddling |
| pangolin | Pasolini | peephole | personae | Piedmont |
| pannikin | passable | peerless | personal | piffling |
| panoptic | passably | pegboard | perspire | pigswill |
| panorama | passbook | peignoir | persuade | pilaster |
| panstick | Passover | Pekinese | pertness | pilchard |
| Pantanal | passport | pellagra | Peruvian | pillager |
| pantheon | password | pellucid | perverse | pillared |
| pantsuit | pastiche | Pembroke | pervious | pilotage |
| Paolozzi | pastille | penalise | Peshawar | pimiento |
| papillae | pastoral | penalize | pétanque | pinafore |
| papillon | pastrami | penchant | Peterson | Pinatubo |
| parabola | patchily | pendular | petition | pinnacle |
| paradigm | patellae | pendulum | Petrarch | Pinochet |
| paradise | patellar | Penelope | pettifog | pinpoint |
| paraffin | patentee | penitent | petulant | pinprick |
| Paraguay | patently | penknife | Phaethon | pinwheel |
| parakeet | paternal | penlight | phalange | pipeclay |
| parallax | pathetic | penology | phantasm | pipeline |
| parallel | pathogen | pensione | Pharisee | pipework |

| | | | | |
|---|---|---|---|---|
| piquancy | plimsole | ponytail | practice | prisoner |
| Piranesi | plimsoll | poolside | practise | prissily |
| piscinae | Pliocene | popinjay | prandial | Pristina |
| Pissarro | Plotinus | poppadom | prankish | pristine |
| pitiable | plotless | poppadum | pratfall | probable |
| pitiably | pluckily | populace | preacher | probably |
| pitiless | plughole | populate | preamble | proceeds |
| pittance | plumbago | populism | precinct | proclaim |
| pixelate | plumbing | populist | precious | procurer |
| pixieish | plumpish | populous | preclude | prodigal |
| pixilate | plurally | porosity | predator | producer |
| pizzeria | Plutarch | porphyry | preexist | profiler |
| placeman | plutonic | porpoise | pregnant | profound |
| placemen | Plymouth | porridge | prejudge | progress |
| placenta | pockmark | Porsenna | prematch | prohibit |
| placidly | podiatry | portable | premiere | prolapse |
| plangent | poetical | porthole | premises | prolific |
| planking | poignant | Portland | premolar | prologue |
| planktic | Poincaré | portrait | prenatal | promisee |
| plankton | pointing | Portugal | preparer | promisor |
| planning | poisoner | Poseidon | presence | promoter |
| plantain | Poitiers | poshness | preserve | prompter |
| plantlet | Polanski | position | pressing | promptly |
| plateaux | polarise | positive | pressman | properly |
| platelet | polarity | positron | pressmen | property |
| platform | polarize | possible | pressure | prophecy |
| platinum | Polaroid | possibly | prestige | prophesy |
| Platonic | polemics | postcard | pretence | propolis |
| platypus | polisher | postcode | Pretoria | proposal |
| playable | politely | postdate | pretreat | proposer |
| playback | politick | postlude | prettify | propound |
| Playfair | politico | postmark | prettily | prorogue |
| playlist | politics | postpone | previous | prosodic |
| playmate | pollster | postural | priapism | prospect |
| playsuit | polluter | potation | prideful | prostate |
| playtime | polonium | Potemkin | priestly | protocol |
| pleading | poltroon | potently | priggish | protract |
| pleasant | polygamy | potholed | primeval | protrude |
| pleasure | polyglot | potholer | primness | Proudhon |
| plebeian | polygyny | Potiphar | primrose | provable |
| plectrum | polymath | potlatch | princely | Provence |
| pleonasm | pomander | potsherd | princess | Proverbs |
| plethora | Pompidou | poultice | printing | provided |
| pleurisy | pondweed | poundage | printout | provider |
| pliantly | Pontormo | powerful | priority | province |

proximal
prudence
Prunella
prurient
pruritic
pruritus
Prussian
psalmist
psalmody
psaltery
ptomaine
pubertal
publican
publicly
puddingy
pudendum
puffball
pugilism
pugilist
puissant
Pulitzer
pullover
punchbag
puncheon
punctual
puncture
punditry
pungency
puniness
punitive
pupation
puppetry
puppyish
purblind
purchase
purifier
purlieux
purplish
purslane
pursuant
purulent
purveyor
pushbike
pushcart
pushover

pussycat
pustular
putative

# Q

quackery
quadrant
quadrate
quagmire
quaintly
quandary
quantify
quantity
quarrier
quartile
quatrain
quayside
queasily
Quechuan
queendom
queerish
quencher
quenelle
question
quickset
quiddity
quietism
quietude
quilling
quilting
quincunx
quipster
quirkily
quisling
quixotic
quoining
quotable
quotient

# R

rabbinic
Rabelais
racecard

racially
raciness
raclette
radially
radiance
radiator
raftered
raggedly
ragstone
railcard
railhead
raillery
railroad
raincoat
raindrop
rainfall
rainwear
Rajneesh
rakishly
rallying
rallyist
Ramadhan
Ramayana
rambutan
Randolph
randomly
rapacity
rapeseed
rapidity
rarefied
rascally
rashness
Rasputin
Rastaman
Rastamen
rateable
rational
Rattigan
rattling
ravening
ravenous
Rawlplug
Rayleigh
reactant
reaction

reactive
readable
readerly
readjust
reaffirm
realness
reappear
rearmost
rearrest
rearward
reasoned
reassert
reassess
reassign
reassure
reattach
reawaken
rebuttal
receiver
recently
receptor
recharge
reckless
recliner
recorder
recourse
recovery
recreant
recreate
rectally
recusant
recycler
redactor
Redditch
redeemer
redefine
redeploy
redesign
Redgrave
redirect
redolent
redouble
redshank
redstart
referent

referral
referrer
refinery
refinish
reforest
reformat
reformer
regality
regicide
regiment
Reginald
regional
register
registry
regrowth
regulate
rehearse
Rehoboam
reindeer
reinfect
reinsure
reinvent
reinvest
rekindle
relation
relative
relaunch
relaxant
releaser
relegate
relevant
reliable
reliably
reliance
reliever
religion
relocate
Remarque
remaster
remedial
remember
reminder
remotely
renderer
renegade

renminbi
renounce
renovate
renowned
rentable
renumber
reoccupy
reoffend
reorient
repairer
repartee
repeater
repeller
repenter
rephrase
replacer
reporter
repoussé
reprieve
reprisal
reproach
republic
requital
research
reselect
reseller
resemble
reserved
resettle
resident
residual
residuum
resinous
resister
resistor
resolute
resolver
resonant
resonate
resource
Respighi
response
restless
restorer
restrain

restrict
restring
restroom
restrung
resupply
retailer
retainer
retarded
retarder
reticent
reticule
retiring
retrench
retrieve
retrofit
returnee
returner
reusable
revealer
reveille
reveller
revenant
reverend
reverent
reversal
reviewer
revision
revivify
revolver
rewinder
Reynolds
rhapsody
rheology
rheostat
rhetoric
Rhiannon
rhinitis
Rhodesia
rhomboid
rhyolite
rhythmic
ribaldry
ribboned
Riccardo
Richards

Richmond
richness
rickrack
rickshaw
ricochet
riddance
rideable
ridicule
Riesling
rifleman
riflemen
rigatoni
rightful
rightish
rightism
rightist
rigidify
rigidity
rigorous
rindless
ringdove
ringside
ringtone
ringworm
riparian
ripeness
ritually
riverbed
riverine
roadkill
roadless
roadshow
roadside
roadster
roadwork
roasting
Robinson
robotics
robotise
robotize
robustly
Rochelle
rocketry
Rockwell
Roderick

roentgen
rollover
romancer
Romanian
romanise
romanize
Romantic
rondavel
rondeaux
roofless
rootless
ropiness
Rosaleen
Rosalind
Rosaline
Rosamond
Rosamund
Roseanna
Roseanne
Rosebery
rosemary
rosewood
rosiness
Roskilde
Rossetti
Rosslare
Rotarian
rotation
rotatory
rotavate
rotundly
roughage
roulette
rounders
roundish
Rousseau
rowdyism
Rowntree
royalism
royalist
rubbishy
rubicund
rubidium
rucksack
rudeness

rudiment
ruefully
ruggedly
Ruisdael
Rumanian
ruminant
ruminate
runabout
runnable
ruralise
rurality
ruralize
Rushmore
rustless
ruthless
Ruysdael
Rwandese
ryegrass

# S

Saarland
sabotage
saboteur
sackable
sacredly
sacristy
saddlery
Sadducee
sadistic
sagacity
Sahelian
sailboat
sailfish
sainfoin
Sakhalin
Sakharov
salaried
saleable
saleroom
salesman
salesmen
salience
saliency
Salinger

| | | | | |
|---|---|---|---|---|
| salinity | saturate | Scorpian | seatless | sensuous |
| Salishan | Saturday | scorpion | seawards | sentence |
| salivary | saucepan | Scorsese | seawater | sentient |
| salivate | Saussure | Scotland | secluded | sentinel |
| Salonica | savagely | Scotsman | secondee | separate |
| saltbush | savagery | Scotsmen | seconder | Sephardi |
| saltless | savannah | Scottish | secondly | Septimus |
| saltness | sawtooth | scouting | secretly | septuple |
| salutary | scabbard | scrabble | secretor | sequelae |
| Salvador | scabious | scraggly | sectoral | sequence |
| salvager | scabrous | scramble | securely | seraglio |
| Salzburg | scaffold | Scranton | security | seraphic |
| Samantha | scalable | scrapper | sedately | seraphim |
| samarium | scallion | scratchy | sedation | serenade |
| sameness | scampish | screamer | sedative | serenely |
| samizdat | scandium | screechy | sediment | serenity |
| samphire | scansion | screener | sedition | sergeant |
| Sancerre | scantily | Scriabin | sedulous | serially |
| sanctify | scapulae | scribble | seedcorn | sermonic |
| sanction | scapular | scrofula | seedless | serology |
| sanctity | scarcely | scrolled | seedling | serrated |
| sandbank | scarcity | scroller | seedsman | servitor |
| sandshoe | Scarlett | scrounge | seedsmen | severely |
| sandwich | scathing | scrubber | seicento | severity |
| sanguine | scavenge | scrunchy | seigneur | sewerage |
| sanitary | scenario | scrutiny | Selangor | sexiness |
| sanitise | schedule | scullery | selector | sexology |
| sanitize | schemata | scullion | selenium | sextuple |
| Sanskrit | Schiller | sculptor | selfhood | sexually |
| Santiago | schizoid | Scythian | selfless | shabbily |
| saponify | Schlegel | seaboard | selfsame | shaddock |
| sapphire | schlocky | seaborne | sellable | shadower |
| saraband | schmaltz | seafarer | selvedge | shaggily |
| Sarajevo | schmooze | seafront | Selznick | shagreen |
| Saratoga | schmoozy | seagoing | semantic | shamanic |
| Sardinia | schnapps | sealable | semester | shambles |
| sardonic | schooner | sealskin | Sémillon | shameful |
| sardonyx | Schröder | Sealyham | seminary | shamrock |
| sargasso | Schubert | seamless | semiotic | Shandong |
| satanism | Schumann | seaplane | semitone | shanghai |
| satanist | sciatica | searcher | semolina | shantung |
| satirise | scimitar | seascape | senility | sharpish |
| satirist | scissors | seashell | señorita | shashlik |
| satirize | scorcher | seashore | sensible | shedload |
| satphone | scornful | seasonal | sensibly | Sheelagh |

| | | | | |
|---|---|---|---|---|
| sheepdog | shrewish | sinfully | slimline | snowdrop |
| sheepish | shrieker | singable | slimness | snowfall |
| sheeting | shrimper | singular | slippage | snowless |
| shelduck | shrunken | sinister | slippery | snowline |
| shelving | shuddery | sinkhole | slipshod | snowshoe |
| Shenyang | shuffler | Sinkiang | slithery | snuggery |
| Shenzhen | shutdown | sinology | slobbery | snugness |
| shepherd | Sibelius | siphonic | slobbish | soakaway |
| Sheraton | Siberian | sirenian | sloppily | soapsuds |
| Sheridan | sibilant | sisterly | slothful | sobriety |
| Shetland | Sicilian | Sisyphus | Slovakia | sociable |
| shiftily | sickener | sitarist | Slovenia | sociably |
| shiitake | sickness | sixpence | slovenly | socially |
| shilling | sickroom | sixpenny | slowdown | societal |
| Shillong | sideburn | sixtieth | slowness | Socrates |
| shimmery | sidekick | sizeable | sluggard | Socratic |
| shingles | sideline | Sizewell | sluggish | sodality |
| shipload | sidelong | skeletal | sluttish | sodomise |
| shipmate | sidereal | skeleton | smallpox | sodomite |
| shipment | sideshow | sketcher | smarmily | sodomize |
| shipping | sidestep | skewbald | smartish | softback |
| shipyard | sidewalk | skewness | smashing | softball |
| shirtily | sideward | Skiathos | smidgeon | softener |
| shocking | sideways | skillful | smocking | softness |
| Shockley | sidewise | skincare | smokable | software |
| shoddily | Sidmouth | skinhead | Smolensk | softwood |
| shoehorn | sighting | skinless | Smollett | solarium |
| shoelace | sightsee | skipjack | smoocher | soldiery |
| shoplift | signally | skirmish | smoothie | solecism |
| shopping | signpost | skirting | smoothly | solemnly |
| shopworn | Sihanouk | skittery | smoulder | solenoid |
| shortage | Sikorsky | skittish | smuggler | solidify |
| shortish | silencer | Skryabin | smugness | solidity |
| Shoshone | silently | skullcap | snappily | Solihull |
| shoulder | silicate | skydiver | snappish | solitary |
| shouldn't | silicone | skylight | snapshot | solitude |
| shoveler | silkworm | skyscape | snatcher | solstice |
| showcase | Sillitoe | skywards | sneakily | solution |
| showdown | Silurian | slapdash | sneaking | solvable |
| showgirl | Silvanus | slaphead | sniffily | solvency |
| showjump | simplify | slattern | snobbery | Somalian |
| showroom | simulate | Slavonic | snobbish | sombrely |
| shrapnel | Sinclair | sleazily | snobbism | sombrero |
| shredder | sinecure | sleepily | snootily | somebody |
| shrewdly | sinfonia | slightly | snowball | Somerset |

| | | | | |
|---|---|---|---|---|
| sometime | sphagnum | squatter | stiletto | stricken |
| somewhat | spheroid | squawker | stimulus | strictly |
| Sondheim | spiffily | squeaker | stingily | stridden |
| songbird | spiffing | squealer | stingray | strident |
| songster | spillage | squeegee | stinking | striking |
| sonogram | Spillane | squeezer | Stirling | strimmer |
| sonority | spinally | squelchy | stirring | stringed |
| sonorous | spinifex | squiggle | stitcher | stringer |
| Sorbonne | spinster | squiggly | stockade | stripper |
| sorcerer | spiracle | squirrel | stockily | stroller |
| sordidly | spirally | Srinagar | stocking | strongly |
| soreness | spirited | stabling | stockist | struggle |
| sorority | spiteful | staccato | stockman | strumpet |
| Sorrento | spitfire | Stafford | stockmen | stubborn |
| soulless | Spithead | stagnant | stockpot | studding |
| soulmate | spittoon | stagnate | Stoicism | studenty |
| soundbox | splatter | stairway | stolidly | studious |
| sounding | splendid | stallion | stonking | stuffily |
| sourness | splinter | stalwart | stooshie | stuffing |
| sourpuss | splitter | stampede | stopcock | stultify |
| southern | splotchy | standard | stopover | stunning |
| southing | splutter | standing | stoppage | stuntman |
| southpaw | spoilage | standout | Stoppard | stuntmen |
| souvenir | spoofery | Stanford | stormily | stupidly |
| spaceman | spookily | Stanhope | storming | sturdily |
| spacemen | spoonful | Stansted | stotinka | sturgeon |
| spacious | sporadic | starfish | stotinki | subframe |
| spandrel | sporting | starkers | stowaway | subgroup |
| Spaniard | sportive | starling | Strachey | subhuman |
| spanking | spotless | starship | straddle | submerge |
| sparkler | spreader | statuary | straggle | submerse |
| sparsely | springer | staysail | straggly | subpoena |
| sparsity | sprinkle | steadily | straight | subsense |
| speaking | sprinter | steading | strained | subsonic |
| specific | spritzer | stealthy | strainer | subtitle |
| specimen | sprocket | steamily | stramash | subtlety |
| specious | spumante | steatite | stranger | subtotal |
| spectate | spurious | steerage | strangle | subtract |
| spectral | spyglass | steering | strategy | suburban |
| spectrum | squabble | Stefanie | stratify | suburbia |
| speculum | squaddie | Stendhal | streaker | succinct |
| speedily | squadron | sterling | streamer | succubus |
| speedway | squander | stickily | strength | suchlike |
| spelling | squarely | stickler | stretchy | suckling |
| Spengler | squarish | stigmata | striated | Sudanese |

suddenly
sufferer
suffrage
suicidal
suitable
suitably
suitcase
Sulawesi
sullenly
Sullivan
sulphate
sulphide
Sumatran
Sumerian
sunbathe
sunblock
sunburnt
sunburst
suncream
sundress
sunlight
sunshade
sunshine
sunshiny
superbly
superbug
supercar
superego
superior
superman
supermen
supernal
supinely
supplant
supplier
suppress
Surabaya
surcease
sureness
surgical
Suriname
surmount
surplice
surprise
surround

surtitle
surveyor
survival
survivor
Susannah
suspense
susurrus
Suwannee
suzerain
Svalbard
Svengali
swannery
swansong
swastika
sweatily
sweeping
sweetish
swelling
swimsuit
swimwear
swindler
swinging
switcher
sybarite
sycamore
Sydenham
syllabic
syllable
syllabub
syllabus
symbolic
symmetry
sympathy
symphony
symposia
synaptic
syncline
syndrome
synonymy
synopsis
synoptic
synovial
syphilis
Syracuse
systemic

systolic
Szczecin
Szechuan
Szechwan

# T

tableaux
tabulate
taciturn
tactical
tactless
taffrail
Tahitian
Taichung
tailback
tailcoat
tailgate
tailless
tailored
tailpipe
tailspin
tailspun
tailwind
takeaway
takeover
taleggio
talented
Taliesin
talisman
talktime
tallness
Tallulah
Talmudic
tamarind
tamarisk
tameness
tamperer
Tamworth
tandoori
tangency
tangible
tangibly
tankless
tantalum

tantalus
tantrism
Tanzania
Taormina
tapenade
tapestry
tapeworm
tappable
tarboosh
tarragon
Tartarus
tartness
Tashkent
Tasmania
tasteful
tattered
tattooer
Tauranga
tautness
Taverner
taxation
taxonomy
taxpayer
teaching
teammate
teamster
teamwork
tearable
tearaway
teardrop
teaspoon
tectonic
teenaged
teenager
Teesside
teetotal
telecast
telecoms
telegram
Telemann
telepath
teleport
teletext
telethon
teletype

televise
telework
telltale
telluric
temerity
template
temporal
tempting
tenacity
tendency
tenderer
tenderly
tenement
Tenerife
Tennyson
tentacle
tepidity
terabyte
teraflop
teriyaki
terminal
terminus
terraced
terrapin
terraria
terrazzo
Terrence
terrible
terribly
terrific
Tertiary
terylene
tesserae
testable
testator
testicle
tetchily
tetrapod
Teutonic
textbook
textural
Thaddeus
Thailand
thalamus
thallium

| | | | | |
|---|---|---|---|---|
| thankful | Thursday | tomahawk | transact | trochaic |
| thatcher | Tiberius | Tombaugh | transect | troilism |
| theistic | Tibullus | tommyrot | transept | Trollope |
| thematic | ticklish | tomogram | transfer | trombone |
| themself | tideline | tomorrow | transfix | tropical |
| Theobald | tidemark | tonality | tranship | trotting |
| Theodora | tidiness | toneless | transmit | trousers |
| Theodore | tiebreak | toothily | trapdoor | trueness |
| theology | Tientsin | topology | trapezia | Truffaut |
| theorise | tigerish | torchlit | trapezii | Trujillo |
| theorist | tillable | toreador | Trappist | trumpery |
| theorize | timbered | torpidly | traumata | truncate |
| theremin | Timbuktu | torridly | traverse | trunking |
| thesauri | timeless | Tórshavn | travesty | trunnion |
| Thesiger | timidity | tortilla | treasure | trustful |
| thespian | timorous | tortoise | treasury | trusting |
| Thessaly | tincture | tortuous | treatise | truthful |
| thiamine | tininess | torturer | treeless | Tsushima |
| thickset | tinkerer | totalise | treeline | tubercle |
| thievery | tinnitus | totality | trembler | tuberose |
| thievish | tinplate | totalize | trencher | tuberous |
| thinking | tinselly | touchily | trendily | tumorous |
| thinners | tinsmith | touching | trespass | tuneless |
| thinness | tinsnips | Toulouse | trialist | tungsten |
| thirteen | Tintagel | touristy | triangle | Tunguska |
| Thompson | tipstaff | towering | Triassic | Tunisian |
| thoracic | tiramisu | townland | tribally | tuppence |
| Thornton | tireless | township | tribunal | tuppenny |
| thorough | Tiresias | townsman | trickery | turbaned |
| thousand | tiresome | townsmen | trickily | turbofan |
| thraldom | titanium | toxaemia | tricorne | turbojet |
| thrasher | Tithonus | toxicant | tricycle | Turgenev |
| threader | Titicaca | toxicity | trifling | turgidly |
| threaten | titivate | tracheae | trillion | turlough |
| threnody | titmouse | tracheal | trimaran | turmeric |
| thresher | toadflax | trachoma | trimming | turncoat |
| thriller | toboggan | trackbed | trimness | turndown |
| throstle | together | tracking | Trimurti | turnover |
| throttle | Togolese | trackway | Trinidad | turnpike |
| thruster | toilette | traction | trioxide | turreted |
| thuggery | toilsome | tradable | triplane | tussocky |
| thuggish | tokenism | Traherne | triptych | tutelage |
| thumping | tolerant | training | tripwire | tutelary |
| thundery | tolerate | tramline | Tristram | tutorial |
| thurible | Toltecan | tranquil | triumvir | Tuvaluan |

tuxedoed
tweezers
twiddler
twilight
twitcher
twittery
twittish
twopence
twopenny
tympanic
tympanum
Tyneside
typecast
typeface
typology
tzatziki

# U

ubiquity
Udmurtia
ugliness
ulcerate
ulcerous
ulterior
ultimacy
ultimata
ultimate
umbilici
umbrella
unabated
unafraid
unawares
unbeaten
unbelief
unbiased
unbidden
unbroken
unbuckle
unbundle
unburden
unburned
unbutton
uncalled
uncapped

uncaring
unclench
uncombed
uncommon
uncooked
uncouple
unctuous
underarm
underbid
undercut
underdog
underfed
underlay
underlie
underlit
underman
underpay
underpin
undersea
undertow
underuse
undimmed
undreamt
undulant
undulate
unearned
uneasily
unedited
unending
unerring
unevenly
unfairly
unfasten
unfilled
unfitted
unforced
unformed
unfreeze
unfrozen
unfunded
ungainly
unglazed
ungulate
unharmed
unheeded

unicycle
unionise
unionism
unionist
unionize
unipolar
uniquely
universe
unjustly
unkindly
unlawful
unleaded
unlearnt
unlikely
unlisted
unlooked
unloosen
unlovely
unmanned
unmarked
unmoving
unopened
unpaired
unperson
unplaced
unproved
unproven
unquoted
unranked
unreason
unsaddle
unsalted
unsealed
unseeded
unseeing
unseemly
unsettle
unshaken
unshaven
unsigned
unsocial
unsolved
unsorted
unspoilt
unspoken

unsprung
unstable
unstated
unsteady
unstring
unstrung
unstuffy
unsubtle
unsubtly
unsuited
unsurely
unswayed
untangle
untapped
untasted
untaught
untended
untested
untidily
untimely
untiring
untitled
untoward
untucked
unusable
unvaried
unversed
unviable
unvoiced
unwanted
unwarily
unwashed
unweaned
unwieldy
unwisdom
unwisely
unwonted
unworked
unworthy
upcoming
upgrader
upheaval
upholder
uplifter
upmarket

uppercut
uprising
upstairs
upstream
upstroke
upthrust
upwardly
urbanely
urbanise
urbanism
urbanist
urbanite
urbanity
urbanize
urethane
urethrae
urethral
urgently
Ursuline
usefully
usurious
uxorious

# V

vacantly
vacation
vagabond
vagrancy
Vajpayee
valanced
Valencia
valerian
Valhalla
validate
validity
Valkyrie
Valletta
valorise
valorize
valorous
valuable
valuably
valvular
vampiric

| | | | | |
|---|---|---|---|---|
| vanadium | veronica | virtuous | walkover | Welshmen |
| Vanbrugh | verrucae | virulent | Wallasey | werewolf |
| vanguard | vertebra | visceral | wanderer | Wesleyan |
| vanquish | vertical | Visconti | Wanganui | westerly |
| vapidity | Verviers | viscount | wantonly | westward |
| vaporise | Verwoerd | Visigoth | wardrobe | Weymouth |
| vaporize | Vesalius | visitant | wardroom | whacking |
| vaporous | Vespucci | visually | wardship | whatever |
| Varanasi | vestment | vitalise | warfarin | wheatear |
| variable | Vesuvius | vitality | warhorse | wheezily |
| variably | vexation | vitalize | wariness | whenever |
| variance | viaticum | vitiligo | warmness | wherever |
| varicose | vibrancy | vitreous | warpaint | Whiggish |
| varietal | vibrator | vivacity | warplane | Whiggism |
| Vasarely | viburnum | vivarium | warranty | whimbrel |
| vascular | vicarage | Vivienne | washable | whinchat |
| vaseline | vicinity | vixenish | washroom | whipcord |
| vastness | Victoria | Vladimir | wasteful | whiplash |
| vaulting | Viennese | Vlaminck | watchdog | whipping |
| vaunting | viewable | vocalise | watchful | whipsawn |
| veganism | vigilant | vocalist | watchman | whiskery |
| vegetate | vigneron | vocalize | watchmen | whispery |
| vehement | vignette | vocation | waterbed | whistler |
| velocity | vigorous | vocative | Waterloo | whitecap |
| venality | vileness | voidable | waterman | whitefly |
| vendetta | villager | volatile | watermen | whitener |
| venerate | villagey | volcanic | waterski | Whittier |
| venereal | villainy | volition | waterway | whomever |
| Venetian | vindaloo | volleyer | waveband | whopping |
| vengeful | vinegary | Voltaire | waveform | whosever |
| venomous | vineyard | volumise | waviness | wickedly |
| venturer | violator | volumize | waxiness | wideness |
| Venusian | violence | Vonnegut | wayfarer | wildfire |
| veracity | Violetta | voracity | weakling | wildfowl |
| Veracruz | Violette | vortical | weakness | wildlife |
| verandah | viperish | Vuillard | weanling | wildness |
| verbally | viperous | vulgarly | weaponry | wilfully |
| verbatim | viraemia | | wearable | wiliness |
| verbiage | virginal | **W** | weaselly | Williams |
| verboten | Virginia | | Wedekind | windfall |
| verdancy | viridian | waiflike | Wedgwood | Windhoek |
| verifier | virility | wainscot | Weismann | windlass |
| Verlaine | virology | waitress | Weizmann | windless |
| vermouth | virtuosi | Waldheim | welcomer | windmill |
| Veronese | virtuoso | walkable | Welshman | windpipe |

windsock
windsurf
windward
wineskin
wingbeat
wingless
wingspan
Winifred
winnable
Winnipeg
wipeable
wireless
wireworm
wiseacre
wishbone
wistaria
wisteria
witchery
withdraw
withdrew
withhold
wizardly
wizardry

woefully
womanise
womanish
womanize
wonderer
wondrous
woodbine
woodchip
woodcock
woodenly
woodland
woodlice
woodruff
woodsman
woodsmen
Woodward
woodwind
woodwork
woodworm
Woolsack
wordless
wordplay
workable

workably
workaday
workbook
workless
workload
workmate
workroom
workshop
wormhole
wormwood
worthily
Worthing
wrangler
wrapping
wrathful
wreckage
wrestler
wretched
wriggler
wringing
writable
writerly
wrongful

Würzburg
Wycliffe

## ✖

Xankändi
Xantippe
Xenophon
Xinjiang

## Y

yachting
Yamamoto
Yamasaki
yarmulka
yarmulke
yearbook
yearling
yearning
Yemenite
yeomanry
Yinchuan

yodeller
yoghourt
Yokohama
youngish
yourself
youthful
Yugoslav
Yuletide

## Z

Zakopane
zaniness
Zanzibar
zealotry
zenithal
Zeppelin
Ziegfeld
ziggurat
Zimbabwe
zodiacal
zucchini
Zurbarán

# **9** LETTERS

## A

abandoned
abasement
abatement
abdominal
abduction
abhorrent
abidingly
abolition
abominate
aborigine
abscissae
absconder
absorbent
absorbing
abstainer

abstinent
absurdism
absurdist
absurdity
abundance
abusively
abysmally
Abyssinia
accession
accessory
accompany
according
accordion
accretion
acellular
acetylene
acidulate

acidulous
Aconcagua
acquiesce
acquittal
acrobatic
acropolis
activator
actualise
actuality
actualize
actuarial
actuation
acuteness
adamantly
adaptable
adaptogen
addiction

addictive
Addington
addressee
addresser
adenoidal
adeptness
adherence
adjacency
adjective
admirable
admirably
Admiralty
admission
admixture
adoptable
adoration
adornment

adrenalin
adsorbent
adulation
adulatory
adulterer
adulthood
adumbrate
advantage
Adventism
Adventist
adventure
adverbial
adversary
adversely
adversity
advertise
advisable

| | | | | |
|---|---|---|---|---|
| advisedly | Aldebaran | amazement | androgyny | antitrust |
| aerialist | Aldeburgh | amazingly | Andromeda | antivenin |
| aerobatic | Aldershot | Amazonian | anecdotal | antiviral |
| aerodrome | aleatoric | ambergris | angelfish | Antonioni |
| aeroplane | alertness | ambiguity | Angelique | anxiously |
| aerospace | Alexander | ambiguous | anglicise | apartheid |
| Aeschylus | Alexandra | ambitious | Anglicism | apartment |
| aesthetic | Alexandre | ambrosial | anglicize | apathetic |
| aetiology | algebraic | ambulance | angostura | Apeldoorn |
| affection | Algeciras | ambuscade | anguished | Aphrodite |
| affective | Algonkian | amendment | angularly | Apocrypha |
| affidavit | Algonquin | Amerasian | anhydrous | apologise |
| affiliate | algorithm | Americana | animalism | apologist |
| affluence | alienable | americium | animality | apologize |
| Afrikaans | alienness | amidships | animation | apostolic |
| Afrikaner | alignment | amorality | animistic | apparatus |
| aftercare | Allahabad | amorously | animosity | appealing |
| afterglow | allegedly | amorphous | Annabella | appellant |
| afterlife | allergist | ampersand | Annabelle | appellate |
| aftermath | alleviate | amphibian | Annapolis | appendage |
| afternoon | alligator | amplifier | Annapurna | appertain |
| afterword | Allistair | amplitude | Anneliese | appetiser |
| Agamemnon | allocable | Amsterdam | annotator | appetizer |
| aggravate | allocator | amusement | announcer | appliance |
| aggregate | allopathy | anabolism | annoyance | applicant |
| aggressor | allotment | anaerobic | annulment | appointed |
| aggrieved | allotrope | analgesia | anomalous | appointee |
| Agincourt | allowable | analgesic | anonymity | apportion |
| agitation | allowance | analogous | anonymous | appraisal |
| agreeable | allowedly | analysand | anorakish | appraisee |
| agreeably | Almodóvar | anarchism | anorectic | appraiser |
| agreement | almshouse | anarchist | Anschluss | apprehend |
| agronomic | aloneness | Anastasia | Antarctic | aquaplane |
| aimlessly | alongside | anatomise | antenatal | aquarelle |
| airstream | aloofness | anatomist | anthology | aquilegia |
| airworthy | Alphonsus | anatomize | anticline | Aquitaine |
| aitchbone | Altdorfer | ancestral | antigenic | arabesque |
| Akhenaten | alternate | anchorage | antipasti | Aramintha |
| Akhenaton | Althusser | anchorite | antipasto | arbitrage |
| Akhetaten | altimeter | anchorman | antipathy | arbitrary |
| Akhmatova | altiplano | anchormen | Antipodes | arbitrate |
| alabaster | aluminise | anciently | antiquary | arboretum |
| albatross | aluminium | ancillary | antiquity | Arbuthnot |
| alchemist | aluminize | Andalusia | antiserum | archangel |
| alcoholic | amaryllis | Androcles | antitoxin | archetype |

Archibald
architect
archivist
Ardizzone
arduously
Argentina
Argentine
Aristotle
Arkwright
Arlington
armadillo
armistice
Armstrong
arriviste
arrogance
arrowroot
arsenical
Artemisia
arthritic
arthritis
arthropod
Arthurian
artichoke
articular
artificer
artillery
artisanal
artlessly
ascendant
ascension
ascertain
Asclepius
asexually
Ashkenazi
Ashkenazy
asparagus
aspartame
aspersion
aspirator
assailant
assembler
assertion
assertive
assiduity
assiduous

assistant
associate
assonance
assurance
assuredly
asthmatic
astrakhan
astrolabe
astrology
astronaut
astronomy
asymmetry
atavistic
atheistic
Athelstan
Athenaeum
athletics
atonality
atonement
atrocious
attainder
attendant
attention
attentive
attenuate
attractor
attribute
attrition
aubergine
aubrietia
audacious
audiology
auditoria
Augustina
Augustine
Aurangzeb
Auschwitz
austerely
austerity
Australia
authentic
authoress
authorial
authorise
authority

authorize
autoclave
autocracy
autofocus
autograph
automatic
automaton
autonomic
autopilot
autoroute
auxiliary
available
avalanche
averagely
avocation
avoidable
avoidably
avoidance
avuncular
awakening
awareness
awestruck
awfulness
awkwardly
axiomatic
ayatollah
Ayckbourn
Aylesbury
Ayurvedic
azimuthal

# B

Babylonia
bacchanal
Bacharach
bacillary
backbench
backcloth
backslash
backslide
backspace
backstage
backstory
backtrack

backwards
backwater
backwoods
bacterial
bacterium
badminton
bagatelle
bagginess
bailiwick
baksheesh
balaclava
balalaika
balconied
baldachin
baldaquin
balefully
Balkanise
Balkanize
balladeer
ballerina
ballistic
Ballymena
Balthasar
Balthazar
Baltimore
Baltistan
bamboozle
bandicoot
bandoleer
bandolier
bandstand
bandwagon
bandwidth
Bangalore
bannister
banquette
baptismal
baptistry
Barbadian
barbarian
barbarism
barbarity
barbarous
Barcelona
barefaced

Barenboim
bargainer
bargepole
barminess
barnacled
barnstorm
barograph
barometer
baronetcy
barracuda
barricade
barrister
Barrymore
bartender
Bartholdi
bashfully
Bashkiria
basically
bastinado
Bathsheba
battalion
battiness
battleaxe
bavaroise
bawdiness
beachhead
beachwear
beanfeast
beardless
Beardsley
beatitude
beauteous
beautiful
becquerel
bedfellow
bedjacket
bedridden
bedsitter
bedspread
beefeater
beefsteak
Beelzebub
Beersheba
Beethoven
beginning

| | | | | |
|---|---|---|---|---|
| behaviour | biohazard | blueberry | bourgeois | bromeliad |
| belatedly | biologist | bluegrass | Bourguiba | bronchial |
| beleaguer | biorhythm | blueprint | bowerbird | Bronowski |
| belemnite | biosphere | bluffness | boyfriend | brotherly |
| bellicose | bioweapon | bluntness | bracingly | browsable |
| bellyache | bipartite | blusterer | brainless | Brunswick |
| bellyflop | birdbrain | boardroom | brainstem | brushwood |
| belvedere | birthdate | boardwalk | brainwash | brushwork |
| Benbecula | birthmark | boathouse | brainwave | brusquely |
| benchmark | bisection | boatswain | brambling | brutalise |
| benighted | bishopric | bobsleigh | brashness | brutalism |
| benignant | bizarrely | Boccaccio | brasserie | brutality |
| benignity | blackball | bodacious | brassiere | brutalize |
| berkelium | blackbird | bodyboard | bratwurst | bubblegum |
| Berkshire | Blackburn | bodyguard | Brazilian | buccaneer |
| Bermudian | Blackfeet | bogginess | breadline | Bucharest |
| benchmark | Blackfoot | boliviano | breakable | buckboard |
| Bernhardt | blackhead | Bollywood | breakaway | bucketful |
| Bernoulli | blackjack | Bolshevik | breakbeat | buckthorn |
| Bernstein | blacklist | bolsterer | breakdown | buckwheat |
| beryllium | blackmail | bombastic | breakfast | budgetary |
| bespatter | Blackmore | bombazine | breakneck | Bujumbura |
| bestially | blackness | bombinate | breathily | Bulgarian |
| Betelgeux | Blackpool | bombshell | brickwork | bulldozer |
| Bethlehem | blameless | Bonaparte | bricolage | bullfight |
| bethought | blandness | bonhomous | bridleway | bullfinch |
| betrothal | blankness | Bonington | briefcase | bullishly |
| betrothed | blaspheme | bookmaker | brigadier | bumblebee |
| Betterton | blasphemy | bookshelf | brilliant | bumptious |
| Beveridge | blatantly | bookstall | brimstone | Bundesrat |
| Bhutanese | Blavatsky | boomerang | briquette | Bundestag |
| bicameral | bleakness | boondocks | briskness | bunkhouse |
| bicyclist | blessedly | boorishly | Britannia | buoyantly |
| bifurcate | blindfold | bootblack | Britannic | burlesque |
| bilateral | blindness | bootstrap | Britisher | burliness |
| bilharzia | blindworm | Borromini | broadband | burningly |
| bilingual | blinkered | Bosanquet | broadcast | Burroughs |
| biliously | blockhead | Bosphorus | broadleaf | Burundian |
| billabong | bloodbath | bossiness | broadloom | bushiness |
| billboard | bloodless | botanical | Broadmoor | bushwhack |
| billiards | bloodline | Botswanan | broadness | Buthelezi |
| billionth | bloodshed | boulevard | broadside | buttercup |
| bimonthly | bloodshot | boundless | brochette | butterfat |
| binocular | blowtorch | bounteous | Broderick | butterfly |
| biodiesel | Bluebeard | bountiful | brokerage | Buxtehude |
| biography | | | | |

bystander
Byzantine
Byzantium

# C

cabinetry
cablegram
cabriolet
cacophony
cadetship
Caesarean
Caesarian
cafeteria
cafetière
Caithness
calabrese
calculate
calendula
calibrate
caliphate
Callaghan
callosity
calloused
callously
calmative
calorific
Calvinism
Calvinist
Cambodian
Cambridge
camcorder
Camembert
cameraman
cameramen
campanile
campanula
campesino
Canaletto
canceller
Cancerian
cancerous
candidacy
candidate
candlelit

Candlemas
candytuft
canniness
cannonade
canonical
cantabile
Cantabria
Canticles
Cantonese
canvasser
canyoning
capacious
capacitor
caparison
capellini
capillary
Capricorn
capsulise
capsulize
captaincy
captivate
captivity
carabiner
Caracalla
carambola
Caratacus
carbonara
carbonate
carbonise
carbonize
carbuncle
carcinoma
cardboard
careerism
careerist
carefully
caretaker
Caribbean
Carinthia
Carmelite
carnality
carnation
carnelian
carnivore
carpaccio

carpenter
carpentry
carpeting
carrageen
Cartagena
Cartesian
carthorse
cartilage
cartouche
cartridge
cartwheel
cashpoint
Casnewydd
Cassandra
casserole
cassoulet
cassowary
castigate
Castilian
Castlebar
castrator
casuistic
casuistry
catabolic
cataclysm
catalepsy
catalogue
Catalonia
catalyser
catalysis
catalytic
catamaran
cataplexy
catarrhal
catatonia
catatonic
catchment
catchword
catechise
catechism
catechist
catechize
categoric
caterwaul
Catharine

catharsis
cathartic
cathedral
Catherine
Caucasian
causality
causation
causative
cauterise
cauterize
cavalcade
Cavendish
cavernous
cavewoman
cavewomen
ceanothus
ceasefire
ceaseless
Ceaușescu
celandine
celebrant
celebrate
celebrity
celestial
Celestine
cellphone
cellulite
celluloid
cellulose
centenary
centésimo
centigram
centipede
centrally
centurion
cerebella
certainly
certainty
certifier
certitude
Cervantes
cessation
Cetshwayo
chaffinch
chairlift

Chaliapin
challenge
chambered
chameleon
chamomile
champagne
Champlain
chandlery
chanteuse
Chanukkah
chaparral
chaperone
charabanc
character
charbroil
chargrill
charlatan
Charleroi
charlotte
Charmaine
charmless
Charolais
chartered
charterer
charwoman
charwomen
Charybdis
Chassidim
chatterer
chauffeur
cheapjack
cheapness
Chechenia
checklist
checkmate
cheekbone
cheerless
chemistry
cheongsam
Cherbourg
Cherenkov
Cherkessk
Chernenko
Chernobyl
Cherubini

| | | | | |
|---|---|---|---|---|
| chevalier | circuitry | coagulant | colosseum | composter |
| chewiness | circulate | coagulate | colostomy | composure |
| Chiangmai | cirrhosis | coalfield | colostrum | computing |
| chicanery | cirrhotic | coalition | colourant | comradely |
| chickweed | citizenry | coastline | colourful | concavity |
| chieftain | cityscape | cobwebbed | colouring | concealer |
| chihuahua | civically | coccygeal | colourist | conceited |
| chilblain | civiliser | cochineal | colourway | concerned |
| childcare | civilizer | cockatiel | coltsfoot | concerted |
| childhood | cladistic | Cockcroft | columbine | concierge |
| childless | claimable | Cockerell | columnist | concisely |
| childlike | clamorous | cockfight | combatant | concision |
| Chinatown | clampdown | cockiness | combative | concordat |
| chipboard | clapboard | cockroach | combustor | concourse |
| chipolata | Clarendon | cockscomb | comfiness | concubine |
| chiropody | clarifier | coenobite | comforter | condenser |
| chitinous | classical | cofferdam | comically | condiment |
| chivalric | classless | cognition | Comintern | condition |
| chlamydia | classmate | cognitive | commander | conducive |
| chocolate | classroom | cognizant | commensal | conductor |
| choirgirl | Claudette | cohabitee | commingle | conferral |
| chopstick | cleanable | coherence | commissar | confessor |
| chorister | cleanness | coiffured | committal | confidant |
| Christian | clearance | Cointreau | committee | confident |
| Christina | clearness | colcannon | commodify | configure |
| Christine | Cleopatra | Coleraine | commodity | confirmed |
| Christmas | clergyman | Coleridge | commodore | Confucian |
| chromatic | clergymen | collation | commotion | Confucius |
| chromatin | Cleveland | colleague | communard | confusion |
| chronicle | clickable | collected | communion | congenial |
| chrysalis | clientele | collector | communism | congeries |
| chthonian | climactic | collegial | communist | congested |
| Churchill | climbable | collegian | community | Congolese |
| churchman | clinician | collinear | commutate | congruent |
| churchmen | clipboard | collision | compactly | congruity |
| Chuvashia | cloakroom | collocate | compactor | congruous |
| cicatrice | clockwise | colloidal | companion | conjugate |
| cicatrise | clockwork | colloquia | compendia | conjuring |
| cicatrize | cloisonné | collusion | competent | Connaught |
| cigarette | closeness | collusive | complaint | connector |
| cigarillo | cloudless | Colombian | complexly | Connemara |
| cinematic | cloyingly | colonelcy | compliant | connexion |
| cinephile | clubbable | coloniser | complicit | connubial |
| cineraria | clubhouse | colonizer | component | conqueror |
| circadian | coachwork | colonnade | composite | conscious |

conscript
consensus
consonant
consortia
constable
Constance
constancy
Constanta
Constanza
constrain
constrict
construal
construct
consulate
contagion
container
contender
contented
continent
continual
continuum
contralto
contrived
contriver
contumacy
contumely
contusion
conundrum
convector
converter
convexity
convincer
convivial
cookhouse
cooperage
cooperate
copiously
copolymer
copyright
Corcovado
cordially
coriander
corkscrew
cormorant
corncrake

Corneille
cornelian
Cornelius
cornetist
cornflake
cornflour
cornicing
corniness
corollary
corporate
corporeal
corpulent
corpuscle
correctly
corrector
Correggio
correlate
corrosion
corrosive
corrugate
corrupter
corruptly
cortisone
coruscate
cosmogony
cosmology
cosmonaut
costumier
cotangent
cotyledon
couchette
countable
countdown
countless
coupledom
courgette
Courrèges
Courtauld
Courtenay
Courteney
courteous
courtesan
courtroom
courtship
courtyard

couturier
covalency
Coverdale
covetable
cowardice
crackdown
crackling
craftsman
craftsmen
craftwork
cranberry
crankcase
crapshoot
crapulent
crapulous
crassness
craziness
credulity
credulous
cremation
crepitate
crescendi
crescendo
cricketer
crimplene
crinoline
crispness
criterion
criticise
criticism
criticize
Crockford
crocodile
croissant
croneyism
crookedly
croquette
crossbill
crossfire
crossness
crossover
crosstalk
crosswalk
crossways
crosswind

crosswise
crossword
crotchety
crucially
cruciform
crudeness
crushable
cryogenic
cubbyhole
cuckoldry
culminate
cultivate
cuneiform
cunningly
curettage
curiosity
curiously
currently
curricula
cursorily
curvature
curviness
custodial
custodian
customary
customise
customize
cutaneous
cuttingly
cybercafe
cyberpunk
cyclopean
cyclotron
Cymbeline
cynically
cytoplasm

**D**

dachshund
daffiness
dairymaid
dalliance
Dalmatian
damnation

damselfly
dancehall
dandelion
dandified
dangerous
d'Annunzio
daredevil
Darjiling
Darmstadt
dartboard
Dartmouth
Darwinian
Darwinism
Darwinist
dashboard
dashingly
dastardly
dauntless
davenport
deaconess
deathless
debarment
debatable
debauched
debenture
debutante
decadence
decahedra
decalitre
Decalogue
Decameron
decametre
decathlon
deceitful
decennial
deception
deceptive
decidable
decidedly
deciduous
decilitre
decimetre
deckchair
déclassée
declivity

| | | | | |
|---|---|---|---|---|
| decoction | demimonde | detection | digitalis | dislocate |
| décolleté | democracy | detective | digitally | dismantle |
| decompose | demystify | detention | digitiser | dismember |
| decorator | dendritic | detergent | digitizer | dismissal |
| découpage | denigrate | determine | dignified | disorient |
| dedicated | denseness | deterrent | dignitary | disparage |
| dedicatee | dentistry | detonator | diligence | disparate |
| dedicator | dentition | detractor | dimension | disparity |
| deducible | deodorant | detriment | dimorphic | dispenser |
| deduction | deodorise | Deucalion | dinginess | dispersal |
| deductive | deodorize | deuterium | dioecious | disperser |
| defaulter | Depardieu | devastate | Dionysiac | displease |
| defeatism | departure | developer | Dionysian | disputant |
| defeatist | dependant | deviation | Dionysius | disregard |
| defection | dependent | devilment | dioptrics | disrepair |
| defective | depiction | deviously | diphthong | disrepute |
| defendant | depilator | devotedly | diplomacy | disrupter |
| defensive | depletion | dexterity | direction | dissector |
| deference | depositor | dexterous | directive | dissemble |
| deferment | depravity | diabolism | directory | dissenter |
| defiantly | deprecate | diabolist | dirigible | dissident |
| deficient | depressed | diaconate | dirigisme | dissipate |
| definable | depthless | diacritic | dirigiste | dissolute |
| deflation | derivable | diaeresis | dirtiness | dissonant |
| deflector | Descartes | Diaghilev | disappear | distantly |
| defoliant | descender | diagnosis | disarming | distemper |
| defoliate | describer | dialectal | disavowal | distiller |
| deformity | Desdemona | dialectic | disbelief | distraint |
| degrading | desecrate | diaphragm | discharge | distraite |
| dehiscent | desertion | diarrhoea | discoidal | disturbed |
| dehydrate | deserving | diastolic | discolour | disunited |
| dejection | desiccate | dichotomy | discomfit | dithyramb |
| Delacroix | designate | Dickinson | discourse | ditziness |
| delegator | designing | dictation | discovery | diurnally |
| delicious | desirable | dietetics | discredit | divergent |
| delighted | desirably | dietician | disembark | diversely |
| delimiter | desperado | dietitian | disengage | diversify |
| delineate | desperate | different | disesteem | diversion |
| delirious | despoiler | difficult | disfavour | diversity |
| deliverer | despotism | diffident | disfigure | divisible |
| demagogic | destitute | diffusely | dishcloth | Dixieland |
| demagogue | destroyer | diffusion | dishonest | dizziness |
| demanding | desuetude | diffusive | dishonour | djellabah |
| demarcate | desultory | digestion | disinfect | Dobermann |
| demeanour | detailing | digestive | disinvest | doctorate |

doctrinal
docudrama
dodecagon
dogmatism
dogmatist
dogsteeth
dogstooth
dolefully
D'Oliveira
dollhouse
dolomitic
dominance
dominator
Dominican
Dominique
Donatello
Doncaster
Donizetti
doodlebug
Doolittle
doomsayer
Dordrecht
dormitory
dosimeter
dosimetry
dosshouse
dottiness
doubtless
dowdiness
dowelling
downgrade
downright
downriver
downscale
downshift
downstage
downtempo
downtrend
downwards
draconian
draftsman
draftsmen
dragonfly
drainpipe
dramatics

dramatise
dramatist
dramatize
Dravidian
dreamboat
dreamless
driftwood
drinkable
dromedary
droppings
dropsical
drugstore
Druidical
drumstick
drunkenly
dualistic
dubiously
Dubrovnik
duckboard
ductility
Dumbarton
dumbfound
Dungarvan
Dunstable
duplicate
duplicity
duskiness
dustiness
dutifully
dynamical
dysentery
dyspepsia
dyspeptic
dysphasia
dysphasic
dysphoria
dysphoric
dysplasia
dyspraxia
dystopian
dystrophy

**E**

eagerness

earliness
earnestly
earthling
earthward
earthwork
earthworm
eastbound
easterner
eastwards
eavesdrop
ebullient
ebusiness
eccentric
ecclesial
echinacea
eclampsia
eclamptic
ecologist
ecommerce
economics
economise
economist
economize
ecosphere
ecosystem
ectoplasm
ecumenism
Eddington
edelweiss
Edgeworth
edibility
Edinburgh
editorial
education
educative
Edwardian
effective
effectual
efficient
effluvium
effortful
effulgent
egomaniac
egotistic
egregious

Ehrenburg
eiderdown
eightieth
Eindhoven
ejaculate
elaborate
elastomer
electable
electoral
electrify
electrode
elegantly
elemental
elevation
elevenses
eliminate
Elisabeth
Elizabeth
Ellington
ellipsoid
Ellsworth
elocution
elopement
eloquence
elsewhere
elucidate
elusively
emaciated
emanation
embarrass
embattled
embellish
embezzler
embrasure
embroider
embryonic
emergence
emergency
eminently
Emmanuela
Emmenthal
emollient
emolument
emotional
emotively

empathise
empathize
emphasise
emphasize
emphysema
empirical
emptiness
emulation
enactment
enameller
encaustic
enchanter
enchilada
enclosure
encompass
encounter
encourage
endearing
endeavour
endlessly
endocrine
endorphin
endoscope
endoscopy
endosperm
endowment
endurable
endurance
energetic
engrained
engraving
enigmatic
enjoyable
enjoyably
enjoyment
enlighten
enquiring
enrapture
enrolment
enteritis
entertain
entourage
entrechat
entrecôte
enumerate

| | | | | |
|---|---|---|---|---|
| enunciate | Esperanto | exchanger | expletive | factually |
| enviously | espionage | exchequer | explicate | faggoting |
| enzymatic | esplanade | exciseman | exploiter | faintness |
| epaulette | essential | excisemen | explosion | Fairbanks |
| ephedrine | establish | excitable | explosive | fairyland |
| ephemeral | estimable | excitably | expositor | faithless |
| Ephesians | estimably | excluding | expounder | falsehood |
| epicentre | estimator | exclusion | expressly | falseness |
| Epicurean | estuarine | exclusive | expulsion | fanatical |
| Epidaurus | eternally | excoriate | expulsive | fanciable |
| epidermal | ethically | excrement | expurgate | fanciness |
| epidermis | Ethiopian | excretion | exquisite | fantasise |
| epilation | ethnicity | excretory | extempore | fantasist |
| epileptic | ethnology | exculpate | extension | fantasize |
| epiphanic | etiolated | excursion | extensive | fantastic |
| epiphytic | etiquette | excusable | extirpate | farmhouse |
| episcopal | etymology | excusably | extortion | farmstead |
| epistemic | eucalypti | execrable | extractor | fascinate |
| epithelia | Eucharist | execrably | extradite | fascistic |
| epitomise | Euclidean | execution | extremely | fastening |
| epitomize | euphemism | executive | extremism | fatefully |
| eponymous | euphonium | executrix | extremist | fattiness |
| equaliser | euphorbia | exemplary | extremity | fatuously |
| equalizer | Euphrates | exemplify | extricate | faultless |
| equipment | Euripides | exemption | extrinsic | favourite |
| equipoise | Europoort | exerciser | extrovert | fearfully |
| equitable | Eurotrash | exfoliant | extrusion | fecundity |
| equitably | evaluator | exfoliate | extrusive | federally |
| equivocal | evaporate | exhauster | exuberant | feedstock |
| eradicate | evasively | exhibitor | exudation | feelingly |
| erectness | eventless | existence | exultancy | felonious |
| ergonomic | eventuate | exogenous | eyeshadow | fenugreek |
| Ernestine | evergreen | exonerate | | Ferdinand |
| erogenous | everybody | exoticism | **F** | Fermanagh |
| erosional | evidently | expansion | | fermenter |
| eroticise | evocation | expansive | | ferocious |
| eroticism | evocative | expatiate | Fabianism | fertilise |
| eroticize | evolution | expectant | Fabianist | fertility |
| erroneous | exactness | expedient | fabricate | fertilize |
| erstwhile | Excalibur | expediter | facecloth | fervently |
| erudition | excavator | expensive | facetious | festively |
| escalator | excellent | expertise | facsimile | festivity |
| Escoffier | excepting | expiation | factional | fetishise |
| Esmeralda | exception | expiatory | factorial | fetishism |
| esoterica | excessive | explainer | factorise | fetishist |
| | | | factorize | |

| | | | | |
|---|---|---|---|---|
| fetishize | flashback | foretaste | Francisco | frugivore |
| feudalism | flashbulb | foretoken | Francoism | fruitcake |
| Feuerbach | flashcard | forewoman | Francoist | fruiterer |
| Fibonacci | flatliner | forewomen | francolin | fruitless |
| fictional | flattener | forgather | frangible | frustrate |
| fiduciary | flatterer | forgetful | franglais | Fulbright |
| fieldfare | flatulent | forgiving | Frankfort | fulfilled |
| fieldwork | flavonoid | forgotten | Frankfurt | fullerene |
| fieriness | fledgling | forlornly | frankness | fulminate |
| fifteenth | fleetness | formalise | fraternal | fulsomely |
| fightback | flexitime | formalism | fraudster | fumigator |
| filigreed | flintlock | formalist | Frederica | fundament |
| filmstrip | flippancy | formality | Frederick | fungicide |
| filovirus | floodgate | formalize | Frederika | funicular |
| financial | flophouse | formation | freeboard | funkiness |
| financier | floristry | formative | freelance | furiously |
| fingering | flotation | formulaic | Freemason | furnished |
| fingertip | flowerpot | formulary | freestyle | furnisher |
| Fionnuala | fluctuate | formulate | freewheel | furniture |
| firebrand | fluoresce | fornicate | freezable | furriness |
| firebreak | fluorspar | forsythia | freighter | furtively |
| firebrick | flyweight | forthwith | Fremantle | fusillade |
| firefight | folkloric | fortifier | Frenchify | fussiness |
| fireguard | following | fortitude | Frenchman | fustiness |
| firehouse | foodstuff | fortnight | Frenchmen | fuzziness |
| firelight | foolhardy | fortunate | frequency | |
| fireplace | foolishly | forwarder | freshener | |
| firepower | foolproof | forwardly | freshness | **G** |
| fireproof | footboard | fossicker | fretfully | |
| firestorm | footbrake | fossilise | fricassée | gabardine |
| firewater | footloose | fossilize | fricative | gaberdine |
| firmament | footplate | fosterage | Friedrich | Gabriella |
| firstborn | footprint | foundling | frightful | Gabrielle |
| fisherman | footstool | fourscore | frigidity | Gaeltacht |
| fishermen | forbidden | fractious | frivolity | gainfully |
| fishplate | forcemeat | fragility | frivolous | Gaitskell |
| fittingly | forebrain | Fragonard | Frobisher | galantine |
| fizziness | foreclose | fragrance | frogmarch | Galatians |
| flagellum | forecourt | frailness | frogspawn | Galbraith |
| flageolet | forefront | frameless | frolicker | galingale |
| flagstaff | foregoing | framework | frontally | gallantly |
| flagstone | foreigner | Francesca | frontward | gallantry |
| flakiness | foreshore | Francesco | frostbite | galleried |
| flambeaux | foresight | franchise | Fructidor | Gallacise |
| flammable | forestall | Francisca | frugality | Gallicism |
| | | | | Gallicize |

| | | | | |
|---|---|---|---|---|
| Gallipoli | geologist | glissandi | gravitate | Guayaquil |
| gallivant | geomancer | glissando | greatcoat | guerrilla |
| gallstone | geomantic | globalise | greatness | guesswork |
| galvanise | geometric | globalism | Greenaway | guidebook |
| galvanize | georgette | globalist | greenback | guideline |
| Galveston | Georgiana | globalize | greengage | Guildford |
| gangplank | Geraldine | glowingly | greenhorn | guildhall |
| garibaldi | Geraldton | gluggable | Greenland | guileless |
| garrulity | geriatric | glutinous | greenness | guillemot |
| garrulous | Géricault | glycerine | greensand | guiltless |
| Gascoigne | Germanise | godfather | Greenwich | Guinevere |
| gasometer | germanium | godliness | greenwood | guitarist |
| gastritis | Germanize | godmother | Grenadian | gumshield |
| gastropod | germicide | godparent | grenadier | guncotton |
| gastropub | germinate | goldcrest | grenadine | gunpowder |
| gatecrash | gestation | goldenrod | Grenville | gunrunner |
| gatehouse | ghettoise | goldfield | greybeard | Gurdjieff |
| Gateshead | ghettoize | goldfinch | greyhound | gustation |
| gathering | Ghislaine | goldsmith | grievance | Gutenberg |
| gaucherie | gibberish | gondolier | grisaille | Gutiérrez |
| gaudiness | Gibraltar | goodnight | gritstone | gutsiness |
| gauntness | giddiness | gooeyness | Groningen | guttering |
| gawkiness | gigahertz | goofiness | grosgrain | Gwendolen |
| gazetteer | gigantism | goosander | grossness | Gwendolyn |
| gearstick | Gilgamesh | Gorbachev | grotesque | gymnasium |
| gearwheel | Gillespie | Göttingen | grouchily | gymnastic |
| gelignite | gimmickry | governess | groundhog | gyrfalcon |
| genealogy | ginormous | graceless | grounding | gyroscope |
| generally | Giorgione | gradation | groundnut | |
| generator | girlishly | gradually | groundsel | **H** |
| genetical | glacially | grandiose | groveller | |
| Genevieve | glaciated | grandness | gruelling | habitable |
| geniality | gladiator | grandsire | gruffness | habituate |
| genitalia | gladiolus | granulate | Grünewald | hackneyed |
| genitally | Gladstone | grapeshot | Grytviken | haematite |
| genocidal | Glamorgan | grapevine | guacamole | haematoma |
| genotypic | glamorise | graphical | Guangdong | hailstone |
| genteelly | glamorize | graphitic | Guangzhou | hairbrush |
| gentility | glamorous | Grappelli | guarantee | hairdrier |
| gentleman | glandular | graspable | guarantor | hairdryer |
| gentlemen | glaringly | grassland | guardedly | hairiness |
| genuflect | glassware | gratingly | guardroom | hairpiece |
| genuinely | gleanings | gratitude | guardsman | hairslide |
| geodesist | gleefully | gravadlax | guardsmen | hairspray |
| geography | Glendower | graveyard | Guatemala | hairstyle |

| | | | | |
|---|---|---|---|---|
| Halesowen | hatchling | Hellenist | hilliness | horniness |
| halfpence | hatefully | Hellenize | Hilversum | horoscope |
| halfpenny | haughtily | hellhound | Himalayan | horseback |
| halitosis | Hauptmann | hellishly | Hindemith | horsehair |
| Halloween | haversack | Helmholtz | hindrance | horseplay |
| Halmahera | Hawksmoor | helpfully | hindsight | horseshoe |
| haltingly | Hawthorne | Hemingway | Hindustan | horsetail |
| hamadryad | haymaking | Henrietta | hippiedom | horsewhip |
| hamburger | hazardous | Henriette | Hiroshima | hortatory |
| Hammurabi | headboard | hepatitis | histamine | hortensia |
| Hampshire | headcount | Heraklion | histology | hosteller |
| Hampstead | headdress | herbalism | historian | hostilely |
| hamstring | headlight | herbalist | Hitchcock | hostility |
| hamstrung | headliner | herbarium | Hitlerian | hourglass |
| handbrake | headphone | herbicide | Hizbullah | houseboat |
| handcraft | headpiece | herbivore | hoariness | housecoat |
| handiness | headscarf | Herculean | hobgoblin | household |
| handiwork | headstone | Hercynian | hobnailed | houseleek |
| handlebar | headwater | hereabout | Hölderlin | housemaid |
| handprint | healthful | hereafter | Holinshed | housemate |
| handshake | healthily | heretical | hollyhock | houseroom |
| handstand | heartache | hereunder | Hollywood | housewife |
| haphazard | heartbeat | heritable | holocaust | housework |
| haplessly | heartburn | heritably | holograph | howsoever |
| happening | heartfelt | hermitage | homebuyer | hoydenish |
| happiness | hearthrug | Herodotus | homemaker | Huascarán |
| harbinger | heartland | hesitance | homeopath | hubristic |
| hardboard | heartless | hesitancy | homeowner | huffiness |
| hardcover | heartsick | heterodox | homestead | humankind |
| hardihood | heartsore | heuristic | homewards | humanness |
| hardiness | heartwood | hexagonal | homicidal | humdinger |
| hardliner | heathland | hexahedra | homiletic | humectant |
| Harlequin | heatproof | hexameter | homograph | humiliate |
| harmfully | heaviness | Heyerdahl | homologue | humongous |
| harmonica | Heaviside | Hezbollah | homophobe | Humphries |
| harmonise | Hebridean | hibernate | homophone | humungous |
| harmonium | hegemonic | Hibernian | homunculi | hunchback |
| harmonize | Heidegger | hidebound | honeycomb | hundredth |
| harpooner | heightism | hideously | honeymoon | Hungarian |
| harquebus | heightist | hierarchy | honeytrap | hurricane |
| harshness | heinously | highlight | honoraria | hurriedly |
| harvester | helically | Highsmith | honorific | hurtfully |
| Hasdrubal | hellebore | hilarious | hopefully | husbandry |
| hastiness | Hellenise | Hildegard | hopscotch | huskiness |
| hatchback | Hellenism | hillbilly | horehound | hybridise |

| | | | | |
|---|---|---|---|---|
| hybridity | illicitly | imprecise | Indianise | inheritor |
| hybridize | Illinoian | impromptu | Indianism | inhibited |
| Hyderabad | illogical | improvise | Indianize | inhibitor |
| hydrangea | imageless | imprudent | indicator | inhumanly |
| hydration | imaginary | impudence | indigence | initially |
| hydraulic | imbalance | impulsion | indignant | initiator |
| hydrofoil | imbecilic | impulsive | indignity | injection |
| hydrology | imbroglio | imputable | indolence | injurious |
| hydrolyse | imitation | inability | Indonesia | injustice |
| hydrolyze | imitative | inamorato | inducible | innermost |
| hydroxide | immanence | inanimate | induction | innkeeper |
| hygienist | immediacy | inanition | inductive | innocence |
| hyperbola | immediate | inaudible | indulgent | innocuous |
| hyperbole | immensely | inaudibly | inebriate | innovator |
| hypericin | immensity | inaugural | ineffable | Innsbruck |
| hypericum | immersion | incapable | ineffably | inoculate |
| hyperlink | immersive | incarnate | inelastic | inorganic |
| hyperreal | immigrant | incaution | inelegant | inpatient |
| hypertext | immigrate | incentive | ineptness | inquorate |
| hyphenate | imminence | inception | inertness | inrushing |
| hypnotise | immodesty | incessant | inexactly | insectile |
| hypnotism | immorally | incidence | infantile | insensate |
| hypnotist | immovable | incipient | infatuate | insertion |
| hypnotize | immovably | inclement | infection | insidious |
| hypocaust | immutable | including | infective | insincere |
| hypocrisy | immutably | inclusion | inferable | insinuate |
| hypocrite | impaction | inclusive | inference | insipidly |
| | impartial | incognito | infertile | insistent |
| **I** | impassive | incommode | infielder | insolence |
| | impatient | incorrect | infirmary | insoluble |
| ibuprofen | impedance | increment | infirmity | insolvent |
| Icelander | imperfect | incubator | inflation | insomniac |
| Icelandic | imperious | inculcate | inflexion | inspector |
| ichneumon | impetuous | incumbent | influence | installer |
| identical | impiously | incurable | influenza | instantly |
| identikit | implement | incurably | informant | instigate |
| ideograph | implicate | incurious | infuriate | institute |
| ideologue | implosion | incursion | infusible | insulator |
| idiomatic | implosive | indecency | ingenious | insurable |
| ignoramus | impolitic | indelible | ingenuity | insurance |
| ignorance | important | indelibly | ingenuous | insurgent |
| illegally | importune | indemnify | ingestion | integrate |
| illegible | imposture | indemnity | inglenook | integrity |
| illegibly | impotence | indenture | ingrained | intellect |
| illiberal | impotency | indexable | ingrowing | intensely |

intensify
intensity
intensive
intention
intercede
intercept
intercity
intercool
intercrop
interdict
interface
interfere
interfuse
interject
interlace
interlard
interline
interlink
interlock
interlude
interment
interplay
interpose
interpret
interrupt
intersect
intervene
interview
interwove
intestacy
intestate
intestine
intricacy
intricate
intriguer
intrinsic
introduce
introvert
intrusion
intrusive
intuition
intuitive
Inuktitut
invalidly
invective

invention
inventive
inventory
Inverness
inversely
inversion
inversive
invidious
inviolate
invisible
invisibly
involuted
ionically
ionisable
ionizable
Iphigenia
irascible
irascibly
iridology
Irishness
irksomely
Ironsides
ironstone
ironworks
irradiate
Irrawaddy
irregular
irrigable
irrigator
irritable
irritably
irruption
irruptive
ischaemia
ischaemic
Isherwood
isinglass
Islamabad
isolation
isomerise
isomerism
isomerize
isometric
isosceles
isotropic

Israelite
Issigonis
itchiness
iteration
iterative
itinerant
itinerary
Izvestiya

**J**

jacaranda
jackfruit
jackknife
Jacquelyn
jacquerie
Jacquetta
jailbreak
jailhouse
Jalalabad
jambalaya
Jamestown
janissary
jargonise
jargonize
jaundiced
jaywalker
jealously
Jeannette
Jefferies
Jefferson
jellyfish
jerkiness
Jerusalem
Jespersen
jessamine
jewellery
jitterbug
jobcentre
jobsworth
jockstrap
jocularly
jolliness
Jordanian
Josephine

Jotunheim
journeyer
joviality
joyriding
judgement
judiciary
judicious
juiciness
jumpiness
Junoesque
juridical
justifier
Justinian
juvenilia
juxtapose

**K**

Kabbalism
Kabbalist
kalanchoe
Kamchatka
Kampuchea
Kandinsky
Kaohsiung
karabiner
Karakoram
Karlsruhe
Karnataka
Katharine
Katherine
Kathmandu
Kauffmann
kerbstone
kerfuffle
Kettering
Keynesian
keystroke
Khakassia
Khalistan
kibbutzim
kickstand
kidnapper
Killarney
killifish

kilohertz
kilojoule
kilolitre
kilometre
kilotonne
Kimberley
kinematic
kingmaker
Kingstown
kinkiness
kinswoman
kinswomen
Kirbigrip
Kirghizia
Kirkcaldy
Kisangani
Kissinger
kissogram
Kiswahili
Kitchener
kittenish
kittiwake
Kitzbühel
Kitzinger
Klemperer
knotgrass
knowingly
knowledge
Kosciusko
Kropotkin
Kshatriya
kundalini
Kurdistan
Kwangchow
Kwangtung

**L**

laborious
Labourite
labyrinth
lachrymal
lactation
Ladysmith
Lafayette

| | | | | |
|---|---|---|---|---|
| Lamartine | leastwise | limelight | Lohengrin | lyonnaise |
| Lambrusco | lecherous | limescale | loincloth | lyrically |
| lambswool | leeriness | limestone | Lombardic | |
| lamebrain | leftwards | limitless | longevity | |
| lamellate | legendary | limousine | longhouse | **M**  |
| lampblack | legionary | limpidity | longingly | |
| Lampedusa | legislate | Lindbergh | longitude | macadamia |
| lamplight | Leibovitz | lineament | longshore | MacArthur |
| lampshade | Leicester | linearity | lookalike | Maccabees |
| Lancaster | leisurely | lineation | looniness | macchiato |
| landowner | leitmotif | lingually | loopiness | MacDonald |
| landscape | leitmotiv | lintelled | looseness | macédoine |
| landslide | lengthily | liquidate | loquacity | Macedonia |
| landwards | leniently | liquidise | lorgnette | machinery |
| Languedoc | Leningrad | liquidity | loudmouth | machinist |
| languidly | lethality | liquidize | Louisiana | macintosh |
| lankiness | lethargic | liquorice | lousiness | Mackenzie |
| lanthanum | lettering | literally | lowermost | Macmillan |
| Lanzarote | leucocyte | litheness | Lowestoft | Macquarie |
| Laodicean | leukaemia | lithology | lowlander | macrocosm |
| Laplander | leukaemic | Lithuania | lowliness | madeleine |
| larcenous | leukocyte | litigator | lubricant | maelstrom |
| largeness | Levantine | litigious | lubricate | Magdalena |
| laryngeal | levelness | litterbug | lubricity | Magdalene |
| laserdisc | leviathan | liturgist | lucrative | Magdeburg |
| lassitude | Leviticus | Liverpool | Ludditism | magically |
| latecomer | lexically | liverwort | ludicrous | magnesium |
| laterally | Lexington | livestock | Luftwaffe | magnetise |
| laudation | leylandii | Ljubljana | lumberman | magnetism |
| laudatory | liability | Llandudno | lumbermen | magnetite |
| laughable | libellous | Llewellyn | luminaire | magnetize |
| laughably | liberally | loadstone | luminance | magnetron |
| Launcelot | liberator | loathsome | luminesce | magnifico |
| launderer | libertine | localiser | lumpiness | magnifier |
| laundress | libidinal | localizer | lumpishly | magnitude |
| Lavoisier | librarian | locatable | lunchtime | maharajah |
| lawlessly | Lichfield | Lockerbie | luridness | Maharishi |
| lawnmower | lifeblood | locksmith | Lusitania | Maidstone |
| laypeople | lifeguard | locomotor | lustfully | mainboard |
| layperson | lifesaver | lodestone | lustiness | mainframe |
| lazybones | lifestyle | lodgement | Luxemburg | Maintenon |
| leafiness | lightless | loftiness | luxuriant | majuscule |
| learnable | lightness | logarithm | luxuriate | makeshift |
| leasehold | lightning | logically | luxurious | malachite |
| leastways | lightship | logistics | lymphatic | maladroit |
| | | | | malathion |

| | | | | |
|---|---|---|---|---|
| Malaysian | marsupial | medically | messianic | milkiness |
| Maldivian | martially | medicinal | messiness | milkshake |
| malformed | Martineau | megahertz | metabolic | millenary |
| malicious | Martinmas | megaphone | metacarpi | millennia |
| malignant | martyrdom | megapixel | metallise | Millicent |
| malignity | masculine | Meghalaya | metallize | milligram |
| malleable | Masefield | Mehitabel | metalwork | millinery |
| mammalian | masochism | Melanesia | metatarsi | millionth |
| mammogram | masochist | Melbourne | meteorite | millipede |
| Manchuria | Massinger | Mélisande | meteoroid | millstone |
| Mancunian | massively | mellotron | methadone | milometer |
| mandatory | masterful | melodious | Methodism | Milosevic |
| mandoline | masticate | melodrama | Methodist | Milwaukee |
| manganese | matchless | Melpomene | methought | mincemeat |
| mangetout | matchlock | meltwater | methylate | minefield |
| manhandle | matchwood | memorable | metonymic | mineshaft |
| manhattan | maternity | memorably | metricate | miniature |
| manically | mateyness | memoranda | metronome | minidress |
| manifesto | matriarch | menagerie | Meyerbeer | minimally |
| manliness | matricide | mendacity | mezzanine | minimiser |
| mannequin | matrimony | Mendeleev | mezzotint | minimizer |
| mannerism | Matsuyama | Mendelian | Michelson | miniskirt |
| mannerist | mattifier | Mendelism | microbial | Minnesota |
| manoeuvre | matutinal | mendicant | microchip | minuscule |
| manometer | Mauritian | menopause | microcode | Mirabella |
| Mansfield | Mauritius | menstrual | microcosm | Mirabelle |
| Maracaibo | mausoleum | mentalist | microfilm | mirthless |
| marcasite | maxillary | mentality | microgram | misbehave |
| marchpane | maximiser | mercenary | microwave | mischance |
| Margareta | maximizer | mercerise | micturate | miscreant |
| margarine | Mayflower | mercerize | middleman | misdirect |
| margarita | mayoralty | merciless | middlemen | miserable |
| marijuana | mayorship | mercurial | Middlesex | miserably |
| Marinetti | McCartney | Mercurian | Middleton | misgiving |
| maritally | McCullers | mercurous | midlander | misgovern |
| Maritimes | meanwhile | merganser | midstream | misguided |
| marketeer | meatiness | merriment | midsummer | mishandle |
| marketing | mechanics | merriness | midwicket | misinform |
| Marmaduke | mechanise | mescaline | midwifery | mismanage |
| marmalade | mechanism | mesmerise | midwinter | misplaced |
| marmoreal | mechanize | mesmerism | migration | misshapen |
| marquetry | medallion | mesmerist | migratory | mistiness |
| Marrakech | medallist | mesmerize | milestone | mistletoe |
| Marrakesh | mediaeval | Messalina | militancy | Mnemosyne |
| marshland | mediation | messenger | militaria | moderator |

modernise
modernism
modernist
modernity
modernize
modulator
Mogadishu
moistness
Moldavian
molecular
molluscan
momentary
momentous
monastery
moneybags
Mongolian
Mongoloid
monikered
monkshood
monobasic
monocoque
monocular
monocycle
monograph
monologue
monomania
monoplane
monotreme
Monsignor
monsoonal
monstrous
Montaigne
Montespan
moodiness
moonlight
moonscape
moonshine
moonstone
moraliser
moralizer
moratoria
morbidity
Mordvinia
Morecambe
Mormonism

mortality
mortgagee
mortgagor
mortician
mosaicist
motivator
motocross
motorbike
motorcade
motorhome
mountable
mousetrap
moustache
mouthpart
mouthwash
mujahedin
Mullingar
mullioned
multicast
multiform
multihull
multipack
multiplex
multitask
multitude
mundanely
mundanity
municipal
munitions
murderess
murderous
murkiness
muscleman
musclemen
muscovado
Muscovite
Musharraf
mushiness
musically
musketeer
muskiness
Mussolini
mustiness
mutilator
mutuality

muzziness
Mycenaean
myelomata
mysticism
mythology

**N**

nakedness
namecheck
nameplate
nanometre
Nantucket
Narayanan
narcissus
narration
narrative
Nashville
nastiness
Nathanael
Nathaniel
naturally
naughtily
navigable
navigator
nebuliser
nebulizer
necessary
necessity
nectarine
neediness
nefarious
Nefertiti
negligent
negotiate
neighbour
neodymium
Neolithic
neologism
neoNazism
neophobia
neophobic
nephritis
Neptunian
neptunium

nerveless
nerviness
nervously
Netanyahu
networker
Neuchâtel
neuralgia
neuralgic
neurology
neutrally
nevermore
Newcastle
Newmarket
newsagent
newsflash
newsgroup
newspaper
newsprint
Newtonian
Nicaragua
Nicholson
Nicolette
nicotiana
Niemöller
Nietzsche
niggardly
nightclub
nightfall
nightgown
nightlife
nightmare
nightside
nightspot
nightwear
ninetieth
nippiness
nitration
nocturnal
noiseless
noisiness
nominally
nominator
nonentity
nonpareil
normalise

normality
normalize
normative
northerly
northland
northward
Norwegian
nosebleed
nostalgia
nostalgic
notepaper
notoriety
notorious
noughties
novelette
noviciate
novitiate
Nuku'alofa
numbskull
numerator
numerical
Nuremberg
nursemaid
nutriment
nutrition
nutritive
Nyasaland
nystagmus

**O**

oarswoman
oarswomen
obbligati
obbligato
obedience
obeisance
obfuscate
objectify
objection
objective
objurgate
obliquely
obliquity
oblivious

| | | | | |
|---|---|---|---|---|
| obnoxious | omissible | otherness | overshoot | Palembang |
| obscenely | onanistic | otherwise | oversight | Palestine |
| obscenity | oncogenic | oubliette | oversized | Palladian |
| obscurely | onlooking | Oudenarde | overskirt | palladium |
| obscurity | onomastic | ourselves | oversleep | palletise |
| obsequies | onrushing | outermost | overslept | palletize |
| observant | onslaught | outfitter | overspend | palliasse |
| obsession | operation | outgrowth | overspent | palmistry |
| obsessive | operative | outnumber | overspill | palpation |
| obstetric | operculum | outrigger | overstate | palpitate |
| obstinacy | opportune | outskirts | oversteer | panatella |
| obstinate | opposable | outsource | overstock | panegyric |
| obtrusive | oppressor | outspoken | overstuff | panelling |
| obviously | optically | outspread | overtaken | panellist |
| occipital | optimally | outwardly | overthrew | panhandle |
| occlusion | optimiser | outworker | overthrow | Pankhurst |
| occlusive | optimizer | ovenproof | overtired | panoramic |
| occultism | optometry | overblown | overtness | pansexual |
| occultist | opulently | overboard | overvalue | Pantaloon |
| occupancy | orangeade | overclass | overwhelm | pantheism |
| oceanaria | Orangeman | overcrowd | overwrite | pantheist |
| octagonal | Orangemen | overdraft | overwrote | pantihose |
| octahedra | oratorial | overdrank | oviparous | pantomime |
| odalisque | orbitally | overdrawn | ovulation | pantyhose |
| odiferous | orchestra | overdress | ownership | paparazzi |
| odourless | ordinance | overdrink | Oxfordian | paparazzo |
| oenophile | organelle | overdrive | oxidation | paperback |
| oesophagi | organiser | overdrove | oxidative | paperless |
| oestrogen | organizer | overdrunk | oxygenate | paperwork |
| Offenbach | orgiastic | overeager | | papillary |
| offensive | orientate | overeaten | **P** | papilloma |
| offertory | orienteer | overexert | | parabolae |
| officiant | originate | overgraze | pacemaker | parabolic |
| officiate | orphanage | overgrown | Pachelbel | parachute |
| officious | orthodoxy | overjoyed | pachyderm | paradisal |
| offspring | orthotics | overladen | packaging | paraglide |
| oleograph | Orwellian | overlarge | packhorse | paragraph |
| olfaction | oscillate | overnight | pageantry | paralegal |
| olfactory | Osnabrück | overpaint | painfully | paralysis |
| oligarchy | osteology | overpower | paintball | paralytic |
| Oligocene | osteopath | overprice | painterly | paramedic |
| oligopoly | ostracise | overreach | paintwork | parameter |
| ombudsman | ostracism | overreact | Pakistani | paramount |
| ombudsmen | ostracize | oversexed | palanquin | paranoiac |
| ominously | Ostrogoth | overshirt | palatable | parapente |

| | | | | |
|---|---|---|---|---|
| parascend | pauperise | peregrine | pettishly | pinstripe |
| parasitic | pauperism | perennial | petulance | piousness |
| parchment | pauperize | perfecter | phagocyte | pipsqueak |
| parentage | Pavarotti | perfectly | phalanger | piquantly |
| pargeting | Pavlovian | perfervid | phalarope | pirouette |
| parhelion | paymaster | perforate | pharaonic | piscatory |
| Parnassus | peaceable | performer | Pharisaic | piscivore |
| parochial | peaceably | perfumery | phenomena | pistachio |
| parquetry | peacetime | perfusion | phenotype | pitchfork |
| parrakeet | peasantry | perihelia | pheromone | piteously |
| parricide | pecuniary | perimeter | philander | pithiness |
| parsimony | pedagogic | perinatal | philately | pitifully |
| parsonage | pedagogue | periphery | philippic | pivotable |
| Parthenon | pederasty | periscope | Phillippa | pixellate |
| partially | pedometer | perishing | philology | pizzicati |
| partition | peevishly | peristyle | Philomena | pizzicato |
| partitive | Pekingese | peritonea | phlebitis | placatory |
| partridge | Pelletier | perkiness | Phoenicia | placement |
| passenger | pelletise | permanent | phonecard | placentae |
| passerine | pelletize | permeable | phonetics | placental |
| passively | pendulous | permutate | phoniness | placidity |
| passivity | peneplain | perpetual | phonology | plainness |
| Pasternak | penetrate | Perpignan | phosphate | plainsong |
| pasturage | penfriend | persecute | phosphine | plaintiff |
| Patagonia | peninsula | persevere | photocall | plaintive |
| patchouli | penitence | persimmon | photocell | planetary |
| patchwork | penniless | personage | photocopy | planetoid |
| paternity | pennywort | personate | photostat | plangency |
| pathology | pensioner | personify | physician | plasmatic |
| patiently | pensively | personnel | physicist | plastered |
| patinated | penstemon | persuader | pianistic | plasterer |
| patriarch | pentagram | pertinent | Pickering | plasticky |
| patrician | pentangle | pertussis | picnicker | plastique |
| patricide | Pentecost | pervasive | pictogram | platitude |
| patrimony | penthouse | pessimism | pictorial | Platonism |
| patriotic | Pentothal | pessimist | piecemeal | Platonist |
| patristic | penumbrae | pesticide | piecework | plausible |
| Patroclus | penumbral | pestilent | piggyback | plausibly |
| patroller | penurious | petersham | pigtailed | playfully |
| patrolman | pepperoni | pethidine | pikestaff | playgroup |
| patrolmen | perceiver | pétillant | pilferage | playhouse |
| patronage | perchance | petroleum | pimpernel | playmaker |
| patroness | percheron | petrology | pinchbeck | plaything |
| patronise | percolate | petticoat | pineapple | plenitude |
| patronize | perdition | pettiness | Pinkerton | plenteous |

| | | | | |
|---|---|---|---|---|
| plentiful | Polynesia | pragmatic | priestess | proofread |
| ploughman | polyphony | pranayama | Priestley | propagate |
| ploughmen | polyploid | prankster | primaeval | propeller |
| plumpness | polyptych | prayerful | primarily | propellor |
| plunderer | polythene | precedent | primitive | prophetic |
| pluralise | Pomerania | precentor | princedom | proponent |
| pluralism | pompadour | preceptor | principal | propriety |
| pluralist | pomposity | precipice | principle | propylene |
| plurality | pompously | precisely | printable | proscenia |
| pluralize | ponderosa | precision | Priscilla | proscribe |
| plutocrat | ponderous | precocity | prismatic | prosecute |
| Plutonian | poorhouse | precursor | Pritchett | proselyte |
| plutonium | popliteal | predation | privateer | prosodist |
| pneumatic | poppycock | predatory | privately | prostatic |
| pneumonia | popularly | predicate | privation | prostrate |
| pneumonic | porbeagle | predictor | privatise | protector |
| Podgorica | porcelain | predigest | privatize | protester |
| poetaster | porcupine | preemptor | privilege | prototype |
| poeticise | porphyria | prefatory | proactive | protozoan |
| poeticism | porringer | prefigure | probation | Provençal |
| poeticize | porterage | pregnancy | probiotic | provender |
| poignancy | portfolio | prejudice | proboscis | provident |
| pointedly | portrayal | premature | procedure | providing |
| pointless | portrayer | Preminger | processor | provision |
| poisonous | possessor | preoccupy | proconsul | provolone |
| pokerwork | posterior | preordain | procreate | proximate |
| polemical | posterity | prerecord | profanity | proximity |
| policeman | posthaste | presbyter | professed | prudently |
| policemen | postilion | preschool | professor | prurience |
| politburo | postnatal | prescient | profiling | pseudonym |
| politesse | postulant | prescribe | profiteer | psoriasis |
| political | postulate | preseason | profusely | psoriatic |
| pollinate | postwoman | presenter | profusion | psychical |
| pollutant | postwomen | presently | prognosis | psychosis |
| pollution | potassium | preserver | programme | psychotic |
| Pollyanna | potboiler | preshrunk | projector | ptarmigan |
| Polokwane | potentate | president | Prokofiev | pterosaur |
| polonaise | potential | presidium | prolixity | Ptolemaic |
| polyamide | potpourri | Prestwick | prolonged | pubescent |
| polyandry | pottiness | pretender | promenade | publicise |
| polyester | poulterer | preterite | prominent | publicist |
| polygonal | powerboat | prevalent | promising | publicity |
| polygraph | powerless | preventer | promotion | publicize |
| polyhedra | practical | previewer | proneness | publisher |
| polymeric | practised | priceless | pronounce | puerility |

puffiness
pugnacity
puissance
pullulate
pulmonary
pulsation
pulverise
pulverize
punchball
punchbowl
punchcard
punchline
punctilio
punctuate
pungently
pupillage
puppeteer
purchaser
purgation
purgative
purgatory
purposely
purposive
pursuance
pushchair
pushiness
pussyfoot
Pygmalion
Pyongyang
pyramidal
pyrethrum
pyromania

**Q**

quadratic
quadrille
quadruped
quadruple
quaffable
Quakerism
qualifier
quarterly
quartette
quartzite

Quasimodo
queenship
queerness
querulous
quicklime
quickness
quicksand
quickstep
quiescent
quietness
quintuple
quittance
quixotism
quizzical
quotation
quotidian

**R**

rabbinate
racehorse
racetrack
racialise
racialism
racialist
racialize
racketeer
raconteur
Radcliffe
radiantly
radiation
radiative
radically
radicchio
radiogram
radiology
radionics
ragpicker
rainmaker
rainstorm
rainswept
rainwater
Rajasthan
Ramillies
rampantly

rancidity
rancorous
randomise
randomize
rapacious
raptorial
rapturous
Rarotonga
rascality
raspberry
ratepayer
rationale
raucously
raunchily
ravishing
razorbill
reachable
reactance
readiness
realistic
reanalyse
reanimate
reappoint
rearguard
rearrange
rearwards
rebalance
rebellion
recapture
reception
receptive
recession
recessive
recharger
recherché
recipient
reckoning
reclusive
recognise
recognize
recollect
recombine
recommend
reconcile
recondite

reconnect
reconvene
reconvert
recording
recordist
recruiter
rectangle
rectifier
rectitude
rectorial
recumbent
recurrent
recursion
recursive
recusancy
redaction
redbreast
redevelop
redingote
redivivus
redolence
reducible
reduction
reductive
redundant
refection
refectory
referable
reference
referenda
refinance
reflation
reflector
reflexion
reflexive
reformism
reformist
refractor
refresher
refulgent
refurbish
refusenik
refutable
regarding
regicidal

registrar
regretful
regularly
regulator
rehearsal
rehydrate
Reichstag
reimburse
reinforce
Reinhardt
reinstate
reinsurer
reiterate
rejection
rejoinder
relevance
relevancy
religiose
religious
reliquary
reluctant
remainder
Rembrandt
remediate
reminisce
remission
remoulade
removable
renascent
rendering
rendition
renewable
renouncer
renovator
repackage
repairman
repairmen
reparable
repayable
repayment
repellant
repellent
repentant
repertory
replenish

repletion
replicate
reportage
repossess
reprehend
represent
repressed
represser
reprimand
reprobate
reprocess
reproduce
reptilian
repudiate
repugnant
repulsion
repulsive
repurpose
reputable
reputably
reputedly
requester
requisite
rescuable
resentful
reservist
reservoir
reshuffle
residence
residency
resilient
resistant
resistive
resonance
resonator
respecter
responder
restfully
restively
restraint
resultant
resurface
resurgent
resurrect
retaliate

retardant
retention
retentive
rethought
Rethymnon
reticence
retinitis
retoucher
retractor
retrieval
retriever
retrodden
retroussé
revealing
reverence
reversion
revetment
revivable
revocable
revulsion
rewarding
rewirable
rewritten
Reykjavik
rhapsodic
rheumatic
Rhineland
Rhodesian
rhymester
ricepaper
Richelieu
riderless
righteous
rightmost
rightness
rightsize
rightward
rigmarole
rillettes
ringingly
ringsider
riotously
riskiness
ritualise
ritualism

ritualize
rivalrous
riverbank
riverboat
riverside
roadblock
roadhouse
roadstead
roaringly
Rochester
rocketeer
Roeselare
roguishly
roisterer
roominess
Roosevelt
rootstock
Roquefort
rosaceous
Rosalinda
Roscommon
Rosemarie
Rosinante
rotatable
rotavator
Rotherham
Rotterdam
rotundity
roughcast
roughneck
roughness
roughshod
roundelay
Roundhead
roundness
roundsman
roundsmen
roundworm
rousingly
routinely
Rovaniemi
rowdiness
rubberise
rubberize
rudbeckia

ruddiness
ruffianly
ruination
ruinously
runaround
Runnymede
Ruritania
rushlight
rusticate
rusticity
rustiness
rustproof
ruthenium

**S**

saccharin
sackcloth
sacrament
sacrifice
sacrilege
sacristan
saddlebag
safeguard
safflower
sagacious
sagebrush
sailboard
sailcloth
sailplane
Sainsbury
sainthood
salacious
Salamanca
salesgirl
Salisbury
saltiness
saltpetre
saltwater
salubrity
salvation
Salvatore
Samaritan
Samarkand
Samarqand

sanatoria
sanctuary
sandalled
sandblast
sandboard
sandglass
Sandhurst
sandpaper
sandpiper
sandstone
sandstorm
sangfroid
Sanhedrim
Sanhedrin
sanitaria
sanitiser
sanitizer
Sansovino
Santander
Santayana
Santorini
sapodilla
sarabande
Saragossa
sarcastic
sarcomata
Sardinian
sargassum
sarkiness
sartorial
Saskatoon
Sasquatch
sassafras
Sassenach
sassiness
satellite
satiation
satinwood
satirical
satisfied
saturated
Saturnian
saturnine
sauciness
Sauternes

| | | | | |
|---|---|---|---|---|
| Sauvignon | scripture | semiotics | severance | shorthand |
| saxifrage | scrivener | senescent | sextuplet | shorthold |
| saxophone | scrounger | seneschal | sexualise | shorthorn |
| scaleable | scrubland | seniority | sexuality | shortlist |
| scallywag | scruffily | sensation | sexualize | shortness |
| scannable | scrummage | senseless | shadeless | shortstop |
| scapegoat | scrunchie | sensitise | shadiness | shoveller |
| scarecrow | sculpture | sensitive | shakedown | showbizzy |
| scarifier | seafaring | sensitize | shakiness | showiness |
| Scarlatti | seasoning | sensorily | shallowly | showpiece |
| scatology | seaworthy | sensually | shamanism | showplace |
| scavenger | sebaceous | sentience | shamateur | shrinkage |
| sceptical | Sebastian | sentiment | shambolic | shrubbery |
| scheduled | secateurs | separable | shameless | sibilance |
| scheduler | secession | separator | shapeless | sibylline |
| schematic | seclusion | Sephardic | shareable | sideboard |
| schilling | secondary | Sephardim | shareware | sidelight |
| Schindler | secretary | September | sharkskin | sideswipe |
| schmaltzy | secretion | septuplet | sharpener | sidetrack |
| schmoozer | secretive | sepulchre | sharpness | sidewards |
| schnauzer | secretory | sequencer | shatterer | Siegfried |
| schnitzel | sectarian | sequester | sheathing | sightless |
| scholarly | sectional | sequinned | sheeplike | sightseer |
| schoolboy | secularly | Seraphina | sheepskin | Sigismund |
| schooling | sedentary | serenader | sheerness | signaller |
| scientist | Sedgemoor | Serengeti | Sheffield | signalman |
| scintilla | seditious | serialise | sheikhdom | signalmen |
| sclerosis | seduction | serialism | shellfire | signatory |
| sclerotic | seductive | serialist | shellfish | signature |
| scorbutic | seediness | seriality | shelllike | signboard |
| scorecard | seemingly | serialize | shiftless | signorina |
| scoreless | segmental | seriously | shininess | siliceous |
| scoreline | segregate | sermonise | Shintoism | silicosis |
| scoundrel | selection | sermonize | Shintoist | silkiness |
| scrambler | selective | serologic | shipboard | silliness |
| scrapbook | selfishly | serotonin | shipshape | siltation |
| scrappily | Selfridge | serration | shipwreck | Silvester |
| scrapyard | Sellotape | serviette | shockable | similarly |
| scratcher | semantics | servilely | shoemaker | simpleton |
| screecher | semaphore | servility | shogunate | simulacra |
| screenful | semblance | servitude | shopfront | simulator |
| screwball | semibreve | sessional | shoreline | simulcast |
| scribbler | semicolon | sevenfold | shoreward | sincerely |
| scrimmage | seminally | seventeen | shortcake | sincerity |
| scrimshaw | semiology | severally | shortfall | singalong |

| | | | | |
|---|---|---|---|---|
| Singapore | smokiness | sophistry | spellbind | stairwell |
| singleton | snakebite | Sophocles | spendable | stalemate |
| Sinhalese | snakehead | sophomore | spherical | staleness |
| sinuosity | snakeskin | soporific | sphincter | Stalinism |
| sinuously | sniveller | soppiness | spiciness | Stalinist |
| sinusitis | snowboard | sorriness | Spielberg | stalklike |
| siphonage | snowbound | sorrowful | spikenard | stammerer |
| sissified | Snowdonia | soubrette | spikiness | stampeder |
| Sisyphean | snowdrift | Soufrière | spillover | stanchion |
| situation | snowfield | soulfully | spindrift | standpipe |
| sixteenth | snowflake | soundless | spineless | starboard |
| Skagerrak | snowstorm | soundness | spininess | starburst |
| skatepark | soapstone | sourdough | spinnaker | starchily |
| skedaddle | sobriquet | southerly | spinneret | starfruit |
| sketchily | socialise | Southport | spiritual | stargazer |
| skilfully | socialism | southward | spirogyra | starkness |
| skinflint | socialist | sou'wester | splendour | starlight |
| skintight | socialite | sovereign | splenetic | startling |
| skydiving | sociality | Sovietise | splintery | statehood |
| skyrocket | socialize | Sovietism | spokesman | stateless |
| slackness | sociology | Sovietize | spokesmen | statement |
| slanderer | sociopath | spaceship | spoonbill | stateroom |
| slantwise | sogginess | spacesuit | sportsman | stateside |
| slapstick | sojourner | spacewalk | sportsmen | statesman |
| slaughter | soldierly | spadework | sportster | statesmen |
| slavishly | solemnise | spaghetti | spotlight | stationer |
| sleekness | solemnity | spareness | sprightly | statistic |
| sleepless | solemnize | sparingly | springbok | statuette |
| sleepover | soleplate | Spartacus | springily | statutory |
| sleepwalk | solicitor | spasmodic | sprinkler | staunchly |
| slenderly | solidness | spatially | spritsail | Stavanger |
| slickness | soliloquy | spatulate | squeamish | steadfast |
| slingback | solipsism | speakeasy | squillion | steamboat |
| slingshot | solipsist | spearhead | stabilise | steamroll |
| slippered | solitaire | spearmint | stability | steamship |
| slivovitz | someplace | specially | stabilize | steelwork |
| sloganeer | something | specialty | stackable | steelyard |
| Slovakian | sometimes | specifier | staffroom | steepness |
| Slovenian | somewhere | spectacle | stageable | steerable |
| slowcoach | sommelier | spectator | stagehand | steersman |
| sluiceway | somnolent | speculate | staginess | steersmen |
| smackeroo | songsmith | speechify | stainable | stegosaur |
| smallness | sonically | speedboat | stainless | Steinbeck |
| smartness | sonneteer | speedster | staircase | stepchild |
| smokeless | sophistic | speedwell | stairlift | Stephanie |

| | | | | |
|---|---|---|---|---|
| sterilise | strangler | sublimity | superstar | symbolise |
| sterility | Stranraer | sublunary | supervene | symbolism |
| sterilize | strapless | submarine | supervise | symbolist |
| sternness | strapline | subnormal | suppliant | symbolize |
| steroidal | strapping | subscribe | supporter | symbology |
| stevedore | Strasberg | subscript | suppurate | symmetric |
| Stevenage | stratagem | subsidise | supremacy | symphonic |
| Stevenson | strategic | subsidize | supremely | symposium |
| Stieglitz | streakily | substance | surcharge | synagogue |
| stiffener | streaking | substrata | surfboard | synchrony |
| stiffness | streaming | substrate | surliness | syncopate |
| stigmatic | streetcar | subtenant | surreally | syncretic |
| stillborn | Streisand | subverter | surrender | syndicate |
| stillness | strenuous | subwoofer | surrogacy | synergism |
| stiltedly | stressful | successor | surrogate | synodical |
| stimulant | stretcher | succulent | suspender | syntactic |
| stimulate | striation | sudorific | suspicion | synthesis |
| stinkhorn | stricture | Suetonius | sustainer | synthetic |
| stipulate | stridency | suffocate | swallower | |
| stitching | stringent | suffragan | swampland | **T** |
| Stockholm | stripling | suffusion | swansdown | |
| stockpile | Stromboli | sugarless | Swaziland | tabbouleh |
| Stockport | strongbox | sulkiness | sweatband | tablature |
| stockroom | strongman | sulphuric | sweatshop | tableland |
| stocktake | strongmen | sultanate | sweetcorn | tableware |
| stockyard | strontium | summarily | sweetener | tabulator |
| stoically | structure | summarise | sweetmeat | tackiness |
| Stokowski | struggler | summarize | sweetness | tactfully |
| stolidity | stupidity | summation | swiftness | tactician |
| stomacher | stuporous | summiteer | Swinburne | tactility |
| stonechat | stutterer | sumptuary | swineherd | tailboard |
| stonecrop | Stuttgart | sumptuous | swingboat | tailgater |
| stonewall | styleless | sunbather | swingeing | tailoring |
| stoneware | stylishly | sunburned | swordfish | tailpiece |
| stonewash | stylistic | sunflower | swordplay | tailplane |
| stonework | styrofoam | sunscreen | swordsman | Taiwanese |
| stopwatch | suaveness | sunstroke | swordsmen | talkative |
| storeroom | subaltern | superbike | sybaritic | talkboard |
| Stornoway | subarctic | supercool | sycophant | Talmudist |
| storybook | subatomic | superglue | syllabify | tamarillo |
| storyline | subdivide | superheat | syllogism | Tamerlane |
| stoutness | subeditor | superhero | sylphlike | tamoxifen |
| stovepipe | subjugate | supernova | Sylvester | tangerine |
| straggler | sublimate | superpose | symbiosis | tanginess |
| strangely | sublimely | supersede | symbiotic | tantalise |

| | | | | |
|---|---|---|---|---|
| tantalize | temporize | thereunto | Tisiphone | tradition |
| Tanzanian | temptress | thereupon | titillate | Trafalgar |
| Taoiseach | tenacious | therewith | titration | tragedian |
| Tarantino | tenderise | thermally | titularly | trainable |
| tarantula | tenderize | thesaurus | toadstool | trainload |
| tardiness | tenebrous | thickener | tolerable | transaxle |
| Tarkovsky | Tennessee | thickness | tolerably | transcend |
| tarnation | tenseness | thingummy | tolerance | transform |
| tarpaulin | tensional | thinkable | tollbooth | transfuse |
| tarriness | tentacled | thinnings | tomboyish | transgene |
| tasteless | tentative | thirstily | tombstone | transient |
| tastiness | tenuously | thirtieth | Tongariro | translate |
| Tatarstan | teratogen | Thomasina | tonsorial | transmute |
| tattiness | termagant | Thorndike | toolmaker | transonic |
| tattooist | terminate | Thorshavn | toothache | transpire |
| tautology | terracing | threefold | toothless | transport |
| tawniness | terraform | threesome | toothpick | transpose |
| taxidermy | terrarium | threshold | toothsome | Transvaal |
| taximeter | territory | thriftily | topically | trapezium |
| taxonomic | terrorise | throatily | tormentor | trapezius |
| teachable | terrorism | throwaway | torpidity | trapezoid |
| teacherly | terrorist | throwback | torsional | trappings |
| tearfully | terrorize | thrusting | Tortelier | trattoria |
| technical | terseness | thumbnail | torturous | traumatic |
| technique | tessitura | thumbtack | Toscanini | travelled |
| tectonics | testament | Thuringia | totaliser | traveller |
| tediously | testimony | tidewater | totalizer | traversal |
| telecomms | testiness | tightness | touchable | treachery |
| telegenic | tetralogy | tightrope | touchdown | treadmill |
| telegraph | textually | timbering | touchline | treasurer |
| telematic | texturise | Timbuctoo | toughness | treatable |
| telemeter | texturize | timepiece | touristic | treatment |
| telemetry | Thackeray | timescale | tournedos | Trebizond |
| teleology | Thaddaeus | timeshare | towelling | Treblinka |
| telepathy | thankless | timetable | townscape | tremulous |
| telephone | theatrics | timidness | townsfolk | trenchant |
| telephony | theocracy | Timişoara | traceable | triallist |
| telesales | Theodoric | timpanist | traceried | triathlon |
| telescope | Theodosia | Tinbergen | trackball | tribalism |
| tellingly | theoretic | tinderbox | trackless | tribalist |
| tellurium | theosophy | tinniness | tracksuit | tribesman |
| temazepam | therapist | tinselled | tractable | tribesmen |
| temperate | Theravada | Tipperary | trademark | tributary |
| temporary | therefore | tipsiness | tradesman | trickster |
| temporise | therefrom | tiredness | tradesmen | tricolour |

| | | | | |
|---|---|---|---|---|
| tricuspid | tyrannous | undaunted | unfitting | unsayable |
| tricyclic | | undeceive | unfocused | unscarred |
| triennial | **U** | undecided | unfounded | unscathed |
| trilobite | | undefined | unguarded | unscented |
| trimester | ufologist | underbite | unhappily | unsecured |
| Tripitaka | Ukrainian | undercoat | unhealthy | unselfish |
| tristesse | Ulsterman | undercook | unheeding | unserious |
| triteness | Ulstermen | underdone | unhelpful | unsettled |
| triturate | ultimatum | underfelt | unhurried | unshackle |
| triumphal | ululation | underfoot | uniformed | unsheathe |
| triumviri | umbilical | underfund | uniformly | unshelled |
| trivially | umbilicus | undergone | unimpeded | unsighted |
| Trondheim | umpteenth | underhand | uninjured | unsightly |
| troopship | unabashed | underlain | uninstall | unskilful |
| troublous | unadopted | underline | uninsured | unskilled |
| trousered | unadorned | underling | uninvited | unsmiling |
| trousseau | unaligned | undermine | Unitarian | unsparing |
| truculent | unalloyed | underpart | universal | unspoiled |
| trumpeter | unaltered | underpass | unknowing | unstained |
| truncheon | unanimity | underplay | unlearned | unstinted |
| trustable | unanimous | underrate | unlimited | unstopper |
| tubbiness | unashamed | undersell | unlivable | unstudied |
| Tullamore | unbalance | undershot | unluckily | unsullied |
| tumescent | unbeknown | underside | unmarried | untainted |
| tunefully | unbending | undersize | unmatched | untenable |
| tunesmith | unbiassed | undertake | unmerited | untenured |
| tunneller | unbounded | undertone | unmindful | unthought |
| turbidity | unbridled | undertook | unmusical | untouched |
| turboprop | uncannily | underwear | unnamable | untracked |
| turbulent | unceasing | underwent | unnatural | untrained |
| turgidity | uncertain | undesired | unnoticed | untreated |
| Turkestan | unchanged | undiluted | unopposed | untrodden |
| Turkistan | uncharted | undivided | unpeopled | untutored |
| turnround | unchecked | undoubted | unpitying | untypical |
| turnstile | unclaimed | undreamed | unplanned | unusually |
| turnstone | uncleared | undressed | unplugged | unuttered |
| turntable | unclimbed | unearthly | unplumbed | unvarying |
| turpitude | unclothed | uneatable | unpopular | unwatched |
| turquoise | unclouded | unelected | unpowered | unwearied |
| tweenager | unconcern | unequally | unreality | unwelcome |
| twelfthly | uncounted | unethical | unrefined | unwilling |
| twentieth | uncovered | unfailing | unrelated | unwitting |
| typically | uncrowded | unfancied | unruffled | unwomanly |
| tyrannise | uncrowned | unfeeling | unsalable | unworldly |
| tyrannize | undamaged | unfeigned | unsavoury | unworried |

unwounded
unwritten
Upanishad
upcountry
updatable
upholster
uplighter
uppermost
uprightly
upwelling
urination
urologist
urticaria
Uruguayan
usability
uselessly
usherette
utterable
utterance
uttermost

**V**

vaccinate
vacillate
vacuously
vaginally
vagueness
vainglory
Valentina
valentine
Valentino
valiantly
valuation
valueless
vampirism
Vancouver
vandalise
vandalism
vandalize
vaporetti
vaporetto
vaporiser
vaporizer
variation

varifocal
variously
vasectomy
vassalage
vectorial
vegetable
vehemence
vehicular
Velázquez
velodrome
velveteen
veneering
venerable
venerator
Venezuela
vengeance
ventilate
ventrally
ventricle
veracious
verbalise
verbalism
verbalize
verbosely
verbosity
verdantly
verdigris
veritable
veritably
vermiform
vermifuge
vermilion
verminous
Véronique
versatile
versifier
vertebrae
vertebral
vesicular
Vespasian
vestibule
vestigial
vexatious
viability
vibrantly

vibration
vibratory
vicarious
viceregal
viciously
Vicksburg
victimise
victimize
Victorian
videodisc
videotape
Vientiane
viewpoint
vigilance
vigilante
vindicate
violation
violently
violinist
virginity
virtually
virtuosic
virulence
viscosity
visionary
visualise
visualize
Vitellius
vitriolic
Vitruvius
vivacious
vividness
voiceless
voicemail
volcanism
Volgograd
voltmeter
voluntary
volunteer
voracious
vorticity
vouchsafe
voyeurism
vulcanise
vulcanism

vulcanite
vulcanize
vulgarian
vulgarise
vulgarism
vulgarity
vulgarize

**W**

wackiness
waggishly
Wagnerian
wagonload
waistband
waistcoat
waistline
wakeboard
Wakefield
walkabout
wallpaper
warehouse
warmonger
warningly
washbasin
washboard
washstand
waspishly
wasteland
watchable
watchword
waterbird
waterfall
Waterford
waterfowl
Watergate
waterhole
waterless
waterline
watermark
watermill
watershed
waterside
waterweed
wayfaring

waymarker
waywardly
weariness
wearisome
webmaster
Wednesday
weekender
weepiness
Wehrmacht
weightily
weighting
weirdness
Welshness
Wenceslas
westbound
westerner
Westmeath
westwards
whalebone
wheatgerm
wheatmeal
wheelbase
wheelspin
wherefore
wherefrom
whereupon
wherewith
whetstone
whichever
whimsical
whirligig
whirlpool
whirlwind
whiskered
whisperer
whitebait
whitebeam
whitefish
Whitehall
whitehead
whiteness
whitewash
whodunnit
wholefood
wholemeal

| | | | | |
|---|---|---|---|---|
| wholeness | Wisconsin | woodgrain | wrongdoer | Yourcenar |
| wholesale | wisecrack | woodiness | wrongness | ytterbium |
| wholesome | wishfully | woodlouse | Wuppertal | yuppiedom |
| whosoever | wistfully | Woodstock | Wurlitzer | |
| widowhood | withdrawn | Woolworth | Wycherley | **Z** |
| widthways | withstand | wooziness | | |
| widthwise | witlessly | Worcester | **✗** | Zachariah |
| Wiesbaden | witticism | wordiness | | Zacharias |
| willingly | wittiness | wordsmith | Xanthippe | Zakinthos |
| willpower | wittingly | workbench | xenophobe | Zakynthos |
| Wiltshire | Wodehouse | workforce | xylophone | zealously |
| Wimbledon | woebegone | workhorse | | Zechariah |
| windbreak | wolfhound | workhouse | **Y** | Zeebrugge |
| windiness | Wollaston | workpiece | | zeitgeist |
| windproof | wolverine | workplace | yachtsman | Zephaniah |
| Windscale | womanhood | worksheet | yachtsmen | zillionth |
| windstorm | womaniser | workspace | yardstick | Zinfandel |
| windswept | womanizer | worldwide | yellowish | Zinnemann |
| winemaker | womankind | wormwheel | yesterday | zirconium |
| Winnifred | womenfolk | worriedly | Yggdrasil | zookeeper |
| winningly | wonderful | worrisome | Yiddisher | zoologist |
| winsomely | wonkiness | worthless | Yorkshire | Zoroaster |
| winterise | woodblock | wrestling | youngster | |
| winterize | woodchuck | wristband | | |

# **10 LETTERS**

| **A** | absolution | accentuate | accusatory | adjunctive |
|---|---|---|---|---|
| | absolutism | acceptable | accustomed | adjustable |
| abbreviate | absolutist | acceptably | achievable | adjustment |
| abdication | absorbable | acceptance | achromatic | administer |
| Aberdonian | absorbency | accessible | acoustical | admiration |
| aberration | absorption | accessibly | acrophobia | admissible |
| abhorrence | absorptive | accidental | acrophobic | admittance |
| abnegation | abstemious | accomplice | actionable | admonition |
| abnormally | abstention | accomplish | activation | admonitory |
| abominable | abstinence | accordance | adamantine | adolescent |
| abominably | abstracted | accountant | adaptation | adrenaline |
| Aboriginal | abstractly | accounting | additional | adsorption |
| abrasively | abundantly | accumulate | adequately | adulterant |
| abrogation | Abyssinian | accurately | adhesively | adulterate |
| abruptness | accelerant | accusation | adjectival | adulterous |
| absolutely | accelerate | accusative | adjudicate | adventurer |

advertiser
aerobatics
aerogramme
aeronautic
aesthetics
affability
affectedly
affixation
affliction
affordable
affordably
aficionado
Africanise
Africanize
afterbirth
aftershave
aftershock
aftertaste
afterwards
afterworld
aggrandise
aggrandize
aggravated
aggression
aggressive
agronomist
airfreight
alchemical
alcoholism
alderwoman
alderwomen
Alessandro
Alexandria
algebraist
Algonquian
alienation
alimentary
alkalinity
allegation
allegiance
allegorise
allegorist
allegorize
allegretto
allergenic

allocation
allopathic
allotropic
allurement
alluringly
allusively
alpenstock
alphabetic
altarpiece
alteration
alternator
altogether
altruistic
amalgamate
amanuensis
amateurish
amateurism
ambassador
ambivalent
ambulatory
ameliorate
Amerindian
amiability
ammunition
amphibious
amputation
Anabaptist
analogical
analytical
anatomical
anemometer
angiosperm
anglerfish
Anglophile
anglophone
angularity
animadvert
animalcule
animatedly
annexation
annihilate
annotation
annualised
annualized
answerable

antagonise
antagonism
antagonist
antagonize
Antarctica
antebellum
antecedent
anthracite
anthropoid
antibiotic
Antichrist
anticipate
anticlimax
antifreeze
antimatter
antinomian
antiphonal
Antipodean
antiquated
antiseptic
antisocial
antithesis
Antoinette
aphoristic
apiculture
apocalypse
apocryphal
apolitical
apologetic
apophthegm
apoplectic
apostolate
apostrophe
apothecary
apotheosis
apparently
apparition
appearance
appetising
appetitive
appetizing
applicable
applicator
apposition
appreciate

apprentice
aquamarine
arbitrator
archbishop
archdeacon
archetypal
Archimedes
architrave
aristocrat
arithmetic
Armageddon
arrhythmia
arrhythmic
arrogantly
arrogation
artfulness
articulacy
articulate
artificial
asafoetida
asbestosis
ascendancy
asceticism
ascription
Ashkenazim
asphyxiate
aspidistra
aspiration
assemblage
assessment
asseverate
assignment
assimilate
assistance
assortment
assumption
astigmatic
astounding
astringent
astrologer
astronomer
astronomic
astuteness
asymmetric
asynchrony

atmosphere
attachable
attachment
attainable
attainment
attendance
attractant
attraction
attractive
atypically
auctioneer
audibility
auditorium
auspicious
Austerlitz
Australian
authorship
autocratic
autodidact
autoimmune
automation
automatism
automobile
automotive
autonomous
autostrada
autostrade
avaricious
aviculture
Azerbaijan

# B

Babylonian
babysitter
backbiting
backgammon
background
backhanded
backhander
backpacker
backslider
backstairs
backstitch
backstreet

backstroke
backwardly
bafflement
Bainbridge
Balanchine
balderdash
Balenciaga
Ballantyne
ballistics
balloonist
balustrade
bandleader
Banffshire
Bangladesh
banishment
bankruptcy
baptistery
Barbarossa
barbershop
Barbirolli
barefooted
bareheaded
barometric
barramundi
barrenness
bartending
Basilicata
basketball
basketwork
Basseterre
bassoonist
bastardise
bastardize
Basutoland
Battenberg
Batticaloa
battledore
battlement
battleship
Baudelaire
Beaujolais
beautician
becomingly
bedchamber
bedclothes

bedraggled
beefburger
beforehand
behindhand
bejewelled
Belarusian
believable
believably
belladonna
bellflower
bellwether
belongings
Belorussia
Belshazzar
bemusement
benefactor
beneficent
beneficial
benevolent
Berlusconi
Bernadette
Bertolucci
Bessarabia
bestiality
bestridden
Betelgeuse
betterment
biannually
biblically
biennially
bimetallic
binoculars
biochemist
biodegrade
biographer
biological
biomorphic
biowarfare
bipartisan
bipolarity
Birkenhead
Birmingham
birthplace
birthright
birthstone

Birtwistle
bitchiness
bitterness
bituminous
blackamoor
blackberry
blackboard
blackguard
blackshirt
blacksmith
Blackstone
blackthorn
blancmange
blanketing
blasphemer
blindingly
blissfully
blistering
blitheness
blithering
blitzkrieg
blockhouse
bloodhound
bloodiness
bloodstock
Bloomsbury
bluebottle
boastfully
Boccherini
boisterous
Bolshevism
Bolshevist
bombardier
boneshaker
Bonhoeffer
bookbinder
bookkeeper
boondoggle
bootlegger
bootlicker
borderline
bothersome
Botticelli
bottleneck
bottomless

bottommost
bounciness
bourgeoise
bowdlerise
bowdlerize
brachiopod
brainchild
braininess
brainstorm
Bratislava
breadcrumb
breadfruit
breadstick
breakwater
breastbone
breastfeed
breastwork
breathable
breathless
breeziness
bricklayer
bridegroom
bridesmaid
bridgehead
Bridgetown
brigandage
brigantine
brightness
brilliance
broadcloth
broadsheet
broadsword
brokenness
bronchiole
bronchitic
bronchitis
broodiness
Brooklands
broomstick
browbeaten
brownfield
Brownshirt
brownstone
Brundtland
bruschetta

Bucephalus
Buchenwald
bucketload
budgerigar
buffoonery
buffoonish
bullheaded
Bundesbank
Buonaparte
burdensome
bureaucrat
burglarise
burglarize
buttermilk
buttonhole

## C

cadaverous
Caernarfon
Caernarvon
Caerphilly
caipirinha
calamitous
calcareous
calciferol
calculable
calculated
calculator
Caledonian
calibrator
California
calumniate
calumnious
camouflage
campaigner
candelabra
candlewick
candyfloss
cannelloni
cannonball
canonicity
cantaloupe
Canterbury
cantilever

| | | | | |
|---|---|---|---|---|
| cantonment | cautiously | chaplaincy | chivalrous | clavichord |
| capability | cavalierly | Chardonnay | chlamydiae | Clemenceau |
| Capablanca | cavalryman | charentais | chlorinate | Clementina |
| capitalise | cavalrymen | chargeable | chloroform | clementine |
| capitalism | cavitation | chargehand | chocaholic | clerestory |
| capitalist | celebrator | charioteer | chocoholic | clerically |
| capitalize | cellophane | charismata | chocolatey | cleverness |
| capitation | cellulosic | charitable | choosiness | clinginess |
| capitulate | censorious | charitably | choppiness | clinically |
| Cappadocia | censorship | charleston | choucroute | clodhopper |
| cappuccino | centennial | charmingly | Christabel | cloistered |
| capricious | centesimal | chartreuse | Christiana | clothespin |
| Caractacus | centigrade | chatelaine | Christlike | cloudburst |
| caramelise | centilitre | chatterbox | chromosome | cloudiness |
| caramelize | centimetre | Chatterton | chronicler | clumsiness |
| Caravaggio | centralise | chattiness | Chronicles | coarseness |
| caravanner | centralism | chauvinism | chronology | coastguard |
| carcinogen | centralist | chauvinist | chubbiness | coatimundi |
| cardiogram | centrality | cheapskate | chunkiness | cockatrice |
| cardiology | centralize | checkpoint | churchyard | cockchafer |
| carelessly | centrefold | cheekiness | churlishly | codswallop |
| caricature | centrifuge | cheerfully | Cincinnati | coelacanth |
| carjacking | Cephalonia | cheeriness | Cinderella | coexistent |
| Carmarthen | cephalopod | cheesecake | cinquefoil | cogitation |
| Carmichael | ceramicist | cheesiness | circuitous | cognisance |
| carotenoid | cerebellar | Chelmsford | circularly | cognizance |
| Carrington | cerebellum | Cheltenham | circulator | coherently |
| Carthusian | cerebrally | chemically | circumcise | coincident |
| cartoonist | Ceredigion | chequebook | circumflex | Colchester |
| Cartwright | ceremonial | chessboard | circumvent | collarbone |
| Casablanca | chairwoman | Chesterton | Cistercian | collarless |
| Cassiopeia | chairwomen | chestiness | citronella | collateral |
| castration | chalcedony | Chichester | cladistics | collection |
| casualness | chalkboard | chickenpox | clamminess | collective |
| catabolism | challenged | chiffchaff | clangorous | collegiate |
| catafalque | challenger | chiffonier | clanswoman | colloquial |
| cataleptic | chalybeate | childbirth | clanswomen | colloquium |
| cataloguer | chamaeleon | childishly | classicise | colonially |
| Catalonian | chancellor | chilliness | classicism | colonnaded |
| catchiness | chandelier | Chimborazo | classicist | coloration |
| catchpenny | Chandigarh | chimerical | classicize | coloratura |
| catechesis | changeable | chimpanzee | classified | colossally |
| categorise | changeless | chinchilla | classifier | Colossians |
| categorize | changeling | chirpiness | classiness | colourless |
| cautionary | changeover | Chittagong | Clausewitz | colposcopy |

| | | | | |
|---|---|---|---|---|
| combustion | complicate | congestion | contritely | costliness |
| comeliness | complicity | contrition | contrition | councillor |
| comestible | compliment | congregant | controller | counsellor |
| commandant | compositor | congregate | controvert | counteract |
| commandeer | compounder | congruence | convalesce | countryman |
| commanding | comprehend | coniferous | convection | countrymen |
| commentary | compressor | conjecture | convective | courageous |
| commentate | compromise | connection | convenient | coursebook |
| commercial | compulsion | connective | convention | coursework |
| comminuted | compulsive | connivance | convergent | courthouse |
| commissary | compulsory | conscience | conversant | cousinship |
| commission | concentric | consecrate | conversely | couverture |
| commitment | conception | consensual | conversion | covalently |
| commodious | conceptual | consequent | conveyance | covenantal |
| commonalty | concerning | consistent | conviction | covetously |
| commonness | concertina | consistory | convincing | cowcatcher |
| commonweal | concession | consonance | convoluted | crabbiness |
| communally | conciliate | consortium | convulsion | craftiness |
| communiqué | conclusion | conspectus | convulsive | cranesbill |
| commutable | conclusive | conspiracy | cooperator | crankiness |
| commutator | concoction | constantly | cooptation | crankshaft |
| compaction | concordant | constitute | coordinate | crashingly |
| comparable | concretely | constraint | Copenhagen | creaminess |
| comparably | concretion | consultant | Copernicus | creatively |
| comparator | concurrent | consumable | copulation | creativity |
| comparison | concussion | consummate | copulatory | credential |
| compassion | condescend | contagious | copywriter | creditable |
| compatible | condolence | contention | coquettish | creditably |
| compatibly | conduction | contestant | cordiality | creepiness |
| compatriot | conductive | contextual | Corinthian | crematoria |
| compelling | confection | contiguity | Coriolanus | crenellate |
| compendium | conference | contiguous | cornflower | Cretaceous |
| compensate | conferment | continence | cornucopia | cricketing |
| competence | confession | contingent | coronation | criminally |
| competency | confidence | continuity | corpulence | crispbread |
| competitor | confiscate | continuous | correction | critically |
| complacent | conflation | contortion | corrective | crosspatch |
| complainer | confluence | contraband | correspond | crosspiece |
| complement | conformism | contractor | corroboree | crossroads |
| completely | conformist | contradict | corruption | crosstrees |
| completion | conformity | contraflow | corruptive | Cruikshank |
| completist | confounded | contrarian | corselette | crustacean |
| complexion | confusable | contrarily | corybantic | crustiness |
| complexity | confusedly | contravene | cosmically | cryogenics |
| compliance | congenital | contribute | cosmogonic | cryptogram |

cryptology
cultivable
cultivator
culturally
Cumberland
cumbersome
cummerbund
cumulation
cumulative
Cunningham
curatorial
curmudgeon
curricular
curriculum
curvaceous
cussedness
cuttlefish
cybercrime
cybernetic
cyberspace
cyclically
cyclopedia
cytologist

# D

daintiness
damascened
Darjeeling
Darlington
daughterly
daydreamer
dazzlement
deactivate
deadliness
deadweight
dealership
debasement
debauchery
debilitate
debriefing
decadently
decahedron
decapitate
decathlete

decelerate
decimalise
decimalize
decimation
decisively
declassify
declension
decolonise
decolonize
decompress
decoration
decorative
decorously
decryption
dedication
dedicatory
deductible
deescalate
defacement
defamation
defamatory
defecation
defendable
defensible
deficiency
defilement
definitely
definition
definitive
deflection
deformable
degeneracy
degenerate
degradable
dehiscence
dehumanise
dehumanize
dehumidify
dejectedly
delectable
delectably
delegation
deliberate
delicately
delightful

delinquent
deliquesce
delphinium
delusional
dementedly
demobilise
demobilize
Democratic
demodulate
demography
demoiselle
demolition
demonetise
demonetize
demoniacal
demonology
demoralise
demoralize
demotivate
demureness
denigrator
denominate
denotation
denouement
dentifrice
denudation
deodoriser
deodorizer
department
dependable
dependably
dependence
dependency
depilation
depilatory
deplorable
deplorably
deployable
deployment
depopulate
deportment
depositary
deposition
depository
depreciate

depressant
depressing
depression
depressive
deputation
deracinate
derailleur
derailment
Derbyshire
deregulate
derisively
derivation
derivative
dermatitis
derogation
derogatory
desalinate
descendant
descendent
desecrator
deservedly
déshabillé
desiderata
designator
designedly
desolation
despicable
despicably
despondent
detachable
detachment
detainment
detectable
detectably
determined
determiner
deterrence
detestable
detonation
detoxifier
detraction
devastator
devilishly
devitalise
devitalize

devolution
Devonshire
devotional
diabolical
diagnostic
diagonally
dialogical
diaphanous
diarrhoeal
Dickensian
dictionary
didgeridoo
dielectric
difference
difficulty
diffidence
digestible
digitalise
digitalize
digression
digressive
dilatation
dilettante
dilettanti
diligently
diminuendi
diminuendo
diminution
diminutive
dimorphism
Diocletian
diphtheria
diplodocus
diplomatic
dipsomania
directness
disability
disappoint
disapprove
disarrange
disastrous
disbarment
disbelieve
disbenefit
discerning

discharger
discipline
disclaimer
disclosure
discomfort
discommode
discompose
disconcert
disconnect
discontent
discordant
discounter
discourage
discoverer
discreetly
discrepant
discretely
discretion
discursive
discussant
discussion
disdainful
diseconomy
disembowel
disempower
disenchant
disgusting
dishabille
disharmony
dishearten
dishonesty
dishwasher
disinherit
disjointed
dislikable
disloyally
disloyalty
dismantler
dismissive
disorderly
dispassion
dispatcher
dispensary
dispersant
dispersion

dispersive
displeased
disposable
dispossess
disputable
disqualify
disrespect
disruption
disruptive
dissection
dissembler
dissension
disservice
dissidence
dissimilar
dissipated
dissipator
dissociate
dissoluble
dissonance
dissuasion
dissuasive
distension
distillate
distillery
distinctly
distortion
distracted
distraught
distressed
distribute
disyllabic
disyllable
divergence
divination
divinatory
divisional
Djiboutian
doggedness
dominantly
domination
dominatrix
doomsaying
doorkeeper
Dorchester

Dostoevsky
doubleness
doubtfully
downcurved
downmarket
downstairs
downstream
downtowner
downwardly
dramaturgy
drawbridge
drawstring
dreadfully
dreadlocks
dreaminess
dreamscape
dreariness
dressmaker
drippiness
driveshaft
droopiness
drosophila
drowsiness
dumbstruck
dunderhead
duodecimal
duplicator
durability
Düsseldorf
Dutchwoman
Dutchwomen
dysmorphia
dysmorphic
dysplastic
dysprosium
dystrophic
Dzerzhinsk

# E

earthbound
earthiness
earthquake
earthwards
Eastbourne

eastwardly
ebullience
echinoderm
ecological
economical
ecotourism
ecotourist
Ecuadorean
ecumenical
editorship
effacement
effeminacy
effeminate
effervesce
effeteness
efficiency
effortless
effrontery
effulgence
effusively
egocentric
Egyptology
eighteenth
Eisenhower
Eisenstadt
Eisenstein
eisteddfod
ejaculator
elasticity
elasticise
elasticize
elderberry
elecampane
electorate
electrical
electronic
elementary
elevenfold
eliminator
elliptical
elongation
eloquently
emaciation
emancipate
emasculate

embankment
emblematic
embodiment
embonpoint
embroidery
embryology
emendation
emigration
empathetic
Empedocles
empiricism
empiricist
employable
employment
emulsifier
enablement
encampment
encasement
encashment
enchanting
encourager
encryption
encyclical
endangered
endearment
endogenous
endorsable
endoscopic
enervation
engagement
engagingly
engineless
Englishman
Englishmen
engulfment
enlistment
enormously
enrichment
entailment
enterprise
enthusiasm
enthusiast
enticement
entombment
entomology

| | | | | |
|---|---|---|---|---|
| entrapment | Eurovision | expandable | factitious | fickleness |
| enumerable | euthanasia | expatriate | Fahrenheit | fictionist |
| enumerator | evacuation | expectable | fairground | fictitious |
| epiglottis | evaluation | expectancy | Faisalabad | fieldcraft |
| episcopacy | evaluative | expedience | faithfully | fiendishly |
| episcopate | evanescent | expediency | fallacious | fierceness |
| episiotomy | Evangelina | expedition | familiarly | figuration |
| epistolary | Evangeline | expellable | fanaticism | figurative |
| epithelium | evangelise | expendable | fancifully | figurehead |
| equability | evangelism | experience | farcically | filariasis |
| equanimity | evangelist | experiment | Fassbinder | filibuster |
| equatorial | evangelize | expiration | fastidious | filterable |
| equestrian | evaporator | expiratory | fatalistic | filthiness |
| equilibria | eventually | explicable | fatherhood | filtration |
| equitation | everything | explicator | fatherland | fingerless |
| equivalent | everywhere | explicitly | fatherless | fingermark |
| equivocate | evidential | exploitive | fathomable | fingernail |
| eradicator | eviscerate | exportable | fathomless | fingerpick |
| eremitical | exacerbate | exposition | favourable | fingerpost |
| ergonomics | exactitude | expository | favourably | Finisterre |
| ericaceous | exaggerate | expression | fearlessly | finiteness |
| Ermintrude | exaltation | expressive | fearsomely | fishmonger |
| Ermyntrude | exasperate | expressway | feathering | fisticuffs |
| erotically | excavation | expurgator | fecklessly | fitfulness |
| erotomania | excellence | extendable | federalism | Fittipaldi |
| eructation | excellency | extendible | federalist | FitzGerald |
| erysipelas | excitation | extensible | federation | flabbiness |
| escalation | excitatory | exteriorly | feebleness | flaccidity |
| escapement | excitement | externally | feistiness | flagellate |
| escapology | excitingly | extinction | felicitous | flagrantly |
| escarpment | excludable | extinguish | Felixstowe | flamboyant |
| escritoire | execration | extraction | fellowship | flameproof |
| escutcheon | executable | extractive | femaleness | flashiness |
| espadrille | exegetical | extramural | femininely | flashlight |
| especially | exfoliator | extraneous | femininity | flashpoint |
| estimation | exhalation | exuberance | fertiliser | flatulence |
| ethereally | exhaustion | exultantly | fertilizer | flavourful |
| ethnically | exhaustive | exultation | fetchingly | flavouring |
| ethologist | exhibition | eyewitness | fettuccine | flawlessly |
| eucalyptus | exhilarate | | feverishly | fledgeling |
| eugenicist | exhumation | **F** | fibreboard | fleetingly |
| eulogistic | exobiology | | fibreglass | fleshiness |
| euphonious | exorbitant | fabricator | fibrillate | flightless |
| Eurodollar | exothermic | fabulously | fibrinogen | flimsiness |
| Eurotunnel | exotically | facilitate | fibroblast | flintiness |

| | | | | |
|---|---|---|---|---|
| Flintshire | forthright | fruitiness | geophysics | government |
| flippantly | fortissimi | frustrated | Georgetown | gracefully |
| flirtation | fortissimo | fulfilling | geothermal | graciously |
| floatation | fortuitous | fulfilment | geriatrics | gradualism |
| floatplane | foundation | fumigation | germicidal | gradualist |
| flocculent | fourteenth | functional | Gettysburg | graduation |
| floodlight | fractional | fundholder | ghostwrite | graffitist |
| floorboard | fragranced | fungicidal | ghostwrote | graininess |
| Florentine | fragrantly | furnishing | ghoulishly | grammarian |
| floribunda | franchisee | futuristic | Giacometti | gramophone |
| fluffiness | franchiser | futurology | giftedness | grandchild |
| flugelhorn | Franciscan | | Gilbertine | grandstand |
| fluoridate | frangipane | **G** | Gillingham | grapefruit |
| fluorinate | frangipani | | gingivitis | graphology |
| flycatcher | fraternise | gadolinium | girlfriend | gratefully |
| Folkestone | fraternity | Galsworthy | glaciation | gratuitous |
| folklorist | fraternize | gamekeeper | glasshouse | gravestone |
| folksiness | fratricide | gangbuster | glasspaper | gravimeter |
| follicular | fraudulent | ganglionic | Glaswegian | greasiness |
| fontanelle | freakiness | gangmaster | Gleneagles | greediness |
| footballer | freebooter | gangrenous | Glenrothes | greenfield |
| footbridge | freeholder | gargantuan | glimmering | greenfinch |
| footlights | freelancer | garishness | glitterati | greenhouse |
| forbearing | freeloader | gastronome | gloominess | Greenpeace |
| forbidding | freestyler | gastronomy | gloriously | greenshank |
| forcefully | Frenchness | gatekeeper | glossiness | greenstone |
| foreboding | frenziedly | gaucheness | Gloucester | greensward |
| forecaster | frequenter | gelatinous | gluttonous | gregarious |
| forecastle | frequently | Gelderland | glycolysis | Grenadiers |
| forefather | freshwater | generalise | glyphosate | gridlocked |
| forefinger | friability | generalist | gnomically | grievously |
| foregather | frictional | generality | Gnosticism | grindingly |
| foreground | friendless | generalize | goalkeeper | grindstone |
| foremother | friendlily | generation | goalscorer | grisliness |
| foreordain | friendship | generative | gobsmacked | grittiness |
| forerunner | frightened | generosity | gobstopper | grogginess |
| foreshadow | frightener | generously | gonorrhoea | grooviness |
| forfeiture | fritillary | geneticist | gooseberry | grottiness |
| forgivable | frizziness | gentlefolk | gooseflesh | groundless |
| Formentera | frolicsome | gentleness | gorgeously | groundling |
| formidable | frontwards | gentrifier | Gorgonzola | groundsman |
| formidably | frostiness | geocentric | gormlessly | groundsmen |
| formulator | frothiness | geographer | Gothenburg | groundwork |
| fornicator | fruitarian | geographic | governable | grubbiness |
| fortepiano | fruitfully | geological | governance | gruesomely |

grumpiness
Guanajuato
guardhouse
Guatemalan
guestimate
Guggenheim
guillotine
guiltiness
guineafowl
Gulbenkian
gunfighter
gunrunning
gunslinger
gutturally
Gwendoline
gymnastics
gymnosperm
gypsophila
gyroscopic

# H

habiliment
habitation
habitually
hairspring
halberdier
hallelujah
Hammerfest
hammerhead
hammerlock
handicraft
handmaiden
handsomely
handspring
Hanoverian
hantavirus
harassment
hardbitten
Hargreaves
harmlessly
harmonious
harmoniser
harmonizer
Harrisburg

hartebeest
Hartlepool
harvestman
harvestmen
Hatshepsut
hauntingly
headbanger
headhunter
headmaster
headstrong
heartbreak
heartiness
heartsease
heathenish
heathenism
heatstroke
heavenward
hectically
hedonistic
heedlessly
Heidelberg
Heisenberg
helicopter
Heligoland
heliograph
heliotrope
Hellespont
hellraiser
helplessly
hemiplegia
hemiplegic
hemisphere
henceforth
hendecagon
Hephaestus
heptahedra
heptathlon
herbaceous
hereabouts
hereditary
heretofore
herniation
heroically
hesitantly
hesitation

heterodoxy
hexahedral
hexahedron
hibernator
hiddenness
hieroglyph
Hieronymus
hierophant
highlander
highwayman
highwaymen
Hildegarde
Hildesheim
Hindenburg
Hindustani
hinterland
hippodrome
Hippolytus
Hispaniola
historical
histrionic
hoarseness
hodgepodge
hollowness
Holofernes
holography
homecoming
homeliness
homeopathy
homeworker
homoeopath
homoerotic
homogenise
homogenize
homologate
homologise
homologize
homologous
homonymous
homophobia
homophobic
homosexual
homunculus
honorarium
honourable

honourably
hopelessly
horizontal
Horkheimer
hormonally
hornblende
horologist
horrendous
horridness
horseflesh
horsepower
horsewoman
horsewomen
hospitable
hospitably
hostelling
hotchpotch
housebound
housewares
hovercraft
hullabaloo
humaneness
humanistic
Humberside
humbuggery
humidifier
humiliator
humorously
humourless
humpbacked
hungriness
Huntingdon
husbandman
husbandmen
Hyacinthus
hydraulics
hydrologic
hydrolysis
hydrolytic
hydrometer
hydropathy
hydrophone
hydroplane
hydroponic
hygrometer

hyperbaric
hyperbolae
hyperbolic
hyperdrive
hypermedia
hypersonic
hyperspace
hypodermic
hypotenuse
hypothesis
hysterical

# I

iatrogenic
iconically
iconoclasm
iconoclast
icosahedra
idealistic
identifier
ideologist
idolatrous
ignorantly
illegality
illiteracy
illiterate
illuminate
illuminati
illusorily
illustrate
imaginable
imaginably
imaginings
imbecility
immaculacy
immaculate
immaterial
immaturely
immaturity
immemorial
imminently
immiscible
immobilise
immobility

| | | | | |
|---|---|---|---|---|
| immobilize | imputation | indisposed | ingredient | insobriety |
| immoderate | inaccuracy | indistinct | inhabitant | insolently |
| immodestly | inaccurate | individual | inhalation | insolvency |
| immolation | inactivate | indolently | inherently | insouciant |
| immorality | inactivity | Indonesian | inhibition | inspection |
| immunology | inadequacy | inducement | inhibitory | inspissate |
| impairment | inadequate | inductance | inhumanely | instalment |
| impalement | inapposite | indulgence | inhumanity | instigator |
| impalpable | inaugurate | industrial | inhumation | instructor |
| impalpably | incapacity | ineducable | inimically | instrument |
| impassable | incautious | inelegance | inimitable | insularity |
| impatience | incendiary | ineligible | inimitably | insulation |
| impeccable | incestuous | ineptitude | iniquitous | insurgence |
| impeccably | inchoately | inequality | initialism | insurgency |
| impediment | incidental | inevitable | initiation | intactness |
| impenitent | incinerate | inevitably | initiative | intangible |
| imperative | incisively | inexorable | initiatory | intangibly |
| imperially | incitement | inexorably | injectable | integrable |
| impersonal | incivility | inexpertly | injunction | integrally |
| impervious | inclemency | infallible | injunctive | integrator |
| impishness | incoherent | infallibly | innateness | integument |
| implacable | incomplete | infamously | innocently | intentness |
| implacably | inconstant | infarction | innovation | interbreed |
| implicitly | incredible | infectious | innovative | interfaith |
| impolitely | incredibly | infelicity | innovatory | interferer |
| importable | incubation | infernally | innumeracy | interferon |
| importance | incumbency | infidelity | innumerate | interiorly |
| imposingly | indecently | infighting | inoculator | Interlaken |
| imposition | indecision | infiltrate | inoperable | interleave |
| impossible | indecisive | infinitely | inordinate | interloper |
| impossibly | indecorous | infinitive | inquisitor | intermarry |
| impotently | indefinite | infinitude | insanitary | intermezzi |
| impoverish | indelicacy | inflatable | insatiable | intermezzo |
| impregnate | indelicate | inflection | insatiably | intermodal |
| impresario | indexation | inflexible | insecurely | internally |
| impression | Indianness | inflexibly | insecurity | internment |
| impressive | indication | infliction | inseminate | internship |
| imprimatur | indicative | influencer | insensible | interregna |
| improbable | indictable | informally | insensibly | interspace |
| improbably | indictment | infraction | insentient | interstate |
| improperly | indigenise | infrasonic | insertable | interstice |
| improvable | indigenize | infrasound | insightful | intertwine |
| improviser | indigenous | infrequent | insipidity | intervener |
| imprudence | indirectly | inglorious | insistence | interweave |
| impudently | indiscreet | ingratiate | insistency | interwoven |

intestinal
intimately
intimation
intimidate
intolerant
intonation
intoxicant
intoxicate
intramural
intrepidly
introducer
inundation
invalidate
invalidism
invalidity
invaluable
invaluably
invariable
invariably
invertible
investable
investment
inveteracy
inveterate
invigilate
invigorate
invincible
invincibly
inviolable
inviolably
invitation
invitingly
invocation
inwardness
ionisation
ionization
ionosphere
iridescent
Irishwoman
Irishwomen
ironically
ironmonger
irrational
irrelevant
irreligion

irresolute
irreverent
irrigation
irritating
irritation
Islamicise
Islamicize
isometrics
isomorphic
isothermal
Italianate
Italianise
Italianize

**J**

jackanapes
jackbooted
jackhammer
jackrabbit
Jacobitism
Jacqueline
jaggedness
janitorial
jardinière
Jaruzelski
jauntiness
Jehosaphat
jeopardise
jeopardize
Jesuitical
Jewishness
jingoistic
jocularity
Jogjakarta
journalese
journalism
journalist
journeyman
journeymen
joyfulness
joyousness
jubilantly
jubilation
judicature

judicially
juggernaut
juvenility

**K**

Kafkaesque
Kalgoorlie
Kalimantan
Kantianism
Kazakhstan
Kebnekaise
Kensington
kettledrum
keyboarder
Khrushchev
kibbutznik
Kieslowski
Kilmarnock
kilogramme
kilometric
kindliness
kinematics
kingfisher
Kiritimati
Klagenfurt
Klanswoman
Klanswomen
knighthood
knobkerrie
knockabout
kookaburra
Kristiania
krugerrand
Kuomintang
Kyrgyzstan

**L**

laboratory
laceration
lachrymose
lacklustre
lacustrine
ladykiller

Lamarckian
Lamarckism
lamentable
lamentably
lamination
Lancashire
lanceolate
landholder
landlocked
landlubber
landowning
landscaper
languorous
lanthanide
laparotomy
laryngitis
lascivious
Launceston
laundrette
laundromat
lavatorial
lavishness
lawbreaker
lawfulness
lawrencium
leaderless
leadership
Lebensraum
lederhosen
legalistic
legibility
legislator
legitimacy
legitimate
legitimise
legitimize
leguminous
lengthways
lengthwise
lenticular
leprechaun
lesbianism
letterhead
Leverhulme
Leverkusen

levitation
liberalise
liberalism
liberality
liberalize
liberation
liberatory
libidinous
librettist
Libreville
licensable
licentiate
licentious
lieutenant
lifelessly
lighthouse
likelihood
Lilienthal
liminality
limitation
linguistic
liquidator
liquidiser
liquidizer
liquidness
lissomness
listenable
listlessly
literalism
literalist
literature
lithograph
Lithuanian
litigation
littleness
Littlewood
liturgical
livebearer
livelihood
liveliness
loadmaster
lobotomise
lobotomize
locational
locomotion

locomotive
locomotory
loganberry
loggerhead
logistical
loneliness
Longfellow
lopsidedly
loquacious
lordliness
loudhailer
Louisville
loveliness
lovemaking
lubricator
lubricious
Ludendorff
lugubrious
lumberjack
luminosity
luminously
lumpectomy
lusciously
lustreless
lustrously
Luxembourg
luxuriance
lymphocyte
lymphomata

# **M**

Maastricht
Mabinogion
Macdiarmid
Macedonian
maceration
machinable
mackintosh
macrocarpa
Madagascan
Madagascar
magistracy
magistrate
Magnificat

maidenhead
mainspring
mainstream
maintainer
maisonette
makeweight
malcontent
malefactor
maleficent
malevolent
malignancy
malingerer
malodorous
Malplaquet
Malthusian
manageable
management
manageress
managerial
Manchester
Mandelbrot
Mandelstam
mandragora
mangosteen
maniacally
Manichaean
manicurist
manifestly
manipulate
manservant
manuscript
manzanilla
maraschino
Margaretta
marginalia
marginally
Marguerita
marguerite
marination
marionette
marketable
marrowbone
Marseilles
martingale
Martinican

Martinique
marvellous
mascarpone
masquerade
mastectomy
mastermind
masterwork
masturbate
matchboard
matchmaker
matchstick
materially
maternally
matriarchy
matricidal
Matterhorn
maturation
Maupassant
Mauretania
Mauritania
Maximilian
Mayakovsky
mayonnaise
McGonagall
meagreness
meaningful
measurable
measurably
mechanical
meddlesome
medicament
medication
medievally
mediocrity
meditation
meditative
meerschaum
megalithic
meitnerium
melancholy
Melanesian
membership
membranous
memorandum
mendacious

meningitis
menopausal
menstruate
mercantile
mercifully
meridional
meritocrat
Merseyside
Mesolithic
mesosphere
Messallina
messianism
metabolise
metabolism
metabolize
metacarpal
metacarpus
metallurgy
metaphoric
metaphysic
metastasis
metatarsal
metatarsus
methedrine
methodical
Methuselah
meticulous
metrically
metronomic
metropolis
Metternich
Michaelmas
Michelozzo
microfibre
microfiche
micrograph
microlight
microlitre
micrometer
micrometre
Micronesia
microphone
microscope
microscopy
middlebrow

midfielder
Midlothian
midshipman
midshipmen
Midwestern
mightiness
mignonette
mileometer
militantly
militarily
militarise
militarism
militarist
militarize
militiaman
militiamen
millennial
millennium
millilitre
millimetre
millstream
mimeograph
mindlessly
mineralogy
minestrone
minimalism
minimalist
miniseries
ministrant
minstrelsy
minuteness
miraculous
mirrorball
misaligned
miscellany
misconduct
misericord
misfortune
misleading
misogynist
missionary
mistakenly
mitigation
Mitterrand
mixologist

mizzenmast
mochaccino
moderately
moderation
moderniser
modernizer
modernness
Modigliani
modishness
modularity
modulation
Mohammedan
moisturise
moisturize
molybdenum
monarchism
monarchist
Monégasque
monetarily
monetarism
monetarist
moneymaker
monochrome
monoclonal
monoecious
monogamist
monogamous
monolithic
monomaniac
monophonic
monopolise
monopolist
monopolize
monotheism
monotheist
monotonous
Monsignori
monstrance
Montenegro
Montessori
Monteverdi
Montevideo
Montgomery
Montmartre
Montpelier

Montserrat
monumental
moonstruck
moralistic
moratorium
Morayshire
morganatic
moroseness
morphology
mortadella
motherhood
motherland
motherless
motionless
motivation
motiveless
motorcycle
motormouth
mouldboard
mouldiness
mountebank
mournfully
mousseline
moustached
mouthpiece
Mozambican
Mozambique
mozzarella
Mpumalanga
muckraking
Muhammadan
mujaheddin
mujahideen
multimedia
multiparty
multiplier
multistage
multiverse
munificent
muscularly
musicality
musicianly
musicology
Mussorgsky
mustachios

mutability
mutational
mutilation
mutinously
muttonhead
mycologist
myocardial
myocardium
mysterious
mystically
mythically
mythomania
mythopoeia
mythopoeic

## N

Nairnshire
nanosecond
Napoleonic
narcissism
narcissist
narcolepsy
narrowboat
narrowcast
narrowness
nasturtium
nationally
nationwide
naturalise
naturalism
naturalist
naturalize
naturopath
nauseously
nautically
navigation
Neapolitan
nebulosity
necromancy
necropolis
needlecord
needlessly
needlework
negatively

negativity
neglectful
negligence
negligible
negligibly
negotiable
negotiator
neoclassic
nepotistic
nethermost
nettlerash
neurologic
neurotoxin
neutralise
neutrality
neutralize
newfangled
newscaster
newsletter
newsreader
newsworthy
Ngorongoro
Nicaraguan
nightdress
nightshirt
nightstick
nihilistic
nincompoop
nineteenth
noblewoman
noblewomen
nominalism
nominalist
nomination
nominative
nonchalant
nonplussed
northbound
northerner
notability
notational
noteworthy
noticeable
noticeably
notifiable

notionally
Nottingham
Nouakchott
novelistic
nucleation
numberless
numeration
numerology
numerously
numismatic
nurseryman
nurserymen
nutcracker
nutritious

## O

obdurately
obediently
obituarist
obligation
obligatory
obligingly
obliterate
obsequious
observable
observance
obstetrics
obstructor
obtainable
obtuseness
occasional
occidental
occupation
occurrence
oceanarium
octahedral
octahedron
odiousness
odontology
oenologist
oesophagus
oestradiol
officially
officiator

| | | | | |
|---|---|---|---|---|
| offshoring | outstation | palatinate | parvovirus | pentathlon |
| oftentimes | outstretch | Palestrina | passageway | pentatonic |
| Oireachtas | overactive | palimpsest | passionate | peppercorn |
| Okeechobee | overbridge | palindrome | pasteboard | peppermint |
| oleaginous | overburden | palliation | pastellist | percentage |
| oligarchic | overcharge | palliative | pasteurise | percentile |
| omnipotent | overcommit | Palmerston | pasteurize | perception |
| omniscient | overdosage | paltriness | pasticheur | perceptive |
| omnisexual | overdriven | Panamanian | Patagonian | perceptual |
| omnivorous | overexcite | pancreatic | patchiness | percipient |
| oncologist | overexpose | panhandler | patentable | percolator |
| onomastics | overextend | panjandrum | paternally | percussion |
| ontologist | overground | pantaloons | pathfinder | percussive |
| opalescent | overgrowth | pantograph | pathogenic | perdurable |
| ophthalmia | Overijssel | paperknife | pathologic | peremptory |
| ophthalmic | overlander | Paracelsus | patination | perfection |
| oppositely | overlocker | paradiddle | patisserie | perfidious |
| opposition | overmantel | paraglider | patriarchy | perforator |
| oppression | overmaster | Paraguayan | patriotism | pericardia |
| oppressive | overridden | Paralympic | patronymic | peridotite |
| opprobrium | overriding | Paramaribo | pawnbroker | perihelion |
| optimality | overshadow | paramecium | peacefully | perilously |
| optimistic | overstrain | parametric | peacemaker | periodical |
| optionally | overstress | paranormal | peccadillo | peripheral |
| Oranjestad | oversupply | parapenter | peculation | perishable |
| oratorical | overthrown | paraphrase | peculiarly | peritoneal |
| orchestral | overweight | paraplegia | pederastic | peritoneum |
| ordinarily | overwinter | paraplegic | pedestrian | periwinkle |
| ordination | ovipositor | parasitise | pedicurist | permafrost |
| Ordovician | oxygenator | parasitism | Peenemunde | permanence |
| orientally | oxymoronic | parasitize | pejorative | permanency |
| originally | | paratroops | Penderecki | permeation |
| originator | **P** | pardonable | penetrable | permission |
| ornamental | | parentally | penetrator | permissive |
| ornateness | pacesetter | parenthood | penicillin | Pernambuco |
| oscillator | Paderewski | Parisienne | peninsular | pernicious |
| osculation | paediatric | parliament | penitently | pernickety |
| ostensible | paedophile | Parmigiano | penmanship | peroration |
| ostensibly | pagination | paroxysmal | pennyroyal | perpetrate |
| osteopathy | painkiller | parricidal | pennyworth | perpetuate |
| outlandish | painlessly | parrotfish | penologist | perpetuity |
| outpatient | paintbrush | partiality | pentagonal | perplexity |
| outperform | Palaeocene | participle | pentameter | perquisite |
| outpouring | Palaeozoic | particular | pentaprism | persecutor |
| outrageous | palatially | parturient | Pentateuch | Persephone |

| | | | | |
|---|---|---|---|---|
| Persepolis | phylloxera | plebiscite | polytheism | Praxiteles |
| persiflage | physically | plentitude | polytheist | prearrange |
| persistent | physiology | pleonastic | polytunnel | prebendary |
| personable | pianissimi | pliability | polyvalent | precarious |
| personably | pianissimo | ploughable | Pomeranian | precaution |
| personally | pianoforte | pluckiness | ponderable | precedence |
| personalty | picaresque | pluperfect | pontifical | precession |
| persuasion | Piccadilly | plutocracy | popularise | preciosity |
| persuasive | piccalilli | pneumatics | popularity | preciously |
| Perthshire | pickpocket | Pocahontas | popularize | preclusion |
| pertinence | pictograph | pocketable | population | precocious |
| perversely | pigeonhole | pocketbook | portamenti | precursory |
| perversion | pigmentary | podiatrist | portamento | predaceous |
| perversity | piledriver | poetically | portcullis | predacious |
| Pestalozzi | pilgrimage | poignantly | portentous | predecease |
| pestilence | pillowcase | poinsettia | Portlaoise | predestine |
| petitioner | pillowslip | polemicise | portliness | prediction |
| petroglyph | pincushion | polemicist | Portsmouth | predictive |
| petrolatum | pinstriped | polemicize | Portuguese | predispose |
| Petronella | Pirandello | politeness | positional | preeminent |
| Petronilla | pitilessly | politician | positively | preemption |
| petulantly | Pittsburgh | politicise | positivism | preemptive |
| phagocytic | pixelation | politicize | positivist | prefecture |
| phalangeal | plagiarise | Pollaiuolo | positivity | preferable |
| phantasmal | plagiarism | pollinator | possession | preferably |
| pharmacist | plagiarist | polyanthus | possessive | preference |
| pharyngeal | plagiarize | polychrome | postbellum | preferment |
| phenomenal | plainchant | polychromy | postchaise | prehensile |
| phenomenon | planchette | Polyclitus | postcoital | prehistory |
| philatelic | planetaria | polycotton | posthumous | prejudiced |
| Philippine | plangently | polygamist | postillion | premarital |
| Philistine | planktonic | polygamous | postmaster | prenatally |
| philosophy | plantation | polygynous | postmodern | prenuptial |
| phlebotomy | plasticine | polyhedral | postmortem | prepackage |
| phlegmatic | plasticise | polyhedron | postpartum | prepayment |
| Phoenician | plasticity | Polyhymnia | postscript | preprogram |
| phonograph | plasticize | polymathic | potability | prepuberty |
| phosphoric | playground | polymerase | potentiate | presbytery |
| phosphorus | playscheme | polymerise | potentilla | prescience |
| photogenic | playschool | polymerize | powerfully | presidency |
| photograph | playwright | Polynesian | powerhouse | pressurise |
| photometer | pleadingly | polynomial | praesidium | pressurize |
| photometry | pleasantly | Polyphemus | praetorian | presumable |
| phrenology | pleasantry | polyphonic | pragmatism | presumably |
| phylactery | pleasingly | polyrhythm | pragmatist | presuppose |

pretension
prettiness
prevalence
prevention
preventive
previously
priesthood
primordial
princeling
principled
printmaker
prioritise
prioritize
prissiness
pristinely
privileged
prizefight
procedural
procession
proclivity
Procrustes
proctology
procurable
procurator
prodigally
prodigious
producible
production
productive
profession
proficient
profitable
profitably
profitless
profligacy
profligate
profoundly
profundity
progenitor
prognostic
programmer
projectile
projection
projective
promenader

Promethean
Prometheus
promethium
prominence
promontory
promptness
promulgate
pronominal
pronounced
pronouncer
propaganda
propagator
propellant
propensity
propertied
propitiate
propitious
proportion
propounder
proprietor
propulsion
propulsive
proscenium
prosciutto
prosecutor
Proserpina
Proserpine
prospector
prospectus
prosperity
prosperous
prosthesis
prosthetic
prostitute
protectant
protection
protective
Protestant
protoplasm
protractor
protrusion
provenance
provençale
proverbial
providence

provincial
provitamin
proximally
prudential
pruriently
psephology
psilocybin
psittacine
psychiatry
psychology
psychopath
pubescence
publishing
pufferfish
pugilistic
pugnacious
pulveriser
pulverizer
punctually
punishable
punishment
punitively
puritanism
purposeful
pursuivant
putatively
putrescent
puttanesca
puzzlement
pyracantha
pyridoxine
pyrography
pyromaniac
Pythagoras

## Q

quadrangle
quadriceps
quadruplet
quaintness
quantifier
quarantine
Quaternary
quatrefoil

queasiness
Queensland
quesadilla
questioner
quiescence
Quintilian
quintuplet
quirkiness
quizmaster

## R

rabbinical
racecourse
radicalism
radicalise
radicalize
radiograph
radiologic
radiometer
radiometry
Rafsanjani
ragamuffin
rainforest
rallycross
ramshackle
randomness
rapporteur
rationally
rattletrap
ravenously
Rawalpindi
razzmatazz
reacquaint
reactivate
reactivity
readership
realisable
realizable
reanalysis
reappraise
rearmament
reasonable
reasonably
reassemble

reassembly
rebellious
rebirthing
receivable
receptacle
rechristen
recidivism
recidivist
reciprocal
recitalist
recitation
recitative
recklessly
reclassify
reclinable
recommence
recompense
reconsider
recordable
recoupable
recoupment
recreation
rectorship
recumbency
recuperate
recurrence
recyclable
redcurrant
redecorate
redeemable
redemption
redemptive
rediscover
redundancy
referendum
refillable
refinement
reflection
reflective
refraction
refractive
refractory
refreshing
refulgence
refundable

| | | | | |
|---|---|---|---|---|
| refutation | reorganize | respecting | rheostatic | Rubinstein |
| regardless | repairable | respective | rhetorical | rudderless |
| regenerate | reparation | respirable | rheumatics | ruefulness |
| regimental | reparative | respirator | rheumatism | ruffianism |
| regionally | repatriate | respondent | rheumatoid | ruggedness |
| registrant | repeatable | responsive | rhinestone | rumination |
| regression | repeatedly | restaurant | rhinoceros | ruminative |
| regressive | repellence | restlessly | rhomboidal | Ruritanian |
| regularise | repellency | restorable | rhythmical | rustically |
| regularity | repentance | restrained | rhythmless | Rutherford |
| regularize | repertoire | restrainer | Ribbentrop | ruthlessly |
| regulation | repetition | restricted | riboflavin | |
| regulative | repetitive | resumption | Richardson | **S** |
| regulatory | replicable | resurgence | Richthofen | |
| reinforcer | replicator | retainable | ridiculous | sabbatical |
| rejuvenate | repopulate | retaliator | rightfully | sabretooth |
| relational | reportable | reticently | rightwards | saccharine |
| relatively | reposition | retirement | rigorously | sacerdotal |
| relativise | repository | retractile | rijsttafel | Sacramento |
| relativism | repression | retraction | ringleader | sacredness |
| relativist | repressive | retransmit | ringletted | sacrosanct |
| relativity | reproducer | retrograde | ringmaster | saddleback |
| relativize | republican | retrospect | risibility | salamander |
| relaxation | repudiator | retroviral | ritardandi | saleswoman |
| releasable | repugnance | retrovirus | ritardando | saleswomen |
| relegation | repugnancy | returnable | roadworthy | salivation |
| relentless | reputation | revanchism | robustness | salmonella |
| relevantly | resaleable | revanchist | rockabilly | salopettes |
| relinquish | reschedule | revelation | roisterous | salubrious |
| relocation | rescission | revelatory | rollerball | salutation |
| reluctance | resealable | revengeful | rollicking | sanatorium |
| remarkable | researcher | reverently | rollocking | sanctimony |
| remarkably | resentment | reversible | Romanesque | sandalwood |
| remarriage | reservable | reversibly | Rossellini | sandbagger |
| remediable | reservedly | reviewable | rotational | sandcastle |
| remittance | resettable | revitalise | Rothschild | sanderling |
| remorseful | residually | revitalize | rotisserie | Sandinista |
| remortgage | resilience | revivalism | rottenness | sandpapery |
| remoteness | resistance | revivalist | Rottweiler | Sangiovese |
| remunerate | resistible | revocation | roundabout | sanguinary |
| renascence | resolutely | revolution | roundhouse | sanitarium |
| rendezvous | resolution | rewritable | Roussillon | sanitation |
| renovation | resolvable | rhapsodise | roustabout | saprophyte |
| reoffender | resonantly | rhapsodize | Rowlandson | sarcophagi |
| reorganise | respectful | rheologist | rubberneck | saturation |

| | | | | |
|---|---|---|---|---|
| Saturnalia | scrutinize | separatist | shrewishly | smartphone |
| sauerkraut | sculptural | Septuagint | Shrewsbury | smattering |
| Savonarola | Scunthorpe | sepulchral | shrillness | smelliness |
| sawtoothed | scurrility | sequential | shrinkable | Smithfield |
| saxophonic | scurrilous | serologist | Shropshire | smokestack |
| scaffolder | seaborgium | serpentine | sickliness | smoothness |
| scandalise | seamanlike | serviceman | sidewinder | snapdragon |
| scandalize | seamanship | servicemen | signwriter | snappishly |
| scandalous | seamlessly | servomotor | Silchester | sneakiness |
| scarlatina | seamstress | settlement | silhouette | snobbishly |
| scathingly | searchable | seventieth | silverfish | snootiness |
| scattergun | seasonable | sexologist | silverside | snorkeller |
| scattering | seasonally | Seychelles | similarity | snowmobile |
| scenically | Sebastopol | shabbiness | similitude | snowplough |
| scepticism | secondment | Shackleton | simpleness | solicitous |
| schematise | secretaire | shadowland | simplicity | solicitude |
| schematize | secularise | shadowless | simplistic | solidarity |
| schismatic | secularism | shagginess | simulacrum | solubility |
| Schliemann | secularist | shamefaced | simulation | sombreness |
| Schoenberg | secularize | shamefully | sinfulness | somersault |
| scholastic | sedateness | shearwater | Singhalese | somnolence |
| schoolgirl | seductress | sheepishly | singleness | songwriter |
| schoolmarm | sedulously | sheepshank | singularly | sonography |
| schoolmate | seemliness | Shenandoah | sinisterly | sonorously |
| Schumacher | seersucker | Shetlander | sinologist | soothsayer |
| Schweitzer | seismicity | shibboleth | sisterhood | sophomoric |
| scientific | seismology | shiftiness | skateboard | sordidness |
| scintillae | selectable | shillelagh | skeletally | soubriquet |
| scoreboard | selflessly | shipwright | sketchbook | soundboard |
| scoresheet | Sellafield | shirtiness | skinniness | soundcheck |
| scornfully | semicircle | shirtwaist | skirmisher | soundproof |
| scorzonera | seminarian | shockingly | skittishly | soundscape |
| Scotswoman | semiquaver | shockproof | skyscraper | soundtrack |
| Scotswomen | senatorial | shoddiness | slanderous | sousaphone |
| Scotticism | Senegalese | shoestring | slatternly | southbound |
| scrambling | Senegambia | shopaholic | sleaziness | southerner |
| screenplay | senescence | shopfitter | sleepiness | southwards |
| scriptural | sensitiser | shopkeeper | sleeveless | spacecraft |
| scriptures | sensitizer | shoplifter | slightness | spaciously |
| scrofulous | sensualist | shorewards | slipstream | sparseness |
| scrollable | sensuality | shortbread | sloppiness | spasticity |
| scrollwork | sensuously | shortening | sluggardly | spatchcock |
| scrupulous | separately | showground | sluggishly | spatiality |
| scrutineer | separation | showjumper | slumberous | specialise |
| scrutinise | separatism | shrewdness | smarminess | specialism |

| | | | | |
|---|---|---|---|---|
| specialist | squareness | stinginess | subaqueous | supergrass |
| speciality | squeezable | stochastic | subculture | superhuman |
| specialize | squirrelly | stockiness | subheading | supermodel |
| speciation | Srebrenica | stockinged | subjection | supernovae |
| speciously | stabiliser | stodginess | subjective | superpower |
| spectacled | stabilizer | Stonehenge | subliminal | supersonic |
| spectacles | stablemate | stonemason | submariner | superstate |
| spectrally | stagecoach | storefront | submersion | superstore |
| speculator | stagecraft | storehouse | submission | supervisor |
| speechless | stagnation | storminess | submissive | superwoman |
| speediness | stalactite | storyboard | suboptimal | superwomen |
| speleology | stalagmite | strabismus | suboptimal | supineness |
| spellcheck | Stalingrad | Stradivari | subSaharan | supplanter |
| spermaceti | standardly | straighten | subscriber | supplement |
| spermicide | standpoint | straightly | subsection | suppleness |
| spheroidal | standstill | straitened | subsequent | supplicant |
| spiracular | Stanislaus | Strasbourg | subsidence | supplicate |
| spiritedly | starvation | strategist | subsidiary | supportive |
| spiritless | starveling | strathspey | subspecies | supposedly |
| spirituous | statecraft | Stravinsky | substation | suppressor |
| spirometer | statically | strawberry | substitute | surfactant |
| spirometry | stationary | streamline | substratum | surgically |
| spitefully | stationery | streetwise | subterfuge | Surinamese |
| splashback | statistics | strengthen | subtropics | surrealism |
| splendidly | statuesque | strictness | subvention | surrealist |
| splutterer | steadiness | stridently | subversion | survivable |
| spoilsport | stealthily | stridulate | subversive | suspension |
| spokeshave | steaminess | strikingly | successful | suspicious |
| spoliation | steeliness | Strindberg | succession | sustenance |
| spongelike | steelworks | stringency | successive | Sutherland |
| spongiform | stentorian | striptease | succinctly | suzerainty |
| sponginess | stepfather | stroganoff | succulence | sweatiness |
| spookiness | Stephenson | stronghold | suddenness | sweatpants |
| spoonerism | stepladder | strongroom | sufferance | sweatshirt |
| sportiness | stepmother | structural | sufficient | Swedenborg |
| sportingly | stepsister | strychnine | suffragist | sweepingly |
| sportswear | stereotype | stubbornly | suggestion | sweepstake |
| spotlessly | stertorous | studiously | suggestive | sweetbread |
| spreadable | stewardess | stuffiness | suicidally | sweetheart |
| Springboks | stickiness | stunningly | sullenness | swimmingly |
| springless | stiflingly | stuntwoman | sulphurous | switchable |
| springlike | stigmatise | stuntwomen | summertime | switchback |
| springtime | stigmatize | stupendous | Sunderland | switchgear |
| sprinkling | stillbirth | sturdiness | sunglasses | swordstick |
| spuriously | stimulator | stylistics | supergiant | sycophancy |

sympathise
sympathize
symphonist
syncretise
syncretism
syncretist
syncretize
synecdoche
synergetic
synonymous
synthesise
synthesist
synthesize
syphilitic
systematic

# T

tabernacle
tablecloth
tablespoon
tabulation
tachograph
tachometer
taciturnly
tactically
tactlessly
Tajikistan
talentless
talismanic
Talleyrand
Tamaulipas
tambourine
Tanganyika
tangential
Tannhäuser
tantamount
tapestried
tarantella
targetable
tartrazine
taskmaster
tastefully
tastemaker
tattersall

tattletale
tawdriness
taxidermic
taxonomist
technetium
technician
technicist
technocrat
technology
telecaster
telegraphy
Telemachus
telematics
telemetric
telepathic
telephonic
telescopic
television
televisual
teleworker
temperance
temporally
temptation
tenderfeet
tenderfoot
tenderiser
tenderizer
tenderloin
tenderness
tendinitis
tendonitis
tentacular
tenterhook
Tereshkova
terminable
terminally
terminator
terracotta
Tertullian
tessellate
testicular
tetchiness
tetrahedra
tetrameter
textuality

thankfully
theatrical
themselves
theocratic
theodolite
theologian
theologist
thereabout
thereafter
thereunder
thermionic
thermistor
thermostat
thickening
thimbleful
thirteenth
thoroughly
thoughtful
thousandth
threadbare
threadworm
threepence
threescore
thriftless
thrombosis
thrombotic
throughout
throughput
Thucydides
thumbprint
thumbscrew
thundering
thunderous
tiddlywink
tiebreaker
timberline
timekeeper
timelessly
timeliness
timorously
Tinseltown
Tintoretto
tirelessly
tiresomely
titivation

tocopherol
toiletries
tokenistic
tolerantly
toleration
tomfoolery
tomography
toothbrush
toothpaste
topgallant
topicality
topography
torchlight
Torquemada
torrential
Torricelli
tortellini
tortuosity
tortuously
touchiness
touchingly
touchpaper
touchstone
tourmaline
tournament
tourniquet
Townsville
townswoman
townswomen
toxicology
Tradescant
trafficker
tragically
tragicomic
traitorous
trajectory
tramontana
trampoline
tranquilly
transcribe
transcript
transducer
transexual
transferee
transferor

transgenic
transgress
transience
transiency
transistor
transition
transitive
transitory
translator
transplant
transverse
trashiness
traumatise
traumatize
travelator
travelogue
travertine
travolator
trawlerman
trawlermen
treasonous
tremendous
trenchancy
trendiness
trespasser
Trevithick
triacetate
triangular
triathlete
trichology
trickiness
triflingly
trifoliate
trilateral
trilingual
trillionth
tripartite
triplicate
triplicity
trisection
triumphant
Trivandrum
trivialise
triviality
trivialize

troglodyte
trolleybus
trombonist
tropically
Trotskyism
Trotskyist
Trotskyite
troubadour
trousseaux
Trowbridge
truculence
truncation
trustfully
trustingly
truthfully
Tskhinvali
tubercular
tuberculin
tumbledown
tumbleweed
tumescence
tumultuous
tunelessly
turbulence
turkeycock
turnaround
turnbuckle
turpentine
turtleneck
tweediness
typescript
typesetter
typewriter
typicality
typography
typologist
tyrannical
Tyrrhenian

# U

Übermensch
ubiquitous
ulceration
ulcerative

ultimately
ultralight
ultrasonic
ultrasound
umbellifer
unabridged
unaccented
unaffected
unAmerican
unanswered
unapproved
unarguable
unarguably
unassisted
unassuming
unattached
unattended
unavailing
unbearable
unbearably
unbeatable
unbeatably
unbecoming
unbeliever
unbleached
unblushing
uncaringly
unchanging
uncoloured
uncommonly
unconfined
uncritical
unctuously
uncultured
undefeated
undefended
undeniable
undeniably
underbelly
underbrush
underclass
undercover
undercroft
underdress
underglaze

underneath
underpants
underscore
undershirt
undershoot
undersized
underskirt
underspend
underspent
understaff
understand
understate
understeer
understudy
undertaken
undertaker
undervalue
underwater
underwhelm
underwired
underworld
underwrite
underwrote
undeserved
undetected
undeterred
undigested
undirected
undismayed
undisputed
undulation
undulatory
uneasiness
uneconomic
unedifying
uneducated
unemployed
unenclosed
unenviable
unequalled
unerringly
unevenness
uneventful
unexamined
unexciting

unexpected
unexploded
unexplored
unfairness
unfaithful
unfamiliar
unfeasible
unfeasibly
unfettered
unfinished
unflagging
unfocussed
unforeseen
unfriendly
ungenerous
ungraceful
ungracious
ungrateful
unheralded
unhygienic
unicameral
unicyclist
uniformity
unilateral
unimpaired
uninformed
uninspired
unintended
uninviting
uninvolved
uniqueness
university
unkindness
unknowable
unlabelled
unladylike
unlamented
unlawfully
unleavened
unlettered
unlicensed
unlikeness
unmannerly
unmerciful
unmetalled

unmissable
unnameable
unnumbered
unobserved
unoccupied
unofficial
unoriginal
unorthodox
unplayable
unpleasant
unploughed
unpolished
unprepared
unprompted
unprovoked
unpunished
unreactive
unreadable
unreadably
unrealised
unrealized
unreasoned
unrecorded
unreleased
unreliable
unreliably
unrelieved
unremarked
unreported
unrequited
unreserved
unresolved
unrivalled
unromantic
unruliness
unsaleable
unsanitary
unschooled
unscramble
unscreened
unscripted
unseasonal
unseasoned
unseeingly
unshakable

unsinkable
unskillful
unsociable
unspecific
unsporting
unsteadily
unstinting
unstressed
unsuitable
unsuitably
unsureness
unsurfaced
unswerving
untameable
untestable
unthinking
untidiness
untiringly
untroubled
untruthful
unverified
unwavering
unwearying
unwinnable
unwontedly
unworkable
unworthily
unwrinkled
unwritable
unyielding
upbringing
upholstery
uplighting
uproarious
upstanding
urethritis
urogenital
urological
usefulness
usurpation
utilisable
utilizable
utopianism
Uzbekistan

## V

vacationer
validation
Valladolid
Valparaíso
Vanderbilt
vanquisher
variegated
vaudeville
Vegeburger
vegetarian
vegetation
vegetative
vehemently
velocipede
veneration
Venezuelan
vengefully
venomously
ventilator
verifiable
vermicelli
vernacular
Versailles
vertebrate
vertically
Verulamium
vestibular
veterinary
vibraphone
victimhood
victimiser
victimizer
victimless
Victoriana
victorious
victualler
videophile
videophone
Vietnamese
viewership
viewfinder
viewscreen
vigilantly

vigorously
villainous
villanelle
vindictive
violaceous
virologist
virtualise
virtuality
virtualize
virtuosity
virtuously
virulently
viscerally
visibility
visitation
visualiser
visualizer
viviparity
viviparous
vivisector
Vlissingen
vocabulary
vocational
vociferous
voiceprint
volatilise
volatility
volatilize
volitional
volleyball
volubility
volumetric
voluminous
voluptuary
voluptuous
vulnerable
vulnerably

## W

Wallenberg
wallflower
Walsingham
wanderings
wanderlust

wantonness
wardenship
Warrington
Washington
wastefully
watchfully
watchmaker
watchtower
watercraft
watercress
waterfront
Waterhouse
watermelon
waterproof
waterskier
waterspout
watertight
waterwheel
waterworks
wavelength
weatherman
weathermen
weedkiller
weightless
Weimaraner
wellington
wellspring
Welshwoman
Welshwomen
westernise
westernize
Westphalia
whatsoever
wheatgrass
Wheatstone
wheelchair
wheelhouse
wheeziness
whensoever
whereafter
whiteboard
Whitehorse
wholesaler
wholewheat
whomsoever

wickedness
wickerwork
widescreen
widespread
Wiesenthal
wildebeest
wilderness
wilfulness
Wilhelmina
Willemstad
Williamson
willowherb
winceyette
Winchester
Windermere
windjammer
windowless
windowpane
windscreen
windshield
windsurfer
winegrower
winemaking
wingspread
wingstroke
Winterthur
wintertime
wirelessly
witchcraft
withdrawal
withholder
Wittenberg
wobbliness
womenswear
wonderland
wonderment
wondrously
woodcarver
woodcutter
woodenness
woodpecker
woodturner
woodworker
woolliness
Wordsworth

workaholic     wraithlike     **X-Z**         yesteryear     zidovudine
workaround     wrathfully                     Yogyakarta     Zimbabwean
Workington     wretchedly     xenophobia      youthfully     zoological
Worshipful     wristwatch     xenophobic      Yugoslavia     zoomorphic
worshipper     wrongdoing     xerography      zabaglione
worthiness     wrongfully     yellowness      Zeffirelli
worthwhile     wunderkind

# **11** LETTERS

### A

| | | | |
|---|---|---|---|
| | acquirement | aggravation | anaesthesia |
| | acquisition | aggregation | anaesthetic |
| abandonment | acquisitive | agnosticism | anarchistic |
| abdominally | acrimonious | agoraphobia | anchorwoman |
| abnormality | acupressure | agoraphobic | anchorwomen |
| abomination | acupuncture | agriculture | androgynous |
| abortionist | adaptogenic | ahistorical | anecdotally |
| abracadabra | addictively | aimlessness | angelically |
| abridgement | addressable | aircraftman | angioplasty |
| absenteeism | adjournment | aircraftmen | Anglicanism |
| abstraction | adjudicator | Albuquerque | Anglophilia |
| academician | adolescence | Aldermaston | animalistic |
| academicism | adrenalised | alexandrine | animatronic |
| accelerandi | adrenalized | algorithmic | annihilator |
| accelerando | adumbration | allegorical | anniversary |
| accelerator | advancement | alleviation | anomalously |
| accessorise | adventurism | alphabetise | anonymously |
| accessorize | adventurist | alphabetize | answerphone |
| acclamation | adventurous | altercation | antechamber |
| acclimatise | adversarial | alternately | anthologist |
| acclimatize | advertising | alternation | anthologise |
| accommodate | advertorial | alternative | anthologize |
| accompanist | aerobically | ambiguously | anticipator |
| accordingly | aerodynamic | ambitiously | anticyclone |
| accountable | aeronautics | ambivalence | antiheroine |
| accountancy | affectation | amenability | antioxidant |
| acculturate | affiliation | amenorrhoea | antipyretic |
| accumulator | affirmation | Americanise | antiquarian |
| acerbically | affirmative | Americanism | antirrhinum |
| achievement | Afghanistan | Americanize | anxiousness |
| acidophilus | afterburner | amontillado | apatosaurus |
| acknowledge | agglomerate | amphetamine | aphrodisiac |
| acquiescent | agglutinate | anachronism | apocalyptic |

| | | | |
|---|---|---|---|
| Apollinaire | atomisation | Beckenbauer | boilerplate |
| apologetics | atomization | behavioural | bombardment |
| apotheosise | atrociously | Beiderbecke | bookbinding |
| apotheosize | attentively | belatedness | bookkeeping |
| appallingly | attenuation | Bellerophon | boorishness |
| apparatchik | attestation | bellicosity | botanically |
| appealingly | attitudinal | belligerent | bountifully |
| appeasement | attribution | Benedictine | Bourbonnais |
| appellation | attributive | benediction | bourgeoisie |
| application | attritional | benefaction | Bournemouth |
| appointment | audaciously | beneficence | boysenberry |
| appreciable | audiologist | beneficiary | braggadocio |
| appreciably | Australasia | benevolence | Brahmaputra |
| appreciator | averageness | bereavement | Brahminical |
| approbation | avicultural | Bernardotte | Brandenburg |
| appropriate | avoirdupois | bewitchment | Brazzaville |
| approximate | awkwardness | bibliophile | breadwinner |
| arbitrageur | Azerbaijani | bicarbonate | breastplate |
| arbitrarily | | bicentenary | breathalyse |
| arbitration | **B** | bifurcation | Breconshire |
| archaeology | | bilaterally | bricklaying |
| archaically | Bacchanalia | bilingually | brilliantly |
| archduchess | backbencher | biliousness | Britishness |
| archipelago | backslidden | billionaire | brittleness |
| arduousness | bacterially | biochemical | broadcaster |
| Argentinian | Ballesteros | bioengineer | broadleaved |
| Argyllshire | balletomane | biofeedback | brontosauri |
| aristocracy | Baluchistan | birdwatcher | brotherhood |
| arraignment | balustraded | bisexuality | brucellosis |
| arrangeable | Bangladeshi | bittersweet | brushstroke |
| arrangement | bankability | bizarreness | brusqueness |
| arrestingly | Bannockburn | blackmailer | bulletproof |
| arrividerci | barbarously | bladderwort | bullfighter |
| articulator | barbiturate | blameworthy | bullishness |
| assassinate | Bartholomew | blasphemous | bumptiously |
| assertively | Baryshnikov | blessedness | bureaucracy |
| assiduously | bashfulness | blockbuster | bushwhacker |
| assignation | bathysphere | bloodlessly | businessman |
| assimilable | battledress | bloodstream | businessmen |
| association | battlefield | bloodsucker | buttercream |
| associative | Baudrillard | blunderbuss | Butterfield |
| astigmatism | beachcomber | boardsailor | Byelorussia |
| astringency | beastliness | bodyboarder | |
| athleticism | beautifully | bodybuilder | |
| atmospheric | Beaverbrook | Bohemianism | |

**C**

cabbalistic
cacophonous
Cadwallader
Caerfyrddin
caffeinated
calciferous
calcination
calculating
calculation
calendrical
calibration
Californian
californium
Callicrates
calligraphy
callipygian
callousness
calorimeter
calorimetry
calumniator
Calvinistic
camaraderie
Cameroonian
campanology
Canadianism
candelabrum
candidature
candlelight
candlepower
candlestick
cannibalise
cannibalism
cannibalize
canonically
capacitance
capillarity
capitulator
captivation
carabiniere
carabinieri
caravanning
carbonation
carborundum

carbuncular
carburetted
carburettor
Carcassonne
carcinomata
cardiograph
carefulness
caressingly
caricatural
carminative
carnivorous
Carolingian
carriageway
cartography
castellated
castigation
Castlereagh
casuistical
cataclysmic
catastrophe
catchphrase
categorical
caterpillar
catfighting
Catholicism
catholicity
cauliflower
caustically
ceaselessly
celebration
celebratory
celestially
cementation
centenarian
centigramme
centreboard
centrepiece
centrifugal
centripetal
cerebration
ceremonious
certifiable
certifiably
certificate
Cesarewitch

chairperson
chamberlain
chambermaid
chameleonic
Champollion
chancellery
chanterelle
chaotically
charcuterie
charismatic
charlatanry
Charlemagne
cheerleader
cheesecloth
chiaroscuro
chieftaincy
childminder
chinoiserie
Chippendale
chiropodist
chitterling
chlorophyll
chloroplast
chocolatier
cholesterol
choreograph
Christendom
christening
Christiania
Christopher
chromosomal
chronically
chronograph
chronometer
chucklehead
churchwoman
churchwomen
circularise
circularity
circularize
circulation
circulatory
circumpolar
circumspect
Cirencester

citizenship
clairvoyant
clamdiggers
clandestine
classically
cleanliness
clergywoman
clergywomen
cliffhanger
climacteric
climatology
coagulation
coalescence
cobblestone
cockleshell
codependent
coeducation
coefficient
coexistence
coextensive
cognitively
cognoscenti
coincidence
collaborate
collapsible
collectable
collectible
collocation
colonialism
colonialist
colonoscopy
colouration
colourfully
colouristic
combatively
combination
combustible
comeuppance
comfortable
comfortably
commandment
commemorate
commendable
commendably
commentator

| | | | |
|---|---|---|---|
| comminution | conditional | consultancy | Corinthians |
| commiserate | conditioner | consumerism | cornerstone |
| commonality | condominium | consumerist | cornucopian |
| commonplace | conductance | consumption | corporately |
| communality | conductress | consumptive | corporation |
| communicant | confabulate | contactable | corporatism |
| communicate | confederacy | containable | corporatist |
| communistic | Confederate | containment | corpuscular |
| commutation | confidently | contaminant | correctable |
| commutative | confinement | contaminate | correctness |
| compactness | conformance | contemplate | correlation |
| comparative | confutation | contentedly | correlative |
| compartment | congenially | contentious | corroborate |
| compendious | congressman | contentment | corrugation |
| compensator | congressmen | contestable | corruptible |
| competently | conjectural | continental | coruscation |
| competition | conjugation | contingency | cosignatory |
| competitive | conjunction | continually | cosmogonist |
| compilation | conjunctiva | continuance | cosmography |
| complacency | conjunctive | contractile | cosmologist |
| complainant | conjuncture | contraction | coterminous |
| complaisant | Connecticut | contractual | cotoneaster |
| compliantly | connoisseur | contraption | countenance |
| complicated | connotation | contrariety | counterfeit |
| comportment | consciously | contrastive | counterfoil |
| composition | consecutive | contravener | countermand |
| compression | consequence | contretemps | counterpane |
| compressive | conservancy | contributor | counterpart |
| compromiser | conservator | contrivance | countersign |
| comptroller | considerate | controversy | countersink |
| compunction | considering | conurbation | countersunk |
| computation | consignment | convenience | countervail |
| computerise | consistence | conventicle | countrified |
| computerize | consistency | convertible | countryfied |
| comradeship | consolation | conveyancer | countryside |
| concatenate | consolatory | convivially | countrywide |
| concealment | consolidate | convocation | courteously |
| conceivable | consonantal | convolution | courtliness |
| conceivably | conspicuous | convolvulus | craftswoman |
| concentrate | conspirator | cooperation | craftswomen |
| conciliator | Constantine | cooperative | craftworker |
| conciseness | constipated | coordinator | crashworthy |
| concomitant | constituent | copiousness | creationism |
| concordance | constrictor | copperplate | creationist |
| concurrence | constructor | coprocessor | credibility |

credulously
crematorium
crepitation
crepuscular
crestfallen
criminalise
criminality
criminalize
criminology
crookedness
cruciferous
crucifixion
crunchiness
cryosurgery
cryptically
crystalline
crystallise
crystallize
culmination
culpability
cultivation
Cumbernauld
cumulonimbi
curtailment
curvilinear
customarily
cybernetics
cyclopaedia
cylindrical
cytological
cytoplasmic

# D

dangerously
Dardanelles
deafeningly
debouchment
decalcified
decarbonise
decarbonize
deceitfully
deceptively
declamation
declamatory

declaration
declarative
declination
décolletage
deconstruct
decrepitude
deerstalker
defalcation
defectively
defenceless
defensively
deferential
defoliation
deformation
degradation
degradative
dehydration
deification
delectation
deleterious
deliciously
delightedly
delineation
delinquency
deliriously
deliverable
deliverance
demagnetise
demagnetize
demagoguery
demarcation
demigoddess
democratise
democratize
demodulator
demographer
demographic
demonically
demonstrate
Demosthenes
demountable
demutualise
demutualize
deniability
denigration

denominator
deoxygenate
dependently
deportation
deprecation
deprecatory
depreciable
depredation
deprivation
derangement
dereliction
dermatology
describable
description
descriptive
desecration
desegregate
deselection
desensitise
desensitize
desiccation
desideratum
designation
desperately
desperation
despondency
destabilise
destabilize
destination
destitution
destruction
destructive
desultorily
deteriorate
determinacy
determinant
determinate
determinism
determinist
detestation
detrimental
detumescent
Deuteronomy
Deutschland
Deutschmark

devaluation
devastating
devastation
developable
development
deviousness
dexterously
diacritical
diagnosable
dialectical
diametrical
diamorphine
dichotomous
dicotyledon
dictatorial
didacticism
differently
diffidently
diffraction
diffractive
dilapidated
dipsomaniac
directional
directorate
directorial
disablement
disaffected
disapproval
disarmament
disarmingly
disassemble
disassembly
disbeliever
discernible
discernment
discography
discontinue
discordance
discotheque
discourtesy
discrepancy
discussable
disembodied
disentangle
disgraceful

| | | | |
|---|---|---|---|
| disgruntled | domesticity | egotistical | encumbrance |
| disgustedly | domiciliary | egregiously | endearingly |
| dishevelled | doorstopper | einsteinium | endlessness |
| dishonestly | Dostoyevsky | ejaculation | endometrial |
| disillusion | doublespeak | ejaculatory | endometrium |
| disinclined | doublethink | elaborately | endorsement |
| disinterest | doubtlessly | elaboration | endothermic |
| disjunction | downhearted | elaborative | enforceable |
| disjunctive | downtrodden | elastically | enforcement |
| dislocation | drastically | elasticated | enfranchise |
| disobedient | draughtsman | elastomeric | engineering |
| disobliging | draughtsmen | elderflower | Englishness |
| dispensable | dreadlocked | electioneer | engorgement |
| dispersible | dreadnought | electorally | enhancement |
| displeasure | dressmaking | electrician | enigmatical |
| disposition | drunkenness | electricity | enlargement |
| disputation | dubiousness | electrocute | Enniskillen |
| disquieting | Dunfermline | electrolyte | ennoblement |
| disquietude | duplication | electronica | enquiringly |
| disseminate | duplicitous | electronics | enslavement |
| dissentient | dynamically | elegiacally | entablature |
| dissimulate | dynamometer | elephantine | entertainer |
| dissipation | dysfunction | elevational | enthralment |
| dissipative | Dzerzhinsky | elicitation | entitlement |
| dissolution | | eligibility | enumeration |
| dissolvable | **E** | elimination | enunciation |
| distasteful | | Elizabethan | envelopment |
| distensible | earnestness | ellipsoidal | environment |
| distinction | earthenware | ellipticity | ephemerally |
| distinctive | earthliness | elucidation | episcopally |
| distinguish | easternmost | elusiveness | equidistant |
| distraction | ebulliently | embarkation | equilateral |
| distressful | eclecticism | embarrassed | equilibrium |
| distributor | econometric | embraceable | equinoctial |
| distrustful | ectoplasmic | embrocation | equivalence |
| disturbance | edification | embroiderer | equivalency |
| dithyrambic | editorially | emotionally | equivocally |
| diverticula | educational | emotionless | eradication |
| doctrinaire | effectively | empanelment | erotomaniac |
| doctrinally | effectually | empirically | erratically |
| documentary | efficacious | emplacement | erroneously |
| dodecahedra | efficiently | empowerment | erythrocyte |
| dogfighting | egalitarian | encapsulate | eschatology |
| dolphinaria | egocentrism | enchantment | Esperantist |
| domesticate | egomaniacal | enchantress | essentially |

Estremadura
ethereality
ethnography
ethnologist
ethological
etymologist
Eucharistic
euphemistic
Eurocentric
Europeanise
Europeanism
Europeanize
evanescence
evangelical
evaporation
evaporative
evasiveness
eventuality
everlasting
examination
exceedingly
exceptional
excessively
exclamation
exclamatory
exclusively
exclusivity
excoriation
excremental
excrescence
exculpation
exculpatory
exdirectory
executioner
exercisable
exfoliation
exhaustible
exhortation
existential
exogenously
exoneration
exoskeleton
expansively
expatiation
expectantly

expectation
expectorant
expectorate
expediently
expeditious
expenditure
expensively
experienced
explainable
explanation
explanatory
explication
exploitable
exploration
exploratory
explosively
exponential
exportation
expostulate
expressible
expropriate
expurgation
exquisitely
extemporary
extemporise
extemporize
extensional
extensively
extenuating
extenuation
exterminate
externalise
externalize
extirpation
extractable
extradition
extrapolate
extravagant
Extremadura
extrication
extroverted
exuberantly

**F**

fabrication
facetiously
facilitator
fallibility
falsifiable
familiarise
familiarity
familiarize
fanatically
fantabulous
fantastical
farinaceous
Farnborough
farthermost
farthingale
fascinating
fascination
fashionable
fashionably
fashionista
fatuousness
faultlessly
favouritism
fearfulness
feasibility
featureless
feloniously
fermentable
ferociously
ferruginous
fetishistic
fictionally
fictiveness
fiddlestick
filamentary
filamentous
filmography
financially
fingerboard
fingerprint
fingerstall
finickiness
firecracker

firefighter
firelighter
fissionable
flabbergast
flamboyance
flannelette
flavourless
flavoursome
flexibility
flightiness
flirtatious
floriferous
fluctuation
fluorescent
fluoroscope
fluoroscopy
fomentation
foolhardily
foolishness
footballing
forbearance
foreclosure
foreignness
foreseeable
foreseeably
foreshorten
foresighted
forestation
forethought
Forfarshire
forgetfully
forgettable
forgiveness
forlornness
formational
formatively
formulation
fornication
forthcoming
fortnightly
fortunately
forwardness
fractiously
fragmentary
Francophile

francophone
Frankenfood
frankfurter
frantically
franticness
fraternally
fratricidal
fraudulence
Fredericton
freemasonry
freethinker
freewheeler
Frenchwoman
Frenchwomen
freneticism
fretfulness
Freudianism
frightfully
frivolously
frostbitten
frugivorous
fruitlessly
frustration
fulmination
fulsomeness
functionary
fundamental
fundholding
furtherance
furthermore
furthermost
furtiveness
Furtwängler

## G

gallimaufry
gangsterism
garrulously
gastronomic
gatecrasher
gendarmerie
genealogist
generically
genetically

gentlemanly
gentlewoman
gentlewomen
genuineness
geometrical
geophysical
geopolitics
germination
gerontocrat
gerontology
gerrymander
gestational
gesticulate
ghastliness
Ghirlandaio
ghostwriter
gilliflower
gillyflower
gimcrackery
gingerbread
glamorously
Glastonbury
Glittertind
glossolalia
goalscoring
gobsmacking
godchildren
godforsaken
gourmandise
gourmandize
gracelessly
gradational
gradualness
grammatical
grandfather
grandiflora
grandiosely
grandiosity
grandmaster
grandmother
grandparent
granularity
granulation
graphically
grasshopper

gravedigger
gravimetric
gravitation
greasepaint
greengrocer
greenkeeper
Greenlander
grotesquely
groundsheet
groundswell
groundwater
gruellingly
Guadalajara
Guadalcanal
guesstimate
guilelessly
guiltlessly
gullibility
gutlessness
guttersnipe
gynaecology
gyrocompass

## H

haberdasher
habituation
haematology
haematomata
haemoglobin
haemophilia
haemorrhage
haemorrhoid
hagiography
hairdresser
hairstyling
hairstylist
hallucinate
Hammerstein
handicapped
handshaking
handwriting
handwritten
haphazardly
Hardecanute

harmfulness
harpsichord
harvestable
hatefulness
haughtiness
hazardously
headquarter
healthfully
healthiness
heartbroken
heartlessly
heavenwards
heavyweight
Hegelianism
heinousness
heliosphere
Hellenistic
hellishness
helpfulness
Helsingborg
hemispheric
Hepplewhite
heptahedron
heptathlete
herbivorous
Hercegovina
Herculaneum
hereinafter
heretically
hermeneutic
herpesvirus
herpetology
herringbone
Herzegovina
hexadecimal
hibernation
hideousness
highfalutin
highlighter
hilariously
hillwalking
Hippocrates
hippopotami
hirsuteness
Hispanicise

Hispanicize
histologist
historicise
historicism
historicist
historicity
historicize
hobbledehoy
holographic
homeopathic
homeostasis
homeostatic
homesteader
homoeopathy
homogeneity
homogeneous
homogeniser
homogenizer
honeymooner
honeysuckle
hooliganism
hopefulness
horological
horseradish
hospitalise
hospitality
hospitalize
hospitaller
houndstooth
householder
housekeeper
housemaster
housewifely
housewifery
hucksterism
humiliation
hummingbird
Humperdinck
hunchbacked
hundredfold
hydrocarbon
hydrogenate
hydrography
hydrologist
hydropathic

hydrophilic
hydrophobia
hydrophobic
hydroponics
hydrosphere
hydrostatic
hygroscopic
hyperactive
hypermarket
hypertrophy
hyphenation
hypotension
hypotensive
hypothalami
hypothecate
hypothermia
hypothesise
hypothesize
hypothyroid

# I

ichthyology
ichthyosaur
iconography
iconostasis
icosahedral
icosahedron
identically
ideological
idiotically
idolisation
idolization
idyllically
ignominious
illimitable
illimitably
illogically
illuminator
illusionism
illusionist
illustrator
illustrious
imaginarily
imagination

imaginative
imitatively
immediately
immigration
immobiliser
immobilizer
immortalise
immortality
immortalize
immunologic
impartially
impassioned
impassively
impassivity
impatiently
impeachable
impeachment
impecunious
impedimenta
impenitence
imperfectly
imperialism
imperialist
imperiously
impermanent
impermeable
impersonate
impertinent
impetuosity
impetuously
impingement
implausible
implausibly
implementer
implication
implicative
importantly
importation
importunate
importunity
impoundment
impractical
imprecation
imprecisely
imprecision

impregnable
impregnably
impropriety
improvement
improvident
imprudently
impulsively
impulsivity
inadvertent
inadvisable
inalienable
inalienably
inattention
inattentive
inaugurator
inauthentic
incantation
incantatory
incarcerate
incarnation
incentivise
incentivize
incertitude
incessantly
incinerator
incipiently
inclination
inclusively
incoherence
incoherency
incompetent
incongruent
incongruity
incongruous
inconstancy
incontinent
incorporate
incorporeal
incorrectly
incredulity
incredulous
incremental
incriminate
inculcation
incuriosity

| | | | |
|---|---|---|---|
| incuriously | infatuation | inspiration | interrogate |
| indefinable | inferential | inspiratory | interrupter |
| indefinably | inferiority | instability | intersexual |
| indemnifier | infertility | instantiate | intersperse |
| indentation | infestation | instigation | intertribal |
| independent | infiltrator | instinctive | interviewee |
| indifferent | inflammable | instinctual | interviewer |
| indigestion | influential | institution | intimidator |
| indignantly | infomercial | instruction | intolerable |
| indignation | informality | instructive | intolerably |
| indirection | informatics | insuperable | intolerance |
| individuate | information | insuperably | intractable |
| indivisible | informative | integration | intractably |
| indivisibly | infrequency | integrative | intravenous |
| indomitable | ingeniously | intelligent | intrepidity |
| indomitably | ingenuously | intemperate | intricately |
| indubitable | ingratitude | intenseness | introverted |
| indubitably | inhabitable | intensifier | intrusively |
| inductively | inheritable | intensively | intuitively |
| inductivism | inheritance | intentional | inventively |
| inductivist | injudicious | interaction | investigate |
| indulgently | innocuously | interactive | investiture |
| industrious | innumerable | interceptor | invidiously |
| inebriation | inoculation | intercessor | invigilator |
| ineffective | inoffensive | interchange | involuntary |
| ineffectual | inoperative | intercooler | involvement |
| inefficient | inopportune | intercourse | ionospheric |
| inelegantly | inquisition | interesting | ipecacuanha |
| ineluctable | inquisitive | interfacing | iridescence |
| ineluctably | inscription | interfusion | iridologist |
| inequitable | inscrutable | interiorise | ironmongery |
| inequitably | inscrutably | interiority | irradiation |
| inescapable | insecticide | interiorize | irredentism |
| inescapably | insectivore | interlinear | irredentist |
| inessential | inseminator | interlining | irreducible |
| inestimable | insensitive | intermingle | irreducibly |
| inestimably | insentience | internalise | irrefutable |
| inexactness | inseparable | internality | irrefutably |
| inexcusable | inseparably | internalize | irregularly |
| inexcusably | insidiously | internecine | irrelevance |
| inexpensive | insincerely | interpolate | irrelevancy |
| infanticide | insincerity | interpreter | irreligious |
| infantilism | insinuation | interracial | irremovable |
| infantryman | insistently | interregnum | irreparable |
| infantrymen | insouciance | interrelate | irreparably |

irreverence
irrevocable
irrevocably
isomorphism
isomorphous

**J**

jargonistic
Jehoshaphat
jitteriness
joblessness
Judaisation
Judaization
judgemental
judiciously
juridically
justiciable
justifiable
justifiably

**K**

Kabbalistic
Kalashnikov
Kaliningrad
Kierkegaard
Kilimanjaro
kilocalorie
kinesiology
kinetically
kinetoscope
kitchenette
kitchenware
kitesurfing
kitschiness
kittenishly
kleptomania
knowingness
knucklehead
Kulturkampf
kwashiorkor

**L**

laboriously
laconically
laicisation
laicization
Lakshadweep
lamentation
lammergeier
lammergeyer
Lanarkshire
Lancastrian
landlordism
landscapist
langoustine
laparoscope
laparoscopy
latitudinal
latticework
launderette
lawlessness
leaseholder
leatherette
lecherously
lectureship
Leeuwenhoek
legendarily
legerdemain
legionnaire
legislation
legislative
legislature
leisurewear
Leoncavallo
Lepidoptera
letterpress
libertarian
libertinism
lickspittle
lieutenancy
ligamentous
lightweight
Lilliputian
limitlessly
Lindisfarne

linguistics
lionhearted
lionisation
lionization
lipoprotein
liposuction
liquidation
listeriosis
literalness
lithography
lithosphere
liveability
Livingstone
localisable
localizable
logarithmic
Londonderry
loosestrife
loudspeaker
lovableness
lubrication
lucratively
lucubration
ludicrously
luminescent
lumpishness
lustfulness
Lutheranism
Lutosławski
luxuriantly
luxuriously
lycanthrope
lycanthropy

**M**

Machiavelli
machination
macrobiotic
macrocosmic
macroscopic
Maeterlinck
magisterial
magnanimity
magnanimous

magnificent
Mahabharata
Maharashtra
maidservant
maintenance
Makhachkala
maladjusted
malapropism
malediction
malevolence
malfeasance
malfunction
maliciously
malpractice
mammography
managership
mandatorily
Mandelshtam
mandolinist
Manichaeism
manipulable
manipulator
mantelpiece
mantelshelf
manufactory
manufacture
manumission
marchioness
marginalise
marginality
marginalize
marketplace
Marlborough
marlinspike
marshmallow
Martiniquan
martyrology
masculinity
Mashonaland
masochistic
massiveness
masterclass
masterfully
masterpiece
mastication

masturbator
materialise
materialism
materialist
materiality
materialize
mathematics
matriarchal
matriculate
matrilineal
matrimonial
Mauritanian
McCarthyism
McCarthyite
meadowsweet
meaningless
measureless
measurement
mechanistic
Mecklenburg
medicinally
medievalise
medievalist
medievalize
megalomania
megalopolis
melancholia
melancholic
Melanchthon
mellifluous
melodically
membraneous
memorabilia
memorialise
memorialist
memorialize
menaquinone
mendelevium
Mendelssohn
mensuration
mentholated
merchandise
merchandize
merchantman
merchantmen

mercilessly
meritocracy
meritorious
merrymaking
mésalliance
Mesopotamia
metamorphic
metaphysics
meteorology
methodology
methylation
metrication
metrosexual
Mezzogiorno
microbrewer
microcosmic
Micronesian
microscopic
microsecond
micturition
millenarian
milligramme
millionaire
millisecond
Milquetoast
minesweeper
miniaturise
miniaturist
miniaturize
miniskirted
ministerial
Minneapolis
mirthlessly
misalliance
misanthrope
misanthropy
misbegotten
miscarriage
miscellanea
mischievous
misconceive
misconstrue
misdiagnose
miserliness
misidentify

Mississippi
Missolonghi
mistrustful
mockingbird
modernistic
moisturiser
moisturizer
molestation
mollycoddle
momentarily
momentously
monarchical
monasticism
moneylender
moneymaking
monoculture
monographic
monolingual
Monseigneur
monstrosity
monstrously
Montenegrin
Montesquieu
Montgolfier
Montpellier
moonlighter
motherboard
mountaineer
mountainous
Mountbatten
Moussorgsky
multicolour
multiracial
multitasker
multivalent
municipally
munificence
murderously
muscularity
musculature
mycological
mythologise
mythologist
mythologize
mythomaniac

mythopoetic
myxomatosis

# N

Namaqualand
naphthalene
narcoleptic
narratively
nationalise
nationalism
nationalist
nationality
nationalize
naturalness
naturopathy
naughtiness
Navratilova
Neanderthal
nearsighted
necessarily
necessitate
necessitous
neckerchief
necromancer
necromantic
necrophilia
necrophobia
necrotising
necrotizing
needlepoint
needlewoman
needlewomen
negotiation
neighbourly
neocolonial
neonatology
nervousness
Netherlands
netherworld
neuroleptic
neurologist
neuroticism
newbuilding
nickelodeon

Nietzschean
nightingale
nightmarish
nitrogenous
nocturnally
nomadically
nonchalance
nondescript
nonetheless
nonsensical
Northampton
Northcliffe
Northumbria
northwardly
Nostradamus
nothingness
noticeboard
notoriously
nourishment
Novosibirsk
numerically
numismatics
numismatist
nutritional
nymphomania

# O

obfuscation
obfuscatory
objectively
objectivity
objurgation
obliqueness
obliviously
obnoxiously
obscuration
observation
observatory
obsessional
obsessively
obsolescent
obstinately
obstruction
obstructive

obtrusively
obviousness
odoriferous
oenological
oesophageal
offensively
officialdom
officialese
officiation
officiously
oligopolist
ominousness
omnipotence
omnipresent
omniscience
oncological
ontological
opalescence
operational
operatively
opinionated
Oppenheimer
opportunely
opportunism
opportunist
opportunity
opprobrious
optionality
optometrist
orchestrate
orderliness
organically
orientalism
orientalist
orientation
originality
origination
ornithology
ornithopter
orthodontic
orthography
orthopaedic
oscillation
oscillatory
ostentation

osteologist
osteopathic
Ouagadougou
outbuilding
outdistance
outstanding
overachieve
overbalance
overbearing
overdevelop
overgarment
overindulge
overnighter
overpayment
overproduce
overstaffed
overstretch
overweening
overwritten
overwrought
overzealous
Oxfordshire
oxidisation
oxidization
oxygenation

# P

pacifically
paediatrics
paedophilia
painfulness
painkilling
painstaking
Palestinian
palindromic
palpitation
pamphleteer
pandemonium
Panglossian
pantalettes
Pantelleria
pantheistic
paperweight
papillomata

paracetamol
parachutist
paradoxical
paragliding
parallactic
parallelism
Paralympics
paramedical
paramountcy
parascender
parasitical
parathyroid
paratrooper
paratyphoid
parenthesis
parenthetic
parishioner
parlourmaid
participant
participate
participial
particulate
partnership
parturition
passionless
passiveness
pastoralism
patchworked
paternalism
paternalist
paternoster
pathologist
patriarchal
peacekeeper
peacemaking
pearlescent
peculiarity
pedunculate
peevishness
pelargonium
Peloponnese
penetration
penetrative
penitential
penological

| | | | |
|---|---|---|---|
| pensionable | persuadable | plasticizer | precipitant |
| pensiveness | pertinacity | playfulness | precipitate |
| pentathlete | pertinently | pleasurable | precipitous |
| Pentecostal | pervasively | pleasurably | preciseness |
| penultimate | pessimistic | Pleistocene | predecessor |
| penuriously | pestiferous | plentifully | predicament |
| perambulate | petrodollar | ploughshare | predication |
| perceivable | petrography | pluralistic | predicative |
| perceptible | petrologist | plutocratic | predictable |
| perceptibly | Pharisaical | pneumococci | predictably |
| percipience | pharyngitis | pocketknife | predominant |
| percolation | philanderer | pointillism | predominate |
| peregrinate | philatelist | pointillist | preeminence |
| perennially | Philippians | pointlessly | preexistent |
| perestroika | Philippines | poisonously | prefectural |
| perfectible | philodendra | policewoman | prehistoric |
| perforation | philologist | policewomen | prejudicial |
| performable | philosopher | politically | preliminary |
| performance | philosophic | pollination | preliterate |
| perfunctory | phosphorous | poltergeist | prematurely |
| pericardial | photocopier | polyandrous | prematurity |
| pericardium | photography | polymorphic | premeditate |
| perinatally | photometric | polypeptide | premiership |
| periodicity | phototropic | polystyrene | premonition |
| peripatetic | phraseology | polytechnic | premonitory |
| periphrasis | phylloxerae | pomegranate | preparation |
| perishingly | physicality | ponderously | preparative |
| peristalsis | physiognomy | Pondicherry | preparatory |
| peristaltic | pictorially | pontificate | preposition |
| peritonitis | picturesque | populariser | preprandial |
| permanently | pipistrelle | popularizer | prepubertal |
| permissible | piscatorial | pornography | prerogative |
| permutation | piscivorous | portability | presbyteral |
| perpetrator | pitchblende | portmanteau | presciently |
| perpetually | piteousness | portraitist | presentable |
| perpetuator | pitifulness | portraiture | preservable |
| persecution | plagiariser | possibility | prestigious |
| persistence | plagiarizer | postulation | Prestonpans |
| personalise | plaintively | potentially | prestressed |
| personality | planetarium | powerlessly | presumption |
| personalize | planetology | practicable | presumptive |
| personation | Plantagenet | practicably | pretentious |
| perspective | plasterwork | practically | prevaricate |
| perspicuity | plastically | prayerfully | preventable |
| perspicuous | plasticiser | Precambrian | primatology |

primitively
primitivism
primitivist
principally
printmaking
proactively
probability
probationer
problematic
proceedings
procreation
procreative
Procrustean
procurement
prodigality
profanation
professedly
proficiency
profiterole
progestogen
prognathous
progression
progressive
Prohibition
prohibitive
prohibitory
prolegomena
proletarian
proletariat
proliferate
prominently
promiscuity
promiscuous
promisingly
promotional
promulgator
proofreader
propagation
prophetical
prophylaxis
propinquity
proposition
proprietary
prorogation
prosaically

prosecution
proselytise
proselytism
proselytize
prospective
prosthetics
prosthetist
prostration
protagonist
protectress
protraction
protuberant
providently
provisional
provocation
provocative
psittacosis
psychedelia
psychedelic
psychiatric
psychically
psychodrama
psychopathy
pterodactyl
publication
publishable
pulchritude
punctilious
punctuality
punctuation
purchasable
purgatorial
puritanical
purportedly
purposeless
purposively
pyroclastic
pyrotechnic
Pythagorean

**Q**

quadraphony
quadrennial
quadrillion

quadrupedal
qualitative
quarrelsome
quarterback
quarterdeck
querulously
quicksilver
quiescently
quincuncial
quinquereme
quintillion
quizzically
quotability

**R**

Rabelaisian
Rachmaninov
radioactive
radiocarbon
radiography
radiologist
radiometric
radiophonic
Radnorshire
raggamuffin
rallentandi
rallentando
Ramakrishna
rangefinder
rapaciously
rapscallion
rapturously
Rastafarian
ratatouille
ratiocinate
rationalise
rationalism
rationalist
rationality
rationalize
rattlesnake
raucousness
raunchiness
ravishingly

razzamatazz
reactionary
realignment
realisation
realization
realpolitik
reanimation
reappraisal
reassertion
reassurance
rebarbative
recalculate
recantation
receptivity
recessional
reciprocate
reciprocity
recirculate
reclamation
recognition
recombinant
recondition
reconfigure
reconnoitre
reconstruct
recoverable
recruitment
rectangular
rectifiable
rectilinear
recurrently
redeveloper
redirection
rediscovery
redoubtable
redoubtably
reductively
redundantly
reduplicate
referential
reflectance
reflexively
reflexivity
reflexology
reformation

reformatory
reformulate
refreshment
refrigerant
refrigerate
refulgently
regenerator
regionalise
regionalism
regionalist
regionalize
registrable
regretfully
regrettable
regrettably
regroupment
regurgitate
rehydration
reification
reincarnate
reinfection
reinsurance
reintegrate
reinterpret
reintroduce
reinvention
reiteration
rejuvenator
relatedness
reliability
religiosity
religiously
reluctantly
remediation
remembrance
reminiscent
remonstrate
remorseless
Renaissance
renegotiate
reorganiser
reorganizer
reorientate
repellently
repetitious

replaceable
replacement
replenisher
replication
repossessor
repressible
reproachful
reprobation
repudiation
repulsively
requirement
requisition
rescindable
reselection
resemblance
resentfully
reservation
residential
resignation
resiliently
resistivity
resourceful
respectable
respectably
respiration
respiratory
resplendent
responsible
responsibly
restitution
restitutive
restiveness
restoration
restorative
restriction
restrictive
restructure
resuscitate
retaliation
retaliative
retaliatory
retardation
retentively
retentivity
reticulated

retinopathy
retractable
retribution
retributive
retributory
retrievable
retroactive
retrorocket
revaluation
revealingly
Revelations
reverberant
reverberate
reverential
revisionary
revisionism
revisionist
rewardingly
rheological
rhetorician
rheumaticky
rhinoplasty
rhombohedra
rhythmicity
ricketiness
Riefenstahl
righteously
Rijksmuseum
riotousness
ritualistic
roadholding
Robespierre
robotically
Rockefeller
Rockhampton
Roddenberry
rodenticide
rodomontade
roguishness
rollerblade
romanticise
romanticism
romanticist
romanticize
Rosicrucian

rudimentary
rumbustious
rustication

## S

Saarbrücken
sabbatarian
sacramental
sacrificial
sagaciously
Sagittarian
Sagittarius
sailboarder
saintliness
saintpaulia
salaciously
saleability
salespeople
salesperson
salmonellae
Salvadorean
salvageable
sandblaster
sandboarder
saprophytic
sarcophagus
sardonicism
sartorially
satirically
saturnalian
saxophonist
scaffolding
scalability
Scandinavia
Scarborough
scaremonger
scattershot
scholarship
schoolchild
schoolhouse
schottische
Schrödinger
Schwarzkopf
Scientology

| | | | |
|---|---|---|---|
| scintillant | sexological | socialistic | sportswomen |
| scintillate | Seychellois | sociologist | spreadeagle |
| scleroderma | shadowiness | sociopathic | spreadsheet |
| scoundrelly | Shaftesbury | soliloquise | springboard |
| scrappiness | Shakespeare | soliloquize | Springfield |
| screamingly | shallowness | solipsistic | springiness |
| screwdriver | shamanistic | solmisation | Springsteen |
| scruffiness | shamelessly | solmization | squeamishly |
| scrumptious | shapelessly | somnolently | squirearchy |
| searchlight | shapeliness | sonographic | stagflation |
| seasickness | shareholder | soothsaying | stakeholder |
| seasonality | shenanigans | sophistical | stallholder |
| secondarily | shepherdess | sorrowfully | standardise |
| secretarial | shipbuilder | soulfulness | standardize |
| secretariat | shirtsleeve | Southampton | starchiness |
| secretively | shoplifting | sovereignty | startlingly |
| sedimentary | shortcoming | spacewalker | stateliness |
| seductively | showerproof | Spanishness | stateswoman |
| segregation | showjumping | sparrowhawk | stateswomen |
| seigneurial | showmanship | spastically | statistical |
| seismically | shuttlecock | specialness | statutorily |
| seismograph | sickeningly | specifiable | steadfastly |
| seismometer | sightseeing | specificity | steamroller |
| selectively | significant | spectacular | steeplejack |
| selectivity | signwriting | speculation | stegosaurus |
| selfishness | silveriness | speculative | stepbrother |
| semiologist | silversmith | speechifier | stephanotis |
| semiotician | Silverstone | speedometer | stereoscope |
| sempiternal | Singaporean | spellbinder | stethoscope |
| senatorship | singularity | spendthrift | stewardship |
| Sennacherib | situational | spermatozoa | stickleback |
| sensational | skeletonise | spermicidal | stiltedness |
| senselessly | skeletonize | spherically | stimulation |
| sensibility | sketchiness | spinelessly | stimulatory |
| sensitively | skilfulness | spinsterish | stipendiary |
| sensitivity | skulduggery | spiritually | stipulation |
| sententious | slaughterer | Spitsbergen | stockbroker |
| sentimental | sleepwalker | spokeswoman | Stockhausen |
| septicaemia | slenderness | spokeswomen | stockholder |
| sequestrate | smallholder | spondulicks | stockinette |
| serendipity | smithereens | spondylitis | stocktaking |
| seriousness | smokescreen | sponsorship | stoneground |
| serological | smorgasbord | spontaneity | stonewashed |
| serviceable | snowboarder | spontaneous | storyteller |
| seventeenth | sociability | sportswoman | strangeness |

strangulate
Strathclyde
streakiness
strenuously
stringently
stroboscope
studentship
stylishness
stylisation
stylization
subassembly
Sub-Atlantic
subcategory
subcontract
subcultural
subdivision
subjugation
subjunctive
sublimation
submergence
submersible
subordinate
subservient
subsistence
substandard
substantial
substantive
subtraction
subtractive
subtropical
suburbanise
suburbanite
suburbanize
succulently
Sudetenland
sufficiency
suffocation
suffragette
suggestible
suitability
sumptuously
supercharge
superficial
superfluity
superfluous

superimpose
superintend
superiority
superlative
supermarket
superscript
supertanker
supervision
supervisory
supportable
supposition
suppository
suppressant
suppression
suppressive
suppuration
suppurative
supremacism
supremacist
surpassable
survivalism
survivalist
susceptible
susceptibly
suspenseful
Susquehanna
sustainable
sustainably
sustainment
susurration
swallowtail
swarthiness
swashbuckle
switchblade
switchboard
Switzerland
sycophantic
syllogistic
symmetrical
sympathetic
sympathiser
sympathizer
symptomatic
synchromesh
synchronise

synchronism
synchronize
synchronous
syncopation
syndicalism
syndicalist
syndication
syntactical
synthesiser
synthesizer
systematise
systematist
systematize

# T

tachycardia
taciturnity
tactfulness
tagliatelle
Tailleferre
talkatively
Tallahassee
Tamburlaine
tangibility
tarnishable
tastelessly
tautologous
taxidermist
Tchaikovsky
tearfulness
technically
Technicolor
technocracy
technophile
technophobe
technospeak
tediousness
teetotalism
teetotaller
Tegucigalpa
telecommute
telegrapher
telegraphic
telekinesis

telekinetic
telemessage
telephonist
teleprinter
temperament
temperature
tempestuous
temporarily
tenaciously
tendentious
tentatively
tenuousness
teratogenic
termination
terminology
Terpsichore
terrestrial
Territorial
testimonial
tetrahedral
tetrahedron
thalidomide
thanatology
Thatcherism
Thatcherite
thenceforth
Theodorakis
theological
theoretical
theosophist
therapeutic
thereabouts
thermogenic
thermometer
Thermopylae
thickheaded
thingamabob
thingamajig
thirstiness
thistledown
thoughtless
threatening
throatiness
thunderbolt
thunderclap

thunderhead
timekeeping
titanically
titillation
toastmaster
tobacconist
tomographic
tonsillitis
topographer
topographic
topological
totalisator
totalizator
townspeople
tracheotomy
traditional
tragicomedy
trailblazer
traineeship
transaction
transceiver
transcriber
transdermal
transection
transferral
transfigure
transformer
transfusion
transgender
transgenics
transhumant
transiently
Transjordan
translation
translocate
translucent
transmittal
transmitter
transparent
transponder
transporter
transsexual
transuranic
trapezoidal
traversable

treacherous
treasonable
treecreeper
tremulously
trenchantly
trencherman
trenchermen
trendsetter
trepanation
trepidation
triangulate
tribeswoman
tribeswomen
tribulation
triceratops
triennially
Trincomalee
Trinidadian
Trinitarian
trituration
triumvirate
troglodytic
troposphere
troubleshot
troublesome
truculently
trusteeship
trustworthy
tuberculous
tunefulness
turbocharge
turbulently
Tutankhamen
Tutankhamun
twelvemonth
twopenn'orth
typesetting
typewriting
typewritten
typographer
typographic
typological
tyrannicide

# U

Ulaanbaatar
Ulsterwoman
Ulsterwomen
ultramarine
ultrasonics
ultraviolet
umbilically
unabashedly
unaccounted
unadvisedly
unaesthetic
unalterable
unalterably
unambiguous
unambitious
unanimously
unannounced
unappealing
unashamedly
unassertive
unavailable
unavoidable
unavoidably
unawareness
unbeknownst
unbelieving
unblemished
unbreakable
uncastrated
unceasingly
uncertainly
uncertainty
unchristian
uncivilised
uncivilized
unclimbable
uncluttered
unconcealed
unconcerned
unconfident
unconfirmed
uncongenial
unconnected

unconscious
uncontested
uncontrived
unconvinced
uncountable
undecidedly
undefinable
undemanding
undercharge
underexpose
underground
undergrowth
underhanded
undersigned
understated
understorey
undertaking
underweight
underwriter
undescended
undeserving
undesirable
undesirably
undeveloped
undeviating
undiagnosed
undignified
undisclosed
undisguised
undisturbed
undoubtedly
undrinkable
unemotional
unendurable
unequivocal
unessential
unethically
unexplained
unexpressed
unfailingly
unfaltering
unfermented
unflappable
unflinching
unforgiving

unfortunate
unfulfilled
unfurnished
ungodliness
unhappiness
unhealthily
unhelpfully
unhurriedly
unicellular
unidiomatic
unification
unimportant
unimpressed
uninhabited
uninhibited
uninitiated
uninspiring
uninstaller
uninsurable
universally
unjustified
unknowingly
unmitigated
unmoderated
unmotivated
unnaturally
unnavigable
unnecessary
unobtrusive
unorganised
unorganized
unorthodoxy
unpalatable
unpatriotic
unperturbed
unplumbable
unpopulated
unpractised
unprintable
unprocessed
unpromising
unprotected
unpublished
unqualified
unreachable

unrealistic
unreasoning
unreceptive
unregulated
unrehearsed
unrelenting
unremitting
unrepentant
unrewarding
unsatisfied
unsaturated
unscheduled
unselfishly
unshakeable
unshockable
unskilfully
unsmilingly
unsolicited
unsparingly
unspeakable
unspeakably
unspecified
unstoppable
unstoppably
unsupported
unsurpassed
unsuspected
unsweetened
untarnished
Untermensch
unthinkable
unthinkably
untouchable
untraceable
untreatable
untypically
unusualness
unutterable
unutterably
unvarnished
unvaryingly
unwarranted
unwatchable
unwelcoming
unwholesome

unwillingly
unwittingly
upgradeable
upholsterer
uprightness
uselessness
utilitarian
utilisation
utilization
Uttaranchal

**V**

vacationist
vaccination
vacillation
vacuousness
valediction
valedictory
vanishingly
variability
variational
variegation
variousness
Vendemiaire
ventilation
ventilatory
ventricular
ventriloquy
venturesome
Vereeniging
vermiculite
versatility
verticality
vertiginous
vestigially
vibrational
vicariously
vichyssoise
viciousness
vicissitude
victimology
videography
vigilantism
vinaigrette

vindication
viniculture
violoncello
viridescent
virological
viscountess
viticulture
vivaciously
vivisection
Vladikavkaz
Vladivostok
volcanology
voluntarily
voluntarism
voluntarist
voraciously
voyeuristic
vulcanology

**W**

wainscoting
wakeboarder
wakefulness
warrantable
washerwoman
washerwomen
waspishness
watchmaking
watercolour
watercourse
waterlogged
waywardness
weathercock
weathervane
weighbridge
weightiness
Weissmuller
Wensleydale
westerniser
westernizer
westernmost
Westminster .
Westmorland
wheelbarrow

wheelwright
whereabouts
wheresoever
wherewithal
whimsically
Whitsuntide
Whittington
wholesomely
widdershins
Wilberforce
willingness
Winckelmann

windcheater
windsurfing
winsomeness
wintergreen
wiretapping
wisecracker
wistfulness
witheringly
witlessness
womanliness
wonderfully
woodcarving

woodturning
woodworking
workability
workaholism
workmanlike
workmanship
workstation
worldliness
worthlessly

# X-Z

xerographic
yachtswoman
yachtswomen
Yellowknife
Yevtushenko
Yugoslavian
Zarathustra
zealousness
zillionaire
Zoroastrian

# **12** LETTERS

## A

abbreviation
abolitionism
abolitionist
abrasiveness
abstemiously
abstractedly
academically
acceleration
accentuation
accidentally
accomplished
accordionist
accoutrement
accumulation
accumulative
acoustically
acquaintance
acquiescence
adaptability
additionally
adhesiveness
adjudication
administrate
admonishment
adulteration
advantageous
adventitious

advisability
aerodynamics
aeronautical
aestheticism
aetiological
affectionate
Afrikanerdom
afterthought
aggressively
agribusiness
agricultural
agrochemical
alliteration
alliterative
allusiveness
alphabetical
alphanumeric
amalgamation
ambidextrous
ambivalently
amelioration
amortisation
amortization
amphitheatre
anaesthetise
anaesthetist
anaesthetize
analytically
anathematise

anathematize
anatomically
Anglocentric
animatronics
annihilation
announcement
Annunciation
antagonistic
Antananarivo
antediluvian
anthropology
anticipation
anticipatory
anticyclonic
antimacassar
antimalarial
antiparticle
antipathetic
antisocially
antithetical
Anuradhapura
apostrophise
apostrophize
apparatchiki
appendectomy
appendicitis
appreciation
appreciative
apprehension

apprehensive
approachable
appropriator
appurtenance
arachnophobe
archaeologic
archetypical
architecture
Ardnamurchan
aristocratic
Aristophanes
Aristotelian
arithmetical
aromatherapy
aromatically
articulately
articulation
artificially
artistically
Ashurbanipal
asphyxiation
aspirational
asseveration
assimilation
astonishment
astringently
astrobiology
astrological
astronautics

astronomical
astrophysics
asymmetrical
asymptomatic
asynchronous
athletically
atmospherics
Attenborough
attitudinise
attitudinize
attractively
attributable
audiological
augmentation
auscultation
auspiciously
Australasian
authenticate
authenticity
automaticity
autonomously
availability
aviculturist

**B**

bacchanalian
bachelorette
bachelorhood
backslapping
backwardness
backwoodsman
backwoodsmen
bacteriology
Bandaranaike
bantamweight
barbarically
barnstorming
Barranquilla
battleground
battlemented
beatifically
Beaumarchais
Bedfordshire
befuddlement

behaviourism
behaviourist
belligerence
belligerency
benefactress
beneficially
benevolently
Berwickshire
bespectacled
bewilderment
Bhagavadgita
bibliography
bicentennial
bilingualism
Billingsgate
biochemistry
biodiversity
bioflavonoid
biographical
biologically
biosynthesis
biosynthetic
bioterrorism
bioterrorist
birdwatching
blabbermouth
blackcurrant
bladderwrack
blandishment
blisteringly
blockbusting
Bloemfontein
bloodletting
bloodsucking
bloodthirsty
bluestocking
boardsailing
boastfulness
bobsleighing
bodyboarding
bodysnatcher
boisterously
bootylicious
Bougainville
boulevardier

brachiosauri
breakthrough
breaststroke
breathalyser
breathlessly
breathtaking
brilliantine
brinkmanship
brontosaurus
Brunelleschi
buccaneering
Buenaventura
bullfighting
bureaucratic
businesslike
butterscotch

**C**

cabinetmaker
calamitously
calculatedly
calligrapher
calligraphic
calorimetric
camiknickers
canalisation
canalization
cancellation
canonisation
canonization
cantankerous
capercaillie
capitalistic
capitulation
capriciously
Capricornian
caravanserai
carbohydrate
carbonaceous
carcinogenic
cardiography
cardiologist
carelessness
caricaturist

carpetbagger
Cartesianism
Carthaginian
cartographer
cartographic
castellation
catastrophic
cautiousness
ceremonially
championship
characterful
characterise
characterize
charlatanism
chastisement
chauvinistic
cheerfulness
cheeseburger
chemotherapy
chequerboard
cherubically
chesterfield
Chhattisgarh
childishness
chiropractic
chiropractor
chivalrously
chlorination
choreography
Christchurch
Christianity
Christianise
Christianize
chromatogram
chronologist
churchwarden
churlishness
circumcision
circumscribe
circumstance
cirrocumulus
cirrostratus
Citlaltépetl
civilisation
civilization

clairvoyance
clannishness
clapperboard
clarinettist
classifiable
climatically
clubbability
cluelessness
Clytemnestra
coachbuilder
coalitionist
cockfighting
codependence
codependency
codification
coelenterate
cohabitation
cohesiveness
coincidental
collaborator
collaterally
collectively
collectivise
collectivism
collectivist
collectivity
collectivize
colloquially
collywobbles
colonisation
colonization
commandingly
commencement
commendation
commensurate
commercially
commissariat
commissioner
commonwealth
communicable
communicator
companionway
compellingly
compensation
compensatory

complacently
complaisance
completeness
complication
compressible
compromising
compulsively
compulsorily
concentrator
conceptually
conciliation
conciliatory
conclusively
concreteness
concupiscent
concurrently
condemnation
condemnatory
condensation
conductivity
confectioner
confessional
confidential
configurable
confirmation
confirmatory
confiscation
conformation
confoundedly
Confucianism
Confucianist
congeniality
congenitally
conglomerate
congratulate
congregation
connectivity
conquistador
conscription
consecration
consequently
conservation
conservatism
Conservative
conservatory

considerable
considerably
consistently
consolidator
conspiracist
constabulary
constipation
constituency
constitution
constitutive
constriction
construction
constructive
consultation
consultative
consummately
consummation
containerise
containerize
contemporary
contemptible
contemptibly
contemptuous
contextually
continuation
continuously
contractible
contrapuntal
contrariness
contrariwise
contribution
contributive
contributory
controllable
controllably
contumacious
convalescent
conveniently
conventional
conversation
conveyancing
convincingly
conviviality
convulsively
coordination

coquettishly
corespondent
corporeality
correctional
cosmetically
cosmographer
cosmological
cosmopolitan
costermonger
counterblast
counterclaim
counterpoint
counterpoise
countrywoman
countrywomen
courageously
covetousness
cowardliness
crackbrained
creativeness
creditworthy
crenellation
cryptography
cryptologist
cultivatable
cumulatively
cumulonimbus
curmudgeonly
customisable
customizable
Czechoslovak

# D

daguerrotype
deactivation
debilitation
decapitation
deceleration
decentralise
decentralize
decipherable
decipherment
decisiveness
decommission

decompressor
decongestant
deconsecrate
decoratively
decorousness
deescalation
defenestrate
defibrillate
definiteness
definitional
definitively
deflationary
degeneration
degenerative
dehumidifier
deliberately
deliberation
deliberative
delicatessen
delightfully
delimitation
deliquescent
demilitarise
demilitarize
demodulation
demonisation
demonization
demonstrable
demonstrably
demonstrator
demoralising
demoralizing
demotivation
denaturation
Denbighshire
denomination
denouncement
denunciation
denunciatory
departmental
depoliticise
depoliticize
depopulation
depreciation
depressingly

depressurise
depressurize
deracination
deregulation
deregulatory
derivational
derogatorily
desalination
desirability
despoliation
despondently
dessertspoon
destructible
determinable
determinedly
dethronement
detumescence
devilishness
diabolically
diagrammatic
diatomaceous
dictatorship
didactically
differential
digitisation
digitization
dilapidation
dilatoriness
dilettantish
dilettantism
directorship
disaccharide
disadvantage
disaffection
disagreeable
disagreeably
disagreement
disallowance
disambiguate
disappointed
disassociate
disastrously
disbursement
discipleship
disciplinary

discomfiture
discomposure
disconnected
disconsolate
discontented
discourteous
discoverable
discreteness
discriminate
discursively
disdainfully
disestablish
disgustingly
dishevelment
disincentive
disinfectant
disinfection
disingenuous
disintegrate
dislodgement
dismissively
disobedience
disorganised
disorganized
disorientate
dispensation
dispiritedly
displacement
disputatious
disquisition
disreputable
dissatisfied
disseminator
dissertation
dissociation
dissociative
distillation
distinctness
distributary
distribution
distributive
diversionary
diverticulum
divertimenti
divertimento

divisibility
divisiveness
dodecahedron
dogmatically
dolphinarium
domestically
doppelgänger
downloadable
dramatically
draughtboard
dunderheaded
dynastically

# E

eavesdropper
eccentricity
Ecclesiastes
ecclesiastic
ecclesiology
echolocation
eclectically
ecologically
econometrics
economically
ecstatically
ecumenically
editorialise
editorialist
editorialize
educationist
effeminately
effervescent
efflorescent
effortlessly
effusiveness
Egyptologist
eisteddfodau
Ekaterinburg
electability
electrically
electrolysis
electrolytic
electroplate
electroscope

electroshock
elementarily
elliptically
elocutionist
emancipation
emancipatory
emasculation
embarrassing
embezzlement
embryologist
emotionalise
emotionalism
emotionalize
emphatically
emulsifiable
encephalitic
encephalitis
enchantingly
encipherment
encirclement
encroachment
encrustation
encyclopedia
encyclopedic
endangerment
endogenously
endoskeleton
enfeeblement
Englishwoman
Englishwomen
enjoyability
enormousness
enshrinement
entanglement
enterprising
entertaining
enthronement
enthusiastic
entomologist
entrancement
entrenchment
entrepreneur
ephemerality
Epicureanism
epidemiology

epigrammatic
episcopalian
episodically
epistemology
equalisation
equalization
equatorially
equidistance
equivalently
equivocation
escapologist
esoterically
estrangement
ethnocentric
ethnographer
ethnographic
ethnological
etymological
euphoniously
euphorically
Eurocentrism
evangelistic
evisceration
evolutionary
evolutionism
evolutionist
exacerbation
exaggeration
exasperation
exchangeable
excitability
exclusionary
excruciating
excursionist
exhaustively
exhilaration
exobiologist
exorbitantly
expansionary
expansionism
expansionist
expatriation
experiential
experimental
experimenter

explicitness
exploitation
exploitative
expositional
expressively
expressivity
expropriator
exserviceman
exservicemen
exterminator
extinguisher
extortionate
extortionist
extramarital
extramurally
extraneously
extravagance
extravaganza
extroversion

## F

fabulousness
facilitation
facilitative
factionalism
faithfulness
fancifulness
fastidiously
fatherliness
fearlessness
fecklessness
felicitously
feminisation
feminization
fenestration
Ferlinghetti
fermentation
fermentative
feverishness
fibrillation
fictionalise
fictionality
fictionalize
figuratively

finalisation
finalization
flagellation
flamboyantly
flammability
floriculture
fluorescence
fluoridation
fluorination
fluoroscopic
followership
forbiddingly
forcefulness
forensically
formaldehyde
forthrightly
fortuitously
foundational
fountainhead
fractionally
Frankenstein
frankincense
fraudulently
frenetically
frictionless
friendliness
frontbencher
frontiersman
frontiersmen
frontispiece
fruitfulness
functionally
futurologist

## G

Gainsborough
galactically
galvanically
galvanometer
gamesmanship
gasification
genealogical
generational
genuflection

geographical
geologically
geometrician
geophysicist
geopolitical
geostrategic
geriatrician
gerontocracy
ghostwritten
ghoulishness
gigantically
gladiatorial
globetrotter
glockenspiel
gloriousness
gobbledegook
gobbledygook
Gondwanaland
gorgeousness
governmental
governorship
gracefulness
graciousness
graphologist
gratuitously
greengrocery
gregariously
grotesquerie
gruesomeness
Guadalquivir
guardianship

# H

haberdashery
habitability
haemophiliac
hagiographer
hagiographic
hairdressing
hallucinogen
Hammarskjöld
handkerchief
handsomeness
happenstance

hardstanding
harlequinade
harmlessness
harmonically
harmoniously
headmistress
headquarters
headshrinker
heartbreaker
heedlessness
heliocentric
Heliogabalus
heliographic
heliospheric
helplessness
henceforward
heraldically
hereditarily
heritability
hermeneutics
hermetically
heterosexism
heterosexist
heterosexual
hierarchical
hieroglyphic
hierophantic
Hillsborough
hindquarters
hippopotamus
histological
historically
Hofmannsthal
Hohenzollern
holidaymaker
homelessness
homesteading
homoeostasis
homologation
homosexually
hopelessness
horizontally
horrendously
horrifically
horsemanship

horticulture
housebreaker
housekeeping
Huddersfield
humanitarian
humanisation
humanization
humorousness
hydrocephaly
hydrodynamic
hydrographer
hydrographic
hydrological
hydrostatics
hydrotherapy
hydrothermal
hygienically
hypertension
hypertensive
hyperthermia
hyperthyroid
hypertrophic
hypnotherapy
hypnotically
hypochondria
hypocritical
hypothalamic
hypothalamus
hypothetical
hysterectomy
hysterically

# I

ichthyosauri
iconoclastic
iconographer
iconographic
idealisation
idealization
identifiable
identifiably
idiosyncrasy
illegibility
illegitimacy

illegitimate
illogicality
illumination
illustration
illustrative
immaculately
immeasurable
immeasurably
immemorially
immoderately
immunisation
immunization
immunologist
immutability
impartiality
impenetrable
impenetrably
impenitently
imperatively
imperfection
imperishable
imperishably
impermanence
impersonally
impersonator
impertinence
imperviously
implantation
implicitness
impoliteness
imponderable
impregnation
impressively
imprisonment
improvidence
inaccessible
inaccessibly
inaccurately
inactivation
inadequately
inadmissible
inadvertence
inapplicable
inarticulacy
inarticulate

| | | | |
|---|---|---|---|
| inaudibility | Indianapolis | insolubility | intervention |
| inauguration | indifference | insouciantly | intimidation |
| inauspicious | indigestible | inspectorate | intimidatory |
| incalculable | indigestibly | inspectorial | intolerantly |
| incalculably | indirectness | installation | intonational |
| incandescent | indiscipline | instillation | intoxication |
| incapability | indiscreetly | instructress | intransigent |
| incapacitant | indiscretion | instrumental | intransitive |
| incapacitate | indisputable | insufferable | intrauterine |
| incautiously | indisputably | insufferably | introduction |
| incendiarism | indissoluble | insufficient | introductory |
| incestuously | indistinctly | insurrection | introversion |
| incidentally | individually | intellectual | invalidation |
| incineration | indoctrinate | intelligence | Invercargill |
| incisiveness | industrially | intelligible | invertebrate |
| inclusionary | ineffability | intelligibly | investigator |
| incoherently | inefficiency | intemperance | inveterately |
| incommodious | inelasticity | interception | invigilation |
| incomparable | ineradicable | intercession | invigoration |
| incomparably | ineradicably | intercessory | invisibility |
| incompatible | inexactitude | interconnect | invulnerable |
| incompetence | inexperience | interdiction | invulnerably |
| incompetency | inexplicable | interestedly | irascibility |
| incompletely | inexplicably | interference | iridescently |
| incompletion | inexpressive | interglacial | irrationally |
| inconclusive | inextricable | interjection | irredeemable |
| incongruence | inextricably | interlinkage | irredeemably |
| inconsequent | infectiously | interlocutor | irregardless |
| inconsistent | infelicitous | intermediacy | irregularity |
| inconsolable | infiltration | intermediary | irrelevantly |
| inconsolably | inflammation | intermediate | irremediable |
| incontinence | inflammatory | interminable | irremediably |
| inconvenient | inflationary | interminably | irresistible |
| incorporator | inflectional | intermission | irresistibly |
| incorrigible | infotainment | intermittent | irresolutely |
| incorrigibly | infrequently | intermixable | irresolution |
| increasingly | infringement | intermixture | irresolvable |
| indebtedness | ingratiating | interpolator | irrespective |
| indecisively | ingratiation | interrogator | irreverently |
| indefensible | inharmonious | interruption | irreversible |
| indefensibly | inhospitable | interruptive | irreversibly |
| indefinitely | inordinately | intersection | irritability |
| indelicately | insalubrious | interstellar | Islamophobia |
| independence | insecticidal | interstitial | Islamophobic |
| independency | insemination | intertextual | isolationism |

isolationist

## J

Jacksonville
Johannesburg
journalistic
jurisdiction

## K

kaleidoscope
Kanchenjunga
Keynesianism
Khachaturian
Kinchinjunga
kindergarten
kiteboarding
kleptomaniac
klipspringer
knowledgable
Krishnamurti
Kristiansand

## L

labyrinthine
Lamentations
languorously
laparoscopic
lasciviously
Latinisation
Latinization
laureateship
leatheriness
legalisation
legalization
legitimately
legitimation
Léopoldville
lepidopteran
lexicography
licentiously
Lichtenstein
lifelessness

Lilliburlero
Lincolnshire
liquefaction
Lisdoonvarna
listlessness
literalistic
literariness
lithographer
lithographic
lithological
lithospheric
liturgically
Liverpudlian
localisation
localization
lollapalooza
longitudinal
longshoreman
longshoremen
lopsidedness
Loughborough
lovesickness
lubriciously
Ludwigshafen
lugubriously
luminescence
lusciousness
lustrousness
Luxembourger
lycanthropic

## M

machicolated
Mademoiselle
magnetically
magnetometer
magnificence
magniloquent
maintainable
majestically
majoritarian
malevolently
malformation
malleability

malnourished
malnutrition
maltreatment
malversation
manipulation
manipulative
manoeuvrable
manslaughter
manufacturer
marksmanship
marlinespike
marriageable
Marseillaise
marvellously
masturbation
masturbatory
Matabeleland
mathematical
maximisation
maximization
meaningfully
mechanically
meditatively
megalomaniac
melodramatic
mendaciously
menstruation
merchandiser
merchantable
meretricious
meritocratic
mesmerically
Mesopotamian
metalanguage
metallically
metallurgist
metamorphism
metamorphose
metaphorical
metaphysical
methodically
meticulously
metropolitan
Michelangelo
microbiology

microbrewery
microcircuit
microclimate
microgravity
micropayment
microscooter
microsurgery
middleweight
Midwesterner
militaristic
millefeuille
mindlessness
mineralogist
minicomputer
minimisation
minimization
ministration
miraculously
misadventure
misalignment
misanthropic
misbehaviour
miscalculate
misdemeanour
misdiagnosis
misdirection
miserabilism
miserabilist
misinterpret
misjudgement
misogynistic
mispronounce
misquotation
misrepresent
misstatement
mistranslate
mistreatment
mitochondria
mobilisation
mobilization
modification
monastically
monetisation
monetization
monopolistic

monosyllabic
monosyllable
monotheistic
monotonously
Montparnasse
monumentally
morphologist
motherliness
motivational
motorcycling
motorcyclist
motorisation
motorization
mountainside
mournfulness
mucilaginous
mulligatawny
multifaceted
multifarious
multilateral
multilayered
multilingual
multimillion
multiplicand
multiplicity
municipality
munificently
Murrumbidgee
musicianship
musicologist
mysteriously
mythological

**N**

narcissistic
nasalisation
nasalization
naturalistic
naturopathic
navigability
navigational
necrophiliac
neoclassical
Netherlander

neurochemist
neurological
neurosurgeon
neurosurgery
neurotically
nevertheless
Newfoundland
nidification
nightclothes
nomenclature
nomenklatura
nonagenarian
nonchalantly
northernmost
notification
novelisation
novelization
numerologist
nutritionist
nutritiously
nymphomaniac

**O**

Oberammergau
obliteration
obscurantism
obscurantist
obsequiously
obsolescence
obstetrician
obstreperous
occasionally
occupational
oceanography
octogenarian
odontologist
omnipresence
omnisciently
omnivorously
onomatopoeia
onomatopoeic
operatically
oppositional
oppressively

optimisation
optimization
orchestrally
orchestrator
orchidaceous
ordinariness
organisation
organization
orienteering
ornamentally
orthodontics
orthodontist
orthographic
orthopaedics
oscilloscope
ossification
ostentatious
osteological
osteoporosis
osteospermum
outmanoeuvre
outplacement
outrageously
overachiever
overactivity
overcapacity
overcautious
overdramatic
overemphasis
overestimate
overexertion
overexposure
overfamiliar
overgenerous
overinflated
overpopulate
overreaction
oversimplify
overtrousers
overwhelming
oxyacetylene

**P**

pacification

paedophiliac
painlessness
palaeography
Palaeolithic
palatability
panchromatic
pancreatitis
pantechnicon
paradigmatic
paradisiacal
paramilitary
paranormally
parascending
parasitology
Parkinsonism
Parmigianino
parochialism
parsimonious
participator
particularly
partisanship
partitionist
passionately
pathetically
pathological
patriarchate
peacefulness
peacekeeping
pedantically
pedestrianly
Peeblesshire
pejoratively
penalisation
penalization
penitentiary
Pennsylvania
peradventure
perambulator
perceptively
perceptually
percipiently
peremptorily
perfidiously
perilousness
periodically

| | | | |
|---|---|---|---|
| peripherally | photographic | postmistress | preservation |
| periphrastic | photogravure | postponement | preservative |
| permaculture | photomontage | postpositive | presidential |
| permanganate | photorealism | postprandial | presumptuous |
| permeability | photorealist | potentiality | pretreatment |
| permissively | phototropism | powerboating | prevaricator |
| perniciously | photovoltaic | practicality | preventative |
| perpetration | phrenologist | practitioner | principality |
| perpetuation | physiologist | praiseworthy | prizefighter |
| perseverance | pictographic | praseodymium | probationary |
| persistently | pigmentation | precancerous | problematise |
| perspectival | pisciculture | precariously | problematize |
| perspicacity | pitilessness | precessional | procedurally |
| perspiration | plasterboard | preciousness | processional |
| persuasively | platonically | precipitator | proclamation |
| pertinacious | plausibility | precociously | proctologist |
| perturbation | pleasantness | precognition | prodigiously |
| perverseness | plebiscitary | precognitive | productively |
| pestilential | pneumococcal | preconceived | productivity |
| Peterborough | pneumococcus | precondition | professional |
| petrifaction | polarisation | predetermine | professorial |
| petrographer | polarization | predilection | proficiently |
| petrographic | policyholder | predominance | progesterone |
| petrological | polyethylene | preeclampsia | programmable |
| pettifoggery | polymorphism | preeclamptic | programmatic |
| pettifogging | polymorphous | preeminently | prolegomenon |
| pharmacology | polyrhythmic | preexistence | prolifically |
| Pheidippides | polysyllabic | prefabricate | prolongation |
| phenomenally | polytheistic | prefectorial | promulgation |
| Philadelphia | polyurethane | preferential | pronominally |
| philadelphus | pontifically | prehistorian | pronouncedly |
| philanthropy | Popocatépetl | prelapsarian | propagandise |
| philharmonic | pornographer | premenstrual | propagandist |
| philistinism | pornographic | preparedness | propagandize |
| philodendron | portentously | preponderant | prophylactic |
| philological | portmanteaux | preponderate | propitiation |
| philosophise | positionally | preposterous | propitiatory |
| philosophize | positiveness | prepubescent | propitiously |
| phlebotomist | positivistic | prerequisite | proportional |
| phonetically | possessively | presbyterial | proportioned |
| phonographic | postcoitally | Presbyterian | propulsively |
| phonological | postdoctoral | prescription | proscription |
| phosphoresce | postfeminist | prescriptive | proscriptive |
| photochromic | postgraduate | presentation | prosecutable |
| photographer | posthumously | presentiment | proselytiser |

proselytizer
prosperously
prostitution
protactinium
protectively
protectorate
protestation
protoplasmic
prototypical
protuberance
proverbially
providential
provincially
prudentially
psephologist
pseudonymity
pseudonymous
psychiatrist
psychoactive
psychobabble
psychologist
psychometric
psychopathic
psychosexual
psychosocial
psychotropic
pumpernickel
punitiveness
purification
purposefully
putrefaction
pyrotechnics

# Q

quadrangular
quadraphonic
quadriplegia
quadriplegic
quadrophonic
quantifiable
quantitative
quarterstaff
quattrocento
questionable

questionably
Quetzalcóatl
quinquennial
quintessence
quixotically
quizzicality

# R

racketeering
radiographer
radiographic
radioisotope
radiological
radionuclide
radiotherapy
rambunctious
ramification
ratification
rationaliser
rationalizer
Rauschenberg
reactivation
readjustment
reappearance
reassessment
reassignment
reattachment
rebelliously
recalcitrant
recapitulate
receivership
receptionist
recessionary
rechargeable
reciprocally
recklessness
recognisable
recognisance
recognizable
recognizance
recollection
recommission
reconcilable
reconnection

reconstitute
reconversion
recreational
recrudescent
recuperation
recuperative
redecoration
redefinition
redeployment
redistribute
reductionism
reductionist
reflationary
reflectively
reflectivity
refractively
refreshingly
refrigerator
regeneration
regenerative
regimentally
registration
regressively
rehabilitate
reimbursable
reinvestment
reinvigorate
rejuvenation
relationship
relentlessly
reminiscence
remonstrance
remorsefully
remuneration
remunerative
renegotiable
renewability
Renfrewshire
renounceable
renouncement
renunciation
reoccupation
reoccurrence
repatriation
repercussion

repetitively
repopulation
repossession
reprehension
repressively
reproachable
reproducible
reproduction
reproductive
reservedness
resettlement
resoluteness
respectfully
respectively
resplendence
responsively
restaurateur
restlessness
restrainable
resurrection
resuscitator
reticulation
retrenchment
revelational
reversionary
Rhadamanthus
rhetorically
rheumatology
rhododendron
rhombohedral
rhombohedron
rhythmically
ridiculously
rightfulness
rigorousness
Risorgimento
rollerblader
Romanisation
Romanization
romantically
rotationally
rubbernecker
ruthlessness

**S**

sacrilegious
sadistically
sailboarding
salesmanship
salinisation
salinization
salubriously
Salvationist
sanctionable
sandboarding
sanitaryware
Sardanapalus
sardonically
sarsaparilla
Saskatchewan
satisfaction
satisfactory
scandalously
Scandinavian
scatological
Scheherazade
Schiaparelli
schoolmaster
Schopenhauer
Scottishness
screenwriter
scriptwriter
scrupulosity
scrupulously
sectarianism
segmentation
seismologist
selflessness
Selkirkshire
semantically
semicircular
semiological
sensuousness
separability
separateness
sepulchrally
sequentially
sequestrator

seraphically
seronegative
seropositive
servicewoman
servicewomen
sexagenarian
shamefacedly
shamefulness
sharecropper
shareholding
sharpshooter
sheepishness
Shevardnadze
shipbuilding
shirtsleeved
shirtwaister
Shostakovich
shrewishness
significance
silviculture
simultaneity
simultaneous
situationism
situationist
skateboarder
skittishness
skullduggery
sledgehammer
slipperiness
slovenliness
sluggishness
smallholding
snappishness
sociobiology
sociological
solicitation
solicitously
solitariness
Solzhenitsyn
somnambulant
somnambulism
somnambulist
sophisticate
southernmost
spaciousness

specifically
speciousness
spectrograph
spectrometer
spectrometry
spectroscope
spectroscopy
speechlessly
speleologist
spellchecker
spermatozoon
spinsterhood
spiritedness
spiritlessly
spiritualise
spiritualism
spiritualist
spirituality
spiritualize
spitefulness
spokespeople
spokesperson
sporadically
sportspeople
sportsperson
spotlessness
spuriousness
stairclimber
stakeholding
Stakhanovite
Stanislavsky
statistician
stealthiness
steeplechase
Stellenbosch
stenographer
stepchildren
stepdaughter
stereophonic
stereoscopic
stertorously
stockbreeder
stockbroking
storytelling
Stradivarius

straightness
straitjacket
stranglehold
stratigraphy
stratocumuli
stratosphere
streetwalker
strengthener
streptococci
streptomycin
stridulation
stroboscopic
structurally
stubbornness
studiousness
stupefaction
stupendously
subcommittee
subconscious
subcontinent
subcutaneous
subjectively
subjectivity
subliminally
submissively
subnormality
subscription
subsequently
subservience
subsidiarity
substantiate
substitution
substructure
subterranean
subversively
successfully
successively
succinctness
sufficiently
suggestively
Sulaymaniyah
sulphonamide
superannuate
supercharger
supercilious

superhighway
superhumanly
supernatural
superstardom
superstition
supervenient
supervention
supplemental
supplication
supplicatory
supportively
surmountable
surprisingly
surrealistic
surroundings
surveillance
suspiciously
swashbuckler
syllabically
symbolically
synchroniser
synchronizer
syncretistic
synonymously
systemically

# T

tactlessness
Tadzhikistan
tangentially
taramasalata
tastefulness
tautological
technicality
technicolour
technobabble
technocratic
technologist
technophilia
technophilic
technophobia
technophobic
tectonically
telecommuter

telegraphist
telemarketer
telemedicine
teleological
telepresence
teleprompter
televisually
tercentenary
tergiversate
terrifically
tessellation
testamentary
testosterone
thankfulness
thanksgiving
theatrically
thematically
theoretician
theorisation
theorization
theosophical
therapeutics
thermocouple
thermography
thermosphere
thermostatic
Thessaloníki
thoroughbred
thoroughfare
thoroughness
thoughtfully
thousandfold
thundercloud
thunderously
thunderstorm
timelessness
timorousness
tirelessness
tiresomeness
togetherness
tolerability
torrentially
tortuousness
totalitarian
toxicologist

toxocariasis
tracheostomy
tractability
tradescantia
trailblazing
trainspotter
tranquillise
tranquillity
tranquillize
transcendent
transduction
transferable
transference
transgressor
transhumance
transitional
transitively
transitivity
transitorily
translatable
translucence
translucency
transmission
transmogrify
transoceanic
transparency
transposable
transversely
transvestism
transvestite
Transylvania
tremendously
trendsetting
trepidatious
triangularly
trichologist
trichromatic
triglyceride
trigonometry
triplication
triumphalism
triumphalist
triumphantly
tropospheric
troublemaker

troubleshoot
Trustafarian
trustfulness
trustingness
truthfulness
tuberculosis
tumultuously
tunelessness
turbocharger
Turkmenistan
typification
tyrannically
tyrannicidal

# U

Übermenschen
ubiquitously
ultramontane
unacceptable
unacceptably
unaccustomed
unacquainted
unaffectedly
unaffiliated
unaffordable
unanswerable
unapologetic
unappetising
unappetizing
unassailable
unassailably
unassociated
unassumingly
unattainable
unattainably
unattractive
unattributed
unauthorised
unauthorized
unavailingly
unbecomingly
unbelievable
unbelievably
unblushingly

unbreathable
unbridgeable
unchallenged
unchangeable
unchangingly
uncharitable
uncharitably
unchivalrous
unclassified
uncommercial
unconsidered
uncontrolled
unconvincing
uncritically
unctuousness
uncultivated
undemocratic
underachieve
underclothes
undercurrent
underfunding
undergarment
underperform
underutilise
underutilize
underwritten
undeservedly
undetectable
undetermined
undiminished
undiplomatic
undiscerning
undiscovered
undocumented
uneconomical
unemployable
unemployment
unencumbered
uneventfully
unexpectedly
unexpurgated
unfaithfully
unfathomable
unfathomably
unfavourable

unfavourably
unfertilised
unfertilized
unflaggingly
unflattering
unforgivable
unforgivably
unfulfilling
ungainliness
ungovernable
ungracefully
ungraciously
ungratefully
unhesitating
unhistorical
unidentified
unilaterally
unimaginable
unimaginably
unimportance
unimpressive
uninterested
unionisation
unionization
Unitarianism
universalise
universalism
universalist
universality
universalize
unlawfulness
unlikelihood
unmanageable
unmanageably
unmercifully
unmistakable
unmistakably
unnoticeable
unobstructed
unobtainable
unofficially
unoriginally
unparalleled
unpardonable
unpardonably

unpleasantly
unpopularity
unprejudiced
unprincipled
unproductive
unprofitable
unquenchable
unquestioned
unreasonable
unreasonably
unrecognised
unrecognized
unregenerate
unregistered
unrelievedly
unremarkable
unrepeatable
unreservedly
unresponsive
unrestrained
unrestricted
unsatisfying
unscientific
unscrupulous
unseasonable
unseasonably
unseemliness
unsportingly
unsteadiness
unstintingly
unstructured
unsuccessful
unsupervised
unsurprising
unsuspecting
unswervingly
unsystematic
unthinkingly
untimeliness
untrammelled
untruthfully
unventilated
unverifiable
unwaveringly
unwieldiness

unworthiness
uproariously
urbanisation
urbanization
uxoriousness

# V

vainglorious
valorisation
valorization
Valpolicella
vaporisation
vaporization
varicoloured
vaudevillian
vegetational
velociraptor
vengefulness
verification
veterinarian
vibraphonist
Victorianism
victoriously
videographer
vigorousness
vilification
vindictively
vinification
viridescence
virtuousness
viticultural
vituperation
vituperative
vivification
vocalisation
vocalization
vocationally
vociferously
volcanically
voluminously
voluptuously

# W

weatherboard
weatherproof

wainscotting
wakeboarding
wallcovering
Warwickshire
wastefulness
watchfulness

weightlessly
weightlifter
welterweight
Westinghouse
whimsicality
whippoorwill

wholehearted
whortleberry
wicketkeeper
Wigtownshire
Williamsburg
Winterhalter
Wittgenstein
wretchedness

# Y-Z

Yamoussoukro
yellowhammer
youthfulness
zoogeography
zoologically

# **13** LETTERS

## A

Aberdeenshire
abortifacient
accelerometer
acceptability
accessibility
accommodating
accommodation
accompaniment
accreditation
acculturation
acidification
acquisitively
acrobatically
actualisation
actualization
acupuncturist
adjustability
administrator
admissibility
adventuresome
adventurously
advertisement
aesthetically
affirmatively
affordability
afforestation
agglomeration
agglutination
agreeableness
agriculturist

aircraftwoman
aircraftwomen
airworthiness
allegorically
alternatively
ambassadorial
amniocentesis
amplification
anachronistic
anaerobically
anglicisation
anglicization
animadversion
anthropophagy
antibacterial
anticlimactic
anticlockwise
anticoagulant
antihistamine
antilogarithm
antimicrobial
antinomianism
antipersonnel
antipsychotic
antiscorbutic
apathetically
aphrodisiacal
applicability
apportionment
appropriately
appropriation
approximately

approximation
arachnophobia
arachnophobic
arbitrariness
arboriculture
archaeologist
archaeopteryx
architectonic
architectural
argumentation
argumentative
arithmetician
artificiality
ascertainable
ascertainment
assassination
assertiveness
astrophysical
atavistically
attentiveness
attributively
audaciousness
authentically
authenticator
authoritarian
authoritative
authorisation
authorization
autobiography
autochthonous
automatically

## B

baccalaureate
Balkanisation
Balkanization
battlecruiser
beatification
believability
belligerently
Berchtesgaden
bibliographer
bibliographic
Bildungsroman
biodegradable
biotechnology
blasphemously
bombastically
bougainvillea
bouillabaisse
brachiosaurus
brainchildren
breathability
brutalisation
brutalization
bumptiousness
bureaucratise
bureaucratize
businesswoman
businesswomen
butterfingers

## C

calcification
callisthenics
campanologist
campylobacter
cannibalistic
Carboniferous
carbonisation
carbonization
Cardiganshire
cardiographer
cardiological
carnivalesque
cartilaginous
casualisation
casualization
categorically
cauterisation
cauterization
centrifugally
centripetally
cerebrospinal
ceremoniously
certification
Chandrasekhar
changeability
characterless
Charlottetown
Chateaubriand
chieftainship
choreographer
choreographic
chromatograph
chronological
chrysanthemum
cinematically
cinematograph
circumambient
circumference
circumspectly
circumvention
clandestinely
clandestinity
clarification

classlessness
climactically
coeducational
collaboration
collaborative
colloquialism
combativeness
combinational
commemoration
commemorative
commensurable
commercialise
commercialism
commerciality
commercialize
commiseration
communication
communicative
communitarian
companionable
companionably
companionship
comparability
comparatively
compartmental
compassionate
compatibility
compendiously
competitively
complementary
complimentary
compositional
comprehension
comprehensive
compressional
computational
concatenation
concentration
conceptualise
conceptualize
concessionary
concomitantly
concupiscence
condescending
condescension

conditionally
confabulation
confectionery
confederation
configuration
conflagration
confraternity
confrontation
congressional
congresswoman
congresswomen
consanguinity
conscientious
consciousness
consequential
conservatoire
considerately
consideration
consolidation
conspicuously
constellation
consternation
contamination
contemplation
contemplative
contextualise
contextualize
contortionist
contraception
contraceptive
contractually
contradiction
contradictory
contravention
controversial
convalescence
convolutional
cooperatively
correspondent
corroboration
corroborative
counteraction
counteractive
counterfeiter
counterweight

courteousness
craftsmanship
criminologist
cruiserweight
cryptographer
cryptographic
cryptological
customisation
customization
cyanobacteria
cybercriminal
cybersquatter
cylindrically

## D

daguerreotype
dangerousness
daughterboard
decaffeinated
deceitfulness
decomposition
decompression
decontaminate
decriminalise
decriminalize
deductibility
defectiveness
defensiveness
deferentially
defibrillator
deforestation
deliciousness
deliquescence
dematerialise
dematerialize
demonstration
demonstrative
demythologise
demythologize
denationalise
denationalize
deoxygenation
dependability
depersonalise

depersonalize
dermatologist
descriptively
desegregation
destructively
deterioration
determination
deterministic
detrimentally
devastatingly
developmental
devolutionary
devolutionist
diagnostician
dialectically
diametrically
diaphragmatic
dictatorially
differentiate
differentness
digestibility
dimensionally
directionless
disappearance
disappointing
discoloration
disconcerting
disconnection
discontinuity
discontinuous
discreditable
discretionary
discriminator
disembodiment
disengagement
disequilibria
disfiguration
disfigurement
disgracefully
disharmonious
dishonourable
dishonourably
disillusioned
disintegrator
disinterested

disinvestment
dismantlement
dismemberment
disobediently
disparagement
dispassionate
disposability
dispossession
disproportion
disrespectful
dissemination
dissimilarity
dissimulation
distastefully
distinctively
distinguished
distributable
distrustfully
documentation
domestication
dramatisation
dramatization
dramaturgical
draughtswoman
draughtswomen
Dumfriesshire
dysfunctional
dysmenorrhoea

# E

eccentrically
educationally
effectiveness
effervescence
efficaciously
efflorescence
egocentricity
egregiousness
Egyptological
electrocution
electromagnet
electromotive
electrostatic
elephantiasis

embarrassment
embellishment
embryological
employability
encapsulation
encephalogram
encouragement
encyclopaedia
encyclopaedic
encyclopedist
endocrinology
endometriosis
energetically
enigmatically
enlightenment
entertainment
entomological
environmental
equestrianism
ergonomically
eroticisation
eroticization
establishment
ethnocentrism
evangelically
everlastingly
exaggeratedly
exceptionable
exceptionally
excessiveness
exclusiveness
excommunicate
exhibitionism
exhibitionist
existentially
expandability
expansiveness
expectoration
expeditionary
expeditiously
expendability
expensiveness
explanatorily
explosiveness
exponentially

expostulation
expressionism
expressionist
expropriation
exquisiteness
extensibility
extensiveness
extermination
extraordinary
extrapolation
extrapolative
extravagantly
extrinsically

# F

facetiousness
factorisation
factorization
faithlessness
falsification
fantastically
fascinatingly
featherweight
felicitations
ferroconcrete
ferroelectric
fertilisation
fertilization
fetishisation
fetishization
flirtatiously
foolhardiness
foreknowledge
forgetfulness
formalisation
formalization
formulaically
fortification
fossiliferous
fossilisation
fossilization
fractionation
fractiousness
fragmentarily

fragmentation
frighteningly
frightfulness
fruitarianism
fruitlessness
functionalism
functionalist
functionality
fundamentally

## G

galvanisation
galvanization
Gelsenkirchen
generalisable
generalissimo
generalizable
geometrically
geomorphology
geostationary
gerontocratic
gerontologist
gesticulation
ghettoisation
ghettoization
glamorisation
glamorization
globalisation
globalization
globetrotting
glorification
governability
gracelessness
grammatically
grandchildren
granddaughter
grandiloquent
graphological
gratification
gravitational
Grossglockner
grotesqueness
groundskeeper
gubernatorial

gynaecologist

## H

haematologist
Halicarnassus
hallucination
hallucinatory
harmonisation
harmonization
healthfulness
heartbreaking
heartlessness
hemispherical
Herefordshire
hermaphrodite
hermeneutical
herpetologist
Hertfordshire
heterogeneity
heterogeneous
heuristically
homoeroticism
homogeneously
homosexuality
horizontality
horticultural
housebreaking
housemistress
hundredweight
hybridisation
hybridization
hydraulically
hydrocephalic
hydrocephalus
hydrochloride
hydrodynamics
hydroelectric
hydrogenation
hymenopterous
hyperactivity
hypercritical
hypertrophied
hypochondriac
hypoglycaemia

hypoglycaemic
hypothecation

## I

ichthyologist
ichthyosaurus
ideologically
idiomatically
idiosyncratic
ignominiously
illusionistic
imaginatively
immateriality
immunological
immunotherapy
impassability
impeccability
impecuniosity
imperceptible
imperceptibly
imperialistic
imperiousness
impermanently
impermissible
impersonality
impersonation
impertinently
imperturbable
imperturbably
impetuousness
implacability
implicational
importunately
impossibility
impracticable
impracticably
impractically
Impressionism
Impressionist
improbability
improvability
improvidently
improvisation
improvisatory

impulsiveness
inadvertently
inappropriate
inattentively
incandescence
incarceration
inclusiveness
incombustible
incommunicado
incompetently
inconceivable
inconceivably
incongruently
incongruously
inconsequence
inconsiderate
inconsistency
inconspicuous
incontestable
incontestably
incontinently
inconvenience
incorporation
incorporative
incorrectness
incorruptible
incredibility
incredulously
incrementally
incrimination
incriminatory
indefatigable
indefatigably
indentureship
independently
indescribable
indescribably
indeterminacy
indeterminate
indifferently
indiscernible
indispensable
indisposition
individualise
individualism

individualist
individuality
individualize
individuation
industrialise
industrialism
industrialist
industrialize
industriously
ineffectively
ineffectually
inefficiently
inelastically
ineligibility
inevitability
inexhaustible
inexhaustibly
inexorability
inexpensively
inexperienced
inexpressible
inexpressibly
infallibility
infinitesimal
inflexibility
inflorescence
influentially
informational
informatively
ingenuousness
injudiciously
inoffensively
inorganically
inquisitively
inquisitorial
insatiability
inscriptional
insectivorous
insensibility
insensitively
insensitivity
insidiousness
insignificant
inspectorship
inspirational

instantaneity
instantaneous
instantiation
instinctively
institutional
instructional
instructively
insubordinate
insubstantial
insufficiency
insupportable
insupportably
insusceptible
intangibility
intelligently
intemperately
intensiveness
intentionally
interactively
interactivity
intercellular
interestingly
intergalactic
interlocution
interlocutory
intermarriage
intermittency
international
interoperable
interpersonal
interpolation
interposition
interpretable
interracially
interrelation
interrogation
interrogative
interrogatory
interruptible
interspersion
intransigence
intransigency
intravenously
intrinsically
introspection

introspective
intrusiveness
intuitiveness
invariability
inventiveness
investigation
investigative
investigatory
invidiousness
invincibility
inviolability
involuntarily
irrationality
irrecoverable
irrecoverably
irreplaceable
irrepressible
irrepressibly
irresponsible
irresponsibly
irretrievable
irretrievably
isometrically

## J

jollification
judgementally
judiciousness
jurisprudence
justification
justificatory
juxtaposition

## K

kaleidoscopic
Kangchenjunga
Kidderminster
Kirkcudbright
knickerbocker
Knightsbridge
knowledgeable
knowledgeably
knuckleduster

Kristallnacht

## L

lackadaisical
landownership
latitudinally
leatherjacket
lecherousness
legislatively
leishmaniasis
leisureliness
lepidopterist
lepidopterous
lethargically
lexicographer
lexicographic
liberationist
librarianship
Liebfraumilch
Liechtenstein
limitlessness
listenability
litigiousness
ludicrousness
luxuriousness

## M

Machiavellian
machicolation
machinability
macromolecule
magisterially
magnanimously
magnification
magnificently
maladminister
maliciousness
Manichaeanism
manifestation
Massachusetts
materfamilias
materialistic
mathematician

matriculation
matrilineally
meaninglessly
mechanisation
mechanization
Mediterranean
mellifluously
merchandising
mercilessness
Messerschmidt
metalliferous
metallography
metallurgical
metamorphosis
metaphysician
meteorologist
microanalysis
microcomputer
micronutrient
microorganism
Middlesbrough
millennialism
millennialist
mineralogical
ministerially
miscegenation
miscellaneous
mischievously
misconception
miserableness
mismanagement
Mississippian
misunderstand
misunderstood
mitochondrial
mitochondrion
modernisation
modernization
mollification
momentousness
Monmouthshire
monochromatic
monocotyledon
monumentality
morphological

mortification
mountainously
multicoloured
multicultural
multinational
multitudinous
mummification
murderousness
musicological
mystification

## N

nationalistic
negotiability
neighbourhood
neoclassicism
neoclassicist
Netherlandish
neurochemical
neurosurgical
nightwatchman
nightwatchmen
nitrification
nomenclatural
nonconformism
nonconformist
nonconformity
nonsensically
noradrenaline
normalisation
normalization
Northallerton
nostalgically
nullification
numerological

## O

objectionable
obliviousness
obnoxiousness
observational
obsessiveness
obtrusiveness

oceanographer
oceanographic
offensiveness
officiousness
oligopolistic
omnicompetent
operationally
ophthalmology
opportunistic
opprobriously
orchestration
orientational
ornamentation
ornithologist
osteomyelitis
outspokenness
outstandingly
overambitious
overconfident
overdetermine
overdramatise
overdramatize
overemotional
overemphasise
overemphasize
overexcitable
overindulgent
overqualified
oversensitive
overstatement
overstimulate
overvaluation
oystercatcher

## P

paediatrician
painstakingly
palaeographer
palaeographic
palaeontology
panoramically
paradoxically
parallelogram
paralytically

paranoiacally
paraphernalia
parasitically
parenthetical
parliamentary
participation
participative
participatory
particoloured
particularise
particularity
particularize
Passchendaele
paterfamilias
paternalistic
patriotically
pedestrianise
pedestrianize
Pembrokeshire
Pennsylvanian
perambulation
perambulatory
percussionist
peregrination
perfectionism
perfectionist
perfunctorily
peripherality
permutational
perpendicular
perspicacious
perspicuously
pervasiveness
petrification
petrochemical
phallocentric
pharmacologic
pharmacopoeia
phencyclidine
phenobarbital
phenomenology
philanthropic
philosophical
photochemical
photocopiable

photoelectric
photoreceptor
phylloquinone
physiological
physiotherapy
phytochemical
phytoplankton
picturesquely
piezoelectric
plaintiveness
platitudinous
pluralisation
pluralization
pneumatically
pointlessness
poliomyelitis
polycarbonate
polychromatic
polypropylene
Portlaoighise
postmodernism
postmodernist
postmodernity
postoperative
potentiometer
powerlessness
pragmatically
precautionary
precipitately
precipitation
precipitously
preconception
predeterminer
predicatively
predominantly
predominately
preferability
prefiguration
preindustrial
premedication
premeditation
preoccupation
preponderance
prepositional
prepossessing

preproduction
Pre-Raphaelite
presumptively
pretentiously
preternatural
prevarication
primatologist
primitiveness
primogeniture
principalship
privatisation
privatization
probabilistic
problematical
procrastinate
proctological
professorship
profitability
progenitorial
prognosticate
progressional
progressively
prohibitively
projectionist
proliferation
proliferative
promiscuously
pronounceable
pronouncement
pronunciation
prophetically
proportionate
propositional
proprietorial
prosecutorial
prospectively
prostaglandin
protectionism
protectionist
Protestantism
provincialism
provinciality
provisionally
provocatively
pseudoscience

psychoanalyse
psychoanalyst
psychokinesis
psychokinetic
psychological
psychometrics
psychosomatic
psychosurgery
psychotherapy
psychotically
punctiliously
purposelessly
purposiveness
pusillanimity
pusillanimous
pyrotechnical

## Q

quadrilateral
quadrillionth
quadripartite
quadruplicate
qualification
qualitatively
quartermaster
querulousness
questionnaire
quincentenary
quintillionth

## R

Radhakrishnan
radioactively
radioactivity
rapaciousness
rapprochement
ratiocination
ratiocinative
reaffirmation
realistically
reappointment
rearrangement
recalcitrance

recalculation
reciprocation
recirculation
recombination
recommendable
recrimination
recrudescence
rectification
redevelopment
reductiveness
reduplication
reflexologist
reforestation
reformulation
refrigeration
refurbishment
regimentation
regretfulness
regurgitation
reimbursement
reincarnation
reinforcement
reinstatement
reintegration
religiousness
reminiscently
remonstration
remorselessly
renegotiation
reorientation
repetitiously
replenishment
reprehensible
reprehensibly
reproachfully
republicanism
repulsiveness
resentfulness
residentially
resourcefully
resplendently
restoratively
restrictively
resuscitation
resuscitative

retentiveness
retroactively
retrogression
retrogressive
retrospection
retrospective
reunification
reverberation
reversibility
revolutionary
revolutionise
revolutionist
revolutionize
righteousness
ritualisation
ritualization
Roxburghshire
rudimentarily
rutherfordium

## S

sacrosanctity
sadomasochism
sadomasochist
Salzkammergut
sanctimonious
sarcastically
scandalmonger
scarification
Schadenfreude
schematically
schizophrenia
schizophrenic
scholasticism
schoolteacher
Scientologist
scintillating
scintillation
screenwriting
scriptwriting
seaworthiness
secretiveness
sedimentation
seductiveness

segregational
seismological
semiconductor
semipermeable
sensationally
senselessness
sensitiveness
sensitisation
sensitization
sententiously
sentimentally
sequestration
serendipitous
serialisation
serialization
Shakespearean
Shakespearian
shambolically
shamelessness
shapelessness
shiftlessness
significantly
signification
silvicultural
socialisation
socialization
sociocultural
solemnisation
solemnization
sophisticated
Sovietologist
spasmodically
specification
spectacularly
spectrometric
spectroscopic
speculatively
speleological
spinelessness
splendiferous
spontaneously
sportsmanlike
sportsmanship
sprightliness
squeamishness

stabilisation
stabilization
Staffordshire
staphylococci
statesmanlike
statesmanship
stationmaster
statistically
steadfastness
steeplechaser
stereotypical
sterilisation
sterilization
strangulation
strategically
stratigraphic
stratocumulus
stratospheric
strenuousness
streptococcal
streptococcus
structuralism
structuralist
Struwwelpeter
stultifyingly
stylistically
subcontractor
subordination
subsidisation
subsidization
substantially
substantively
substitutable
subterraneous
sumptuousness
superabundant
supercomputer
superficially
superfluously
superlatively
supernumerary
superordinate
superposition
superstitious
supplementary

supranational
surreptitious
survivability
swordsmanship
symbolisation
symbolization
symmetrically
synchronicity
synchronously
syntactically
synthetically

## T

tablespoonful
talkativeness
tantalisation
tantalization
tastelessness
technological
telemarketing
teleportation
televangelist
temperamental
tempestuously
temporariness
tendentiously
tenosynovitis
tentativeness
terpsichorean
terrestrially
territorially
theatricality
thenceforward
theologically
theoretically
thermodynamic
thermogenesis
thermographic
thermonuclear
thermoplastic
thermosetting
Thessalonians
thoroughgoing
thoughtlessly

thunderstruck
toastmistress
tonsillectomy
topographical
tortoiseshell
toxicological
toxoplasmosis
traditionally
trainspotting
tranquilliser
tranquillizer
transactional
transatlantic
Transcaucasia
transcendence
transgendered
transgression
transgressive
transistorise
transistorize
transliterate
translocation
transmissible
transmutation
transnational
transparently
transpersonal
transpiration
transportable
transposition
traumatically
treacherously
tremulousness
triangularity
triangulation
trichological
trichromatism
trigonometric
trilingualism
typographical
tyrannosaurus

# U

umbelliferous
unaccompanied
unaccountable
unaccountably
unadulterated
unadventurous
unambiguously
unappealingly
unappreciated
unceremonious
unchallenging
uncharismatic
uncircumcised
uncleanliness
uncomfortable
uncomfortably
uncompetitive
uncomplaining
uncomplicated
unconcernedly
unconditional
unconditioned
unconquerable
unconsciously
unconsecrated
unconstrained
unconsummated
uncontainable
uncontentious
uncooperative
uncoordinated
underachiever
undercarriage
underclothing
underemployed
underestimate
underexposure
undergraduate
understanding
understatedly
undisciplined
unembarrassed
unemotionally

unenforceable
unenlightened
unequivocally
unexceptional
unexplainable
unfalteringly
unfamiliarity
unfashionable
unfashionably
unflinchingly
unforeseeable
unforgettable
unforgettably
unforthcoming
unfortunately
unfulfillable
ungentlemanly
ungrammatical
unhealthiness
unhelpfulness
unilateralism
unilateralist
unimaginative
unimpeachable
unimpeachably
uninformative
uninhabitable
uninhibitedly
unintelligent
unintentional
uninteresting
uninterrupted
unjustifiable
unjustifiably
unknowability
unmentionable
unmistakeable
unmitigatedly
unnaturalness
unnecessarily
unobtrusively
unoriginality
unpasteurised
unpasteurized
unprecedented

unpredictable
unpredictably
unpressurised
unpressurized
unpretentious
unproblematic
unpublishable
unputdownable
unquestioning
unreadability
unrelentingly
unreliability
unremittingly
unrepentantly
unselfishness
unsentimental
unserviceable
unsightliness
unspectacular
unsubstantial
unsuitability
unsupportable
unsurpassable
unsustainable
unsustainably
unsymmetrical
unsympathetic
Untermenschen
unthreatening
untrustworthy
unwarrantable
unwarrantably
unwillingness
unworldliness

# V

vegetarianism
ventriloquial
ventriloquism
ventriloquist
verbalisation
verbalization
versification
vertiginously

victimisation
victimization
visualisation
visualization
viticulturist
vitrification
vitriolically
volcanologist
vulcanisation
vulcanization
vulcanologist

vulgarisation
vulgarization
vulnerability

# W

weightlifting
wholesomeness
Wilhelmshaven
Witwatersrand

Wolverhampton
wonderfulness
worthlessness

# Y-Z

Yekaterinburg
yuppification
zoogeographer
zoogeographic

# Multiple words

## 2 WORDS

### 1-LETTER FIRST WORD

A-bomb
a cappella
à deux
a fortiori
à la
A level
A-line
A-list
a posteriori
a priori
A-side
B-list
B-movie
B-side
D-Day
D notice
E-number
F-word
G-man
G-men
G spot
G-string
H-bomb
I Ching
i-Mode
J-cloth
L-driver
L-plate
m-commerce
O level
T-bone
T-junction
T-shirt
T-square

U-bend
U-boat
U-turn
V-neck
V-necked
V-sign
X chromosome
X-rated
X-ray
Y chromosome
Y-fronts

### 2-LETTER FIRST WORD

ad hoc
ad hominem
ad infinitum
ad-lib
ad litem
ad nauseam
Al-Anon
al dente
Al Fatah
Al Fujayrah
Al Qaeda
Al Qaida
al-Qa'idah
An Najaf
as regards
at anchor
at bay
at best
at bottom
at cost
at ease
at fault

at first
at grass
at gunpoint
at hand
at heart
at heel
at home
at interest
at intervals
at issue
at large
at last
at least
at leisure
at length
at liberty
at loggerheads
at most
at odds
at once
at peace
at present
at random
at rest
at risk
at root
at sea
at sight
at source
at speed
at stake
at times
at will
at work
at worst
au courant

au fait
au gratin
au naturel
au pair
au revoir
bo tree
by acclamation
by appointment
by choice
by comparison
by courtesy
by default
by definition
by degrees
by design
by-election
by extension
by foot
by hand
by heart
by implication
by inches
by jingo
by Jove
by-law
by marriage
by mistake
by name
by numbers
by oneself
by order
by-product
by request
by return
by right
by rights

2 WORDS

MULTI-WORD

by sea
by turns
by water
by wire
da capo
Da Nang
de facto
de jure
de luxe
de' Medici
de novo
de rigueur
De Stijl
de trop
Di Caprio
do battle
do bird
do good
do-gooder
do up
do without
do wonders
du jour
eh up
El Alamein
El Dorado
El Niño
El Paso
El Salvador
en bloc
en cabochon
en croute
en daube
en masse
en passant
en pointe
en route
en suite
et al.
et cetera
et seq.
ex cathedra
ex gratia
ex nihilo
ex officio

ex parte
go about
go-ahead
go astray
go back
go bail
go ballistic
go bananas
go begging
go-between
go-cart
go commando
go down
go Dutch
go far
go figure
go flying
go-getter
go-getting
go-go
go gold
go halves
go-kart
go live
go mad
go native
go nowhere
go off
go out
go over
go overboard
go phut
go places
go platinum
go postal
go public
go round
go shares
go short
go-slow
go sour
go south
go spare
go steady
go straight

go under
go up
go walkabout
go walkies
go west
go without
go wrong
ha-ha
he-man
he-men
hi-fi
hi-tech
in absentia
in action
in addition
in advance
in aggregate
in arms
in arrears
in attendance
in ballast
in bounds
in-box
in brief
in bulk
in business
in cahoots
in camera
in case
in chancery
in character
in charge
in check
in chief
in circulation
in clover
in commission
in common
in company
in comparison
in concert
in conclusion
in condition
in conference
in conjunction

in conscience
in consequence
in contention
in context
in control
in convoy
in credit
in-crowd
in debit
in default
in demand
in-depth
in detail
in dock
in doubt
in drink
in duplicate
in earnest
in eclipse
in effect
in embryo
in essence
in evidence
in excess
in exchange
in extremis
in fact
in fashion
in favour
in fits
in-flight
in flood
in force
in form
in front
in fruit
in full
in fun
in funds
in future
in gear
in general
in goal
in hand
in hardback

| | | | |
|---|---|---|---|
| in harness | in progress | in touch | no fear |
| in heat | in proportion | in tow | no fool |
| in hock | in public | in train | no good |
| in holes | in question | in training | no-hoper |
| in-house | in reach | in tray | no joke |
| in irons | in reality | in trim | no kidding |
| in isolation | in recovery | in triplicate | no less |
| in-joke | in relief | in truth | no longer |
| in key | in reserve | in tune | no matter |
| in kind | in residence | in turn | no mean |
| in-law | in retrospect | in type | no more |
| in league | in return | in utero | no-no |
| in lieu | in reverse | in vain | no-nonsense |
| in-line | in ruins | in view | no object |
| in little | in scale | in vitro | no offence |
| in luck | in secret | in vivo | no one |
| in marriage | in-service | in wait | no picnic |
| in mass | in session | in whole | no place |
| in memoriam | in shore | ju-jitsu | no problem |
| in microcosm | in short | La Gioconda | no-show |
| in midstream | in sight | La Palma | no sweat |
| in miniature | in silhouette | La Paz | no way |
| in mitigation | in situ | La Plata | no-win |
| in moderation | in spades | La Rioja | no wonder |
| in mothballs | in spate | La Rochelle | no worries |
| in opposition | in spirit | La Scala | of course |
| in order | in sport | La Serenissima | of late |
| in outline | in step | La Spezia | of necessity |
| in paperback | in stitches | Le Havre | of note |
| in parallel | in stock | Le Mans | of old |
| in parenthesis | in store | Li-lo | of right |
| in part | in strength | lo-fi | of sorts |
| in particular | in style | my eye | on approval |
| in passing | in substance | my foot | on balance |
| in pawn | in succession | My Lady | on board |
| in perpetuity | in sum | My Lord | on call |
| in person | in summary | my pleasure | on camera |
| in phase | in sync | my word | on course |
| in place | in synch | no-ball | on credit |
| in pocket | in tandem | no-brainer | on cue |
| in practice | in tatters | no chance | on deck |
| in principle | in tears | no comment | on demand |
| in print | in theory | no contest | on deposit |
| in private | in time | no dice | on draught |
| in profile | in toto | no doubt | on duty |

| | | |
|---|---|---|
| on earth | on tick | ro-ro |
| on edge | on time | so-called |
| on file | on tiptoe | so long |
| on fire | on tiptoes | so many |
| on foot | on top | so much |
| on form | on tow | so-so |
| on guard | on track | so there |
| on hand | on trial | St Albans |
| on heat | on view | St Andrews |
| on high | on wheels | St Bernard |
| on hire | op art | St Croix |
| on hold | op. cit. | St David's |
| on horseback | or else | St Émilion |
| on ice | ox tongue | St-Étienne |
| on impulse | po-faced | St Eustatius |
| on loan | re-cover | St George's |
| on oath | re-echo | St Helena |
| on occasion | re-edit | St Helens |
| on occasions | re-educate | St Helier |
| on offer | re-education | St John |
| on order | re-elect | St John's |
| on paper | re-election | St Kilda |
| on parade | re-emerge | St Kitts |
| on pointe | re-emergence | St Lawrence |
| on principle | re-emergent | St Louis |
| on purpose | re-emphasis | St Lucia |
| on record | re-emphasise | St Malo |
| on relief | re-emphasize | St Martin |
| on remand | re-enact | St Moritz |
| on report | re-enactment | St-Nazaire |
| on request | re-engineer | St Nicolas |
| on sale | re-enter | St Paul |
| on schedule | re-entrance | St Petersburg |
| on shore | re-entrant | St Sophia |
| on show | re-entry | St Thomas |
| on side | re-examination | St Trinian's |
| on sight | re-examine | St-Tropez |
| on song | re-export | Te Deum |
| on spec | re-form | to advantage |
| on stream | re-formation | to bits |
| on supply | re-present | to blame |
| on tap | re-presentation | to boot |
| on target | re-release | to date |
| on tenterhooks | re-route | to death |
| on terms | re-sign | to distraction |

2 WORDS

MULTI-WORD

to-do
to excess
to hand
to heel
to hell
to let
to match
to order
to perfection
to scale
to size
to spare
to taste
up north
up sticks
up top
up until
Wi-Fi
ye gods
yo-yo
Yr Wyddfa

## 3-LETTER FIRST WORD

Abu Dhabi
Abu Simbel
ace high
ack-ack
Adi Granth
age-old
aim high
air bag
air bed
air brake
air commodore
air-conditioned
air conditioner
air conditioning
air corridor
air cushion
air force
air-freshener
air gun
air hostess
air kiss

air letter
air marshal
air mile
air pistol
air plant
air pocket
air pump
air quality
air raid
air rifle
all aboard
all-clear
all comers
all ears
all eyes
all found
all hours
all-in
all-inclusive
all out
all right
all-round
all-rounder
all-time
all told
Amu Darya
and Co.
any day
any good
any more
any old
any time
arc lamp
arc light
arm-wrestle
arm-wrestling
art deco
art house
art nouveau
ash blond
ash blonde
Ash Wednesday
Ave Maria
bad blood
bad call

bad debt
bad faith
bad form
bad lot
bad luck
bad-mouth
bad news
bad show
bad-tempered
bag lady
bar billiards
bar chart
bar code
bar graph
bar mitzvah
bar none
bas-relief
bat mitzvah
bay laurel
bay rum
Bay State
bay window
bed-blocking
bed-wetting
bee-eater
bee-keeper
bee-keeping
bee-stung
bel canto
Ben-Gurion
Ben Nevis
Big Apple
big band
Big Bang
Big Ben
Big Brother
big deal
big dipper
big end
big game
big gun
big-head
big-headed
big hitter
big mouth

| | | | |
|---|---|---|---|
| big noise | cop to | dog-leg | eye tooth |
| big picture | cor anglais | dog rose | fag end |
| big shot | cot death | Dog Star | fan belt |
| big smoke | cow parsley | dog-tired | fan club |
| big top | cry foul | dog-tooth | fan-tailed |
| big wheel | cry wolf | Don Juan | Far East |
| bin-end | cub reporter | doo-wop | Far Eastern |
| bit much | Cub Scout | dot-com | far-fetched |
| bit part | cue ball | dot matrix | far-flung |
| bit thick | cue card | dry battery | far from |
| bog-standard | cut corners | dry cell | far gone |
| bon mot | cut glass | dry-clean | far-off |
| bon vivant | cut in | dry dock | far out |
| bon viveur | cut loose | dry fly | far-reaching |
| bon voyage | cut-off | dry ice | far-seeing |
| boo-boo | cut-out | dry out | far-sighted |
| bow-legged | cut-price | dry rot | Far West |
| bow tie | cut short | dry run | fat cat |
| bow window | cut-throat | dry slope | fax machine |
| box clever | cut up | dry up | fed up |
| box girder | dab hand | due to | fee simple |
| box junction | day boy | dum-dum | fig leaf |
| box number | day centre | Dun Laoghaire | fir cone |
| box office | day girl | ear lobe | fit in |
| box pleat | day nursery | ear-piercing | fit up |
| box room | day off | ear-splitting | fly agaric |
| Boy Scout | day release | ear trumpet | fly-fish |
| bug-eyed | day return | eat away | fly-fishing |
| buy it | day room | eat dirt | fly half |
| buy time | day school | eat up | fly-past |
| bye-bye | day surgery | eco-friendly | fly-post |
| bye-law | day trip | eco-label | fly-tip |
| cap sleeve | day tripper | eco-labelling | fob pocket |
| car park | Des Moines | eco-warrior | fob watch |
| car wash | die-cast | eel-like | for aye |
| cat burglar | die hard | egg-nog | for free |
| cat flap | dim sim | egg white | for fun |
| cat litter | dim sum | ego trip | for good |
| cha-cha | dim-witted | end on | for hire |
| con man | doe-eyed | end-user | for keeps |
| con men | dog cart | eye-catching | for love |
| con trick | dog collar | eye-opener | for luck |
| cop off | dog days | eye-popping | for openers |
| cop on | dog-eared | eye socket | for real |
| cop-out | dog-end | eye teeth | for rent |

for sale
for short
for show
for starters
for sure
fox-hunting
fry-up
fun run
fur seal
gap year
gas chamber
gas fire
gas mantle
gas mask
gee-whiz
Gem State
get across
get ahead
get along
get at
get away
get by
get cracking
get even
get hitched
get ideas
get knotted
get lost
get-out
get over
get physical
get real
get religion
get round
get sick
get spliced
get straight
get stuffed
get-together
get unstuck
get-up
get weaving
gin rummy
God bless
god-daughter

God-fearing
God forbid
God knows
God willing
gum arabic
gum tree
gun carriage
gun dog
gun-shy
hag-ridden
ham-fisted
has-been
hat-trick
hay fever
hee-haw
hen night
hen party
her indoors
het up
hey presto
hey up
hip bath
hip bone
hip flask
hip hop
hip-hopper
hit home
hit list
hit man
hit men
hit wicket
hoi polloi
hoo-ha
hot air
hot-blooded
hot button
hot-desking
hot dog
hot flush
hot-headed
hot key
hot money
hot pants
hot potato
hot rod

hot-rodder
hot seat
hot shoe
hot spot
hot stuff
hot-tempered
hot ticket
hot tub
hot-wire
how so
ice age
ice beer
ice-breaker
ice cap
ice cream
ice dancing
ice field
ice hockey
ice lolly
ice pack
ice pick
ice rink
ice skate
ice skater
ice skating
ill-advised
ill-assorted
ill-bred
ill-conceived
ill-disposed
ill-equipped
ill-fated
ill-favoured
ill-founded
ill-gotten
ill-judged
ill-natured
ill-omened
ill-starred
ill-tempered
ill-treat
ill-use
ill will
ion exchange
Ivy League

Iwo Jima
jam-packed
jam tomorrow
jaw-dropping
jet black
jet engine
jet lag
jet-lagged
jet set
jet-setter
jet-setting
jet ski
jet-skier
jet-skiing
jet stream
Jim Crow
jim-jams
jiu-jitsu
job lot
job-share
job-sharer
Kew Gardens
key grip
Key Largo
key money
key ring
key signature
Key West
kid brother
kid sister
Kon-Tiki
lac insect
Lao-tzu
lap dance
lap dancer
lap dancing
lap joint
Las Palmas
Las Vegas
law-abiding
law centre
Law Commission
law court
law lord
Law Officer

Law Society

lay about

lay bare

lay brother

lay-by

lay down

lay into

lay odds

lay-off

lay on

lay out

lay reader

lay sister

lay up

lay waste

Led Zeppelin

lee shore

lee side

leg break

leg iron

leg side

leg-up

leg warmer

let alone

let-down

let drop

let fly

let go

let loose

let off

let on

let-out

let ride

let rip

let slide

let slip

let-up

ley line

Lib Dem

lie detector

lie doggo

lie-down

lie-in

lie low

lie off

lie up

lip-read

lip-reader

lip-sync

lip-synch

lit up

lop-eared

Los Alamos

Los Angeles

Low Church

low comedy

low-down

low-fi

low frequency

low gear

Low German

low-impact

low-key

low-keyed

low-level

low life

low-loader

low-lying

low-profile

low relief

low-rise

low season

low-slung

low spirits

low technology

low tide

low water

mad keen

mah-jong

mah-jongg

man-eating

man-made

Mau Mau

May Day

mea culpa

Met Office

Mid-Atlantic Ridge

Mid Glamorgan

mix-up

mob cap

mob-handed

mod cons

mot juste

Mrs Grundy

Mrs Justice

mud pack

mud-slinging

net profit

New Age

new blood

New Britain

New Brunswick

New Caledonia

New Deal

New Delhi

New England

New Forest

New Georgia

New Guinea

New Guinean

New Hampshire

New Hebrides

New Ireland

New Jersey

New Jerusalem

New Kingdom

new man

new maths

new men

New Mexico

new moon

new one

New Orleans

New Testament

new town

new wave

New World

new year

New York

New Yorker

New Zealand

New Zealander

nil desperandum

nit-pick

nit-picker

nit-picking
non-alcoholic
non-aligned
non-allergenic
non-allergic
non-being
non-believer
non-belligerent
non-combatant
non-commissioned
non-committal
non-committally
non-conducting
non-conductor
non-contributory
non-cooperation
non-drinker
non-essential
non-event
non-existence
non-existent
non-ferrous
non-fiction
non-fictional
non-flammable
non-functional
non-governmental
non-inflammable
non-interference
non-intervention
non-invasive
non-judgemental
non-linear
non-member
non-metal
non-metallic
non-native
non-natural
non-negotiable
non-operational
non-payment
non-person
non-productive
non-productively
non-professional

non-profit
non-proliferation
non-resident
non sequitur
non-slip
non-smoker
non-smoking
non-specific
non-standard
non-starter
non-stick
non-stop
non-technical
non-toxic
non-U
non-uniform
non-verbal
non-violence
non-violent
non-white
not bad
not cricket
not guilty
not half
not necessarily
not out
not proven
now now
nut loaf
nux vomica
oak apple
off base
off beam
off break
off camera
off-colour
off course
off duty
off form
off guard
off-key
off-licence
off-limits
off-peak
off-piste

off-putting
off-ramp
off-road
off season
off side
off-white
oft-times
oil paint
oil painting
oil palm
oil platform
oil rig
oil slick
oil well
old age
old bag
Old Bailey
old bat
old boy
old chestnut
Old Colony
Old Delhi
Old Dominion
Old English
old-fashioned
Old Firm
old girl
Old Glory
old gold
old guard
old hand
old hat
Old Kingdom
old lady
old maid
old man
old master
old men
old moon
old salt
Old Sarum
old stager
Old Testament
old-time
old-timer

old trout
Old Vic
old woman
old women
old-world
one another
one day
one-dimensional
one flesh
one-liner
one nation
one-nighter
one-off
one-shot
one-sided
one-time
one-two
one-upmanship
one-way
Our Father
our kid
Our Lord
out loud
out-take
own brand
own goal
Pac-Man
pak choi
pan-fry
pan pipes
Pap test
par excellence
pay back
pay bed
pay dearly
pay in
pay-off
pay out
pay up
pea coat
pea green
pea jacket
pea-shooter
pea-souper
peg away

peg leg
peg out
pen-name
pen pal
pen-pusher
pep pill
pep talk
per annum
per capita
per cent
per diem
per se
pet name
pia mater
pie chart
pie-eyed
pig-headed
pig iron
pin money
pin-tuck
pin-up
pom-pom
pop art
pop-eyed
pop music
pop-up
pot belly
pot-bound
pot luck
pot plant
pot roast
pro bono
pro-choice
pro forma
pro-life
pro-lifer
pro rata
pro tem
pub crawl
pug nose
put about
put across
put aside
put away
put back

put-down
put forward
put off
put on
put out
put over
put through
put together
put up
put-upon
pye-dog
rag paper
rag-roll
rag rug
rag trade
ram home
ram raid
rat pack
rat race
rat run
raw-boned
raw deal
raw material
raw sienna
raw umber
red admiral
Red Army
red-blooded
red-brick
red card
red carpet
red cell
Red Crescent
Red Cross
red deer
red dwarf
red ensign
red-faced
red flag
red giant
red grouse
red-handed
red-headed
red herring
red-hot

red lead
Red Leicester
red light
red meat
red mullet
red panda
red pepper
red planet
red rose
red salmon
red setter
red snapper
Red Square
red squirrel
red tape
red top
rib-tickler
rig-out
Rig Veda
Rio Grande
rip-off
rip-roaring
rip tide
roe deer
rub along
rub down
rub elbows
rub noses
rub off
rub out
rub shoulders
rum baba
run amok
run amuck
run away
run-down
run dry
run high
run-in
run interference
run low
run-off
run on
run out
run over

run past
run riot
run risks
run short
run-through
run-up
run wild
run with
rye bread
sal volatile
Sam Browne
San Antonio
San Diego
San Francisco
San Jose
San Juan
San Marino
San Salvador
San Sebastián
São Paulo
say cheese
say-so
say when
sci-fi
sea anchor
sea anemone
sea bass
sea bream
sea breeze
sea change
sea cow
sea cucumber
sea dog
sea-green
sea horse
sea lavender
sea level
sea lion
Sea Lord
sea salt
sea shanty
sea squill
sea squirt
sea stack
sea trout

sea urchin
sea wall
see daylight
see fit
see reason
see red
see-saw
see sense
see stars
see-through
set about
set against
set apart
set-aside
set back
set by
set down
set fair
set forth
set in
set off
set on
set out
set piece
set play
set point
set sail
set square
set theory
set-to
set-up
set upon
sex appeal
sex bomb
sex change
sex chromosome
sex hormone
sex kitten
sex life
sex object
sex symbol
sex tourism
sex worker
sin bin
sit back

**MULTI-WORD**

2 WORDS

sit-down
sit-in
sit out
sit tight
sit-up
Six Nations
six-pack
six-shooter
ski jump
ski lift
ski mask
ski pants
sky blue
sky-high
slo-mo
sob story
soi-disant
sol-fa
soy sauce
spa bath
Sri Lanka
Sri Lankan
sub judice
sub lieutenant
sub rosa
sui generis
sum total
sun-baked
sun deck
sun-dry
sun-kissed
tae-bo
tag end
tag wrestling
t'ai chi
Taj Mahal
tap dance
tap dancer
tap-dancing
tax avoidance
tax break
tax-deductible
tax disc
tax evasion
tax exile

tax haven
tax return
tax year
tea bag
tea break
tea chest
tea cloth
tea cosy
tea dance
tea room
tea rose
tea set
tea towel
tea tree
tee-hee
tee shirt
Tel Aviv
Ten Commandments
Tet Offensive
Tex-Mex
tic-tac
tie-back
tie-dye
tie-in
tie into
tie up
tin whistle
tip-off
tip-top
Toc H
toe-tapping
Tom Collins
tom-tom
too bad
too much
top brass
top dog
top dollar
top drawer
top dressing
top flight
top gun
top hat
top-heavy
top-hole

top-level
top-notch
top off
top out
top-secret
top ten
top twenty
top-up
top whack
tow bar
tow-headed
tow rope
toy boy
try-out
try square
tub-thumper
tub-thumping
two-bit
two cheers
two-dimensional
two-faced
two-piece
two-step
two-stroke
two-time
two-way
vas deferens
vin ordinaire
vox pop
wah-wah
war chest
war clouds
war crime
war game
wax lyrical
way back
way-out
web-footed
web page
wet blanket
wet dream
wet fly
wet nurse
wet room
wet rot

win-win
yes-man
yes-men
Yom Kippur
zip code
zip-up

**4**-LETTER FIRST WORD

able-bodied
able seaman
able seamen
acid drop
acid house
acid jazz
acid rain
acid test
Afro-American
Afro-Caribbean
agar-agar
aide-memoire
airy-fairy
Alma-Ata
alma mater
Alma-Tadema
aloe vera
also-ran
amyl nitrite
anal-retentive
anni horribili
anni mirabili
Anno Domini
ante-post
anti-Semite
anti-Semitic
anti-Semitism
aqua regia
aqua vitae
arch-enemy
arch-rival
area code
argy-bargy
arms control
arms race
arum lily

Asia Minor
atom bomb
Aunt Sally
auto-suggestion
Azad Kashmir
baby boom
baby boomer
baby buggy
baby-doll
back boiler
back-breaking
back-burner
back catalogue
back-door
back down
back off
back out
back passage
back-pedal
back room
back-stabbing
back up
back water
bags I
bain-marie
Baja California
bake blind
ball bearing
ball game
ball valve
bang on
bang out
bang up
bank card
bank holiday
bank rate
bare all
bare bones
barn dance
barn owl
base jump
base metal
base rate
bass clef
Bass Strait

Bath bun
bath chair
bath salts
bean counter
bean curd
bean sprout
bear-baiting
bear comparison
bear fruit
bear hug
bear market
bear out
bear up
bear with
beat down
beat generation
beat off
beat time
beat-up
beau monde
beef tomato
beer belly
beer garden
beer gut
beer mat
bee's knees
bell-bottoms
bell jar
bell-ringer
bell-ringing
bend sinister
bent double
best boy
best man
best-seller
best-selling
best wishes
beta blocker
beta particle
beta ray
bête noire
bias binding
bile duct
bird flu
bird table

blow-dry

blow off

blow out

blow over

blow up

blue baby

blue-blooded

blue cheese

blue-chip

blue-collar

blue lias

Blue Nile

Blue Peter

blue riband

blue ribbon

blue-sky

blue tit

blue whale

boat people

boat train

body bag

body blow

body clock

body double

body language

body politic

body shop

body stocking

body warmer

boil down

boil over

bolo tie

bolt-hole

bolt upright

bona fide

bona fides

bond paper

bone china

bone dry

bone idle

bone marrow

bony fish

boob tube

book club

book value

boom boom

boon companion

boot camp

boot-cut

Bora-Bora

born-again

boss-eyed

Boys' Brigade

Bren gun

buck naked

buck teeth

buck tooth

buck-toothed

bulk large

bull bar

bull market

bull-necked

bull terrier

bump-start

bunk bed

burn down

burn out

burn rubber

bush telegraph

bust-up

busy Lizzie

butt heads

butt naked

buzz cut

cack-handed

cafe society

call centre

call collect

call forth

call girl

call in

call off

call sign

call signal

call up

camp bed

Camp David

camp follower

Cape Agulhas

Cape Canaveral

Cape Cod

Cape Finisterre

Cape gooseberry

Cape Horn

Cape Kennedy

Cape Town

Cape Wrath

Cape York

card-carrying

card index

card sharp

card sharper

care worker

case-hardened

case history

case law

case study

cash book

cash card

cash cow

cash crop

cash desk

cash dispenser

cash flow

cash register

cash-strapped

cask-conditioned

cast about

cast around

cast away

cast down

cast iron

cast lots

cast-off

cast on

cat's cradle

cat's paw

Chao Phraya

chat room

chat show

chef-d'oeuvre

chew over

chew up

chip in

chit-chat

choc ice
chop-chop
chop logic
chop suey
chow chow
chow mein
city father
city hall
city slicker
city state
claw hammer
clay pigeon
clip art
clip joint
club class
club feet
club foot
club sandwich
coal gas
coal tar
coal tit
coat hanger
coat-tail
cold-blooded
cold-bloodedly
cold-call
cold chisel
cold comfort
cold cream
cold cuts
cold frame
cold fusion
cold-hearted
cold shoulder
cold sore
cold storage
cold sweat
cold turkey
cold war
cole tit
come about
come across
come again
come back
come clean

come close
come down
come forward
come-hither
come home
come nowhere
come off
come-on
come out
come over
come right
come round
come short
come through
come under
come unglued
come unstuck
come upon
Cook Strait
cool it
copy-edit
copy editor
copy typist
corn dolly
Cosa Nostra
cost accountant
cost accounting
cost-effective
cost-efficient
cost price
Côte d'Ivoire
coup d'état
crab apple
crab lice
crab louse
crew cut
crew neck
crop circle
crop dusting
crop top
cube root
curd cheese
cure-all
dado rail
Dáil Éireann

damp course
damp squib
Dark Ages
dark horse
dark matter
data capture
data protection
Date Line
date palm
date rape
Davy Jones
Davy lamp
dawn chorus
dead duck
dead end
dead hand
dead heat
dead letter
dead loss
dead meat
dead-nettle
dead on
dead reckoning
dead ringer
dead wood
deaf aid
deaf-blind
deaf mute
deed poll
deep-dyed
deep end
deep freeze
deep freezer
deep-froze
deep-frozen
deep-fry
deep-rooted
deep-seated
Deep South
deep space
defy description
déjà vu
desk clerk
dewy-eyed
dial tone

dial-up
ding-dong
dirt bike
dirt cheap
dirt poor
dirt track
disc brake
disc jockey
disk drive
dive-bomb
dive-bomber
dog's life
done deal
done for
done in
done up
down payment
down time
down tools
down town
down under
drag queen
drag race
drag racer
drag racing
draw back
draw blood
draw breath
draw lots
draw out
draw rein
draw straws
draw stumps
draw up
drip-dry
drip-feed
drop anchor
drop back
drop behind
drop cloth
drop curtain
drop-dead
drop goal
drop handlebars
drop hints

drop-in
drop kick
drop-off
drop out
drop scone
drop shot
drop waist
drop zone
drum into
drum kit
drum major
drum majorette
drum roll
drum up
dual carriageway
duct tape
dude ranch
dumb-bell
dumb waiter
dung beetle
dura mater
dust bowl
dust cover
dust jacket
dust sheet
dust storm
dust-up
duty-bound
duty-free
each other
each-way
Earl Grey
East Africa
East African
East Anglia
East Anglian
East Ayrshire
East End
East Indies
East Kilbride
East London
East Lothian
East Renfrewshire
East Side
East Sussex

East Timor
easy chair
easy-going
easy listening
easy meat
easy ride
easy street
easy touch
echo chamber
echo sounder
Eton College
Euro-sceptic
Euro-scepticism
even break
even-handed
even-handedly
even-handedness
even money
even then
even though
ever such
exit poll
eyes front
eyes left
eyes right
face down
face downwards
face mask
face-off
face pack
face-saving
face up
face upwards
face value
fail-safe
fair copy
fair deal
fair dinkum
fair dos
fair enough
fair game
Fair Isle
fair-minded
fair play
fair trade

fait accompli
fall about
fall apart
fall back
fall behind
fall flat
fall for
fall guy
fall in
fall-off
fall out
fall short
fall through
fall upon
fast breeder
fast food
fast forward
fast-talk
fast track
faux pas
fava bean
feel free
feel-good
feel small
fees simple
feet first
feng shui
feta cheese
fill in
fill out
film noir
find against
find fault
find favour
find God
find out
fine art
Fine Gael
fine print
fine-tune
fire alarm
fire away
fire blanket
fire brigade
fire door

fire drill
fire-eater
fire engine
fire escape
fire extinguisher
fire irons
fire practice
fire-raiser
fire station
fire trap
firm hand
fish finger
fish kettle
fish slice
five-spice
flag day
flag-waving
flak jacket
flat-footed
flat iron
flat out
flat-pack
flat race
flea-bitten
flea market
flip chart
flip-flop
flip side
flow chart
flow diagram
foie gras
folk dance
folk etymology
folk music
folk tale
food chain
food poisoning
foot fault
foot soldier
foot-tapping
Fort Knox
Fort William
Fort Worth
foul-mouthed
foul play

foul-up
four-dimensional
four freedoms
four-poster
four-square
four-stroke
Free Church
free enterprise
free fall
free-form
Free French
free hand
free house
free kick
free love
free market
free pardon
free port
free radical
free-range
free ride
free-standing
Free State
free trade
free verse
free vote
free will
from hell
from overseas
from scratch
frou-frou
fuel cell
fuel injection
full blast
full-blooded
full-blown
full board
full-bodied
full bore
full colour
full-fledged
full-frontal
full house
full lock
full marks

full moon
full nelson
full-on
full out
full pelt
full rig
full-scale
full stop
full term
full tilt
full-time
full-timer
full whack
fund-raiser
fund-raising
fuse box
gain ground
gall bladder
game bird
game fish
game on
game over
game plan
game point
game show
game theory
gang agley
gang bang
gang rape
Gaza Strip
gear down
gear lever
gear up
Gell-Mann
gene pool
gene therapy
germ cell
germ warfare
gift token
gift voucher
gift wrap
gilt-edged
Girl Guide
give away
give birth

give blood
give chase
give evidence
give ground
give in
give odds
give out
give over
give pursuit
give tongue
give up
give way
glad-hand
glad-hander
glad rags
Glen More
glow-worm
glue ear
glue-sniffing
goal average
goal difference
goal kick
goal line
goat-antelope
God's gift
God's truth
gold-digger
gold disc
gold dust
gold leaf
gold medal
gold mine
gold plate
gold rush
gold standard
golf club
golf links
good call
good cheer
good deal
good faith
good form
Good Friday
good grief
good-hearted

good-humoured
good job
good-looking
good luck
good money
good-natured
good news
good riddance
good show
good-tempered
good thinking
good-time
good word
gory details
Gran Canaria
grey area
Grey Friar
grey matter
grey seal
grey squirrel
Grim Reaper
gros point
grow apart
grow into
grow up
Grub Street
Gulf Stream
Gulf War
gull-wing
gung-ho
Hail Mary
hair-raising
hair shirt
hair-splitting
hair trigger
Hale-Bopp
half-baked
half binding
half board
half-brother
half-cock
half-cocked
half-crown
half-cut
half-dozen

half-hardy
half-hearted
half-heartedly
half-heartedness
half hitch
half-hour
half-hourly
half-hunter
half-inch
half landing
half-life
half-light
half measure
half-moon
half nelson
half-sister
half-term
half-timbered
half-time
half-title
half-tone
half-track
half-truth
half-volley
half-witted
hand around
hand down
hand grenade
hand in
hand on
hand out
hand over
hand-pick
hand round
hang around
hang back
hang fire
hang-glide
hang-glider
hang-gliding
hang heavily
hang loose
hang on
hang-out
hang ten

hang-up
hara-kiri
hard-boiled
hard cash
hard cheese
hard copy
hard core
hard disk
hard drive
hard feelings
hard going
hard-headed
hard-hearted
hard hit
hard-hitting
hard labour
hard line
hard lines
hard luck
hard-nosed
hard nut
hard palate
hard-pressed
hard put
hard rock
hard roe
hard sell
hard shoulder
hard tack
hard up
hard-wearing
hard-wired
hare-brained
Hare Krishna
hash browns
have kittens
head first
head-on
head start
head teacher
head-turning
hear hear
heat-seeking
heir apparent
heir presumptive

heli-ski
heli-skiing
hell-bent
herd instinct
here goes
hero worship
hidy-hole
high altar
high chair
High Church
high-class
high command
high commission
high commissioner
high court
high explosive
high fashion
high fidelity
high finance
high five
high-flier
high-flown
high-flyer
high frequency
high gear
High German
high ground
high-handed
high-impact
high jinks
high jump
high jumper
high-level
high life
High Mass
high-minded
high-octane
high-powered
high priest
high priestess
high-profile
high relief
high-rise
high road
high roller

high school
high seas
high season
high sheriff
high society
high-spirited
high spirits
high spot
high street
high table
high tea
high-tech
high technology
high-tensile
high tide
high-top
high treason
high water
high wire
hill fort
hill station
hire purchase
hoar frost
hog's back
hold back
hold cheap
hold court
hold dear
hold down
hold fast
hold forth
hold good
hold hands
hold hard
hold off
hold on
hold out
hold over
hold service
hold sway
hold true
hold-up
hold water
hold with
holm oak

Holy Ark
Holy City
Holy Communion
holy day
Holy Family
Holy Father
Holy Ghost
Holy Grail
Holy Island
Holy Land
Holy League
Holy Office
holy orders
Holy Sacrament
Holy Scripture
Holy See
Holy Sepulchre
Holy Spirit
Holy Trinity
holy war
Holy Week
Holy Writ
home brew
home economics
home farm
home-grown
Home Guard
home help
home-made
Home Office
home page
home rule
home run
Home Secretary
home straight
home stretch
home truth
Homo sapiens
Hong Kong
hook-up
horn-rimmed
hors d'oeuvre
how's that
how's tricks
hula hoop

hula-hula
hung-over
hunt counter
hush-hush
hush money
Hyde Park
iced tea
idée fixe
Indo-China
Indo-European
Indo-Pacific
ipso facto
Iron Age
Iron Curtain
iron lung
iron maiden
iron man
iron men
iron pyrites
iron rations
itsy-bitsy
itty-bitty
Jack Frost
jack in
jack pine
jack plug
Jack Russell
jack socket
Jack tar
jack up
Jew's harp
John Bull
John Dory
John o'Groats
join battle
join forces
join hands
joss stick
jump bail
jump jet
jump lead
jump-off
jump rope
jump ship
jump-start

junk bond
junk food
junk mail
jury-rigged
just so
Kama Sutra
Kara Kum
keep back
keep count
keep down
keep faith
keep-fit
keep goal
keep going
keep guard
keep house
keep in
keep mum
keep off
keep on
keep out
keep quiet
keep rank
keep score
keep shtum
keep step
keep time
keep to
keep up
keep watch
keep wicket
kerb-crawler
kerb-crawling
kerb drill
kick against
kick-boxer
kick-boxing
kick in
kick-off
kick oneself
kick-pleat
kick-start
kick up
Kiel Canal
kind-hearted

kind-heartedly
kind-heartedness
kind of
king cobra
King Edward
king high
king post
king prawn
king-size
king-sized
Kirk session
kiss-curl
kiss goodbye
kiwi fruit
knee-jerk
knot garden
know-all
know backwards
know best
know-how
know-nothing
kung fu
Lady chapel
Lady Day
laid-back
Lake School
lame duck
lamp post
land agent
land bridge
land girl
land mass
Land Registry
lash-up
last breath
last-ditch
last-gasp
Last Judgement
last minute
last name
last post
last rites
last straw
Last Supper
last thing

last trump
last word
lava lamp
lawn tennis
lazy eye
lead crystal
lead glass
lead-in
lead shot
lead time
lead-up
leaf litter
leaf mould
lean-to
leap year
left back
Left Bank
left-field
left hand
left-handed
left-hander
left luggage
left wing
left-winger
lèse-majesté
lese-majesty
let's pretend
Lévi-Strauss
life assurance
life cycle
life expectancy
life force
life form
life imprisonment
life insurance
life jacket
life peer
life raft
life sciences
life sentence
life-size
life-sized
life support
life-threatening
lift-off

like clockwork
like crazy
like lightning
like mad
like-minded
like so
lily-livered
lily pad
lily-white
lima bean
lime tree
limp-wristed
line dance
line dancer
line dancing
line drawing
line management
line manager
line-out
line-up
link-up
list price
live-bearing
live dangerously
live down
live-in
live rough
live together
live wire
load factor
load line
loan shark
Loch Lomond
Loch Morar
Loch Ness
loci classici
lock forward
lock horns
lock-in
lock-up
Long Beach
long-distance
long division
long-drawn
long face

long haul
long hundredweight
Long Island
long johns
long jump
long jumper
long leg
long-life
long live
long-lived
Long March
long off
Long Parliament
long-playing
long-range
long shot
long-sighted
long-standing
long-suffering
long suit
long term
long ton
long wave
long-winded
look after
look-in
look lively
look-see
look sharp
look slippy
look small
look smart
look up
loon pants
Lord Advocate
Lord Chamberlain
Lord Chancellor
Lord Justice
Lord Lieutenant
Lord Mayor
Lord Provost
Lord Treasurer
lose count
lose face
lose ground

lose heart
lose height
lose patience
lose sleep
lose touch
lose weight
loss adjuster
loss-leader
lost cause
lost generation
lost soul
love affair
love bite
love child
love children
love handles
love-in
love life
love nest
love seat
lump sum
Lyme disease
lynx-eyed
made-up
mail order
main brace
main clause
main drag
main line
main man
main men
make amends
make-believe
make certain
make-do
make faces
make for
make good
make haste
make hay
make headway
make history
make known
make love
make merry

make off
make out
make over
make peace
make ready
make sail
make sense
make sure
make time
make tracks
make-up
make water
make waves
make way
make whoopee
malt whisky
Manx cat
mark time
mark you
Mars Pathfinder
Marx Brothers
Mary Celeste
Mary Rose
mass-market
mass media
mass noun
mass number
mass-produce
mass production
meal ticket
mean business
mean well
meat loaf
mend fences
mess about
mess around
mess up
mess with
Midi-Pyrénées
midi system
mild steel
milk chocolate
milk fever
milk float
milk pudding

milk round
milk run
milk teeth
milk thistle
milk tooth
mill race
mill wheel
mind-bending
mind-blowing
mind-boggling
mind game
mine host
mini-me
mini-pill
mint sauce
mock-heroic
mock orange
mock-up
modi operandi
modi vivendi
Mona Lisa
mons pubis
mons Veneris
Mont Blanc
moon boot
moon-faced
moss stitch
Most Reverend
moth-eaten
move aside
move in
move mountains
move on
move over
muck sweat
mug's game
mung bean
musk deer
musk ox
must-have
mute swan
nail-biting
nail file
nail polish
nail varnish

name day
name-drop
name-dropping
name names
navy blue
Navy List
neap tide
Near East
Near Eastern
near miss
near thing
near to
nest egg
Neue Sachlichkeit
news agency
news conference
news-stand
next door
next to
nice one
nosh-up
nosy parker
Nova Scotia
oast house
odds-on
ogee arch
olde worlde
once-over
one's all
one's doing
one's last
one's lookout
open day
open-ended
open fire
open-handed
open-hearted
open house
open letter
open market
open marriage
open-minded
open-necked
open-plan
open prison

open season
open secret
open sesame
open-source
open-toed
open-top
open-topped
Open University
open verdict
Opus Dei
oral history
Oval Office
oven-ready
over against
over-egg
over-elaborate
over-optimistic
pack ice
pack in
pack out
pack up
page-turner
page-turning
paid-up
pall-bearer
Palm Beach
Palm Springs
Palm Sunday
palm tree
Palo Alto
part company
part exchange
part-song
part-time
part-way
paso doble
pass judgement
pass key
pass muster
pass off
pass out
pass over
pass up
pass water
past it

past master
past participle
past redemption
path-breaking
Peak District
peak load
pear drop
pear-shaped
peep show
peer group
pell-mell
pent-up
pick apart
pick clean
pick off
pick on
pick out
pick over
pick through
pick up
Pied Piper
pier glass
pile-up
pina colada
pine cone
pine marten
pine nut
pine tree
ping-pong
Pink Floyd
pint-size
pint-sized
pipe cleaner
pipe down
pipe dream
pipe organ
pipe up
pith helmet
play about
play-act
play along
play around
play away
play back
play ball

play dirty
play down
play fair
play favourites
play footsie
play games
play God
play hell
play hookey
play-off
play on
play out
play politics
play possum
play safe
play truant
play up
plea-bargain
plea-bargaining
plot thickens
plug-in
plug into
plum duff
plum pudding
plum tomato
plus fours
plus sign
plus-size
Poet Laureate
pogo stick
poke bonnet
pole dancer
pole dancing
pole position
Pole Star
pole vault
poll tax
polo neck
polo shirt
Pony Express
pony-trekking
pooh-bah
pooh-pooh
poop deck
poor relation

poor white
pork barrel
pork pie
Port Blair
Port Elizabeth
Port Louis
Port Mahon
Port Moresby
Port Said
Port Stanley
Port Sunlight
Port Vila
port wine
post bail
post office
prep school
prie-dieu
prie-dieux
prix fixe
prop forward
puff adder
puff pastry
puff sleeve
pull back
pull down
pull faces
pull in
pull off
pull out
pull over
pull punches
pull rank
pull round
pull strings
pull through
pull together
pull up
pump-action
pump iron
punk rock
punk rocker
pure-bred
pure mathematics
push ahead
push off

push on
push-start
quad bike
Quai d'Orsay
race meeting
race relations
rain check
rake-off
rara avis
rare bird
rare earth
rat's tail
rave-up
read into
read-out
read up
read-write
real ale
real estate
real property
real tennis
real time
rear admiral
rear end
reed mace
reed organ
reef knot
rent boy
rest easy
rest home
ride high
ride on
ride out
ride pillion
ride shotgun
ride up
riff-raff
rift valley
ring binder
ring fence
ring finger
ring main
ring ouzel
ring pull
ring road

Riot Act
risk capital
road hog
road hump
road map
road metal
road pricing
road rage
road tax
road test
Road Town
rock-bottom
rock cake
rock climbing
rock crystal
rock dove
rock face
rock garden
rock music
rock plant
rock pool
rock rose
rock salmon
rock salt
rock-solid
rock wool
role model
role play
role playing
roll back
roll bar
roll-call
roll in
roll-neck
roll-on
roll-out
roll over
roll-up
roly-poly
rood screen
roof rack
room-mate
room service
room temperature
root beer

root canal
root sign
root vegetable
rope ladder
rose-coloured
rose hip
Rose Theatre
rose-tinted
rose water
rose window
Rosh Hashana
Rosh Hashanah
Ross Dependency
ruby wedding
rude boy
Rump Parliament
rush hour
rust belt
rust bucket
safe conduct
safe house
safe keeping
safe period
safe seat
safe sex
sage green
salt cellar
salt flats
salt-glazed
salt lick
salt marsh
salt pan
same difference
sand martin
sans-culotte
sans serif
sash cord
sash window
save face
sawn-off
scot-free
seam bowler
seat belt
seed capital
seed head

seed leaf
seed money
seed pearl
seed potato
self-absorbed
self-absorption
self-abuse
self-addressed
self-adhesive
self-adjusting
self-aggrandizing
self-appointed
self-assemble
self-assembly
self-assertion
self-assertive
self-assertiveness
self-assessment
self-assurance
self-assured
self-aware
self-awareness
self-catering
self-censorship
self-centred
self-centredness
self-certification
self-coloured
self-confessed
self-confidence
self-confident
self-confidently
self-conscious
self-consciously
self-consciousness
self-consistency
self-consistent
self-contained
self-contradiction
self-control
self-controlled
self-deception
self-defeating
self-defence
self-defensive

self-denial
self-denying
self-deprecating
self-deprecation
self-deprecatory
self-destruct
self-destruction
self-destructive
self-destructively
self-determination
self-directed
self-direction
self-discipline
self-disciplined
self-doubt
self-drive
self-educated
self-education
self-effacement
self-effacing
self-employed
self-employment
self-esteem
self-evaluation
self-evident
self-examination
self-explanatory
self-expression
self-fertile
self-fertilisation
self-fertilization
self-fertilize
self-financed
self-financing
self-fulfilling
self-governing
self-government
self-harm
self-harmer
self-help
self-image
self-importance
self-important
self-improvement
self-induced

self-indulgence
self-indulgent
self-inflicted
self-interest
self-interested
self-involved
self-limiting
self-love
self-made
self-medicate
self-medication
self-motivated
self-motivation
self-mutilation
self-opinionated
self-perpetuating
self-pity
self-pitying
self-policing
self-pollinate
self-pollination
self-portrait
self-possessed
self-possession
self-preservation
self-proclaimed
self-propelled
self-propelling
self-realisation
self-realization
self-referential
self-regard
self-regarding
self-regulating
self-regulation
self-regulatory
self-reliance
self-reliant
self-respect
self-respecting
self-restraint
self-righteous
self-righteously
self-righteousness
self-rule

self-sacrifice
self-sacrificing
self-satisfaction
self-satisfied
self-seed
self-seeder
self-seeker
self-seeking
self-service
self-serving
self-starter
self-styled
self-sufficiency
self-sufficient
self-supporting
self-sustained
self-sustaining
self-tanner
self-tanning
self-tapping
self-taught
self-timer
self-willed
self-worth
sell-off
sell-out
sell short
semi-automatic
semi-conscious
semi-detached
semi-double
semi-final
semi-finalist
semi-fluid
semi-liquid
semi-precious
semi-retired
semi-retirement
semi-skilled
semi-skimmed
semi-solid
send down
send in
send-off
send out

send-up
send word
shed blood
shed tears
shih-tzu
Shin Bet
Shin Beth
shin bone
shin splints
ship chandler
shoe leather
shoe tree
shoo-in
shop assistant
shop floor
shop-soiled
shop steward
shot glass
shot-put
shot-putter
shot-putting
show business
show forth
show home
show house
show-off
show-stopper
show-stopping
show trial
show up
show willing
shut down
shut-eye
shut in
shut off
shut out
shut up
sick leave
side effect
side road
side-saddle
side-splitting
side street
side whiskers
side wind

sign away
sign in
sign language
sign off
sign on
sign out
sign over
sign up
Silk Road
Silk Route
silk screen
sine die
Sing Sing
sing-song
Sinn Fein
sitz bath
skew-whiff
skid row
skim milk
skin-deep
skin-dive
skin-diver
skin test
slag heap
slam-dance
slam dunk
slap-up
slip cover
slip knot
slip-on
slip road
slip stitch
slip-up
sloe-eyed
slot machine
slow burn
slow cooker
slow motion
slow-worm
slug pellet
snap-lock
snow blindness
snow geese
snow goose
snow leopard

soap opera
soda bread
soda fountain
soda water
Sod's Law
sofa bed
soft-boiled
soft-core
soft focus
soft fruit
soft furnishings
soft-hearted
soft option
soft palate
soft pedal
soft roe
soft sell
soft-soap
soft target
soft top
soft touch
sola topi
solo whist
song cycle
song thrush
sore point
soul-destroying
soul food
soul music
soul-searching
soup kitchen
sour cream
sour grapes
soya bean
soya milk
spin doctor
spin dryer
spin-off
spin out
spit blood
spit chips
spit-roast
spot check
spot-weld
spur gear

stag beetle
stag night
stag party
star anise
Star Chamber
star-crossed
star sign
star-spangled
star-struck
star-studded
star turn
Star Wars
stay loose
stay put
stay shtum
stem cell
stem ginger
stem stitch
Sten gun
step aerobics
step back
step change
step down
step forward
step in
step out
step up
stir-crazy
stir-fry
stop by
stop dead
stop in
stop-motion
stop off
stop out
stop over
stop payment
stop press
stop short
stop up
stud horse
stun gun
such as
Suez Canal
Suez crisis

sure-fire
sure-footed
sure thing
tail end
tail fin
tail light
take aback
take after
take aim
take amiss
take apart
take away
take back
take care
take chances
take charge
take counsel
take courage
take cover
take down
take fire
take five
take flight
take fright
take guard
take hold
take in
take liberties
take note
take notice
take odds
take-off
take on
take out
take over
take part
take pity
take place
take root
take shape
take ship
take sick
take sides
take silk
take stock

take that
take to
take turns
take umbrage
take-up
take wing
talk back
talk big
talk dirty
talk down
talk radio
talk shop
talk show
talk turkey
talk up
tall order
tall ship
tall story
tall tale
tank engine
tank top
tape measure
tape-record
tape recorder
tape recording
task force
Tate Gallery
taxi cab
taxi rank
taxi stand
teal blue
team player
team spirit
tear apart
tear down
tear duct
tear gas
tear-jerker
tele-evangelist
tell tales
tent stitch
test bed
test card
test case
test-drive

test-driven
test match
test pilot
test tube
text message
text messaging
thin air
tick-tack
time bomb
time capsule
time-consuming
time frame
time-honoured
time lag
time-lapse
time machine
time off
time out
time-server
time sheet
time signature
time switch
time trial
time warp
time-worn
time zone
toby jug
toll gate
tone-deaf
tone poem
toss-up
tote bag
tour operator
town clerk
town council
town councillor
town crier
town hall
town house
town planner
town planning
tree diagram
tree fern
tree house
tree-hugger

| | | |
|---|---|---|
| tree-hugging | vice versa | well oiled |
| tree ring | Vimy Ridge | well preserved |
| tree surgeon | Viti Levu | well-rounded |
| tree surgery | viva voce | well-spoken |
| tree trunk | wait on | well travelled |
| trig point | wait up | well tried |
| trip hammer | wait upon | well trodden |
| troy weight | walk-in | well turned |
| true-blue | walk it | well-wisher |
| true north | walk off | well-worn |
| Tupi-Guarani | walk-on | West Africa |
| turf accountant | walk out | West African |
| turn against | walk over | West Bank |
| turn around | walk tall | West Bromwich |
| turn down | wall bar | West Country |
| turn heads | wall-eyed | West End |
| turn in | Wall Street | West Indian |
| turn-off | warm-blooded | West Indies |
| turn-on | warm down | West Irian |
| turn out | warm-hearted | West Lothian |
| turn round | warm to | West Midlands |
| turn sour | warm up | West Point |
| turn tail | wash out | West Side |
| turn traitor | wash up | West Sussex |
| turn turtle | wasp-waisted | West Virginia |
| turn-up | weak-kneed | what cheer |
| Ugli fruit | wear thin | what gives |
| ugly duckling | well advised | what price |
| Ulan Bator | well appointed | whey-faced |
| unit trust | well away | whip hand |
| upsy-daisy | well-balanced | whip-round |
| uric acid | well-being | Whit Sunday |
| Ursa Major | well bred | whiz-kid |
| Ursa Minor | well built | wide-angle |
| user-friendliness | well disposed | wide awake |
| user-friendly | well-done | wide ball |
| vade mecum | well endowed | wide boy |
| vasa deferentia | well founded | wide-eyed |
| vena cava | well head | wide-ranging |
| Venn diagram | well heeled | wild boar |
| Very light | well known | wild card |
| Very Reverend | well-meaning | wild duck |
| vice admiral | well meant | wild rice |
| vice chancellor | well-nigh | Wild West |
| vice-president | well-off | wind chill |

wind chime
wind down
wind farm
wind instrument
wind tunnel
wind-up
wine bar
wine cellar
wine glass
wine gum
wine list
wine tasting
wine vinegar
wing chair
wing collar
wing commander
wing forward
wing mirror
wing nut
wipe off
wipe out
wire brush
wire gauze
wire-haired
wire service
wire wool
wise guy
wish-fulfilment
with calf
with child
with foal
with interest
with it
with pleasure
with prejudice
wolf whistle
wood alcohol
wood pigeon
wood pulp
wool-gather
wool-gathering
word class
word-perfect
word processor
work ethic

work experience
work off
work out
work permit
work-shy
work up
work wonders
worm cast
worm-eaten
worm gear
worn out
wrap-around
wrap up
writ large
wych elm
Yale University
yard sale
year dot
year-round
Ynys Môn
yule log
zero hour
zero tolerance
zoom lens
zoot suit

**5**-LETTER FIRST WORD

Abbey Theatre
about-face
about time
about to
about-turn
above all
above oneself
above par
above reproach
above suspicion
acute accent
Adam's apple
Addis Ababa
after all
after-effect
after hours
after you

agent noun
agent provocateur
agony aunt
agony column
agony uncle
ahead of
aides-memoire
Alain-Fournier
alarm clock
Alice band
Alice Springs
Allen key
Allen screw
Aloha State
Alpha Centauri
alpha particle
altar boy
alter ego
amino acid
amour propre
angel cake
angel dust
Angel Falls
angel hair
angle bracket
angle grinder
angle iron
Anglo-Catholic
Anglo-Catholicism
Anglo-Indian
Anglo-Irish
Anglo-Saxon
annus horribilis
annus mirabilis
apart from
après-ski
apron stage
armed forces
aside from
asset-stripping
audio frequency
audio tape
audio typist
audio-visual
Audit Commission

avant-garde
avant-gardism
avant-gardist
Ayers Rock
Baath Party
Baden-Baden
Baden-Powell
Baden-Württemberg
badly off
Badon Hill
bains-marie
baked bean
balsa wood
bandy words
Banja Luka
Basse-Normandie
Basse-Terre
bassi profundi
basso profundo
Baton Rouge
baton round
bawdy house
belle époque
Bell's palsy
belly button
belly laugh
below ground
below par
below stairs
bench press
bench test
betel nut
bevel square
Bible Belt
bilge water
billy goat
birth certificate
birth control
birth mother
birth rate
biter bit
biter bitten
black Africa
black art
black bean

black belt
black bile
black box
Black Country
Black Death
black economy
black eye
Black Forest
black hole
black ice
black magic
Black Maria
black mark
black market
black marketeer
black mass
Black Monday
black out
black pudding
Black Rod
black sheep
black spot
Black Stone
black tie
Black Watch
black widow
blank cheque
blank verse
blast furnace
blast-off
Blaue Reiter
bleed dry
bless you
blind alley
blind date
blind drunk
blind side
blind spot
bling-bling
block capital
block letter
block out
block vote
blood brother
blood count

blood-curdling
blood feud
blood group
blood money
blood orange
blood poisoning
blood pressure
blood pudding
blood relation
blood relative
blood sausage
blood sport
blood sugar
blood vessel
board game
booby prize
booby trap
booze-up
boric acid
bossa nova
botch-up
bowel movement
bowie knife
boxer shorts
brain-dead
brain death
brain drain
brain-teaser
brake drum
brake horsepower
brake shoe
brand name
brand new
brass band
brass farthing
brass hat
brass monkey
brass ring
brass rubbing
break away
break bread
break camp
break cover
break-dance
break-dancing

break down
break even
break faith
break ground
break-in
break into
break off
break open
break out
break rank
break ranks
break serve
break service
break ship
break step
break stride
break sweat
break through
break-up
break wind
break with
breed apart
briar pipe
brick red
bring about
bring back
bring down
bring forth
bring forward
bring in
bring off
bring on
bring out
bring up
bring upon
broad bean
broad-brush
Broad Church
broad gauge
broad-minded
brown ale
brown bear
brown belt
brown coal
brown dwarf

brown goods
brown-out
brown owl
brown rice
brown sugar
brown trout
brush-off
Buck's Fizz
build-up
built-in
built-up
bully beef
bully off
bunny girl
Burne-Jones
burnt sienna
burnt umber
cabin boy
cabin cruiser
cabin fever
cable car
cable-knit
cable stitch
cable television
caffè latte
cairn terrier
Calor gas
camel hair
candy-striped
canon law
canon regular
capri pants
cargo pants
carpe diem
carry away
carry forward
carry off
carry-on
carry out
carry over
carry through
carry weight
carte blanche
carve up
catch-all

catch fire
catch it
catch on
catch up
cause célèbre
chain gang
chain letter
chain mail
chain reaction
chain-smoke
chain store
Chang Jiang
chaos theory
charm offensive
chase rainbows
check-in
check into
check on
check out
check-up
chefs-d'oeuvre
chief constable
child benefit
Chile saltpetre
china clay
China syndrome
China tea
chock-full
choux pastry
chuck steak
civic centre
civil defence
civil disobedience
civil engineer
civil law
civil libertarian
civil liberty
Civil List
civil marriage
civil parish
civil rights
civil servant
civil service
civil union
civil war

clasp hands
clasp knife
class action
clean break
clean-cut
clean house
clean-shaven
clean sheet
clean slate
clean-up
clear-cut
clear off
clear-out
clear-sighted
clear up
cleft lip
cleft palate
cling film
clock in
clock out
clock-watcher
close by
close call
close down
close harmony
close in
close on
close ranks
close season
close shave
close thing
close to
close-up
clove hitch
clued-in
clued-up
coach-built
cocoa bean
cocoa butter
comic opera
comic relief
comic strip
Coney Island
conga drum
conic section

Cook's tour
Costa Blanca
Costa Brava
Costa Rica
Costa Rican
couch grass
couch potato
count noun
count out
count sheep
coups d'état
court card
court martial
court order
court shoe
cover charge
cover note
cover-up
cover version
crack cocaine
crane fly
crash-dive
crash helmet
crash-land
crazy paving
cream cheese
cream cracker
cream puff
cream sherry
cream tea
crème brûlée
crème caramel
crème fraiche
crêpe paper
crêpe Suzette
criss-cross
cross-bencher
cross-breed
cross-check
cross-contaminate
cross-contamination
cross-country
cross-current
cross-cut
cross-dress

cross-dresser
cross-examination
cross-examine
cross-eyed
cross-fertilisation
cross-fertilise
cross-fertilization
cross-fertilize
cross-grained
cross hairs
cross-hatch
cross-legged
cross-ownership
cross-party
cross-ply
cross-pollinate
cross-post
cross-question
cross-refer
cross reference
cross section
cross stitch
cross swords
crowd-puller
Crown Colony
Crown Court
Crown Derby
crown green
Crown jewels
Crown prince
Crown princess
crown wheel
crow's feet
crow's foot
crow's-nest
crush bar
crush barrier
Cuban heel
cupro-nickel
curry comb
curry favour
curry powder
Cutty Sark
Czech Republic
daisy chain

daisy wheel
Dalai Lama
dance hall
dance music
Davis Cup
death camp
death certificate
death duty
death knell
death mask
death penalty
death rate
death rattle
death row
death toll
death trap
Death Valley
death wish
debit card
debit side
Dehra Dun
Delta Force
delta wing
depth charge
dicky bow
Diego Garcia
dilly-dally
dirty bomb
dirty look
dirty weekend
dirty word
dirty work
disco music
dizzy heights
Dodge City
doggy bag
doggy-paddle
dolce vita
doll's house
dolly bird
doner kebab
donor card
Dover sole
dower house
Down's syndrome

drawn-out
dress circle
dress down
dress rehearsal
dress sense
dress shirt
dress up
drift net
drink deep
drink-driver
drink-driving
drink to
drive home
drive-in
Drury Lane
dummy run
durum wheat
Dutch auction
Dutch barn
Dutch cap
Dutch courage
Dutch hoe
Dutch oven
Dutch uncle
dwarf star
dying breed
eagle-eyed
eagle owl
early bath
early bird
early doors
Early English
early grave
early hours
early music
early night
early on
earth science
earth-shattering
earth tremor
eaten up
Ebola fever
eider duck
elbow grease
elbow room

elder statesman
elder statesmen
Ellis Island
emery board
empty-handed
empty-headed
empty nester
Empty Quarter
enter on
entre nous
entry-level
envoy extraordinary
epoch-making
epoxy resin
Epsom salts
equal sign
ethyl alcohol
event horizon
extra-curricular
extra time
extra virgin
faint-hearted
fair's fair
fairy cake
fairy godmother
fairy light
fairy ring
fairy story
fairy tale
faith healing
false alarm
false dawn
false economy
false memory
false move
false pretences
false start
false step
fancy dress
fancy-free
fancy man
fancy men
fancy woman
fancy women
Fanny Adams

MULTI-WORD

2 WORDS

fatty acid
feast day
femme fatale
fever pitch
fibre-optic
fibre optics
field day
field event
field glasses
field hockey
field hospital
field marshal
field mice
field mouse
field mushroom
field officer
field sport
field test
field trial
field trip
fifth column
fifth columnist
Fifth Republic
fifty-fifty
final solution
final straw
fines herbes
first aid
first-aider
first blood
first class
first cousin
first-degree
First Empire
first-foot
first-footer
first fruits
first-hand
first lady
first mate
first name
first night
first off
first offender
first officer

first person
first principles
first-rate
first reading
first refusal
First Reich
First Republic
first school
First State
first strike
first thing
First Triumvirate
first up
First World
fixed assets
fixed-wing
flaky pastry
flame-thrower
flash flood
flash memory
Fleet Street
flesh wound
flick knife
flock wallpaper
flood plain
flood tide
floor manager
floor show
fluid drachm
fluid ounce
focal length
focal point
focus group
folic acid
fool's errand
fool's gold
fool's paradise
force-feed
force majeure
forty-five
Fosse Way
frame-up
fresh blood
frock coat
front-bench

front-end
front line
front runner
fruit bat
fruit cocktail
fruit fly
fruit machine
fruit salad
fruit sugar
fuddy-duddy
fully fashioned
fully fledged
funny bone
funny farm
funny peculiar
galia melon
games console
gamma globulin
gamma radiation
gamma ray
garam masala
ghost town
giant-killer
giant-killing
giant panda
giddy-up
given name
glacé icing
glass-blowing
glass ceiling
glass fibre
glass wool
globe artichoke
Globe Theatre
glory be
glory box
glory hole
gloss paint
glove compartment
glove puppet
going concern
going-over
going strong
goody-goody
goose pimples

goose-step
grace note
grade crossing
grade school
Grand Banks
Grand Canal
Grand Canyon
grand duchess
grand duke
Grand Guignol
grand jury
grand mal
Grand Master
Grand National
grand opera
grand piano
Grand Prix
grand slam
grand total
grand tour
grant aid
grant-maintained
grape hyacinth
graph paper
grass roots
grass snake
grass widow
grave accent
gravy boat
gravy train
great ape
great-aunt
Great Basin
Great Bear
Great Britain
great circle
Great Dane
great deal
Great Depression
Great Divide
Great Exhibition
Great Fire
Great Glen
Great Grimsby
great many

great-nephew
great-niece
Great Ouse
Great Plague
Great Schism
Great Scott
great tit
great-uncle
Great War
Great Wen
Greek Church
Greek coffee
Greek cross
green belt
Green Beret
green card
green fingers
green light
Green Paper
green pepper
green revolution
green room
green tea
green woodpecker
gripe water
group captain
group therapy
grown-up
guard hair
guest beer
guest house
guest worker
guide dog
guilt trip
gutta-percha
habit-forming
Hagia Sophia
hair's breadth
hands down
hands-free
hands off
hand's turn
hands up
hanky-panky
happy hour

harum-scarum
hatha yoga
haute couture
haute cuisine
Haute-Normandie
Hawke Bay
heart attack
heart failure
heart-rending
heart-searching
heart-stopping
heart-throb
heart-warming
Heath Robinson
heave-ho
heavy-duty
heavy going
heavy-handed
heavy-hearted
heavy hitter
heavy hydrogen
heavy industry
heavy metal
heavy mob
heavy petting
heavy water
hedge-hop
hedge sparrow
heirs apparent
heirs presumptive
Hell's Angel
hell's bells
Hemel Hempstead
here's to
hidey-hole
Hindu Kush
hitch-hike
hitch-hiker
hobby horse
hocus-pocus
hoity-toity
honky-tonk
horse brass
horse chestnut
horse latitudes

horse laugh
horse sense
horse-trade
horse-trading
house arrest
house-hunt
house-hunter
house husband
house lights
house martin
house mice
house mouse
house music
house officer
house-proud
house-sat
house-sit
house-sitter
house sparrow
house style
house-train
house-warming
Huang Hai
Huang He
Huang Ho
human being
human interest
human nature
human right
hunky-dory
hurdy-gurdy
hurly-burly
icing sugar
idiot savant
index finger
index-linked
India rubber
inert gas
infra dig
inner city
inner ear
Inner House
Inner Mongolia
Inner Temple
inner tube

inter alia
Irian Jaya
Irish coffee
Irish Gaelic
Irish moss
Irish setter
Irish stew
Irish Sweep
Irish Sweepstake
Irish wolfhound
Ivory Coast
ivory tower
jerry-builder
jerry-built
Jesus Christ
jolly boat
Jolly Roger
jolly well
jumbo jet
kauri pine
Khmer Rouge
kirby grip
klieg light
knees-up
knick-knack
knife-edge
knife pleat
knock about
knock around
knock-back
knock-down
knock-kneed
knock-off
knock out
knock together
knock-up
kraft paper
Kuala Lumpur
Kyrie eleison
lacto-vegetarian
lady's maid
lady's man
lady's mantle
lady's men
lady's slipper

lager lout
lamb's lettuce
lamb's-tails
lance corporal
Land's End
lapis lazuli
lardy cake
large calorie
large intestine
large-scale
laser printer
Lassa fever
latch on
Latin America
Latin American
leave alone
leave go
leave off
leave out
leave school
leave standing
leave-taking
legal aid
legal separation
legal tender
leger line
lemon balm
lemon curd
lemon grass
lemon sole
level crossing
level-headed
level-headedly
level-headedness
level pegging
liege lord
light bulb
light-fingered
light flyweight
light-footed
light-headed
light-hearted
light-heartedly
light heavyweight
light industry

light meter
light middleweight
light on
light pen
light pollution
light touch
light welterweight
light year
likes of
linen basket
lived-in
liver sausage
liver spot
local anaesthetic
local authority
local derby
local government
local time
locus classicus
logic bomb
lollo rosso
loose box
loose cannon
loose cover
loose end
loose forward
loose-leaf
loose scrum
Lords Advocate
Lords Chamberlain
Lords Lieutenant
Lords Provost
lotus-eater
lotus position
Lough Neagh
Louis-Napoleon
lovey-dovey
lower case
lower chamber
lower class
lower court
lower house
lucky devil
lucky dip
lunar eclipse

lunar month
lupus erythematosus
lupus vulgaris
lymph gland
lymph node
Machu Picchu
macro lens
magic carpet
magic lantern
magic mushroom
magic realism
Magna Carta
Magna Charta
magna opera
major-domo
major general
Malay Archipelago
Malay Peninsula
Malin Head
manic depression
manic-depressive
Maori Wars
maple leaf
maple syrup
Mappa Mundi
March hare
Mardi Gras
mare's nest
mare's tail
Marie Celeste
marry money
Marsh Arab
marsh gas
marsh mallow
marsh marigold
match play
match point
Mauna Kea
Mauna Loa
mealy bug
mealy-mouthed
means test
Melba toast
Menai Strait
metal detector

mezzo-soprano
Midas touch
milch cow
miles away
Milky Way
mince matters
mince pie
minus sign
mixed bag
mixed blessing
mixed economy
mixed farming
mixed grill
mixed marriage
mixed metaphor
mixed-up
mixer tap
modal verb
modus operandi
modus vivendi
money-grubbing
money market
money order
money spider
money-spinner
money supply
money talks
Monte Carlo
Monte Cassino
moral majority
moral philosophy
Moral Rearmament
moral victory
moray eel
Moray Firth
Morse code
motor boat
motor car
motor racing
motor scooter
motor vehicle
mount guard
mouse mat
mouth organ
mouth-watering

multi-purpose
multi-storey
multi-track
multi-utility
mumbo-jumbo
music centre
music hall
mynah bird
namby-pamby
nanny goat
navel-gazing
navel orange
Nazca Lines
needs must
nerve cell
nerve centre
nerve gas
nerve-racking
nerve-wracking
never-ending
never fear
never mind
newel post
newly-wed
night light
night owl
night safe
night school
night soil
night-time
nitty-gritty
Noah's ark
Nobel Prize
noble gas
noble rot
noble savage
noise pollution
North Africa
North African
North America
North American
North Ayrshire
North Carolina
North Channel
North Dakota

north-east
north-easterly
north-eastern
north-eastward
north-eastwards
North Island
North Korea
North Lanarkshire
North Lincolnshire
North Minch
North Pole
North Star
North Uist
North Utsire
north-west
north-westerly
north-western
north-westward
north-westwards
North Yorkshire
Notre-Dame
nudge nudge
nurse shark
nutty about
objet d'art
Ocean State
ocean trench
Offa's Dyke
olive branch
olive drab
olive green
olive oil
opera buffa
opera glasses
opera house
opera seria
optic nerve
orang-utan
orang-utang
order arms
Order Order
Order Paper
organ-grinder
oriel window
orris root

other half
other place
other ranks
other woman
other-worldly
Ouija board
Outer House
outer space
owing to
owner-occupier
oxbow lake
ozone hole
ozone layer
paddy field
panda car
panel beater
panel game
panel pin
panel saw
panel truck
panic attack
panic button
panic stations
panne velvet
pants suit
paper boy
paper clip
paper girl
paper money
paper round
paper route
paper-thin
paper tiger
paper trail
Parma ham
party line
party politics
party-pooper
party to
party wall
paste-up
patch pocket
patch test
patio door
Peace Corps

peace dividend
peace offering
peach Melba
Peach State
pearl barley
Pearl Harbor
pease pudding
pedal pusher
penal servitude
penny black
penny dreadful
penny-farthing
penny-pincher
penny-pinching
penny whistle
Peter Pan
petit bourgeois
petit bourgeoisie
petit four
petit mal
petit point
Petri dish
petty bourgeois
petty bourgeoisie
petty cash
petty officer
Phnom Penh
phone book
phone-in
photo finish
photo opportunity
piani nobili
piano accordion
piano nobile
piggy bank
pilot light
pilot officer
pilot whale
pince-nez
Pinot Blanc
Pinot Noir
pinto bean
piped music
Piper Alpha
pitch-black

pitch-dark
pitch in
pitch into
pitch pine
pitch up
place kick
place-kicker
place setting
Plaid Cymru
plain chocolate
plain clothes
plain flour
plain sailing
plain-spoken
plane tree
plate glass
plumb line
Poets' Corner
Poets Laureate
point-blank
point duty
poker face
polar bear
poles apart
polka dot
Poppy Day
porky-pie
Porto Novo
poste restante
pound cake
pound sterling
power broker
power cut
power line
power pack
power plant
power station
power steering
prawn cracker
press charges
press conference
Press Council
press flesh
press gang
press home

press release
press stud
press-up
price tag
prima ballerina
prima donna
prima facie
prime minister
prime mover
prime time
print run
prior to
Privy Council
privy counsellor
privy purse
privy seal
proof positive
proof spirit
Puffa jacket
Puget Sound
punch-drunk
punch-up
puppy fat
puppy love
purse seine
pussy willow
Queen Anne
queen bee
queen consort
queen high
queen mother
queen post
queen-size
queen-sized
queue-jump
quick-fire
quick march
quick one
quick-tempered
quick-witted
quids in
quite something
quote unquote
radar gun
radar trap

radio astronomy
radio-controlled
radio ham
radio-telephone
radio telescope
radio wave
rainy day
raise anchor
raise Cain
raise hell
rake's progress
ranch house
razor shell
razor wire
ready-made
ready-mixed
ready money
ready reckoner
Rhode Island
Rhône-Alpes
ridge tent
right angle
right-angled
right away
right back
Right Bank
right hand
right-handed
right-hander
Right Honourable
right-minded
right on
right one
Right Reverend
right stuff
right-thinking
right whale
right wing
right-winger
rigor mortis
Robbe-Grillet
rogan josh
Rolls-Royce
Roman Britain
Roman candle

Roman Catholic
Roman Catholicism
Roman Empire
Roman law
Roman nose
Roman numeral
Roman Republic
rough diamond
rough edges
rough-hew
rough-hewn
rough-house
rough justice
rough ride
rough trade
round about
round dance
round off
round on
round out
round robin
round-table
round trip
round-up
Royal Academy
Royal Ballet
royal blue
Royal Commission
royal icing
Royal Institution
royal jelly
Royal Mint
Royal Navy
Royal Society
royal warrant
rugby football
rugby league
rugby union
rumpy pumpy
Ryder Cup
sabre-rattling
Saint-Denis
Saint-Exupéry
Saint John
Saint-Saëns

Saint-Simon
salad cream
sales clerk
Santa Barbara
Santa Claus
Santa Cruz
Santa Fe
Santa Monica
Santa Sophia
Santo Domingo
satin stitch
sauce boat
Saudi Arabia
Saudi Arabian
sawed-off
scale insect
Scapa Flow
scoop neck
score points
Scots pine
Scout Association
scrag-end
scrap heap
screw propeller
screw thread
screw up
scrum half
scuba-dive
scuba-diving
Sears Tower
sedge warbler
sense organ
Sepoy Mutiny
Serbo-Croat
Serbo-Croatian
serio-comic
serve notice
shake down
shake hands
shake off
shake on
shake-out
shake-up
shape-shifter
shape-shifting

share option
sharp end
sharp practice
sharp-tongued
sharp-witted
shawl collar
sheep dip
sheet lightning
sheet metal
sheet music
shelf life
shell-less
shell pink
shell shock
shell-shocked
shell suit
shire horse
shirt dress
shirt tail
shish kebab
shock absorber
shock tactics
shock therapy
shock treatment
shock troops
shock wave
shoot down
shoot-out
shoot through
shoot up
shore leave
short-change
short circuit
short commons
short cut
short division
short for
short fuse
short fuze
short-handed
short haul
short head
short hundredweight
short-lived
short of

Short Parliament
short-range
short shrift
short-sighted
short-sightedly
short-sightedness
short-staffed
short-tempered
short term
short-termism
short ton
short wave
short-winded
shove off
shove up
siege mentality
sight line
sight-read
sight screen
silly season
siren call
siren song
sixth sense
skean-dhu
skeet shooting
slack water
slave-driver
slave labour
slave trade
sleep easy
sleep rough
sleep tight
slide rule
sling beer
sling hash
sling plates
slope arms
slush fund
smack bang
small arms
small calorie
small change
small end
small fortune
small fry

small hours
small intestine
small-minded
small potatoes
small print
small-scale
small talk
small-time
small wonder
smart alec
smart aleck
smart card
smash hit
smear test
smell blood
smoke alarm
snail mail
snake charmer
snare drum
snarl-up
snowy owl
snuff movie
socio-economic
socio-political
Sogne Fjord
solar battery
solar cell
solar eclipse
solar energy
solar flare
solar panel
solar plexus
solar power
solar system
solar wind
solar year
solid-state
sonic boom
sotto voce
sound barrier
sound bite
sound effect
sound system
sound wave
South Africa

South African
South America
South American
South Australia
South Ayrshire
South Bank
South Carolina
South Dakota
south-east
south-easterly
south-eastern
south-eastward
south-eastwards
South Georgia
South Island
South Korea
South Lanarkshire
South Pole
South Seas
South Shields
South Uist
South Utsire
south-west
south-westerly
south-western
south-westward
south-westwards
space age
space bar
space cadet
space capsule
space probe
space shuttle
space station
space-time
spare rib
spare tyre
spark out
spark plug
speak out
speak up
speak volumes
speed bump
speed camera
speed dating

speed dial
speed hump
speed limit
sperm count
sperm whale
Spice Girl
Spice Girls
spill blood
spina bifida
spine-chiller
spine-chilling
spine-tingling
spiny anteater
splay-footed
split end
split hairs
split infinitive
split-level
split pea
split pin
split screen
split second
spoon-feed
sport utility
spray gun
squad car
squat thrust
staff nurse
staff officer
staff sergeant
stage direction
stage door
stage fright
stage left
stage-manage
stage management
stage manager
stage name
stage right
stage-struck
stage whisper
stake-out
stamp duty
stand-alone
stand aside

stand back
stand bail
stand by
stand comparison
stand down
stand easy
stand for
stand guard
stand-in
stand-off
stand-offish
stand on
stand out
stand over
stand sentry
stand surety
stand tall
stand to
stand trial
stand-up
stark naked
start off
start out
start over
start-up
State Department
state house
state school
steak tartare
steam bath
steam engine
steam iron
steel band
steel drum
steel pan
steel wool
Stern Gang
stick around
stick at
stick by
stick insect
stick out
stick shift
stick to
stick together

stick-up
stick with
stiff-necked
still life
stink bomb
stock car
stock cube
stock exchange
stock market
stock-still
Stone Age
stone circle
stone me
stony-broke
stool pigeon
storm cloud
storm door
storm drain
storm petrel
storm sewer
storm trooper
storm window
straw poll
straw vote
strip light
strip mine
strip-search
stuck-up
stuff it
sugar beet
sugar cane
sugar-coat
sugar daddy
Sugar Loaf
sugar snap
sugar soap
swear blind
swear word
sweat blood
sweat buckets
sweat bullets
sweet bay
sweet chestnut
sweet cicely
sweet pea

sweet pepper
sweet potato
sweet sixteen
sweet-talk
sweet tooth
sweet william
sweet woodruff
swept-back
swine fever
swing bridge
swing door
swipe card
Swiss chard
Swiss Confederation
Swiss roll
table d'hôte
table manners
table skittles
table tennis
table wine
taken short
tally-ho
tally stick
Tamil Nadu
taste blood
taste bud
tawny owl
teach school
teddy bear
Teddy boy
teeny-bopper
teeny-weeny
tempt fate
tempt providence
tenon saw
terra firma
terra incognita
thank God
thank goodness
thank heavens
that's life
theme park
theme tune
thigh bone
think again

think aloud
think back
think big
think fit
think on
think out
think over
think tank
think twice
think up
third age
third class
third-degree
third-generation
third man
third men
third party
third person
third-rate
third reading
Third Reich
Third Republic
third way
Third World
thole pin
three cheers
three-dimensional
three parts
three-piece
three-quarter
three Rs
throw away
throw-in
throw off
throw open
throw out
throw overboard
throw together
throw up
thumb index
tidal bore
tidal wave
tiger economy
tiger lily
tiger moth

tiger prawn
tiger shrimp
tight corner
tight-fisted
tight-knit
tight-lipped
tight place
tight spot
tippy-toe
tithe barn
title deed
title role
today week
tommy gun
tonic water
tooth fairy
topsy-turvy
torch song
total eclipse
total war
totem pole
touch base
touch bottom
touch down
touch judge
touch off
touch on
touch screen
touch-tone
touch-type
touch up
touch upon
touch wood
tough love
tough luck
tough-minded
tough nut
tower block
Tower Bridge
trace element
track event
track record
trade deficit
trade down
trade in

trade name
trade-off
trade on
trade places
trade plates
trade surplus
trade union
trade unionism
trade unionist
trade up
trade wind
trail arms
trail mix
trans-ship
trans-shipment
trash can
trash talk
trash talker
trawl net
tread water
trial run
troop carrier
trump card
trunk call
trust company
trust fund
tulip tree
tummy button
Turin Shroud
tutti-frutti
ultra vires
Uncle Tom
under-age
under arms
under canvas
under control
under cover
under debate
under fire
under foot
under guard
under load
under oath
under par
under protest

under-report
under-represent
under-resourced
under sail
under siege
under steam
under suspicion
under water
under way
Union flag
Union Jack
Union Territory
upper case
upper chamber
upper class
upper house
upper school
Upper Volta
urban legend
urban myth
Uttar Pradesh
Valle d'Aosta
value judgement
venae cavae
Venus flytrap
vicar general
video game
video recorder
Vigée-Lebrun
Villa-Lobos
vinho verde
viral marketing
vital force
vital signs
vital statistics
vocal cords
vocal folds
voice box
voice-over
volte-face
wafer-thin
Wagga Wagga
wagon-lit
waste words
water bailiff

water-based
water birth
water biscuit
water boatman
water boatmen
water buffalo
water cannon
water chestnut
water closet
water diviner
water feature
water ice
water level
water lily
water main
water meadow
water pistol
water polo
water rat
water-resistant
water table
water tower
water vole
water wings
waxed paper
weigh anchor
weigh-in
weigh into
weigh on
weigh up
Weil's disease
Welsh corgi
Welsh rarebit
Wendy house
what's up
wheel clamp
white ant
white belt
White Book
white-bread
white cell
white Christmas
white-collar
white dwarf
white elephant

white feather
white flag
white gold
white goods
white heat
white hope
white horses
white-hot
White House
white knight
white-knuckle
white lie
white light
white magic
white meat
White Nile
white noise
white-out
White Paper
white rose
White Russia
White Russian
White Sands
white sauce
white slave
white spirit
white tie
white trash
white water
white wedding
white witch
whizz-kid
whole number
whole tone
willy-nilly
Windy City
wiped out
wishy-washy
witch doctor
witch hazel
witch-hunt
World Bank
world-beater
world-beating
world-class

World Cup
world English
world music
world order
world power
world-ranking
World Series
World Service
world-shaking
world war
world-weary
worry beads
worse luck
worse off
worth while
would-be
write-off
write-up
wrong-foot
wrong-headed
Yalta Conference
ylang-ylang
young blood
young gun
young offender
Young Turk
yours faithfully
yours sincerely
yours truly
youth centre
youth club
youth hostel
Yukon Territory
zebra crossing

**6**-LETTER FIRST WORD

absent-minded
absent-mindedly
absent-mindedness
Abukir Bay
acetic acid
across country
across from
action painting

**MULTI-WORD**

**2 WORDS**

action replay
action stations
active service
Actors' Studio
Afghan coat
Afghan hound
Afrika Korps
Aghios Nikolaos
Aigues-Mortes
Alaska Peninsula
almond paste
Alsace-Lorraine
ancien régime
Andhra Pradesh
angina pectoris
animal magnetism
answer to
Appian Way
Arabic numeral
Arctic Circle
armour plate
armour-plated
asking price
aspect ratio
Atkins diet
atomic bomb
atomic number
atomic theory
atomic weight
attorn tenant
aurora australis
aurora borealis
Badger State
Baffin Bay
Baffin Island
Bailey bridge
baking powder
baking soda
baleen whale
Baltic Exchange
bamboo shoot
banana republic
banana split
barbed wire
barley sugar

barley water
barrel organ
barrel vault
basket case
Basque Country
basset hound
Bayeux Tapestry
Beagle Channel
beauty contest
beauty pageant
beauty parlour
beauty queen
beauty salon
beauty sleep
beauty spot
Beaver State
beetle-browed
before time
beggar belief
beggar description
behind bars
behind schedule
behind time
Belize City
belles-lettres
Bering Strait
Berlin airlift
Berlin Wall
beside oneself
better half
better-known
better-off
beyond belief
beyond description
beyond measure
beyond reason
beyond recall
beyond reproach
bichon frise
bikini line
billet-doux
bitter aloes
bitter lemon
bitter orange
bitter pill

Bloody Mary
bloody-minded
Bloody Sunday
bodice-ripper
boiled sweet
boiler suit
Bombay duck
Bombay mix
bomber jacket
boogie board
boogie-woogie
Booker Prize
borrow trouble
Bosnia-Herzegovina
Botany Bay
bottle bank
bottle-feed
bottle green
bottom drawer
bottom feeder
bottom line
bounty hunter
Bourke-White
Boxing Day
Boyle's law
brains trust
Brands Hatch
brandy butter
brandy snap
Brazil nut
breath test
breech birth
breeze block
bridge loan
bridge roll
bridle path
bright spark
broken-down
broken-hearted
broken home
broker-dealer
Bronze Age
bronze medal
bubble bath
bubble wrap

bucket seat
bucket shop
Buenos Aires
buffer solution
bulgar wheat
Bulwer-Lytton
bumper car
bungee cord
bungee jump
bungee jumper
bungee jumping
Bunker Hill
Bunsen burner
butter bean
butter icing
button mushroom
button-through
buyer's market
caddis fly
Caesar salad
camera obscura
camera-ready
camper van
Canada geese
Canada goose
canary yellow
canine teeth
canine tooth
cannon fodder
canons regular
carbon black
carbon copy
carbon dating
carbon dioxide
carbon fibre
carbon monoxide
carbon paper
carbon sink
carbon steel
carbon tax
carnal knowledge
carpet bag
carpet-bomb
carpet slipper
Carson City

cashew nut
Castel Gandolfo
caster sugar
castor oil
castor sugar
cattle grid
cattle guard
caught short
caveat emptor
cavity wall
centre back
centre forward
centre half
centre stage
Chagos Archipelago
chaise longue
chaise lounge
Champs Élysées
change colour
change down
change hands
change over
change step
change up
charge card
chargé d'affaires
charge nurse
cheese-paring
Chenin blanc
cheque card
cherry brandy
cherry-pick
cherry tomato
Chesil Bank
Chesil Beach
cheval glass
cheval mirror
chilli pepper
chilli powder
chorus girl
Church Army
Cinque Ports
citric acid
citrus fruit
cloche hat

closed season
closed shop
cloven feet
cloven foot
cloven hoof
clutch bag
coarse fish
cobalt blue
cocked hat
cocker spaniel
coffee table
coitus interruptus
colour-blind
colour blindness
colour fast
colour scheme
colour sergeant
colour supplement
combat trousers
commis chef
common denominator
Common Era
common good
common ground
common knowledge
common law
common market
common noun
Common Prayer
common property
common room
common salt
common sense
common soldier
common time
common touch
Comoro Islands
compos mentis
conger eel
Copper Age
copper beech
copper-bottomed
copper sulphate
Coptic Church
cordon bleu

cordon sanitaire
corned beef
corner kick
corner shop
corona discharge
Corpus Christi
cosmic ray
cotter pin
cotton bud
Cotton State
cotton wool
county council
county councillor
county court
County Durham
county seat
county town
courts martial
Covent Garden
cowboy boot
Coyote State
cradle-snatcher
credit card
credit union
creepy-crawly
crêpes Suzette
Cresta Run
Crohn's disease
croque-monsieur
cruise control
cruise missile
cuckoo clock
cuckoo pint
cuckoo spit
Cupid's bow
custom-built
custom house
custom-made
cystic fibrosis
danger money
Danish blue
Danish pastry
dapple grey
dating agency
deadly nightshade

deadly sin
dearie me
deckle edge
decree absolute
decree nisi
dengue fever
dental floss
dental surgeon
desert island
devil's advocate
devil's dozen
Devil's Island
devil's own
dialog box
diesel oil
dimmer switch
dining car
dining room
dinner jacket
direct action
direct current
direct debit
direct mail
direct object
direct speech
direct tax
dirndl skirt
dismal science
Divine Office
diving bell
diving board
diving suit
Dogger Bank
dollar mark
dollar sign
dolman sleeve
domino effect
Donald Duck
donkey jacket
donkey work
dormer window
double act
double agent
double-barrelled
double bass

double bill
double bind
double-blind
double bluff
double boiler
double bond
double-book
double-breasted
double-check
double chin
double cream
double-cross
double-dealing
double-decker
double Dutch
double-edged
double entendre
double-entry
double exposure
double fault
double figures
double-glaze
double glazing
Double Gloucester
double-header
double helix
double jeopardy
double-jointed
double negative
double-park
double pneumonia
double standard
double take
double time
double vision
double whammy
duffel bag
duffel coat
dugout canoe
dumdum bullet
dumper truck
dunce's cap
Dunmow flitch
Dunnet Head
Ealing Studios

earned income
Easter Day
Easter egg
Easter Island
Easter Rising
Easter Sunday
eating apple
Eccles cake
Eiffel Tower
either way
eleven-plus
Elysée Palace
Emilia-Romagna
empire line
Empire State
enfant terrible
engine block
envoys extraordinary
equals sign
escape clause
escape key
estate agency
estate agent
estate car
ethnic cleansing
ethnic minority
excess baggage
excuse me
exeunt omnes
factor eight
fallen angel
fallow deer
family credit
Family Division
family jewels
family name
family planning
family tree
family values
feeble-minded
fellow feeling
fellow-traveller
fellow-travelling
Ferris wheel
Fianna Fáil

fiddle-faddle
figure-hugging
figure on
figure out
figure skater
figure skating
filler cap
filter tip
finger bowl
finger food
finger-paint
finnan haddock
firing blanks
firing line
firing squad
fiscal year
flight attendant
flight deck
flight feather
flight lieutenant
flight path
flight recorder
flight sergeant
floppy disk
flower head
flower power
flying boat
flying buttress
Flying Dutchman
flying fish
flying fox
flying officer
flying picket
flying saucer
Flying Scotsman
flying squad
flying start
flying trapeze
Folies-Bergère
follow on
follow suit
follow-through
follow-up
forage cap
forced landing

forced march
forked lightning
formic acid
fossil fuel
fourth dimension
Fourth Republic
Fourth World
freeze-dry
freeze-frame
French bean
French bread
French Canadian
French chalk
French dressing
French Guiana
French horn
French kiss
French kissing
French knickers
French letter
French polish
French Polynesia
French Revolution
French stick
French toast
French window
fridge-freezer
fright wig
frigid zone
fringe benefit
frying pan
future perfect
future shock
Gaelic coffee
gaffer tape
galley proof
Gallup poll
Galway Bay
garage sale
garden centre
garden city
garden party
Garden State
garden-variety
garter snake

garter stitch
gastro-enteritis
gather dust
Geiger counter
Geneva Convention
genito-urinary
George Town
German Bight
German Empire
German measles
German shepherd
ghetto blaster
Giant's Causeway
ginger ale
ginger beer
ginger group
ginger nut
Global Surveyor
global village
global warming
Godwin-Austen
goggle-box
goggle-eyed
goings-on
golden age
golden boy
Golden Delicious
golden eagle
Golden Fleece
Golden Gate
golden geese
golden girl
golden goose
golden handcuffs
golden handshake
Golden Hind
Golden Horn
golden jubilee
golden mean
golden oldie
golden retriever
golden rule
Golden State
golden syrup
golden wedding

Gopher State
gospel music
gospel truth
gossip column
gothic novel
Grande Comore
grande dame
Grands Prix
granny flat
granny knot
Granny Smith
Granth Sahib
graven image
grease gun
greasy spoon
Gretna Green
ground control
ground down
ground elder
ground floor
ground frost
ground glass
ground rent
ground rule
ground speed
ground squirrel
ground zero
growth hormone
growth industry
growth ring
growth stock
guard's van
Guides Association
Guinea-Bissau
guinea pig
gutter press
habeas corpus
halter-neck
hammer beam
hammer drill
hammer home
hammer toe
hanger-on
hansom cab
Harlem Renaissance

Harley Street
Harrow School
Hawke's Bay
hazard lights
header tank
health centre
health club
health farm
health food
health service
health tourism
health visitor
Heaven forbid
heaven knows
heaven-sent
Hebrew Bible
heebie-jeebies
helter-skelter
hermit crab
herpes simplex
herpes zoster
Heyhoe-Flint
hiatus hernia
hidden agenda
hidden depths
higher court
higher education
highly commended
highly strung
hoisin sauce
honest Injun
honour bright
Hooray Henry
housey-housey
Hudson Bay
hugger-mugger
humble-bee
hunger strike
hunter-gatherer
immune response
immune system
income support
income tax
Indian club
Indian corn

Indian file
Indian ink
Indian Mutiny
Indian subcontinent
Indian summer
injury time
inkjet printer
Inland Revenue
inside job
inside leg
inside of
inside out
jacket potato
Jacob's ladder
Jersey City
Jockey Club
Joshua tree
Julian calendar
jumble sale
jumped-up
junior college
junior school
Kansas City
Kariba Dam
Kelvin scale
Khyber Pass
kidney bean
kidney machine
kidney stone
killer whale
kipper tie
kitten heel
knight commander
knight errant
Komodo dragon
Korean War
Kuwait City
labour camp
Labour Day
labour exchange
labour force
labour-intensive
Labour Party
labour-saving
labour union

lactic acid
ladder-back
ladies' fingers
ladies' man
ladies' men
ladies' room
Lammas Day
lancet window
lateen sail
latent heat
latent image
latter-day
leader board
league table
ledger line
Leptis Magna
lesser evil
letter bomb
letter box
Leyden jar
lights out
lignum vitae
likely story
limbic system
limpet mine
linear equation
lingua franca
liquid paraffin
litmus paper
litmus test
litter lout
Little Bear
Little Bighorn
Little Englander
little finger
Little Minch
Little Ouse
little people
Little Rhody
Little Rock
little wonder
livery stable
living room
living wage
living will

Lloyd's Register
locker room
London pride
lonely heart
losing battle
lounge bar
lounge lizard
lounge suit
lovely jubbly
loving cup
lumbar puncture
Lutine Bell
Madhya Pradesh
magnum opus
maiden name
maiden over
mailed fist
maître d'hôtel
malice aforethought
mangel-wurzel
Marble Arch
market garden
market gardener
market-maker
market research
market researcher
market town
market value
marram grass
marron glacé
masked ball
Massif Central
master key
master stroke
Maundy money
Maundy Thursday
medium term
medium wave
mental age
mental attitude
mental block
mental handicap
method acting
methyl alcohol
metric hundredweight

metric system
metric ton
metric tonne
Mexico City
Mickey Finn
Mickey Mouse
mickey-taking
middle age
middle-aged
Middle Ages
Middle America
middle C
middle class
middle distance
middle ear
Middle East
Middle Eastern
Middle England
Middle English
middle ground
Middle Kingdom
middle name
middle school
Middle Temple
Middle West
Milton Keynes
minute steak
mirror image
mirror site
mistle thrush
mobile home
mobile phone
Möbius strip
modern languages
modern pentathlon
monkey business
monkey nut
monkey puzzle
monkey suit
monkey wrench
Monroe doctrine
morris dance
morris dancer
morris dancing
mortar board

mother country
mother lode
mother ship
Mother Superior
mother tongue
motion picture
motive power
Moulin Rouge
mucous membrane
muddle-headed
Munich Agreement
muscle-bound
museum piece
Muslim Brotherhood
narrow gauge
narrow-minded
nation state
Native American
native speaker
nature reserve
nature trail
nether regions
Nicene Creed
nickel silver
nickel steel
Nikkei index
niminy-piminy
Nissen hut
nitric acid
Nizhni Novgorod
noises off
Nordic skiing
Norman Conquest
notary public
Novaya Zemlya
number cruncher
number one
number plate
Number Ten
number two
Nutmeg State
object lesson
objets d'art
Occam's razor
octane number

octane rating
Orange Lodge
Orange Order
orange pekoe
orange stick
Oregon Trail
Orient Express
Orion's Belt
otitis media
oxalic acid
Oxford bags
Oxford Group
Oxford Movement
Oxford University
oxygen bar
oxygen mask
oyster mushroom
packed lunch
packed out
packet boat
paddle boat
paddle steamer
paddle wheel
palace coup
Pallas Athena
Pallas Athene
pampas grass
Panama Canal
Panama City
papier mâché
parade ground
pardon me
parish council
parish-pump
parish register
parrot-fashion
pasque flower
passer-by
patent leather
patent medicine
patron saint
paving stone
paying guest
peanut butter
Pearly Gates

pearly king
pearly queen
pearly whites
pebble-dash
Peking duck
pelvic floor
pelvic girdle
pencil skirt
people carrier
pepper spray
peptic ulcer
period piece
Peters projection
petite bourgeoisie
petits pois
petrol blue
petrol bomb
phoney war
phrase book
pickup truck
pigeon-toed
pillar box
pillow talk
pincer movement
pineal body
pineal gland
pistol-whip
pitter-patter
plasma screen
played out
please God
please yourself
plough back
plunge pool
pocket borough
pocket gopher
pocket money
pocket watch
poetic justice
poetic licence
poison ivy
poison pill
Poitou-Charentes
police officer
police state

police station
Polish Corridor
pollen count
pommes frites
Popish Plot
portal vein
postal code
postal order
poster paint
potato chip
potato crisp
powder blue
powder keg
powder puff
powder room
Prague Spring
praise be
prayer wheel
pretty penny
Prince Charming
prince consort
prince royal
prison camp
prison officer
profit margin
profit-sharing
proper fraction
proper name
proper noun
public bar
public company
public corporation
public defender
public enemy
public eye
public house
public nuisance
public prosecutor
public relations
public school
public sector
public servant
public-spirited
public transport
public utility

Puerto Limón
Puerto Plata
Puerto Rican
Puerto Rico
Purple Heart
purple laver
purple passage
purple patch
purple prose
quarry tile
quartz clock
Quebec City
Queen's Bench
Queen's Counsel
Queen's English
Queen's evidence
Queen's Guide
Queen's highway
Queen's Scout
Queen's Speech
rabbit punch
rabble-rouser
racing car
racing driver
radial keratotomy
radial symmetry
ragged robin
raggle-taggle
raison d'être
random access
Ranger Guide
rattle sabres
razzle-dazzle
record-breaker
record-breaking
record player
reefer jacket
reflex camera
reform school
Regius professor
relief map
relief road
remote control
remote-controlled
remote controller

return match
rhesus factor
rhesus monkey
rhesus negative
rhesus positive
Rhodes Scholar
Rhodes Scholarship
rhythm method
rhythm section
ribbon development
riding crop
riding habit
rights issue
Rimsky-Korsakov
rising damp
Robben Island
rocket science
rocket scientist
rodent ulcer
rogues' gallery
rolled gold
rolled oats
roller bearing
roller blind
roller coaster
roller rink
roller skate
roller skater
roller skating
roller towel
romper suit
Rotary International
rotten borough
rotten luck
rowing boat
rowing machine
rubber band
rubber bullet
rubber johnny
rubber plant
rubber stamp
rubber tree
rumble strip
runner bean
runner-up

Sacred College
sacred cow
saddle horse
saddle soap
saddle-sore
saddle stitch
safari park
safari suit
safety belt
safety catch
safety curtain
safety first
safety glass
safety match
safety net
safety pin
safety razor
safety valve
sailor suit
saint's day
salade niçoise
salmon trout
saving grace
savoir faire
Saxony-Anhalt
Scotch broth
Scotch egg
Scotch whisky
Scout's honour
screen-print
screen saver
screen test
scroll bar
Seanad Eireann
search engine
search me
search party
search warrant
season ticket
second best
second class
Second Coming
second-degree
Second Empire
second-generation

second-guess
second-hand
second name
second nature
second person
second-rate
second-rater
second reading
Second Reich
Second Republic
second sight
second string
second thought
Second Triumvirate
second wind
secret agent
secret police
secret service
secret society
secure arms
seeing double
seeing things
select committee
senile dementia
senior aircraftman
senior aircraftmen
senior aircraftwoman
senior aircraftwomen
senior citizen
senior registrar
Senior Service
sentry box
septic tank
serial number
sewage farm
sewage works
sewing machine
sexual harassment
sexual intercourse
sexual politics
shades of
shadow-box
shadow economy
shanty town
sheath dress

2 WORDS

MULTI-WORD

sheath knife
shilly-shally
shrink-wrap
Shrove Tuesday
Sierra Leone
Sierra Leonean
Sierra Madre
Sierra Nevada
signal box
signet ring
silent majority
silent partner
silent treatment
silica gel
silver birch
silver jubilee
silver medal
silver plate
silver service
Silver State
silver tongue
silver-tongued
silver wedding
simnel cake
simple fracture
simple-minded
simple time
single bond
single-breasted
single combat
single cream
single currency
single file
single-handed
single-handedly
single malt
single market
single-minded
single-mindedly
single-mindedness
single parent
sketch pad
skinny-dip
skinny-rib
slaked lime

Sloane Ranger
slouch hat
sluice gate
smooth snake
smooth-talk
smooth-talker
snooze button
Social Charter
social climber
social compact
social contract
social democracy
social fund
social market
social realism
social science
social security
social service
social studies
social work
social worker
sodium bicarbonate
sodium chloride
sodium hydroxide
sodium lamp
softly-softly
Solway Firth
Somali Peninsula
Sooner State
Soviet Union
sparks fly
speech day
speech impediment
speech recognition
speech therapist
speech therapy
spider crab
spider mite
spider monkey
spider plant
spinal column
spinal cord
spiral-bound
spirit gum
spirit lamp

spirit level
spirit world
spoken for
sponge bag
sponge pudding
sports car
sports jacket
spread betting
spring balance
spring chicken
spring clean
spring greens
spring-loaded
spring onion
spring roll
spring tide
square-bashing
square dance
square deal
square leg
square meal
square measure
square mile
square number
square off
square-rigged
square root
square up
squash rackets
starry-eyed
Staten Island
state's evidence
static electricity
status quo
status symbol
steady on
sticky fingers
sticky wicket
stone's throw
strait-laced
street credibility
street-smart
street value
strike back
strike-breaker

strike home
strike lucky
strike out
strike rate
strike up
string along
string bass
string bean
string course
string out
string quartet
string up
string vest
stroke play
strong-arm
strong meat
strong on
strong stomach
strung out
studio flat
sucker punch
sudden death
summer house
Summer Palace
summer pudding
summer school
Sunday best
Sunday school
Sunset Boulevard
supply-side
Sutton Coldfield
Sutton Hoo
tables d'hôte
tabula rasa
tailor-made
talcum powder
talent scout
tannic acid
tartar sauce
teensy-weensy
tenant farmer
tender-hearted
tender mercies
tennis elbow
tenpin bowling

thanks to
thrash metal
thrift shop
thrift store
thumbs down
thumbs up
ticker tape
ticket tout
timber wolf
Tirich Mir
tissue culture
tissue paper
tittle-tattle
toffee apple
toffee-nosed
toggle switch
toilet bag
toilet-train
toilet water
tongue-lashing
tongue-tied
tongue-twister
Torres Strait
torrid zone
touchy-feely
trades union
trance music
travel agency
travel agent
travel light
travel-sick
travel-sickness
treble clef
trench coat
trench warfare
triple bond
Triple Crown
Triple Entente
triple jump
triple point
triple time
Trojan Horse
Trojan War
trompe l'œil
Truman Doctrine

tsetse fly
tufted duck
tumble dryer
tuning fork
tunnel vision
turned out
turtle dove
United Artists
United Kingdom
United Nations
United States
upside down
upward of
vacant possession
vacuum cleaner
vacuum flask
vacuum-pack
vacuum tube
Valley Forge
vanity case
vanity unit
vapour trail
veggie burger
Velvet Underground
verbal noun
vervet monkey
Vestal Virgin
vested interest
vicars general
Vinson Massif
Virgin Birth
vulgar fraction
vulgar Latin
Walker Cup
walkie-talkie
walrus moustache
Walvis Bay
warble fly
Warner Brothers
Warsaw Pact
washed out
washed-up
weasel words
weaver bird
weight training

weight-watcher
Weimar Republic
wheely bin
widow's mite
widow's peak
widow's weeds
Wiener schnitzel
willow pattern
window box
window dressing
window frame
window ledge
window seat
window-shop
window-shopper
window sill
winkle-picker
winter aconite
Winter Olympics
Winter Palace
winter sport
Winter War
wisdom teeth
wisdom tooth
within reach
Women's Institute
women's lib
women's liberation
wooden spoon
worlds apart
Yankee Doodle
yellow-bellied
yellow-belly
yellow card
yellow fever
yellow jack
yellow jersey
Yellow Pages
yellow peril
yeoman service
Yeoman Warder
Zimmer frame
Zuider Zee

### 7-LETTER FIRST WORD

abandon ship
Aboukir Bay
Academy award
account for
acrylic acid
aeolian harp
African American
African Union
African violet
against nature
aliquot part
Amnesty International
anyone's game
anyone's guess
applied mathematics
aqueous humour
Arabian Gulf
Arabian Nights
Arabian peninsula
assault course
assault rifle
attaché case
Austria-Hungary
backhoe loader
backing track
balance sheet
Ballets Russes
banoffi pie
barrage balloon
barrier cream
barrier method
barrier reef
bascule bridge
basking shark
basmati rice
bathing costume
bathing suit
bedding plant
bedside manner
Beehive State
Belgian endive
Belisha beacon

beneath contempt
Bermuda shorts
Bermuda Triangle
Berners-Lee
between ourselves
between times
between whiles
Beverly Hills
bichons frise
billets-doux
blanket stitch
Blessed Sacrament
boiling point
Bolshoi Ballet
Bonfire Night
botanic garden
bottoms up
boulder clay
bounden duty
bouquet garni
Boutros-Ghali
bowling alley
bowling green
bowling rink
brassed off
breathe again
breathe fire
Brenner Pass
Bristol Channel
British Academy
British Columbia
British Council
British Empire
British Honduras
British India
British Legion
British Library
British Museum
brought forward
brought up
Brownie Guide
brownie point
Brussel sprout
bubonic plague
Buckeye State

bulimia nervosa
bulldog clip
Burmese cat
busman's holiday
cabbage white
Caesar's wife
calcium carbonate
calling card
capital gain
capital goods
capital punishment
capital sum
Capitol Hill
Carnaby Street
carried away
carrier bag
carrier pigeon
carrion crow
Cartier-Bresson
cartoon strip
Cascade Range
cascara sagrada
Castell-Nedd
casting vote
cathode ray
caustic soda
cavalry twill
cayenne pepper
Central America
central bank
Central Command
central heating
Central Park
central processor
central reservation
chafing dish
chaises longues
chamber music
chamber pot
chamois leather
Channel Four
channel-hop
Channel Tunnel
Charity Commission
charnel house

charter flight
Chelsea boot
Chelsea bun
Chelsea pensioner
chewing gum
Chichén Itzá
chicken feed
chicken wire
chimney breast
chimney piece
chimney pot
chimney stack
chimney sweep
Chinese burn
Chinese cabbage
Chinese chequers
Chinese lantern
Chinese leaves
Chinese puzzle
Chinese wall
Chinese whispers
circuit-breaker
clapped-out
clinker-built
clothes horse
clothes line
clothes moth
clothes peg
clotted cream
cluster bomb
coconut ice
coconut milk
coconut shy
codling moth
coeliac disease
collect dust
Colonel Blimp
colonic irrigation
combine harvester
Comédie Française
command economy
command performance
compact disc
compare notes
Compton-Burnett

concert performance
concert pitch
conning tower
contact lens
contact print
contact sport
contour line
control tower
convent school
cooling tower
Corinth Canal
Cornish pasty
costume drama
costume jewellery
cottage cheese
cottage hospital
cottage industry
cottage loaf
cottage pie
council tax
counter-attack
counter-espionage
counter-intuitive
Counter-Reformation
counter-revolution
counter-revolutionary
counter-tenor
country club
Country Code
country cousin
country dance
country music
cracked wheat
Crimean War
cropped top
crumple zone
crushed velvet
crystal ball
crystal clear
crystal-gazing
Crystal Palace
crystal set
culture shock
culture vulture
curling iron

curling tongs
current account
current assets
curtain call
curtain-raiser
curtain wall
custard apple
custard pie
customs house
customs union
cutting edge
decimal place
decimal point
decrees absolute
decrees nisi
deltoid muscle
deposit account
dernier cri
derring-do
descant recorder
desktop publishing
despair of
dessert wine
diamond jubilee
Diamond State
diamond wedding
digital audiotape
digital camera
digital signature
docking station
donkey's years
Doppler effect
Doppler shift
Douglas fir
Douglas-Home
Downing Street
drawing board
drawing pin
drawing room
Dresden china
driving licence
driving range
ducking stool
dynamic range
Eastern bloc

Eastern Cape
Eastern Church
Eastern Empire
Eastern hemisphere
economy class
ectopic pregnancy
ejector seat
elastic band
Emerald Isle
emperor penguin
English breakfast
English Channel
English Heritage
English muffin
English Pale
English rose
Entente Cordiale
esparto grass
Estuary English
Eternal City
evening primrose
evening star
expense account
express train
extreme unction
factory farming
factory floor
factory outlet
falling-off
falling-out
falling star
Father's Day
feather bed
feather-brained
feature film
Federal Reserve
feeding frenzy
Fertile Crescent
fiddler crab
filling station
finance company
finance house
finders keepers
Fingal's Cave
Fischer-Dieskau

fishing line
fishing rod
fitting room
Flodden Field
foreign body
foreign exchange
Foreign Legion
Foreign Office
Foreign Secretary
forlorn hope
fortune-teller
fortune-telling
forward-looking
forward-thinking
Franche-Comté
freedom fighter
Freedom Trail
friends with
frigate bird
fromage blanc
fromage frais
frontal lobe
fuller's earth
funeral director
funeral home
funeral parlour
further education
gallows humour
gastric flu
gastric juice
gateleg table
general anaesthetic
general election
general meeting
General Motors
general practice
general practitioner
general-purpose
general staff
general strike
genetic code
genetic engineering
gentian violet
genuine article
getting on

glacial period
glottal stop
Goodwin Sands
Gordian knot
grammar school
granary bread
Granite State
graphic art
graphic design
graphic equaliser
graphic equalizer
graphic novel
Greater London
Greater Manchester
grizzly bear
growing pains
guelder rose
gunboat diplomacy
gunning for
hacking cough
hacking jacket
hackney carriage
hairpin bend
halfway house
Halley's Comet
Hammond organ
Hampton Court
hangers-on
hanging valley
Hansen's disease
Harpers Ferry
Harvard University
harvest mice
harvest moon
harvest mouse
hatchet-faced
hatchet job
hatchet man
hatchet men
Hawkeye State
hearing aid
hearing things
heavens open
helping hand
Heralds' College

herring gull
Highway Code
Hobson's choice
holding company
holding pattern
holiday camp
honours list
Hoosier State
hopping mad
housing estate
Hundred Flowers
hunting ground
Iberian peninsula
iceberg lettuce
immoral earnings
inertia reel
insider dealing
insider trading
inverse proportion
inverse ratio
ironing board
Islamic Jehad
Islamic Jihad
itching palm
Jameson Raid
jiggery-pokery
Jodrell Bank
jugular vein
Karlovy Vary
Kellogg Pact
keyhole surgery
killing field
kindred spirit
kinetic energy
kissing cousin
kitchen cabinet
kitchen garden
kitchen paper
kitchen roll
kitchen-sink
knights errant
knuckle sandwich
KwaZulu-Natal
lacquer tree
laissez-faire

Lambeth Palace
landing craft
landing gear
landing stage
lantern-jawed
lantern slide
lateral thinking
Lateran Council
Lateran Treaty
leading aircraftman
leading aircraftmen
leading aircraftwoman
leading aircraftwomen
leading article
leading edge
leading light
leading question
leading seaman
leading seamen
lecture theatre
leisure centre
lending library
letters patent
Liberal Democrat
Liberty Bell
license plate
limited company
limited liability
Lincoln Memorial
linseed oil
loading dock
lobster pot
lobster thermidor
Locarno Pact
lodging house
Lombard Street
looking glass
loyalty card
lunatic asylum
lunatic fringe
machine code
machine gun
machine language
machine-readable
machine tool

machine translation
Madeira cake
Madison Avenue
magical realism
Maginot Line
mailing list
maîtres d'hôtel
Malabar Coast
Maltese cross
mansion block
Mansion House
Mariana Trench
Marston Moor
Martha's Vineyard
martial art
martial law
Marxism-Leninism
masking tape
massage parlour
Masters Tournament
mastoid process
matinee coat
matinee idol
medical certificate
medical officer
medulla oblongata
melting point
melting pot
memento mori
Merthyr Tydfil
Mexican wave
mineral oil
mineral water
minimum wage
miracle play
missing link
mission creep
mission statement
Molotov cocktail
monitor lizard
Montego Bay
morning after
morning coat
morning dress
morning glory

morning sickness
morning star
mortise lock
Mother's Day
mother's ruin
mummers' play
mumming play
Murphy's Law
musical box
musical chairs
musical instrument
mustard gas
mutatis mutandis
mystery play
mystery tour
Nagorno-Karabakh
natural gas
natural history
natural law
natural logarithm
natural number
natural philosophy
natural resource
natural science
natural selection
natural wastage
Nelson's Column
nervous breakdown
nervous system
nervous wreck
neutron bomb
neutron star
Niagara Falls
nitrous acid
nitrous oxide
nobody's fool
nodding acquaintance
nominal value
Norfolk Broads
Norfolk Island
Norfolk jacket
Norwich School
nothing daunted
nothing doing
Notting Hill

nouveau riche
nowhere near
nuclear family
nuclear fuel
nuclear physics
nuclear power
nuclear reactor
nuclear waste
nuclear winter
nucleic acid
nursery nurse
nursery rhyme
nursery school
nursery slope
nursing home
Ockham's razor
October Revolution
October War
Oedipus complex
oilseed rape
Olduvai Gorge
Olympic Games
opinion poll
optical fibre
optical illusion
orbital sander
ordinal number
Ottoman Empire
outside broadcast
outside chance
outside interest
Outward Bound
Pacific Rim
package deal
package holiday
package tour
packing case
painted lady
palazzo pants
palette knife
Pancake Day
parking meter
parking ticket
parlour game
parson's nose

parting shot
passers-by
passion flower
passion fruit
passion play
passive resistance
passive smoking
peacock blue
peacock butterfly
pecking order
peeping Tom
pelican crossing
Pelican State
penalty area
penalty box
penalty kick
Pennine Chain
perfect fifth
perfect pitch
Persian carpet
Persian Gulf
Persian lamb
phantom limb
phantom pregnancy
phrasal verb
picture messaging
picture-postcard
picture rail
picture window
pinking shears
pitched battle
pitcher plant
planned economy
plaster cast
plastic bullet
plastic explosive
plastic surgery
playing card
playing field
popping crease
popular front
postage stamp
Potsdam Conference
potter's wheel
potting shed

poverty-stricken
poverty trap
prairie dog
Prairie State
praying mantis
Premium Bond
present arms
present participle
prickly heat
prickly pear
primary care
primary colour
primary industry
princes royal
printed circuit
printed word
private company
private detective
private enterprise
private eye
private investigator
private life
private means
private member
private parts
private school
private secretary
private sector
private soldier
product placement
proving ground
provost marshal
Proxima Centauri
prussic acid
pudding basin
pudding club
punched card
putting green
pyramid selling
quality control
quality time
quantum computer
quantum jump
quantum leap
quantum mechanics

quantum theory
quarter day
quarter-final
quarter-finalist
quarter-hour
quarter-light
quarter sessions
quarter-tone
radical chic
radical sign
railway engine
Rainbow Bridge
rainbow coalition
rainbow trout
raisons d'être
Rathlin Island
reading age
regular canon
request stop
reserve bank
reserve currency
reserve judgement
reserve price
respite care
reverse arms
reverse engineering
reverse gear
rewrite history
rhyming slang
Richter scale
rocking chair
rocking horse
rolling drunk
rolling mill
rolling pin
rolling stock
rooming house
rosebay willowherb
Rosetta Stone
rummage sale
runners-up
running battle
running-board
running commentary
running head

running mate
running repairs
running stitch
running total
Russian doll
Russian Federation
Russian Revolution
Russian roulette
sailing boat
Saronic Gulf
sausage dog
sausage meat
sausage roll
savings account
savings bank
Savings Bond
Scafell Pike
scarlet fever
scarlet woman
scarlet women
scatter cushion
sciatic nerve
science fiction
Science Museum
science park
scratch card
screech owl
sealing wax
season's greetings
selling point
service area
service break
service charge
service flat
service industry
service provider
service road
service station
session musician
seventy-eight
Seville orange
Shangri-La
sheriff court
Shining Path
shotgun marriage

shotgun wedding
shuttle diplomacy
Siachen Glacier
Siamese cat
Silbury Hill
silicon chip
Silicon Valley
sinking feeling
sinking fund
sinking ship
Sistine Chapel
sitting duck
sitting pretty
sitting room
sitting tenant
skimmed milk
sliding scale
slipped disc
smoking gun
smoking jacket
snaggle-toothed
sniffer dog
solvent abuse
Spanish America
Spanish Armada
Spanish chestnut
Spanish fly
Spanish guitar
Spanish Inquisition
Spanish Main
Spanish omelette
Spanish onion
Spanish Town
Special Branch
special constable
special effects
special forces
special needs
special pleading
spotted dick
squeaky-clean
squeeze box
staging post
stained glass
Stanley Cup

Stanley knife
starter home
stately home
station wagon
statute book
statute law
statute mile
staying power
stealth tax
stearic acid
Stewart Island
stirrup pump
stomach pump
storage heater
streets ahead
stretch mark
stuffed shirt
subject matter
subpost office
success story
Suffolk punch
suicide pact
sulphur dioxide
summing-up
supreme court
surface tension
suspend disbelief
suspend payment
swagger stick
swallow dive
swizzle stick
systems analysis
systems analyst
tableau vivant
tabulae rasae
Taiping Rebellion
talking book
talking head
talking point
talking shop
talking-to
Tammany Hall
tangled web
tartare sauce
Teachta Dála

telling-off

tensile strength

tequila slammer

tequila sunrise

thermal imaging

thermal inversion

thermal spring

thought police

Thunder Bay

thyroid gland

tickety-boo

tickled pink

tightly knit

Tollund Man

tongues wag

toothed whale

Topkapi Palace

topping out

torpedo boat

torsion bar

tourist class

Tourist Trophy

tractor trailer

trading card

trading estate

trading post

traffic calming

traffic cone

traffic island

traffic jam

traffic light

traffic warden

trailer trash

trailer truck

trestle table

Tribune Group

trickle-down

trigger-happy

Trinity House

trolley car

trolley wheel

trouble spot

trouser suit

truckle bed

tubular bells

Turkish bath

Turkish coffee

Turkish delight

turning circle

turning point

twelfth man

Twelfth Night

twinkle-toed

typhoid fever

uillean pipes

Umbrian School

unitary authority

unitary council

unknown quantity

Unknown Soldier

utility room

utility truck

utility vehicle

vampire bat

Vandyke beard

vantage point

Vatican City

vending machine

venture capital

Venture Scout

veteran car

vicious circle

Vietnam War

vintage car

virtual memory

virtual reality

virtual storage

vitamin A

vitamin B

vitamin C

vitamin D

vitamin E

vitamin K

Wailing Wall

waiting list

waiting room

Waldorf salad

walking frame

walking stick

Wallace Collection

warrant officer

washing machine

washing powder

washing soda

washing-up

Watling Street

weather-beaten

weather station

wedding band

wedding breakfast

wedding cake

wedding march

wedding ring

weeping willow

welfare state

Wembley Stadium

Western Australia

Western Cape

Western Church

Western Empire

Western Front

Western hemisphere

Western Isles

Western Sahara

Western Wall

wheeler-dealer

wheeler-dealing

wheelie bin

whipper-in

whistle-blower

whistle-stop

whoopee cushion

whooper swan

winding sheet

Windsor Castle

winning post

wishing well

without cease

without ceremony

without doubt

without end

without fail

without limit

without number

without peer

without prejudice
without price
without tears
witness box
witness stand
working capital
working class
working group
working party
worldly goods
worldly possessions
worldly wealth
worldly-wise
Wounded Knee
writer's block
writer's cramp
wrought iron
Yucatán Peninsula

## **8**-LETTER FIRST WORD

Aberdeen Angus
absolute majority
absolute pitch
absolute temperature
absolute zero
Académie française
Achilles heel
Achilles tendon
acquired taste
adhesive tape
Admiral's Cup
advanced level
Agrarian Revolution
aircraft carrier
Aladdin's cave
altitude sickness
American dream
American football
American Indian
American Legion
American Revolution
American robin
American Samoa
America's Cup

amniotic fluid
anabolic steroid
Anglican communion
anorexia nervosa
Antonine Wall
anybody's guess
Apostles' Creed
approved school
Armenian Church
articled clerk
ascorbic acid
assembly line
athlete's foot
Atlantic Charter
Attorney General
Augsburg Confession
Austrian blind
Bactrian camel
Bakewell tart
ballroom dancing
Balmoral Castle
balsamic vinegar
banoffee pie
barbecue sauce
Barbican Centre
Barbizon School
barnacle geese
barnacle goose
baseball cap
Beaufort scale
billiard table
birthing pool
bleeding heart
Blenheim Palace
blotting paper
boarding house
boarding school
Bodleian Library
borlotti bean
Bosworth Field
boutique hotel
Bramley's seedling
bridging loan
broderie anglaise
Brownian motion

Brussels sprout
building society
bulletin board
business end
Cabernet Sauvignon
cabriole leg
calendar year
Campbell-Bannerman
Canadian Shield
carbolic acid
carbonic acid
cardinal humour
cardinal number
cardinal point
cardinal sin
cardinal virtue
carriage clock
carrying-on
Castilla-León
casualty department
cellular phone
cerebral cortex
cerebral hemisphere
cerebral palsy
cervical smear
Chancery Division
Charles's law
Charles's Wain
chastity belt
chemical bond
chemical element
chemical engineering
chemical formula
chemical formulae
Cheshire cat
cinerary urn
cinnabar moth
circular saw
Citizens' Band
clearing bank
clearing house
clerical collar
clerical error
Clermont-Ferrand
climbing frame

clinical psychology
coaching inn
Colorado beetle
Columbia University
commedia dell'arte
compound fracture
compound time
computer animation
computer-literate
computer virus
conclude missives
concrete jungle
consumer durable
contract bridge
conveyor belt
coronary thrombosis
corporal punishment
courtesy title
covering letter
creative accountancy
creative accounting
creature comforts
criminal record
critical mass
Cromarty Firth
crowning glory
cruciate ligament
Cultural Revolution
cupboard love
cylinder block
cylinder head
dangling participle
daylight robbery
definite article
delirium tremens
demerara sugar
depleted uranium
designer baby
dialling code
dialling tone
dialogue box
director general
Dispatch Box
dispatch rider
distance learning

district attorney
district nurse
divining rod
division lobby
division sign
Domesday Book
domestic fowl
domestic science
doubting Thomas
draining board
dramatis personae
dressing-down
dressing gown
dressing room
dressing table
drinking chocolate
drinking fountain
duchesse potatoes
duchesse satin
dwelling place
economic migrant
educated guess
ejection seat
electric blanket
electric blue
electric chair
electric eel
electric fence
electric fire
electric guitar
electric shock
electron microscope
eleventh hour
enlisted man
enlisted men
Equality State
European Commission
European Community
European Council
European Parliament
European Union
exchange contracts
exchange rate
exercise bike
exercise book

extended family
external ear
fallings-off
fallings-out
familiar spirit
fighting chance
fighting fit
finished article
fireside chat
Flinders Island
floating-point
floating rib
floating voter
football pool
forensic medicine
Forestry Commission
forklift truck
fountain pen
freezing point
friendly society
fruiting body
function key
Glorious Revolution
goldfish bowl
goodness knows
Governor General
guardian angel
Hadrian's Wall
heavenly body
Heimlich manoeuvre
higgledy-piggledy
Highland cattle
Highland dress
Highland fling
Himachal Pradesh
historic present
Hodgkin's disease
honeydew melon
hospital trust
humpback bridge
hydrogen bomb
hydrogen peroxide
hydrogen sulphide
Icknield Way
identity parade

imperial gallon
improper fraction
Inchcape Rock
inclined plane
indecent assault
indecent exposure
indirect object
indirect question
indirect speech
informed consent
integral calculus
interior angle
interior decoration
interior decorator
interior design
interior designer
internal exile
internal market
inverted comma
inverted snobbery
Jehovah's Witness
jeunesse dorée
junction box
juvenile delinquency
juvenile deliquent
kangaroo court
Kentucky bluegrass
Keystone State
kilowatt-hour
knacker's yard
knitting needle
Labrador Peninsula
Labrador retriever
language laboratory
latchkey child
latchkey children
laughing gas
laughing hyena
laughing stock
lavender water
learning curve
learning difficulties
Lincoln's Inn
linoleic acid
literary criticism

literary lion
lollipop lady
lollipop man
lollipop men
Lonsdale belt
luncheon meat
luncheon voucher
Lutheran Church
magnetic field
magnetic mine
magnetic north
magnetic pole
magnetic storm
magnetic tape
Magnolia State
majority rule
majority verdict
mandarin collar
mandarin duck
marching orders
Maritime Provinces
marrying kind
Marshall Plan
Martello tower
medicine ball
medicine man
medicine men
medullae oblongatae
mentally handicapped
Mercator projection
merchant bank
merchant marine
merchant navy
Midgard's serpent
midnight blue
midnight sun
Military Cross
military honours
Military Medal
military police
mirabile dictu
morality play
Mosquito Coast
mosquito net
mountain ash

mountain bike
mountain goat
mountain lion
mountain sickness
Mountain State
multiple-choice
multiple sclerosis
muscular dystrophy
mushroom cloud
National Assembly
national curricula
national curriculum
national debt
National Front
National Gallery
national grid
National Guard
National Health
National Hunt
National Insurance
national park
national service
National Socialism
National Trust
nativity play
nautical mile
negative equity
negative pole
nicotine patch
nitrogen cycle
nitrogen dioxide
nitrogen fixation
noblesse oblige
Northern Cape
northern hemisphere
Northern Ireland
Northern Lights
Northern Territory
notaries public
nouvelle cuisine
occluded front
official receiver
official secret
Oklahoma City
opposite number

opposite sex
ordinary grade
ordinary level
ordinary seaman
ordinary seamen
ordinary share
Ordnance Survey
original sin
Orthodox Church
Orthodox Judaism
overflow pipe
overhead projector
paddling pool
Palmetto State
Pandora's box
paradigm shift
paraffin oil
paraffin wax
parallel bars
parallel imports
parietal bone
parietal lobe
Parthian shot
particle board
pathetic fallacy
Peasants' Revolt
pectoral muscle
Pentland Firth
periodic table
personal assistant
personal column
personal computer
personal organiser
personal organizer
personal pension
personal pronoun
personal property
personal stereo
Peterloo massacre
Petronas Towers
physical chemistry
physical education
physical geography
physical science
physical therapist

physical therapy
Piltdown man
pinafore dress
Pitcairn Island
planning permission
platinum blonde
platinum disc
Plimsoll line
Plymouth Brethren
Plymouth Rock
poisoned chalice
Pompidou Centre
Portland cement
Portland stone
positive pole
positive vetting
precious few
precious little
precious metal
precious stone
pressure cooker
pressure group
primrose path
princess royal
printing press
prodigal son
promised land
Prussian blue
quantity surveyor
question mark
question master
question time
rateable value
received pronunciation
recorded delivery
recovery position
referred pain
Reformed Church
register office
registry office
reported speech
ringside seat
sandwich board
sandwich course
sanitary napkin

sanitary towel
Schengen agreement
Scotland Yard
Scottish Borders
Scottish Gaelic
Scottish terrier
Security Council
Security Service
sergeant major
Shetland pony
shifting sands
shocking pink
shooting gallery
shooting star
shooting stick
shopping centre
shoulder arms
shoulder bag
shoulder blade
shoulder pad
shoulder strap
Sicilian Vespers
sickness benefit
sidereal time
sideways on
Skeleton Coast
skeleton key
skipjack tuna
skipping rope
skirting board
slanging match
sleeping bag
sleeping car
sleeping partner
sleeping pill
sleeping policeman
sleeping policemen
sleeping sickness
slippery elm
slippery slope
smelling salts
software library
solitary confinement
Solomon's seal
sounding board

sounding line
Southern Cross
southern hemisphere
Southern Lights
specific gravity
spinning jenny
spinning wheel
splendid isolation
splinter group
sporting chance
springer spaniel
sprocket wheel
squadron leader
stalking horse
stamping ground
standard-bearer
Standard Grade
standard lamp
standard time
standing joke
standing order
standing ovation
standing stone
starting block
starting gate
starting price
starting stall
steering column
steering committee
steering group
steering wheel
stepping stone
sterling area
sterling silver
sticking plaster
sticking point
stinging nettle
stocking cap
stocking stitch
stoppage time
Stormont Castle
straight angle
straight away
straight edge
straight face

straight-faced
straight fight
straight-laced
straight man
straight men
straight off
straight out
straight up
summings-up
Sunshine State
surgical spirit
swimming costume
swimming pool
swimming trunks
switched-on
symphony orchestra
talkings-to
Tamworth Manifesto
Tarpeian Rock
tartaric acid
teaching hospital
Teachtai Dála
teething problems
teething ring
teething troubles
tellings-off
temporal bone
temporal lobe
tenement house
terminal velocity
tertiary industry
toasting fork
tomorrow week
Toulouse-Lautrec
traction engine
trailing edge
training college
training shoe
treasure hunt
Treasure State
treasure trove
Treasury bill
tropical cyclone
tropical storm
troubled waters

tubercle bacilli
tubercle bacillus
tungsten carbide
twopenny-halfpenny
unearned income
upwardly mobile
vaulting horse
venereal disease
venetian blind
Victoria Peak
Victoria plum
Victoria sandwich
Victoria sponge
Virginia creeper
virtuous circle
visiting card
vitreous humour
volatile oil
volcanic glass
Volstead Act
Waltzing Matilda
watching brief
watering can
watering hole
watering place
whatever next
whippers-in
whipping boy
whooping cough
windfall tax
witching hour

## 9-LETTER FIRST WORD

activated carbon
activated charcoal
Aesthetic Movement
Alexander Archipelago
Alexander technique
alligator pear
alternate angles
ambulance-chaser
amplitude modulation
amusement arcade
amusement park

Angostura bitters
answering machine
Antarctic Circle
Antarctic Peninsula
Arunachal Pradesh
Ascension Island
Ashmolean Museum
Asperger's syndrome
Attorneys General
automatic pilot
auxiliary verb
ballistic missile
ballpoint pen
Barebones Parliament
battering ram
Beardmore Glacier
Béarnaise sauce
Beaubourg Centre
beefsteak tomato
beginner's luck
Bluegrass State
botanical garden
breathing space
brigadier general
broadside on
butterfly nut
butternut squash
Byzantine Empire
Caesarean section
Cambridge University
capillary action
capillary tube
carryings-on
cartridge paper
catalytic converter
catchment area
Catherine wheel
celestial equator
celestial pole
celestial sphere
cellulose acetate
Champagne-Ardenne
character actor
Charlotte Amalie
Charlotte Dundas

chequered flag
Children's Crusade
chocolate-box
Christian Aid
Christian era
Christian name
Christian Science
Christian Scientist
Christmas cacti
Christmas cactus
Christmas cake
Christmas Day
Christmas Island
Christmas pudding
Christmas rose
Christmas tree
cognitive therapy
combining form
committee stage
community care
community centre
community service
condensed milk
conjoined twin
crocodile clip
crocodile tears
curricula vitae
curricula vitarum
detention centre
directors general
Dobermann pinscher
Dominican Republic
Edinburgh Festival
eightsome reel
electoral college
electoral register
electoral roll
Ellesmere Island
Ellesmere Port
endowment mortgage
Episcopal Church
essential oil
Evergreen State
extension lead
Falklands War

Fallopian tube
favourite son
Fibonacci number
Fibonacci series
financial year
finishing school
finishing touch
flotation tank
Forbidden City
forbidden degrees
forbidden fruit
Frankfurt School
frequency modulation
geometric mean
geometric progression
Gladstone bag
glandular fever
governing body
Governors General
Granville-Barker
grappling hook
grappling iron
graveyard shift
Greenwich meridian
Greenwich Village
greetings card
Gregorian calendar
Gregorian chant
Grenadier Guards
Guatemala City
Gunpowder Plot
handlebar moustache
Hanseatic League
heartbeat away
hepatitis A
hepatitis B
hepatitis C
Household Cavalry
household name
household word
hurricane lamp
immersion heater
induction coil
induction loop
insurance policy

intensive care
interlock fabric
Jefferson City
Jerusalem artichoke
Judgement Day
knowledge base
knowledge worker
landscape architecture
landscape gardening
Languedoc-Roussillon
leveraged buyout
lightning conductor
lightning rod
listening post
longshore drift
Louisiana Purchase
lymphatic system
Manhattan Project
marrowfat pea
menstrual period
microwave oven
Midsummer Day
molecular biology
molecular weight
Morecambe Bay
mortality rate
Mothering Sunday
necessary evil
nicotinic acid
Northwest Territories
Nullarbor Plain
obsessive-compulsive
operating profit
operating room
operating system
operating table
operating theatre
orchestra pit
pantomime dame
paragraph mark
parchment paper
paternity suit
Permanent Secretary
permanent wave
permanent way

**MULTI-WORD**

2 WORDS

perpetual motion
personnel carrier
petroleum jelly
pituitary body
pituitary gland
political correctness
political prisoner
political science
polyvinyl chloride
ponderosa pine
postviral syndrome
potassium hydroxide
potential difference
potential energy
practical joke
preferred share
Princeton University
principal boy
probation officer
proboscis monkey
promenade concert
Ptolemaic system
Ptolemaic theory
puerperal fever
pulmonary emphysema
quotation mark
radiation sickness
radiation therapy
rearguard action
reception room
recurring decimal
refectory table
reference library
reference point
repayment mortgage
repertory company
resolving power
retaining wall
returning officer
revolving door
rheumatic fever
Rorschach test
Sackville-West
Sagebrush State
salicylic acid

Salvation Army
satellite dish
satellite television
Sauvignon Blanc
scheduled caste
sebaceous gland
secondary colour
secondary industry
secondary picketing
secretary bird
Secretary General
sensitive plant
severance pay
sheltered accommodation
sheltered housing
shepherd's pie
shrinking violet
Siegfried Line
signature tune
sincerely yours
situation comedy
smokeless zone
snowball's chance
soldering iron
Solicitor General
spaghetti Bolognese
spaghetti western
stainless steel
stovepipe hat
stumbling block
suffragan bishop
sulphuric acid
Sunflower State
surrogate mother
suspended animation
suspended ceiling
suspender belt
swaddling clothes
Sydenham's chorea
Tasmanian devil
technical college
technical knockout
telegraph pole
telephone box
telephone directory

2 WORDS

MULTI-WORD

telephone exchange
telephone number
telephoto lens
temperate zone
Tiananmen Square
Tourette's syndrome
Trafalgar Square
transport cafe
Tunbridge Wells
umbilical cord
universal joint
Vancouver Island
vanishing point
vegetable oil
voluntary-aided
voluntary-controlled
voluntary school
Volunteer State
whirligig beetle
whirlpool bath
witchetty grub
Wolverine State
Worcester sauce
Yorkshire pudding
Yorkshire terrier

## 10-LETTER FIRST WORD

Abominable Snowman
Alcoholics Anonymous
alimentary canal
Alzheimer's disease
ankylosing spondylitis
Archimedes' principle
arithmetic progression
arithmetic series
artificial insemination
artificial intelligence
artificial respiration
Associated Press
asymmetric bar
Athanasian Creed
Australian Rules
Authorised Version
Authorized Version

Babylonian Captivity
barbituric acid
Battleborn State
biological clock
biological control
bituminous coal
blackwater fever
Bloomsbury Group
Buckingham Palace
Caledonian Canal
cannellini bean
Canterbury bell
carboxylic acid
Centennial State
Challenger Deep
Chesapeake Bay
chinagraph pencil
collateral damage
collective bargaining
collective farm
collective noun
commercial traveller
compressed air
compulsory purchase
confidence trick
congestion charge
connecting rod
connective tissue
consenting adult
consistory court
conspiracy theory
continuous assessment
Copacabana Beach
Copernican system
Copernican theory
Cornhusker State
Coromandel Coast
Coronation stone
Cumberland sausage
curriculum vitae
deficiency disease
Democratic Party
department store
designated driver
developing country

diplomatic bag
diplomatic immunity
diplomatic recognition
dispensing optician
disposable income
downwardly mobile
electrical storm
electronic publishing
elementary school
Equatorial Guinea
Eustachian tube
evaporated milk
foundation course
foundation garment
foundation stone
functional food
generation gap
Generation X
Generation Xer
gentleman's agreement
Gettysburg address
gramophone record
greenhouse effect
greenhouse gas
greenstick fracture
Guantánamo Bay
Hallelujah Chorus
herbaceous border
Hindenburg Line
honourable mention
housemaid's knee
Immaculate Conception
impersonal pronoun
incidental music
indefinite article
indefinite pronoun
industrial action
industrial estate
industrial park
industrial relations
Industrial Revolution
industrial-strength
ingeminate peace
integrated circuit
investment trust

Lancashire hotpot
Laurentian Plateau
Leamington Spa
liberation theology
lieutenant colonel
lieutenant commander
lieutenant general
loggerhead turtle
lumberjack shirt
Maastricht Treaty
magnifying glass
maidenhair fern
management accountant
management accounting
maraschino cherry
mechanical drawing
mechanical engineering
methylated spirit
methylated spirits
Michaelmas daisy
Midsummer's Day
millennium bug
monosodium glutamate
monumental mason
natterjack toad
nineteenth hole
operations room
ophthalmic optician
Palmerston North
Parkinson's disease
Parkinson's law
Peninsular War
peppercorn rent
percussion cap
performing arts
pernicious anaemia
phosphoric acid
ploughman's lunch
Pontefract cake
possessive determiner
possessive pronoun
praetorian guard
preference share
prevailing wind
primordial soup

princesses royal
procurator fiscal
production line
promissory note
propelling pencil
proscenium arch
Protestant ethic
Pythagoras' theorem
recreation ground
reflecting telescope
refracting telescope
refractive index
registered post
reinforced concrete
Republican Party
resistance movement
retirement pension
rheumatoid arthritis
saturation point
shortcrust pastry
simplicity itself
situations vacant
situations wanted
Solicitors General
strawberry blonde
submachine gun
suspension bridge
sweetheart neckline
technology transfer
television set
thermionic valve
threepenny bit
transistor radio
transition metal
transition series
traveller's cheque
travelling salesman
travelling salesmen
veterinary surgeon
wellington boot
whispering campaign
windscreen wiper
yesterday's man
yesterday's men
yesterday's news

## 11-LETTER FIRST WORD

affirmative action
alternating current
alternative energy
alternative medicine
Association Football
Brandenburg Gate
Carolingian Renaissance
caterpillar track
cauliflower ear
centrifugal force
centripetal force
Christingle service
combination lock
consolation prize
continental breakfast
continental climate
Continental Divide
continental drift
continental quilt
continental shelf
controlling interest
convenience food
corporation tax
crystalline lens
diminishing returns
exclamation mark
exclamation point
Feldenkrais method
Flamborough Head
fundamental note
genetically modified
grandfather clock
Hippocratic oath
hollandaise sauce
Huntington's disease
hydrocyanic acid
inferiority complex
information superhighway
information technology
inheritance tax
leatherback turtle
marshalling yard

Munchausen's syndrome
Neanderthal man
nictitating membrane
opportunity knocks
pantothenic acid
performance art
performance artist
personality disorder
politically correct
porterhouse steak
portmanteau word
preparatory school
procurators fiscal
proprietary name
proprietary term
qualitative analysis
Queensberry Rules
radiocarbon dating
Remembrance Day
Remembrance Sunday
Renaissance man
Renaissance men
respiratory tract
restrictive practice
ribonucleic acid
Sandringham House
Secretaries General
sentimental value
Sharpeville massacre
significant figure
Smithsonian Institution
spontaneous combustion
stakeholder pension
subordinate clause
subsistence level
subsistence wage
Territorial Army
territorial waters
Townswomen's Guild
Underground Railroad
Unification Church
Westminster Abbey

## 12-LETTER FIRST WORD

astronomical unit
Commonwealth Games
Conservative Party
Constitution State
constructive dismissal
craniosacral therapy
differential calculus
differential equation
displacement ton
extrasensory perception
functionally illiterate
Glyndebourne Festival
hydrochloric acid
hydrothermal vent
intellectual property
intelligence quotient
intrauterine device
legionnaires' disease
metaphysical poet
metropolitan county
occupational hazard
occupational therapist
occupational therapy
philosopher's stone
photographic memory
premenstrual syndrome
professional foul
quantitative analysis
registration document
registration mark
registration number
semicircular canal
simultaneous equation
synchronised swimming
synchronized swimming
Threadneedle Street
unemployment benefit
Yellowhammer State

## 13-LETTER FIRST WORD

accommodation address
cartilaginous fish
cerebrospinal fluid
communication cord
compassionate leave
complementary angle
complementary colour
complementary medicine
concentration camp
conscientious objector
decompression chamber
decompression sickness

dishonourable discharge
electromotive force
Frankenstein's monster
International Brigade
international community
international law
international style
Knickerbocker Glory
Mediterranean climate
neighbourhood watch
Peloponnesian War
photoelectric cell
psychological warfare
reciprocating engine

# 3 WORDS

## 1-LETTER FIRST WORD

a cut above
à la carte
à la mode
D and C
I dare say
I should coco
I should cocoa

## 2-LETTER FIRST WORD

as a rule
as a whole
as far as
as good as

as one man
as things stand
at a glance
at a lick
at all costs
at a loss
at a minimum
at an angle
at any cost
at any price
at any rate
at a pinch
at a premium
at a price
at a profit
at a push

at a stretch
at a stroke
at a time
at close quarters
at cross purposes
at daggers drawn
at death's door
at every turn
at first blush
at first glance
at first hand
at first sight
at full blast
at full pelt
at full stretch
at full tilt

at long last
at one's back
at one's best
at one's command
at one's convenience
at one's disposal
at one's ease
at one's elbow
at one's expense
at one's feet
at one's fingertips
at one's leisure
at one's peril
at one's pleasure
at one's risk
at one's service
at one's side
at one's worst
at second hand
at short notice
at the coalface
at the double
at the least
at the most
at the outside
at the ready
by all means
by and by
by and large
by a nose
by any chance
by any means
by dint of
by main force
by no means
by one's fingertips
by one's side
by reason of
by that token
by the book
by the by
by the bye
by the truckload
by the way
by the yard

by this token
by virtue of
by way of
by your leave
de nos jours
do a bunk
do a runner
do away with
do duty as
do duty for
do-it-yourself
do justice to
do one's best
do one's bit
do one's damnedest
do oneself justice
do one's nut
do one's utmost
do one's worst
do-or-die
do-si-do
do the honours
do the trick
do to death
ex post facto
go along with
go back on
go belly up
go easy on
go for broke
go for it
go great guns
go hard with
go in for
go it alone
go one better
go one's way
go pear-shaped
go the distance
go the rounds
go through fire
go through with
go to court
go to earth
go to ground

go to hell
go to law
go too far
go to pieces
go to pot
go to press
go to prove
go to sea
go to seed
go to show
go to sleep
go to town
go to war
go to waste
go without saying
if need be
I'm a Dutchman
in a body
in accordance with
in accord with
in actual fact
in a flash
in a hole
in a hurry
in aid of
in all weathers
in a nutshell
in any case
in a row
in a spot
in a trice
in a twinkling
in a twitter
in a way
in a whirl
in a wink
in a word
in bed with
in broad daylight
in case of
in cold blood
in common with
in deep water
in deep waters
in due course

in excess of
in favour of
in flagrante delicto
in for it
in full cry
in full fig
in full flight
in full flood
in full flow
in full sail
in full spate
in full swing
in full view
in God's name
in good company
in good standing
in good time
in high dudgeon
in holy orders
in honour bound
in honour of
in hot pursuit
in hot water
in keeping with
in line for
in line with
in living memory
in loco parentis
in memory of
in mint condition
in name only
in one piece
in one's blood
in one's bones
in one's confidence
in one's cups
in one's debt
in one's face
in one's gift
in one's hair
in one's head
in one's keeping
in one's lap
in one's name
in one's pocket

in one's shirtsleeves
in one's shoes
in one's sights
in one's sleep
in one's tracks
in one's turn
in one's way
in one's wisdom
in open court
in order to
in other words
in Queer Street
in safe hands
in seventh heaven
in short order
in small doses
in spite of
in stockinged feet
in the altogether
in the bag
in the balance
in the betting
in the black
in the buff
in the can
in the clear
in the club
in the dark
in the doghouse
in the end
in the event
in the field
in the flesh
in the frame
in the groove
in the know
in the loop
in the main
in the mass
in the money
in the nude
in the offing
in the picture
in the pink
in the pipeline

in the race
in the raw
in the red
in the right
in the road
in the rough
in the round
in the running
in the soup
in the swim
in the wars
in the wash
in the way
in the wings
in the works
in the wrong
in two minds
in two shakes
in view of
in your dreams
in-your-face
Ku Klux Klan
la-di-da
me and mine
my giddy aunt
my heart bleeds
my honourable friend
ne plus ultra
no amount of
no can do
no-claims bonus
no end of
no expense spared
no flies on
no-go area
no great shakes
no holds barred
no laughing matter
no-man's-land
no oil painting
no strings attached
no thanks to
of easy virtue
of good cheer
of like mind

of one mind
of the essence
of unsound mind
on a budget
on all fours
on a loser
on and off
on and on
on a plate
on a platter
on a promise
on a roll
on a sixpence
on a string
on automatic pilot
on bended knee
on bended knees
on borrowed time
on cloud nine
on cloud seven
on collision course
on course to
on every hand
on firm ground
on no account
on nodding terms
on one's account
on one's back
on one's case
on one's conscience
on one's doorstep
on one's feet
on one's game
on one's guard
on one's hands
on one's haunches
on one's head
on one's knees
on one's lonesome
on one's mettle
on one's mind
on one's own
on one's plate
on one's tail
on one's tiptoes

on one's tod
on one's toes
on one's uppers
on one's way
on pain of
on speaking terms
on the air
on the ball
on the bench
on the blink
on the block
on the bone
on the books
on the breadline
on the button
on the cadge
on the cards
on the carpet
on the cheap
on the contrary
on the defensive
on the dole
on the doorstep
on the dot
on the double
on the fiddle
on the Flat
on the fly
on the game
on the go
on the hoof
on the hop
on the house
on the job
on the latch
on the level
on the line
on the lookout
on the loose
on the make
on the march
on the mark
on the mat
on the mend
on the move

on the nail
on the nod
on the nose
on the offensive
on the prowl
on the q.t.
on the quiet
on the rack
on the rails
on the razzle
on the rebound
on the record
on the rise
on the road
on the rocks
on the ropes
on the run
on the scent
on the scrounge
on the shelf
on the side
on the skids
on the sly
on the spot
on the table
on the take
on the tiles
on the town
on the trot
on the turn
on the waggon
on the wagon
on the wane
on the warpath
on the watch
on the whole
on the wing
on thin ice
on tippy-toe
on tippy-toes
on top of
on your bike
on your marks
ox-eye daisy
so-and-so

St Bernard Pass
St Elmo's fire
St George's Channel
St George's cross
St Gotthard Pass
St James's Palace
St John Ambulance
St John's wort
St Lawrence Seaway
St Mark's Cathedral
St Paul's Cathedral
St Peter's Basilica
St Swithin's day
St Vitus's dance
to a degree
to a man
to a nicety
to a T
to a turn
to be sure
to die for
to kingdom come
to one's bones
to one's cost
to one's credit
to one's disadvantage
to one's face
to one's feet
to one's fingertips
to one's liking
to one's satisfaction
to reckon with
to the bad
to the bone
to the contrary
to the core
to the death
to the finish
to the fore
to the full
to the gills
to the good
to the gunwales
to the hilt
to the letter

to the marrow
to the nines
to the point
to the skies
to the winds
up against it
up and about
up-and-comer
up-and-coming
up and doing
up-and-over
up and running
up for grabs
up in arms
up one's sleeve
up one's street
up the ante
up the creek
up the duff
up the pole
up the river
up the spout
up the stick
up-to-date
up to par
up to scratch
up to snuff
up to speed
us and them
va-va-voom

## 3-LETTER FIRST WORD

Act of Settlement
Act of Succession
Act of Supremacy
Act of Uniformity
Act of Union
act one's age
act the fool
add one's twopenn'orth
age of consent
aid and abet
air chief marshal
Air Force One

air-sea rescue
air traffic control
air traffic controller
air vice-marshal
Aix-en-Provence
all and sundry
all at sea
all in all
all-in-one
all-in wrestling
All Saints' Day
All Souls' Day
all the best
all the way
Arc de Triomphe
arm in arm
ask for trouble
bad hair day
bag and baggage
bag of nerves
bay for blood
Bay of Bengal
Bay of Biscay
Bay of Fundy
Bay of Pigs
Bay of Plenty
bed and board
bed and breakfast
beg the question
beg to differ
big with child
bit by bit
bit of rough
bob and weave
bob for apples
bow and scrape
bow one's knee
bow the knee
box one's ears
boy next door
can of worms
cap in hand
car boot sale
cat and mouse
cod liver oil

cop hold of
coq au vin
cri de cœur
cul-de-sac
cut a caper
cut a dash
cut a deal
cut and dried
cut and paste
cut and run
cut and thrust
cut a tooth
cut both ways
cut it fine
cut it out
cut no ice
cut one's losses
cut one's teeth
cut out for
cut the cackle
cut the cord
cut the mustard
cut the ribbon
cut things fine
cut-throat razor
cut to ribbons
cut up rough
Dar es Salaam
day and night
day by day
day-care centre
day of obligation
day of reckoning
die a death
die in harness
die is cast
die like flies
die the death
dig the dirt
dig up dirt
dog eat dog
dos and don'ts
Dow Jones average
Dow Jones index
dry as dust

dry-ski slope
eat humble pie
eat one's dust
eat one's words
eau de cologne
eau de Nil
eau de toilette
eau de vie
eff and blind
Eid ul-Adha
Eid ul-Fitr
end in tears
end it all
end of story
end to end
far and away
far and near
far and wide
far cry from
fin de siècle
fit the bill
fit to bust
fly a kite
fly-by-night
fly-by-wire
fly the coop
fly the flag
fly the nest
for all seasons
for a song
for dear life
for good measure
for grim death
for my money
for one's country
for one's life
for one's liking
for one's pains
for one's sins
for pity's sake
for the asking
for the birds
for the nonce
for the record
for the ride

for the taking
fur will fly
get a grip
get a life
get away with
get back at
get back to
get carried away
get down to
get hold of
get itchy feet
get off on
get one's breath
get one's cards
get one's goat
get one's jollies
get one's oats
get one's way
get out of
get rid of
get round to
get shot of
get stuck in
get stuck into
get the bird
get the boot
get the hump
get the message
get the nod
get the picture
get the push
get the shove
get up speed
get up steam
get up to
get wind of
get worked up
Guy Fawkes Night
hat in hand
hem and haw
his and hers
hit a nerve
hit it off
hit the bottle
hit the hay

hit the jackpot
hit the mark
hit the road
hit the roof
hit the sack
hit the scene
hit the skids
hit the spot
hit the trail
hit the wall
hot cross bun
hot to trot
hot-water bottle
how-de-do
how-d'ye-do
how say you
hue and cry
hum and haw
Île-de-France
ill at ease
Inn of Court
ins and outs
it's your funeral
jog one's memory
Koh-i-noor
lah-di-dah
lap of honour
law and order
law of averages
law of nature
law unto oneself
lay about one
lay an egg
lay claim to
lay down arms
lay eyes on
lay hands on
lay hold of
lay hold on
lay on thick
lay siege to
lay store by
lay store on
lay to rest
lay to waste

let go of
let it drop
let it pass
let it rest
let off steam
let oneself go
let up on
let well alone
lie in state
low-water mark
mad cow disease
man and boy
man-at-arms
Man Booker Prize
man enough to
man of parts
man-of-war
man-o'-war
man the barricades
man to man
men-at-arms
men in suits
men-of-war
men-o'-war
mix and match
mix one's drinks
New Age traveller
New Model Army
New South Wales
New Stone Age
New Year's Day
New Year's Eve
nip and tuck
nom de guerre
nom de plume
Non-Aligned Movement
non compos mentis
not a hope
not all there
not a sausage
not a whit
not before time
not mince words
not much cop
not one's day

not one's scene
now and again
now and then
now or never
now you're talking
odd-job man
odd-job men
odd man out
odd one out
off and on
off one's case
off one's chump
off one's face
off one's feet
off one's game
off one's hands
off one's head
off one's nut
off one's rocker
off one's trolley
off the air
off the boat
off the bone
off the cuff
off the hook
off the map
off the mark
off the pace
off the peg
off the record
off the shelf
off the waggon
off the wagon
off the wall
oil and water
oil of cloves
oil of turpentine
oil of wintergreen
oil the wheels
old-age pensioner
old boy network
old boys' network
Old English sheepdog
Old Line State
old man's beard

**MULTI-WORD**

3 WORDS

Old Stone Age
old wives' tale
one after another
one and all
one and only
one-armed bandit
one by one
one-day wonder
one for one
one-horse race
one-horse town
one jump ahead
one-man band
one-night stand
one of us
one or two
one step ahead
one-to-one
one-track mind
one-trick pony
out and about
out-and-out
out for blood
out of action
out of bounds
out of breath
out of character
out of circulation
out of commission
out of condition
out of contention
out of context
out of control
out-of-court
out of danger
out-of-date
out of doors
out of fashion
out of favour
out of form
out of gear
out of hand
out of humour
out of it
out of joint

out of key
out of kilter
out of line
out of luck
out of nowhere
out of order
out of phase
out of place
out of plumb
out of pocket
out of practice
out of print
out of proportion
out of reach
out of service
out of sight
out of sorts
out of square
out of step
out of stock
out of sync
out of synch
out of temper
out of time
out of touch
out of training
out of true
out of tune
out of turn
out of whack
out to lunch
out with it
Pan-Africanist Congress
pas de deux
pay court to
pay its way
pay one's dues
pay one's respects
pay one's way
pay-per-view
pay the score
pen and ink
pit-a-pat
pit bull terrier
ply for hire

pop one's clogs
pop the question
pot-au-feu
pot of gold
put behind one
put down roots
put down to
put flesh on
put into action
put it about
put money on
put oneself about
put on weight
put paid to
put store by
put store on
put to bed
put to flight
put to rights
put to sea
put to sleep
put up with
Ras al Khaimah
rat-tat-tat
Red Army Faction
red blood cell
red-hot poker
red-letter day
red-light district
Rio de Janeiro
Rub' al Khali
rub it in
rub one's hands
run a mile
run an errand
run around with
run a temperature
run away with
run for it
run foul of
run its course
run out of
run out on
run the gamut
run the gauntlet

run the risk
run the show
run to earth
run to ground
run to ruin
run to seed
sad to say
San Andreas fault
say a mouthful
say no more
say one's piece
say the word
Sea of Azov
Sea of Galilee
Sea of Japan
Sea of Marmara
see the light
see the world
set eyes on
set fire to
set foot in
set foot on
set in concrete
set in stone
set on fire
set store by
set store on
set the agenda
set the pace
set the scene
set to rights
set up home
set up shop
sit in for
sit in judgement
Six Day War
six feet under
son et lumière
son-in-law
Son of Man
tae kwon do
t'ai chi ch'uan
tam-o'-shanter
tan one's hide
tar and feather

Tar Heel State
tea and sympathy
Tel Aviv-Jaffa
ten a penny
ten-gallon hat
ten to one
the penny dropped
the real McCoy
the whole caboodle
the whole shebang
tic-tac-toe
tie the knot
Tin Pan Alley
tip one's hand
tip one's hat
tip the balance
tip the scales
Tir-na-nog
tit for tat
toe the line
toe to toe
top and tail
try for size
try it on
try one's best
try one's damnedest
try one's luck
tug of love
tug of war
tug one's forelock
two a penny
two-by-four
two by two
two or three
two-way mirror
two-way street
Umm al Qaiwain
ups-a-daisy
ups and downs
use-by date
use one's loaf
Van Allen belt
vis-à-vis
vol-au-vent
wax and wane

way back when
way to go
Wee Free Kirk
wet one's whistle
who goes there
win one's spurs
win on points
win the day
woe is me
Yom Kippur War
you and yours

**4-LETTER FIRST WORD**

ages of consent
aide-de-camp
auld lang syne
auto-da-fé
ayes have it
back and forth
back of beyond
back-seat driver
back-to-back
back to front
ball of fire
bang away at
bang on about
bang to rights
Bank of England
Bard of Avon
bare one's soul
bare one's teeth
bear down on
bear ill will
bear in mind
bear testimony to
bear witness to
beat a retreat
beat one's breast
beat the bounds
beat the clock
beat the rap
beat the system
bell the cat
belt and braces

bend one's ear
bend one's knee
bend over backwards
bend the knee
best of five
best of luck
best of three
bide one's time
bill and coo
bill of exchange
bill of fare
bill of lading
Bill of Rights
bird has flown
bird of paradise
bird of passage
bird of prey
bite one's lip
bite one's nails
bite one's tongue
bite the bullet
bite the dust
blot one's copybook
blow a fuse
blow a gasket
blow-by-blow
blow itself out
blow off steam
blow one's mind
blow one's nose
blow one's stack
blow one's top
blow one's trumpet
blow the gaff
blue-eyed boy
blue-green algae
blue on blue
Bob's your uncle
body and soul
boil down to
bold as brass
bone of contention
Book of Kells
Book of Proverbs
born and bred

born in wedlock
bowl of cherries
bric-a-brac
buck stops here
bums on seats
burn one's boats
burn one's bridges
bury the hatchet
bust a gut
call a halt
call attention to
call in question
call into play
call into question
call it quits
call of nature
call one's bluff
call the shots
call the tune
call to arms
call to mind
call to order
call to witness
can't be bothered
Cape Breton Island
Cape St Vincent
case in point
cash and carry
cash in hand
cash on delivery
cast aspersions on
cast light on
c'est la vie
chew the cud
chew the fat
chew the scenery
chip away at
chop and change
City of London
City Technology College
clap eyes on
clap hold of
coat of arms
coat of mail
cock-a-hoop

cock-a-leekie
come a cropper
come and go
come down on
come down to
come down with
come full circle
come in for
come in handy
come into line
come into question
come of age
come off it
come one's way
come on strong
come on to
come out with
come over big
come to blows
come to grief
come to life
come to light
come to mind
come to naught
come to nothing
come to pass
come to rest
come up roses
come up smiling
come up trumps
come up with
come what may
cook one's goose
cook the books
cool one's heels
cost of living
coup de grâce
Cox's orange pippin
cris de cœur
culs-de-sac
curl one's lip
damp-proof course
Davy Jones's locker
dead and buried
dead as mutton

dead men's shoes
dead of night
dead of winter
dead spit of
dead to rights
debt of honour
deed of covenant
deep-vein thrombosis
deus ex machina
dice with death
Dien Bien Phu
Diet of Worms
dish the dirt
done and dusted
don't ask me
don't mention it
doom and gloom
door to door
down and dirty
down and out
down-at-heel
down the hatch
down the line
down the road
down-to-earth
drag and drop
drag one's feet
drag one's heels
draw a blank
draw oneself up
draw one's fire
drop a brick
drop a curtsey
drop a curtsy
drop a hint
drop a stitch
drop like flies
drop like ninepins
drop one's aitches
drop one's guard
drop one's serve
drop one's trousers
drop the ball
drum and bass
duck and dive

duck-billed platypus
dull as dishwater
dull as ditchwater
dust and ashes
earn one's keep
earn one's spurs
ease one's mind
East India Company
east-north-east
east-south-east
easy as ABC
easy does it
eaux de cologne
eaux de toilette
eaux de vie
ever and anon
face the music
fair and square
fair-weather friend
fall back on
fall foul of
fall in line
fall into line
fall into place
fall into step
fall in with
fall like ninepins
fall over backwards
fall prey to
fall short of
fall to pieces
fall victim to
fast and furious
feel-good factor
feel one's age
feel the draught
feel the pinch
feet of clay
felt-tipped pen
felt-tip pen
fill one's boots
fill one's shoes
fill the bill
find its level
find one's feet

find one's level
find one's tongue
fine-tooth comb
fine-toothed comb
fire and brimstone
Fire of London
five-a-side
five o'clock shadow
flex one's muscles
flip one's lid
fold one's arms
food for thought
fore and aft
Fort-de-France
foul one's nest
four-by-four
four-in-hand
four-letter word
four noble truths
four-poster bed
four-wheel drive
free and easy
free-for-all
free of charge
from day one
from now on
from on high
from the dead
from the floor
from the heart
from the top
full of beans
full of oneself
full speed ahead
full steam ahead
full to overflowing
gain ground on
game is up
Gang of Four
gift of tongues
gild the lily
gird one's loins
Girl Guides Association
girl next door
give a hand

give and take
give colour to
give it laldy
give it large
give it up
give me strength
give oneself airs
give on to
give or take
give place to
give rise to
give up on
give voice to
give way to
good as gold
good as new
good for her
good for him
good-for-nothing
good for you
good on her
good on him
good on you
grit one's teeth
grow on trees
grow out of
Gulf of Aden
Gulf of Alaska
Gulf of Aqaba
Gulf of Bothnia
Gulf of California
Gulf of Carpentaria
Gulf of Corinth
Gulf of Darien
Gulf of Finland
Gulf of Guinea
Gulf of Mexico
Gulf of Oman
Gulf of Sidra
Gulf of Thailand
Gulf of Tonkin
Gulf War syndrome
Guru Granth Sahib
half a chance
half a crown

half a dozen

half-and-half

half an eye

half an hour

half the battle

Hall of Fame

hall of residence

hand in glove

hand in hand

hand-me-down

hand-to-hand

hand to mouth

hang a left

hang a right

hang around with

hang one's hat

hang one's head

hang on to

Hang Seng index

hang up on

hard and fast

hard as nails

hard at it

hard done by

hard of hearing

hate one's guts

hats off to

have a ball

have a bellyful

have a butcher's

have a care

have a cow

have a fit

have a heart

have a word

have been around

have designs on

have down pat

have eyes for

have had it

have in common

have in mind

have it away

have itchy feet

have it coming

have it easy

have it large

have it made

have it out

have mercy on

have mercy upon

have no business

have no idea

have nothing on

have one's bellyful

have one's ear

have one's moments

have one's number

have one's uses

have one's way

have the hump

head of hair

head of state

head over heels

head-to-head

hear tell of

hell for leather

here and now

here and there

here to stay

hide-and-seek

high and dry

high and low

high and mighty

high-water mark

hold at bay

hold in derision

hold one's breath

hold one's ground

hold one's hand

hold one's nose

hold one's own

hold one's peace

hold one's serve

hold one's service

hold one's tongue

hold on to

hold out for

hold out on

hold the field

| | | |
|---|---|---|
| hold the fort | jury is out | kith and kin |
| hold the line | just in case | know better than |
| hold the ring | just the job | know inside out |
| hold the stage | keen as mustard | know-it-all |
| hold to ransom | keep at bay | know no bounds |
| hold your horses | keep bad time | know one's onions |
| holy of holies | keep company with | know the ropes |
| Holy Roman Empire | keep good time | know the score |
| home and dry | keep in with | know what's what |
| home from home | keep late hours | know who's who |
| home sweet home | keep on about | lady-in-waiting |
| hook and eye | keep on at | Lamb of God |
| Hook of Holland | keep one's cool | Land of Enchantment |
| hope against hope | keep one's distance | land of Nod |
| hope springs eternal | keep one's feet | Land of Opportunity |
| Horn of Africa | keep one's figure | laps of honour |
| horn of plenty | keep one's head | laws of nature |
| hors de combat | keep one's temper | lead the field |
| how's your father | keep one's word | lead the way |
| huff and puff | keep pace with | lean over backwards |
| inch by inch | keep tabs on | leap to conclusions |
| Inns of Court | keep the peace | left for dead |
| into the bargain | keep the score | left-hand drive |
| into the groove | keep to oneself | left to oneself |
| Iran-Contra affair | keep track of | lend a hand |
| Iran-Contra scandal | keep up appearances | lend an ear |
| Iran-Iraq War | keep up with | lend colour to |
| Isle of Ely | kick into touch | lick into shape |
| Isle of Man | kick one's heels | lick one's chops |
| Isle of Portland | kick the bucket | lick one's lips |
| Isle of Wight | kick the habit | lick one's wounds |
| jack-o'-lantern | kick up dust | life and limb |
| Jack Russell terrier | kill oneself laughing | lift a finger |
| Jack the Lad | kill or cure | lift a hand |
| joie de vivre | kill the messenger | like a demon |
| join the club | King Charles spaniel | like a dream |
| jump for joy | King James Bible | like a flash |
| jump the gun | King James Version | like a leech |
| jump the queue | King of Arms | like a shot |
| jump the rails | king of beasts | like as not |
| jump the shark | King of Kings | like a streak |
| jump the track | Kirk of Scotland | like greased lightning |
| jump through hoops | kiss and tell | like grim death |
| jump to conclusions | kiss goodbye to | like nobody's business |
| jump to it | kiss the rod | like pulling teeth |

like the clappers
like the devil
like the wind
line of battle
line one's pocket
line one's stomach
live in hope
live in sin
live it up
live to regret
live up to
Loch Ness monster
lock on to
Lone Star State
long-drawn-out
look a fright
look a picture
look a treat
look daggers at
look down on
look for trouble
look forward to
look kindly on
look one's age
look the part
look up to
loop the loop
Lord Chief Justice
Lord of Appeal
Lord Privy Seal
lose a wicket
lose one's cool
lose one's figure
lose one's grip
lose one's head
lose one's life
lose one's marbles
lose one's mind
lose one's patience
lose one's rag
lose one's shirt
lose one's temper
lose one's thread
lose one's tongue
lose one's way

lose sight of
lose the plot
lose the thread
lose the way
lose track of
loss of face
lost for words
love-lies-bleeding
made of money
made-to-measure
maid of honour
make a difference
make a face
make a fortune
make a fuss
make a hit
make a killing
make allowance for
make a match
make a move
make an appearance
make an entrance
make a noise
make a pile
make a pitch
make a row
make a splash
make away with
make common cause
make ends meet
make free with
make friends with
make fun of
make inroads in
make it big
make it snappy
make light of
make little of
make love to
make mock of
make no difference
make no mistake
make off with
make one's acquaintance
make one's day

make oneself felt
make oneself scarce
make oneself useful
make one's entrance
make one's excuses
make one's fortune
make one's mark
make one's peace
make one's point
make or break
make play of
make play with
make sense of
make so bold
make sport of
make the cut
make the grade
make the running
make tracks for
make up for
make up ground
make up leeway
make up to
make use of
many happy returns
Mars Global Surveyor
mean to say
meat and potatoes
meet one's eye
meet one's eyes
meet one's gaze
meet one's Maker
meet one's match
meet one's Waterloo
meet the case
mend one's fences
mend one's manners
mend one's ways
mess about with
mess around with
Mick the Miller
mile a minute
mile-high club
milk-and-water
mind one's step

mind over matter
mind the shop
mise en scène
miss a beat
miss the boat
miss the bus
miss the cut
mock turtle soup
Mont St Michel
more or less
more the merrier
move in with
move the goalpost
move the goalposts
mum's the word
name the day
near at hand
near the bone
near the knuckle
near to home
neck and neck
ne'er-do-well
next door to
next in line
nice as pie
nine days' wonder
noes have it
noms de guerre
noms de plume
none the less
none the wiser
nose to tail
null and void
nuts and bolts
once for all
once or twice
one's better feelings
one's better nature
one's bounden duty
one's declining years
one's face fits
one's family jewels
one's finer feelings
one's finest hour
one's gorge rises

one's heart's desire
one's heart sinks
one's humble abode
one's last breath
one's last gasp
one's money's worth
one's own lookout
one's own master
open a book
open-heart surgery
open one's eyes
open the batting
open to debate
open to offers
over a barrel
over one's head
over the counter
over the hill
over the moon
over the odds
over the sticks
over the top
over the way
over the wicket
pack a punch
pack it in
pair of hands
pair of scissors
pair of shears
pair of steps
pair of tweezers
part of speech
pass one's lips
pass the baton
pass the buck
pass the hat
pass the parcel
pick a fight
pick a lock
pick and choose
pick a quarrel
pick holes in
pick-me-up
pick one's brain
pick one's brains

pick one's pockets
pick to pieces
pick up on
pick up speed
pick up steam
pied-à-terre
pigs can fly
pigs might fly
Pine Tree State
pins and needles
play a hunch
play a let
play by ear
play catch-up
play for time
play havoc with
play it cool
play it safe
play one's hunch
play on words
play second fiddle
play the field
play the fool
play the game
play the market
play up to
play with fire
plus ça change
poke fun at
Pont du Gard
pork-pie hat
Port-au-Prince
Port-of-Spain
post office box
pots of money
pour it on
pour scorn on
pros and cons
puff and blow
pull a face
pull oneself together
pull one's leg
pull one's punches
pull one's weight
pull the plug

pull the rug
pull the strings
pull to pieces
pump one's hand
push one's luck
push the envelope
quid pro quo
race against time
rack-and-pinion
rack one's brain
rack one's brains
rags to riches
rain or shine
rain stair rods
rant and rave
rate of exchange
read my lips
read one's mind
read one's palm
read one's thoughts
read-only memory
read the runes
read up on
reap the whirlwind
rear its head
rear-view mirror
rear-wheel drive
reel-to-reel
rend the air
rest her soul
rest his soul
rest is history
rest one's case
ride roughshod over
ride to hounds
ring a bell
ring the changes
rise and shine
risk one's neck
road fund licence
road to nowhere
rock and roll
rock 'n' roll
Rock of Gibraltar
rock the boat

roll of honour
roll-top desk
roly-poly pudding
root and branch
root mean square
rose of Sharon
Ross and Cromarty
rule of law
rule of thumb
rule the roost
rush of blood
sale or return
Salt Lake City
save one's bacon
save one's blushes
save one's breath
save one's hide
save one's life
save one's skin
save the day
Saxe-Coburg-Gotha
seal one's fate
seek one's fortune
self-raising flour
sell-by date
sell one's soul
sell the pass
send away for
shed light on
shed one's blood
shot to pieces
show a leg
Show Me State
show one's face
show one's hand
show one's teeth
show the flag
show the way
shut oneself off
shut up shop
shut your face
shut your mouth
shut your trap
sick building syndrome
sick man of

side by side
sine qua non
sink or swim
skin and bone
slow and sure
slow but sure
snap one's fingers
song and dance
Song of Songs
sons-in-law
spin a yarn
spit it out
Star of David
Star-spangled Banner
stay of execution
stay one's hand
stay the course
stay the distance
stay the pace
step by step
step on it
stir one's stumps
stir the blood
stop at nothing
stop one's ears
stop short of
stop the show
suit one's book
take a bath
take a bow
take a butcher's
take account of
take a chance
take a dive
take advantage of
take a flyer
take a hammering
take a hand
take a hike
take a hint
take as read
take a toss
take a wicket
take by storm
take by surprise

take care of
take cognizance of
take delivery of
take exception to
take for granted
take holy orders
take-home pay
take in hand
take in sail
take into account
take issue with
take it easy
take its course
take its toll
take lying down
take no notice
take no prisoners
take on board
take one's chance
take oneself off
take one's fancy
take one's leave
take one's life
take one's medicine
take one's place
take one's point
take one's seat
take one's time
take pleasure in
take the air
take the biscuit
take the cake
take the chair
take the count
take the fall
take the field
take the fifth
take the floor
take the hint
take the liberty
take the mickey
take the offensive
take the plunge
take the rap
take the salute

**MULTI-WORD**

3 WORDS

take the veil
take to extremes
take to flight
take to heart
take up arms
take up with
talk down to
talk sense into
talk the talk
tear oneself away
tear to pieces
tear to ribbons
tear to shreds
Tell el-Amarna
tell me another
tell one's fortune
tell the time
Test-Ban Treaty
test the water
test-tube baby
tête-à-tête
that sinking feeling
them and us
then and there
thin blue line
thin on top
tick-tack-toe
till kingdom come
tilt at windmills
time after time
time and again
time is money
time will tell
toss a pancake
tour de force
Tour de France
tour of duty
Trás-os-Montes
Tree of Life
trim one's sails
true to form
true to life
true to type
tugs of war
turn a corner

turn a trick
turn full circle
turn inside out
turn of mind
turn of speed
turn one's head
turn Queen's evidence
turn state's evidence
turn the balance
turn the corner
turn the knife
turn the scales
turn the screw
turn the screws
turn the tables
turn the tide
turn to advantage
turn up trumps
Tyne and Wear
vale of tears
wake-up call
walk all over
walk off with
walk of life
walk on air
walk on eggshells
walk one's talk
walk the boards
walk the plank
walk the streets
walk the walk
Wall Street Crash
warm as toast
warm up to
Wars of Religion
wash one's hands
wave the flag
wear the trousers
well and truly
well-to-do
west-north-west
West Point Academy
west-south-west
what possessed you
what the hell

when in Rome
whip into shape
wide area network
wild and woolly
wild goose chase
wind of change
with a bang
with a bump
with a difference
with apologies to
with a vengeance
with a will
with bad grace
with bated breath
with bells on
with both barrels
with flying colours
with forked tongue
with good grace
with knobs on
with one accord
with one's compliments
with one voice
with open arms
with open eyes
with reference to
with regard to
with respect to
word for word
word of honour
word of mouth
work a treat
work like Trojans
work of art
work one's passage
work to rule
work up to
worm will turn
wrap it up
yard of ale
year-on-year
yell bloody murder
yell blue murder
your humble servant
your obedient servant

## **5**-LETTER FIRST WORD

above the line
after a fashion
after a sort
after the fact
again and again
agree to differ
ahead of schedule
ahead of time
aides-de-camp
alive and kicking
along the line
angel food cake
Anglo-Boer War
Anglo-Irish Agreement
Anglo-Irish Treaty
apple-pie order
April Fool's Day
argue the toss
autos-da-fé
Baile Átha Cliath
basal metabolic rate
beast of burden
bells and whistles
below the belt
below the line
Bight of Benin
bills of exchange
bills of fare
bird's-eye view
bird's nest soup
birds of paradise
birds of passage
birds of prey
black and white
black one's eye
blind man's bluff
blind man's buff
block and tackle
blood and guts
blood and thunder
blown off course
borne in on
borne in upon

bound up in
bound up with
brace and bit
brave new world
break a leg
break a sweat
break fresh ground
break new ground
break of day
break of serve
break one's back
break one's duck
break one's heart
break one's serve
break one's service
break one's stride
break out in
break the bank
break the habit
break the ice
break the mould
breed like rabbits
bring home to
bring into line
bring into play
bring into question
bring to bear
bring to life
bring to light
bring to mind
bring to naught
bring to pass
built on sand
bully for her
bully for him
bully for you
burst into flame
burst into flames
burst one's bubble
carry the can
carry the day
carry the flag
catch a cold
catch a crab
catch at straws

catch one's breath
catch one's death
catch one's eye
catch one's fancy
catch sight of
catch the light
catch the sun
catch up with
chase a rainbow
chase one's tail
chase the dragon
chase the game
cheap and cheerful
check up on
cheek by jowl
cheek to cheek
chest of drawers
chief of staff
Child Support Agency
chill one's blood
chock-a-block
chuck it down
claim to fame
clasp one's hands
clean one's plate
clear as day
clear as mud
clear one's throat
clear the air
clear the decks
clear the way
click one's fingers
cloak-and-dagger
close the books
close to home
cloud cuckoo land
coals to Newcastle
coast is clear
coats of mail
comme il faut
corps de ballet
Costa del Sol
could care less
count one's blessings
count the cost

count the days
count the hours
count the pennies
coups de grâce
court of law
Court of Protection
Court of Session
cover one's back
cover one's tracks
crack a bottle
crack of dawn
crack of doom
cramp one's style
crash and burn
cream of tartar
crème de cassis
crème de menthe
crêpe de Chine
crock of gold
cross my heart
cross one's fingers
cross one's mind
cross one's path
cross the floor
Crown Prosecution Service
Cuban Missile Crisis
daddy-long-legs
Daman and Diu
dance attendance on
Darby and Joan
death by misadventure
death-watch beetle
debts of honour
deeds of covenant
devil to pay
dribs and drabs
drink and drive
drink one's health
droit de seigneur
drown one's sorrows
drunk and disorderly
Duchy of Cornwall
Duchy of Lancaster
ducks and drakes
Dutch elm disease

Edict of Nantes
enter one's name
enter the lists
every man jack
every which way
fancy one's chances
feast or famine
fetch and carry
fight one's corner
fight or flight
fight shy of
first among equals
first and foremost
first-day cover
first-degree relative
first of all
First Sea Lord
first things first
First World War
Firth of Clyde
Firth of Forth
Firth of Tay
Fleet Air Arm
flesh and blood
fleur-de-lis
fleur-de-lys
float one's boat
folie à deux
folie de grandeur
force one's hand
force the bidding
force the issue
force the pace
forty-ninth parallel
Franz Josef Land
freak of nature
front-wheel drive
funny ha-ha
gloom and doom
goods and chattels
grace and favour
Grand Canyon State
grasp at straws
grasp the nettle
great and small

Great Australian Bight
Great Barrier Reef
Great Dividing Range
Great Lake State
Great Leap Forward
Great Red Spot
Great Rift Valley
Great White Way
Greek Orthodox Church
Green Mountain State
green with envy
gross domestic product
gross national product
Group of Eight
guard of honour
guest of honour
guilt by association
Halls of Fame
halls of residence
happy as Larry
happy-go-lucky
happy hunting ground
heads of state
heads will roll
Heart of Dixie
heart of stone
heart-to-heart
hedge one's bets
hoist the flag
Homer sometimes nods
horns of plenty
Horst Wessel Song
House of Commons
House of Keys
House of Lancaster
House of Lords
House of Orange
House of York
house-to-house
Human Genome Project
Irish Free State
Irish Republican Army
Jammu and Kashmir
knock into shape
knock it off

knock oneself out
knock on wood
knock spots off
large as life
latch on to
laugh a minute
laugh oneself silly
leave a mark
leave hold of
leave it out
leave its mark
leave of absence
leave one's mark
leave well alone
level of attainment
level playing field
Lewis and Harris
Lewis with Harris
light a fuse
light of day
light the fuse
local area network
Lords of Appeal
Lords Privy Seal
lower one's sights
maids of honour
Mason-Dixon Line
Mazar-e-Sharif
means of production
merry-go-round
might is right
mises en scène
mixed up in
mixed up with
money for jam
month of Sundays
more's the pity
motor neuron disease
mouth to feed
mouth-to-mouth
muddy the waters
neat's-foot oil
never a one
never a whit
never-never land

never say die
never you mind
night and day
North Atlantic Drift
North East Lincolnshire
North-East Passage
north-north-east
north-north-west
North Rhine-Westphalia
North Star State
North-West Passage
odour of sanctity
offer one's hand
order of magnitude
Order of Merit
Papua New Guinea
parts of speech
Peace Garden State
Peace of Utrecht
Perth and Kinross
piece by piece
pièce de résistance
pieds-à-terre
pinch the pennies
plain as day
pluck up courage
point of order
point of view
point the finger
point-to-point
pound of flesh
pound the beat
power of attorney
press the button
press the flesh
pride of place
prime the pump
Punch and Judy
punch the clock
queer one's pitch
raise a laugh
raise an eyebrow
raise one's eyebrows
raise one's glass
raise one's hand

3 WORDS

MULTI-WORD

raise one's hat
raise one's sights
raise the ante
raise the devil
raise the roof
raise the standard
rates of exchange
ready-to-wear
refer to drawer
rhyme or reason
right as rain
right-hand drive
right-hand man
right-hand men
right of abode
right of way
right-to-life
roman-à-clef
Roman Catholic Church
rough and ready
rough and tumble
round the bend
round the clock
round the corner
round the twist
Royal Air Force
Royal British Legion
Royal Greenwich Observatory
Royal Leamington Spa
Royal Shakespeare Company
Royal Tunbridge Wells
Royal Victorian Chain
Royal Victorian Order
Rugby Football Union
Russo-Japanese War
sabre-toothed tiger
screw up courage
seize the day
sense of direction
sense of proportion
serve its turn
serve one's turn
serve two masters
seven-day wonder
Seven Years War

shake a leg
shake one's booty
shake one's hand
shake one's head
shame on you
Shatt al-Arab
shift for oneself
shift one's ground
shirt of Nessus
shoot a line
shoot it out
shoot one's cuffs
shoot the breeze
shoot the messenger
short and sweet
short of breath
shout the odds
sight to behold
sixth-form college
slash-and-burn
sleep on it
slice of life
sling one's hook
smack one's lips
small claims court
small is beautiful
smash-and-grab
smell a rat
smoke and mirrors
smoke-filled room
sorry for oneself
South Sea Bubble
south-south-east
south-south-west
spare no expense
spare one's blushes
speak evil of
speak for oneself
speak for yourself
speak ill of
speak in tongues
speak one's mind
speak up for
speak well of
spend a penny

spick and span
spike one's guns
spill one's blood
spill one's guts
spill the beans
split one's sides
split the difference
split the vote
sport of kings
sport the oak
sport utility vehicle
staff of life
stake a claim
stand a chance
stand and deliver
stand-off half
stand on ceremony
stand one's ground
stand the pace
stand up for
stand up to
stark raving mad
stark staring mad
Stars and Bars
Stars and Stripes
start a family
start a hare
start in on
state of affairs
state of emergency
state of grace
state of play
state of war
steal one's heart
steal one's thunder
steal the show
steer clear of
stick at nothing
stick 'em up
stick it to
stick out for
stick up for
stiff upper lip
still small voice
stock-in-trade

Stoke-on-Trent
Stone of Scone
stone the crows
strut one's stuff
Sturm und Drang
sugar snap pea
sugar the pill
sunny side up
sweat it out
sweep the board
sweet-and-sour
sweet as pie
sweet Fanny Adams
swing into action
swing the lead
sword of Damocles
sword of justice
Synod of Whitby
terms of reference
that's done it
that's torn it
thick and fast
thick as thieves
think better of
think for oneself
think ill of
think little of
think nothing of
third time lucky
three-legged race
three-line whip
Three Mile Island
three-point turn
three-ring circus
Three Wise Men
throw a fit
throw light on
throw money at
throw oneself at
throw oneself into
throw oneself on
throw oneself upon
throw people together
tired and emotional
tonic sol-fa

touch a chord
touch-and-go
touch a nerve
touch one's forelock
tough it out
tours de force
tours of duty
Tower of Babel
Tower of London
tower of strength
toxic shock syndrome
trail one's coat
Trans-Siberian Railway
tread on air
tread the boards
trial and error
trick or treat
troop the colour
truth to tell
Tsavo National Park
twist one's arm
twist the knife
ultra-high frequency
under a cloud
under a spell
under cover of
under full sail
under one's arm
under one's belt
under one's eyes
under one's feet
under one's nose
under one's spell
under one's thumb
under one's wing
under pain of
under penalty of
under plain cover
under separate cover
under starter's orders
under the counter
under the influence
under the knife
under the microscope
under the skin

under the sun
under the table
under the weather
under the wire
Union of Myanmar
until further notice
until further orders
until kingdom come
value added tax
value for money
Venus de Milo
video on demand
vingt-et-un
viola da gamba
Voice of America
walls have ears
warts and all
waste-disposal unit
waste one's breath
watch one's back
watch one's mouth
watch one's step
watch the pennies
watch the time
watch this space
weigh one's words
what's eating her
what's eating him
what's eating you
what's the betting
what's the damage
what's the game
what's the odds
what's your game
what's your pleasure
what's your poison
wheel and deal
wheel of Fortune
where it's at
white blood cell
white man's burden
whole nine yards
whole shooting match
whoop it up
winds of change

woman to woman
words fail me
works of art
World Health Organization
World Trade Center
World Trade Organization
World War I
World Wide Web
worse for drink
worse for wear
worth one's salt
worth one's while
wrack one's brain
wrack one's brains
wring one's hands
wrong way round
yards of ale
you're telling me
Youth Training Scheme

**6**-LETTER FIRST WORD

across the board
actual bodily harm
Argyll and Bute
around the bend
around the clock
around the corner
ascend the throne
asking for trouble
atomic mass unit
Austro-Hungarian empire
Baader-Meinhof Group
Bandar Seri Begawan
barrel of laughs
Battle of Actium
Battle of Agincourt
Battle of Austerlitz
Battle of Balaclava
Battle of Bannockburn
Battle of Borodino
Battle of Bosworth
Battle of Britain
Battle of Crécy
Battle of Culloden

Battle of Edgehill
Battle of Flodden
Battle of Gettysburg
Battle of Hastings
Battle of Jutland
Battle of Lepanto
Battle of Malplaquet
Battle of Marengo
Battle of Naseby
Battle of Navarino
Battle of Nechtansmere
Battle of Oudenarde
Battle of Passchendaele
Battle of Plataea
Battle of Prestonpans
Battle of Ramillies
Battle of Roncesvalles
Battle of Saratoga
Battle of Sedan
Battle of Sedgemoor
Battle of Stalingrad
Battle of Trafalgar
Battle of Verdun
Battle of Waterloo
Battle of Ypres
beasts of burden
before one's eyes
before the fact
before the mast
before the wind
behind closed doors
behind one's back
behind the scenes
behind the times
beside the point
beyond a joke
beyond one's means
beyond the pale
bloody but unbowed
Bosnia and Herzegovina
Boston Tea Party
bottom drops out
bottom falls out
breaks of serve
breath of life

Bridge of Sighs
bubble and squeak
bundle of fun
bundle of laughs
bundle of nerves
burden of proof
bureau de change
Burton-upon-Trent
button one's lip
carpal tunnel syndrome
caught up in
centre of attention
centre of attraction
centre of buoyancy
centre of curvature
centre of excellence
centre of flotation
centre of gravity
centre of mass
centre of pressure
chance one's arm
chance one's luck
change of air
change of heart
change of pace
change of scene
change one's mind
change one's tune
change the subject
checks and balances
chemin de fer
chiefs of staff
chilli con carne
Church of England
Church of Scotland
circle the wagons
clicks and mortar
closed-circuit television
clutch at straws
coffee-table book
comedy of manners
comity of nations
Common Agricultural Policy
common or garden
course of action

course of nature
courts of law
cudgel one's brains
damsel in distress
depart this life
divide and conquer
divide and rule
Doctor of Philosophy
double-edged sword
double or nothing
double or quits
Empire State Building
enough is enough
épater les bourgeois
esprit de corps
excuse my French
famous last words
father-in-law
figure of speech
folies à deux
follow one's nose
forbid the banns
forget-me-not
Franco-Prussian War
freaks of nature
freeze one's blood
Friuli-Venezia Giulia
Garden of Eden
garden of England
Garden of Gethsemane
gather one's wits
gloves are off
grease the skids
grease the wheels
groves of Academe
hammer and sickle
hammer and tongs
Haroun-al-Raschid
hearts and flowers
hearts and minds
Henley Royal Regatta
hither and thither
hither and yon
holier-than-thou
honest-to-God

MULTI-WORD

3 WORDS

honest-to-goodness
horses for courses
Houses of Parliament
Hubble Space Telescope
Indian National Congress
Ismail Samani Peak
Jekyll and Hyde
Jervis Bay Territory
Jewish New Year
johnny-come-lately
junior common room
junior high school
knives are out
Kruger National Park
labour of love
labour the point
larger than life
Latter-Day Saints
Laurel and Hardy
League of Nations
Legion of Honour
letter of credit
liquid crystal display
listen to reason
little by little
little or nothing
living image of
loiter with intent
loosen one's tongue
lowest common denominator
lowest common multiple
master-at-arms
master of ceremonies
matron of honour
matter of course
matter-of-fact
matter of form
matter of opinion
matter of record
ménage à trois
middle of nowhere
Middle Stone Age
moment of truth
mother-in-law
mother-of-pearl

murder will out
Nation of Islam
object of virtu
orders are orders
orders of magnitude
Oxford English Dictionary
packed like sardines
Palace of Minos
Palace of Westminster
Palais de l'Elysée
pardon my French
pepper-and-salt
perish the thought
pièces de résistance
pillar of strength
Plains of Abraham
Pledge of Allegiance
pledge one's troth
plight one's troth
points of view
poison pen letter
powder one's nose
powers of attorney
powers that be
Prince Edward Island
Prince of Darkness
Prince of Wales
public address system
public lending right
public limited company
Puerto Rico Trench
rattle one's cage
retail price index
return the compliment
rhythm and blues
rights of way
romans-à-clef
ruffle one's feathers
school of thought
scrape acquaintance with
scrape the barrel
scream bloody murder
scream blue murder
second in command
Second Sea Lord

second to none
Second World War
Secret Intelligence Service
seeing is believing
senior common room
senior nursing officer
settle accounts with
settle a score
settle one's affairs
settle one's hash
settle the score
shiver my timbers
sickle-cell anaemia
sickle-cell disease
signed and sealed
simple as ABC
Single European Act
single European currency
single-lens reflex
single transferable vote
sister-in-law
slings and arrows
Slough of Despond
slowly but surely
snakes and ladders
Social Democratic Party
social market economy
sodium-vapour lamp
soften the blow
sooner or later
sphere of influence
sphere of interest
spoilt for choice
spread like wildfire
spread one's wings
spring a leak
spring to mind
square accounts with
square the circle
square up to
stands to reason
Statue of Liberty
strain every nerve
Strait of Dover
Strait of Gibraltar

Strait of Hormuz
Strait of Magellan
Strait of Malacca
Strait of Messina
Strait of Otranto
streak of lightning
stream of consciousness
strike a balance
strike a chord
strike a light
strike an attitude
strike a pose
strike it lucky
strike it rich
strike me pink
stroke of luck
supply and demand
swings and roundabouts
Sydney Harbour Bridge
Sydney Opera House
thanks a bunch
thanks a million
Thirty Years War
tickle the ivories
Tierra del Fuego
tongue and groove
tongue in cheek
Trades Union Congress
Treaty of Rome
Treaty of Versailles
tropic of Cancer
tropic of Capricorn
twists and turns
Ulster Unionist Council
United Arab Emirates
United Free Church
United Reformed Church
violas da gamba
visual display unit
wattle and daub
Weston-super-Mare
wheels within wheels
whiter than white
whoops-a-daisy
Wisdom of Solomon

**MULTI-WORD**

**3 WORDS**

within living memory
within one's means
within one's sights
within sight of
within spitting distance
within striking distance
Yankee Doodle Dandy

## 7-LETTER FIRST WORD

absence of mind
Advance Australia Fair
African National Congress
against the grain
against the stream
Ancient of Days
Antigua and Barbuda
article of faith
assault and battery
balance of payments
balance of power
balance of trade
believe you me
Berwick-upon-Tweed
betwixt and between
breathe life into
breathe one's last
British Antarctic Territory
British Expeditionary Force
British National Party
British thermal unit
brittle bone disease
brother-in-law
brought to bed
bureaux de change
Carrick-on-Shannon
castles in Spain
cathode ray tube
Central African Republic
Central Criminal Court
Central Intelligence Agency
central nervous system
central processing unit
Chamber of Commerce
chapter and verse

chapter of accidents
chronic fatigue syndrome
collect one's wits
College of Arms
College of Cardinals
College of Heralds
comrade-in-arms
cooling-off period
couldn't care less
Council of Europe
Council of Trent
counsel of despair
country and western
courses of action
cushion the blow
declare an interest
declare one's interest
deliver the goods
diamond cut diamond
Doctors of Philosophy
dressed to kill
Eastern Orthodox Church
English Civil War
eyeball to eyeball
Faculty of Advocates
fathers-in-law
feather one's nest
figures of speech
flotsam and jetsam
flutter one's eyelashes
getting on for
glutton for punishment
Greater London Council
highest common factor
honours are even
hormone replacement therapy
hostage to fortune
Hudson's Bay Company
hundred per cent
Hundred Years War
Inkatha Freedom Party
Isthmus of Corinth
Isthmus of Suez
letters of credit
Library of Congress

**MULTI-WORD**    **3 WORDS**

massage one's ego
matrons of honour
measure of capacity
measure one's length
measure one's words
meeting of minds
morning-after pill
mothers-in-law
Natural History Museum
nothing for it
nothing to it
outstay one's welcome
peaches and cream
pennies from heaven
People's Liberation Army
persona non grata
plaster of Paris
poacher turned gamekeeper
Premium Savings Bond
prepare the ground
present company excepted
promise the earth
promise the moon
pushing up daisies
redress the balance
reverse the charges
rolling in it
rolling in money
running on empty
Russian Civil War
Russian Orthodox Church
Sadler's Wells Theatre
savings and loan
scratch one's head
scratch the surface
Sequoia National Park
Seventh-Day Adventist
silence is golden
sisters-in-law
sleight of hand
Society of Jesus
Spanish-American War
Spanish Civil War
Special Air Service
Special Boat Service

Special Operations Executive
statute of limitations
strange to say
strange to tell
stretch a point
stretch one's legs
stretch one's wings
suffice to say
sweeten the pill
thrills and spills
through and through
tickled to death
tighten one's belt
tighten the screw
tighten the screws
Tristan da Cunha
twiddle one's thumbs
wheeler and dealer
without a doubt
without a murmur
without further ado
without more ado
wrapped up in
written in stone

## 8-LETTER FIRST WORD

advanced subsidiary level
American Civil War
blessing in disguise
bloodied but unbowed
brothers-in-law
business as usual
Canadian Pacific Railway
Castilla-La Mancha
Chambers of Commerce
children of Israel
climbing the walls
Colossus of Rhodes
contempt of court
daughter-in-law
District of Columbia
division of labour
Dumfries and Galloway
embarras de richesses

engraved in stone
European Economic Community
European Investment Bank
European Monetary System
European Monetary Union
European Recovery Program
European Space Agency
Exchange Rate Mechanism
Festival of Britain
grievous bodily harm
hundreds and thousands
internal-combustion engine
Kingston upon Hull
lighting-up time
magnetic resonance imaging
Massacre of Glencoe
military-industrial complex
Minister of State
Minister without Portfolio
National Health Service
National Portrait Gallery
National Security Agency
National Security Council
needless to say
Official Secrets Act
overplay one's hand
overstay one's welcome
overstep the mark
parallel of latitude
personae non gratae
personal equity plan
practice makes perfect
presence of mind
prisoner of conscience
prisoner of war
recharge one's batteries
reductio ad absurdum
reinvent the wheel
relative atomic mass
renounce the world
Republic of China
Republic of Ireland
Republic of Korea
research and development
Santiago de Compostela

Santiago de Cuba
scorched earth policy
Scottish National Party
seasonal affective disorder
security of tenure
sergeant-at-arms
serjeant-at-arms
shoulder to shoulder
Southend-on-Sea
standard of living
Stockton-on-Tees
straight and narrow
Thousand Island dressing
Trentino-Alto Adige
Trinidad and Tobago
wheeling and dealing
Yosemite National Park

## 9-LETTER FIRST WORD

accidents will happen
according to schedule
attention deficit disorder
automated teller machine
backwards and forwards
commander-in-chief
corridors of power
counselor-at-law
daughters-in-law
delusions of grandeur
different ball game
expecting a baby
Financial Times index
graphical user interface
Greenwich Mean Time
irritable bowel syndrome
Lancaster House Agreement
mentioned in dispatches
Ministers of State
Ministers without Portfolio
overshoot the mark
parallels of latitude
postviral fatigue syndrome
prisoners of conscience
prisoners of war

sackcloth and ashes
secondary modern school
Secretary of State
Strategic Defense Initiative
Stratford-upon-Avon
sweetness and light
Tennessee Valley Authority
Twentieth Century Fox
Verrazano-Narrows Bridge
Voluntary Service Overseas

## 10-LETTER FIRST WORD

acceptable face of
attachment of earnings
Australian Capital Territory
battledore and shuttlecock
commanders-in-chief
confession of faith
conspiracy of silence
counselors-at-law
forewarned is forearmed
Manchester Ship Canal
peripheral nervous system
persistent vegetative state
Protestant work ethic
repetitive strain injury
Shenandoah National Park

strengthen one's hand
university of life

## 11-LETTER FIRST WORD

bicarbonate of soda
contemplate one's navel
Creutzfeldt-Jakob disease
Declaration of Independence
Declaration of Rights
familiarity breeds contempt
miscarriage of justice
Secretaries of State
Yellowstone National Park

## 12-LETTER FIRST WORD

commissioner for oaths
Commonwealth of Nations
Lamentations of Jeremiah
miscarriages of justice
Newfoundland and Labrador

## 13-LETTER FIRST WORD

contradiction in terms
International Date Line
International Monetary Fund
Staffordshire bull terrier

# 4 WORDS

## 1-LETTER FIRST WORD

I beg your pardon
I wasn't born yesterday

## 2-LETTER FIRST WORD

as bold as brass
as clear as day
as clear as mud
as common as muck

as dry as dust
as dull as dishwater
as dull as ditchwater
as easy as ABC
as good as gold
as good as new
as happy as Larry
as keen as mustard
as large as life
as nice as pie
as pleased as Punch

as proud as Punch
as regular as clockwork
as right as rain
as safe as houses
as simple as ABC
as sure as death
as the crow flies
as thick as thieves
as warm as toast
at a loose end
at a low ebb
at each other's throats
at Her Majesty's pleasure
at His Majesty's pleasure
at one fell swoop
at one's earliest convenience
at one's father's knee
at one's mother's knee
at one's own risk
at one's wits' end
at sixes and sevens
at the hands of
at the heels of
at the mercy of
at the receiving end
be one's own boss
be one's own man
be one's own woman
be the death of
be the spit of
by a long chalk
by a long shot
by fits and starts
by leaps and bounds
by return of post
by the back door
by the hands of
by the same token
de haut en bas
do a roaring trade
do oneself a mischief
do one's head in
do one's level best
do one's own thing
go a bundle on

go back to nature
go beyond a joke
go by the board
go down a bomb
go down a storm
go down in history
go down like ninepins
go down the drain
go down the pan
go down the plughole
go down the tube
go down the tubes
go for a burton
go for the burn
go for the jugular
go hot and cold
go like a bomb
go off on one
go off the rails
go one's own way
go one's separate ways
go out the window
go round in circles
go round the houses
go the extra mile
go the whole hog
go through the hoops
go through the mill
go through the motions
go through the roof
go to one's head
go to the bad
go to the barricades
go to the country
go to the dogs
go to the wall
go under the hammer
go under the knife
go up in flames
go up in smoke
go with a swing
go with the flow
go with the territory
Ho Chi Minh City
in a bad way

in a brown study
in a cleft stick
in a delicate condition
in all one's glory
in an interesting condition
in another person's shoes
in at the death
in at the kill
in black and white
in dribs and drabs
in fits and starts
in leaps and bounds
in one fell swoop
in one's bad books
in one's bad graces
in one's birthday suit
in one's black books
in one's good books
in one's good graces
in one's mind's eye
in one's own right
in one's own time
in one's right mind
in one's stockinged feet
in one's wildest dreams
in point of fact
in the course of
in the driver's seat
in the driving seat
in the event of
in the face of
in the family way
in the fast lane
in the first instance
in the first place
in the gift of
in the light of
in the long run
in the melting pot
in the name of
in the neighbourhood of
in the pudding club
in the region of
in the same boat
in the shape of

in the short run
in the teeth of
in the throes of
in the wake of
in with a shout
is the Pope Catholic
it makes no odds
it stands to reason
je ne sais quoi
my lips are sealed
no love lost between
no respecter of persons
no smoke without fire
of all the cheek
of all the nerve
of one's own accord
of the blood royal
of the first magnitude
of the first order
of the first water
on an even keel
on a par with
on a short fuse
on a silver platter
on first-name terms
on one's beam ends
on one's coat-tails
on one's high horse
on one's Jack Jones
on one's last legs
on one's own account
on one's own ground
on one's way out
on the back burner
on the heels of
on the off chance
on the one hand
on the other hand
on the part of
on the qui vive
on the receiving end
on the right track
on the stroke of
on the wrong track
so far so good

so help me God

St Kitts and Nevis

St Valentine's Day Massacre

to beat the band

to cap it all

to coin a phrase

to crown it all

to one's dying day

to one's heart's content

to tell the truth

to the bitter end

to the four winds

to the manner born

to the nth degree

to the tune of

to top it all

up a gum tree

up in the air

up to a point

up to no good

up to one's ears

up to one's elbows

up to one's eyes

up to one's neck

up to the eyeballs

up to the eyes

up to the hilt

up to the mark

up to the nines

up with the lark

we live and learn

### 3-LETTER FIRST WORD

ace in the hole

ace up one's sleeve

add insult to injury

all along the line

all bets are off

all down the line

all fingers and thumbs

all for the best

all hands on deck

all hell breaks loose

all hell broke loose

all in good time

all of a doodah

all of a piece

all of a sudden

all of a tremble

all over the place

all over the shop

all present and correct

all the same to

all things being equal

and all that jazz

Ark of the Covenant

art for art's sake

Bel and the Dragon

bow one's knee to

bow the knee to

can take a joke

cat-o'-nine-tails

cry for the moon

cry from the heart

cry one's eyes out

cut a swathe through

cut a wide swathe

cut out to be

cut the Gordian knot

cut to the bone

cut to the chase

die on one's feet

dig in one's feet

dig in one's heels

dig one's own grave

dip one's toe in

dry as a bone

eat like a bird

eat like a horse

eat one's heart out

end of one's tether

end of the line

end of the road

end of the world

eye of the wind

few and far between

fit as a fiddle

fit as a flea

fit to be tied

4 WORDS

MULTI-WORD

fly in the ointment
fly into a rage
fly into a temper
fly off the handle
fly on the wall
for auld lang syne
for better or worse
for crying out loud
for old times' sake
for the high jump
for the most part
for the time being
get a bead on
get a fix on
get a line on
get a load of
get a move on
get a wiggle on
get back to nature
get beyond a joke
get caught up in
get mixed up in
get mixed up with
get off the ground
get off the mark
get one's act together
get one's back up
get one's breath back
get one's dander up
get one's feet wet
get one's finger out
get one's fingers burnt
get one's hands dirty
get one's head around
get one's head down
get one's head round
get one's just deserts
get one's kit off
get one's own back
get one's own way
get one's skates on
get one's teeth into
get one's tongue round
get on one's nerves
get on one's wick

get on top of
get the ball rolling
get the best of
get the better of
get the goods on
get the hang of
get the measure of
get to first base
get to grips with
get under one's skin
get up one's nose
get with the program
God rest her soul
God rest his soul
God Save the King
God Save the Queen
her lips are sealed
his lips are sealed
hit a brick wall
hit a raw nerve
hit the ground running
hit the panic button
hit the right note
hit the wrong note
hot under the collar
how do you do
how the land lies
how the world wags
I'll drink to that
I'll eat my hat
it's a fair cop
it's a free country
it's Greek to me
law of diminishing returns
law of the jungle
lay at one's door
lay down one's arms
lay down the law
lay one's hands on
lay on the table
leg-of-mutton sleeve
let bygones be bygones
let oneself in for
let one's hair down
let sleeping dogs lie

let the side down
let well enough alone
lie heavy on one
lie of the land
lie through one's teeth
mad as a hatter
man in the moon
man of his word
man of many parts
man of the world
men in grey suits
men in white coats
new broom sweeps clean
new lease of life
new lease on life
nip in the bud
not a dicky bird
not a dog's chance
not a patch on
not a pretty sight
not bat an eye
not bat an eyelid
not blink an eye
not breathe a word
not care a fig
not care a hoot
not care two hoots
not for the world
not get a wink
not give a damn
not give a fig
not give a hang
not give a hoot
not give a monkey's
not give a stuff
not give two hoots
not have a clue
not have an earthly
not have a prayer
not have the faintest
not have the foggiest
not miss a trick
not move a muscle
not on your life
not on your nelly

not sleep a wink
not stand an earthly
not suffer fools gladly
not take kindly to
not the full shilling
not turn a hair
not worth the candle
off one's own bat
off the beaten track
one after the other
one and the same
one for the road
one of a kind
one of these days
one of those days
one way and another
out for one's blood
out for the count
out in the cold
out-of-body experience
out of harm's way
out of keeping with
out of line with
out of one's depth
out of one's hair
out of one's head
out of one's mind
out of one's senses
out of one's skull
out of one's tree
out of one's way
out of the ark
out of the betting
out of the blue
out of the box
out of the frame
out of the loop
out of the ordinary
out of the picture
out of the question
out of the running
out of the true
out of the way
out of the wood
out of the woods

out of this world
out on a limb
out on one's ear
par for the course
pat on the back
pay lip service to
pay one's last respects
pay out of pocket
pay through the nose
pie in the sky
pig in a poke
pig in the middle
pin one's ears back
pin one's faith on
pin one's hopes on
pit of one's stomach
pit of the stomach
pit one's wits against
put a damper on
put a foot wrong
put a lid on
put a premium on
put a stopper on
put back the clock
put in an appearance
put in one's twopenn'orth
put into one's head
put one over on
put one's back into
put one's back up
put one's eyes out
put one's feet up
put one's finger on
put one's foot down
put one's hands on
put one's hands up
put one's hand to
put one's mind to
put one's name down
put one's oar in
put one's seal on
put one's shirt on
put on the map
put on the ritz
put on the table

put our heads together
put out to grass
put out to sea
put out to tender
put pen to paper
put the arm on
put the boot in
put the clocks back
put the clocks forward
put the finger on
put the flag out
put the flags out
put the frighteners on
put their heads together
put the kibosh on
put the kybosh on
put the lid on
put the make on
put the mockers on
put the moves on
put the record straight
put the screws on
put the seal on
put the skids under
put the squeeze on
put the stopper on
put the wind up
put through its paces
put to the sword
put to the test
put to the torch
put up a fight
put up the shutters
put your hands together
put your heads together
rag-and-bone man
ram down one's throat
Río de la Plata
rub of the green
run a tight ship
run into the sand
run off one's feet
run-of-the-mill
run out of gas
run out of steam

run round in circles
run up the flagpole
São Tomé and Príncipe
see eye to eye
see the back of
set one's cap at
set one's face against
set one's hand to
set one's heart on
set one's hopes on
set one's mind to
set one's seal on
set one's sights on
set out one's stall
set pen to paper
set the ball rolling
set the record straight
set the seal on
set the stage for
set the world alight
sit at one's feet
sit below the salt
sit on one's tail
sit on the fence
sit on the stomach
six of the best
sky is the limit
sow one's wild oats
sow the seed of
sow the seeds of
ten out of ten
the life of Riley
tip of an iceberg
tip of the iceberg
tip the scales at
Tom, Dick, and Harry
too clever by half
too close for comfort
top of the morning
top of the tree
try one's hand at
try on for size
two of a kind
two-up two-down
War of American Independence

War of Jenkins's Ear
way of the world
wet behind the ears
wet the baby's head
you and whose army
you live and learn

**4**-LETTER FIRST WORD

Acts of the Apostles
Arts and Crafts Movement
away with the fairies
back at square one
back in the day
back of an envelope
back of one's mind
back the wrong horse
back to square one
bald as a coot
ball-and-socket joint
ball of the foot
ball of the thumb
bang for one's buck
bang people's heads together
bang the drum for
beam in one's eye
beat about the bush
beat a hasty retreat
beat swords into ploughshares
beat the drum for
beat the pants off
bend the knee to
bent out of shape
best of both worlds
best of the bunch
bite at the cherry
bite one's head off
blot on one's escutcheon
blow a hole in
blow away the cobwebs
blow hot and cold
blow one's brains out
blow one's socks off
blow the whistle on
bolt from the blue

born out of wedlock

boys will be boys

buck up one's ideas

burn the midnight oil

burn to a crisp

call it a day

calm before the storm

can't take a joke

Cape of Good Hope

card up one's sleeve

cash in one's chips

cast one's eye over

cast pearls before swine

cast the first stone

chip on one's shoulder

clip the wings of

cock and bull story

cock a snook at

cock of the walk

come back to earth

come into its own

come into the world

come on the scene

come rain or shine

come to a head

come to grips with

come to no harm

come to one's senses

come to terms with

come under the hammer

come with the territory

cool as a cucumber

corn on the cob

damn with faint praise

dead as a dodo

dead as a doornail

dead in the water

dead on one's feet

dead to the world

deaf as a post

dear to one's heart

Dome of the Rock

don't bet on it

don't give houseroom to

don't hold your breath

don't mince one's words

down in the dumps

down in the mouth

down on one's luck

down to the ground

down to the wire

drag through the mud

draw a bead on

draw a veil over

draw in one's horns

draw the line at

draw the short straw

drop in the bucket

drop in the ocean

drop into one's lap

dyed in the wool

earn an honest penny

East Riding of Yorkshire

easy on the ear

easy on the eye

edge of the envelope

eyes out on stalks

fact of the matter

fall between two stools

fall into one's lap

fall on deaf ears

fall on one's feet

fall on stony ground

fall through the net

fate worse than death

feel a million dollars

feel the pulse of

fine kettle of fish

fire in one's belly

fire in the belly

fish out of water

flat as a pancake

flea in one's ear

flog a dead horse

foam at the mouth

foot-and-mouth disease

foul one's own nest

four of a kind

from A to B

from A to Z

from bad to worse
from cover to cover
from day to day
from door to door
from hand to mouth
from head to foot
from head to toe
from pillar to post
from rags to riches
from side to side
from stem to stern
from the horse's mouth
from the word go
from time to time
from top to bottom
from top to toe
gain the upper hand
gift of the gab
gird up one's loins
give it a rest
give me a break
give the game away
give the lie to
give the nod to
give the show away
give up the ghost
grin and bear it
hail-fellow-well-met
hair of the dog
hang by a thread
hard act to follow
hard nut to crack
hard put to it
hard row to hoe
have a down on
have a feel for
have a go at
have a mind to
have an eye for
have an eye to
have another think coming
have a pop at
have a punt at
have a screw loose
have a thick skin

have a thing about
have a thin skin
have a thin time
have a tin ear
have a way with
have got it bad
have got it made
have got no idea
have had its day
have had one's chips
have had one's day
have it both ways
have it in for
have nerves of steel
have nothing to lose
have no truck with
have no use for
have one's eye on
have one's hands full
have one's hands tied
have one's own way
have one too many
have on the brain
have seen better days
have shot one's bolt
have swallowed a dictionary
have the better of
have the drop on
have the goods on
have the hots for
have the last laugh
have the legs of
have the measure of
have the upper hand
have the wind up
have two left feet
have what it takes
head and shoulders above
hear a pin drop
here we go again
hide or hair of
high as a kite
high days and holidays
hold a brief for
hold all the aces

hold all the cards
hold no brief for
hold one's head high
hold the purse strings
hole in the heart
jack-in-the-box
jack of all trades
jobs for the boys
jump down one's throat
jump into bed with
just around the corner
keep a check on
keep a clean sheet
keep a lid on
keep a lookout for
keep an eye on
keep an eye open
keep an eye out
keep a tab on
keep at arm's length
keep one's chin up
keep one's end up
keep one's eye in
keep one's eye on
keep one's eyes peeled
keep one's eyes skinned
keep one's fingers crossed
keep one's hand in
keep one's hands clean
keep one's head down
keep one's mouth shut
keep one's nose clean
keep one's own counsel
keep one's powder dry
keep the ball rolling
keep the lid on
keep the pot boiling
keep under one's hat
keep your hair on
keep your pecker up
keep your shirt on
kick against the pricks
kick in the pants
kick in the teeth
kick over the traces

kick up a fuss
kick up a row
kick up a stink
kick up one's heels
kick up the backside
kill the fatted calf
kiss and make up
lady of the night
land of the free
land on one's feet
last but not least
late in the day
late in the game
lead a merry dance
lead from the front
lead in one's pencil
lead with one's chin
leap in the dark
leap to the eye
left at the post
left holding the baby
left holding the bag
lick and a promise
life of the party
lift the lid off
lift the lid on
like a drowned rat
like a headless chicken
like a scalded cat
like death warmed up
like nothing on earth
like watching paint dry
lily of the valley
line in the sand
line of least resistance
live and let live
live by one's wits
live for the moment
live in the past
live like a king
live like a lord
live like a queen
live off the land
live on one's nerves
long in the tooth

long time no see
look a million dollars
look before you leap
look the other way
look to one's laurels
love-in-a-mist
luck of the draw
lull before the storm
lump in the throat
made of sterner stuff
make a beeline for
make a bolt for
make a break for
make a clean sweep
make a fool of
make a fuss of
make a fuss over
make a game of
make a go of
make a hash of
make a hole in
make a Horlicks of
make a joke of
make a meal of
make a mockery of
make a mock of
make a move on
make an example of
make an issue of
make a play for
make a point of
make a present of
make a virtue of
make both ends meet
make capital out of
make great play of
make great play with
make heavy weather of
make it hot for
make light work of
make no bones about
make one's blood boil
make one's blood curdle
make one's flesh crawl
make one's flesh creep

make one's hackles rise
make one's hair curl
make one's head swell
make one's skin crawl
make one's toes curl
make short work of
make the acquaintance of
make the best of
make the most of
make the welkin ring
make things hot for
make up one's mind
meat and drink to
meat in the sandwich
meet a sticky end
melt in the mouth
milk of human kindness
mind one's own business
mote in one's eye
move heaven and earth
move up a gear
move with the times
much of a muchness
nail in the coffin
name of the game
name to conjure with
near to the mark
neck of the woods
none the worse for
Nord-Pas-de-Calais
once and for all
once upon a time
one's back is turned
one's blood is up
one's days are numbered
one's ears are burning
one's flesh and blood
one's luck is in
one's name is mud
one's nearest and dearest
one's number is up
one's pride and joy
one's star is rising
only game in town
only have eyes for

only time will tell
over and done with
over-egg the pudding
over my dead body
pain in the neck
pare to the bone
part and parcel of
part of the furniture
pass one's eye over
pass on the baton
pass the hat round
pâté de foie gras
path of least resistance
pave the way for
Pays de la Loire
pick of the bunch
pick one's feet up
pick up the baton
pick up the pieces
pick up the slack
pick up the tab
pick up the threads
play a lone hand
play by the rules
play fast and loose
play hard to get
play into one's hands
play it by ear
play it for laughs
play one's cards right
play the devil with
play the old soldier
play to the gallery
poke one's nose into
poor as church mice
poor little rich boy
poor little rich girl
Port of London Authority
pour cold water on
prop up the bar
pull a fast one
pull in one's horns
pull one's finger out
pull one's head in
pull one's socks up

pull the other one
push the boat out
push the panic button
rain cats and dogs
rain on one's parade
rake over old coals
rake over the ashes
read between the lines
read the Riot Act
reap the fruits of
reds under the bed
rest on one's laurels
ring down the curtain
ring up the curtain
rise from the ashes
rise from the ranks
rise through the ranks
rise to the bait
rise to the occasion
rise with the lark
rise with the sun
roll in the hay
roll in the sack
roll-on roll-off
roll up one's sleeves
roll with the punches
roof of the world
rule of the road
safe pair of hands
sail near the wind
salt of the earth
sell like hot cakes
ship of the line
shot across the bows
shot in the arm
shot in the dark
sick and tired of
sick as a parrot
sign of the cross
sign of the times
sing a different song
sing a different tune
sing for one's supper
sing the praises of
sins of the flesh

slap in the face
slap on the back
slap on the wrist
slip of the pen
slip of the tongue
slip through the net
slow off the mark
slow on the uptake
snap one's head off
snug as a bug
stab in the dark
step into one's shoes
step into the breach
step on one's toes
step on the gas
step out of line
suck it and see
swim against the tide
swim with the tide
tail wags the dog
take a back seat
take a chance on
take a fancy to
take a heavy toll
take a pop at
take a punt at
take a rain check
take a running jump
take a shine to
take in good part
take in one's stride
take it for granted
take it in turns
take it out of
take it out on
take one's breath away
take the chequered flag
take the edge off
take the gloves off
take the King's shilling
take the lid off
take the long view
take the measure of
take the part of
take the place of

take the pulse of
take the Queen's shilling
take the shine off
take to one's bed
take to one's heels
take up the baton
take up the cudgels
take up the gauntlet
take up the running
take up the slack
talk a blue streak
talk of the devil
talk out of turn
talk through one's hat
tear one's hair out
tell its own story
tell its own tale
tell t'other from which
thin as a rake
thin on the ground
till hell freezes over
time-and-motion study
time and time again
time of one's life
toad-in-the-hole
trip the light fantastic
turn a blind eye
turn a deaf ear
turn and turn about
turn an honest penny
turn back the clock
turn in one's grave
turn of the screw
turn one's back on
turn one's hand to
turn on one's heel
turn on the charm
turn the other cheek
turn up one's toes
vote with one's feet
want no truck with
Wars of the Roses
wash one's hands of
weak at the knees
well I never did

what the doctor ordered
wide of the mark
will-o'-the-wisp
wipe the floor with
wipe the slate clean
wise after the event
with all guns blazing
with all one's heart
with all one's might
with an eye to
with a view to
with brass knobs on
with might and main
with one eye on
with one's bare hands
with the gloves off
with tongue in cheek
wolf in sheep's clothing
word on the street
word to the wise
work like a charm
work like a Trojan

## 5-LETTER FIRST WORD

after one's own heart
after the fashion of
ahead of its time
ahead of one's time
ahead of the game
apple of one's eye
armed to the teeth
arrow in the quiver
birds and the bees
Black Hole of Calcutta
blast from the past
blind as a bat
break the back of
bring-and-buy sale
bring back to earth
bring home the bacon
bring pressure to bear
bring the house down
bring to its knees
bring to the table

bring up the rear
broad in the beam
broth of a boy
brown as a berry
burnt to a cinder
carry all before one
carry a torch for
catch in the act
champ at the bit
chase one's own tail
cheap at the price
clean as a whistle
clean bill of health
clean up one's act
clear as a bell
clear away the cobwebs
clear the name of
close but no cigar
close to one's heart
close to the bone
close to the mark
Court of St James's
crack of the whip
crème de la crème
cruel to be kind
dance to one's tune
drink a toast to
drink like a fish
drive a hard bargain
drive a wedge between
drunk as a lord
drunk as a skunk
enter into the spirit
every man for himself
every now and again
every now and then
feast one's eyes on
fight a losing battle
fight fire with fire
fight tooth and nail
first past the post
flash in the pan
force down one's throat
fresh as a daisy
froth at the mouth

ghost at the feast

ghost in the machine

grand old man of

Grand Prix de Paris

great and the good

Great St Bernard Pass

Great Wall of China

green about the gills

green around the gills

green at the gills

grind to a halt

grist to one's mill

grist to the mill

happy as a sandboy

house divided cannot stand

icing on the cake

jewel in one's crown

jewel in the crown

joker in the pack

knock one's block off

knock one's socks off

knock people's heads together

knock the socks off

laugh like a drain

laugh one's head off

laugh out of court

laugh up one's sleeve

leave in the dust

leave in the lurch

leave no stone unturned

leave well enough alone

light a fire under

light as a feather

light of one's life

means to an end

money for old rope

Monty Python's Flying Circus

music of the spheres

music to one's ears

nasty bit of work

nasty piece of work

never darken one's door

nudge nudge wink wink

nutty as a fruitcake

opium of the masses

opium of the people

Order of the Bath

order of the day

Order of the Garter

Order of the Thistle

paint the Forth Bridge

paint the town red

penny for your thoughts

piggy in the middle

place a premium on

place in the sun

plain as a pikestaff

point of no return

power behind the throne

price on one's head

prick up one's ears

punch above one's weight

punch one's lights out

putty in one's hands

quake in one's boots

quake in one's shoes

quick as a flash

quick off the mark

quick on the draw

quick on the trigger

quick on the uptake

quiet as a lamb

quiet as a mouse

quiet as the grave

reach for the stars

rough around the edges

Royal Academy of Arts

Royal Canadian Mounted Police

Royal Society of Arts

sands are running out

Santa Fé de Bogotá

saved by the bell

shake in one's boots

shake in one's shoes

shake like a leaf

share and share alike

sharp as a tack

shoot from the hip

shoot one's mouth off

shout from the rooftops

MULTI-WORD | 4 WORDS

sight for sore eyes
sleep like a log
sleep like a top
sleep of the just
slice of the action
smack in the eye
smack in the face
small of the back
smell to high heaven
smoke like a chimney
sober as a judge
sound a note of
sound as a bell
speak of the devil
speak out of turn
speak the same language
stand on one's dignity
stand out a mile
start the ball rolling
state of the art
steal a march on
stick in one's throat
stick-in-the-mud
stick one's neck out
stick one's oar in
stick out a mile
stick to one's guns
stick to one's knitting
stiff as a board
still waters run deep
sting in the tail
stink to high heaven
storm in a teacup
straw in the wind
swear like a trooper
sweep under the carpet
thank one's lucky stars
thick as a plank
thick as two planks
thick on the ground
think nothing of it
think on one's feet
think outside the box

think the world of
thorn in one's flesh
thorn in one's side
those were the days
three of a kind
throw cold water on
throw down the gauntlet
throw in the sponge
throw in the towel
throw of the dice
throw one's hand in
throw one's weight about
throw one's weight around
throw the book at
throw the first stone
throw up one's hands
thumb one's nose at
touch a raw nerve
touch of the sun
tough act to follow
tough nut to crack
tread in one's footsteps
tread on one's toes
treat with kid gloves
twist in the wind
under lock and key
under one's own steam
under the auspices of
under the heel of
until hell freezes over
until one's dying day
upset the apple cart
viper in one's bosom
voice in the wilderness
water on the brain
water under the bridge
what's in a name
white as a sheet
whole new ball game
woman of her word
woman of the world
world and his wife
world is one's oyster

**6**-LETTER FIRST WORD

answer the description of
appear on the scene
arrive on the scene
asleep at the wheel
batten down the hatches
Battle of Aboukir Bay
Battle of El Alamein
Battle of Little Bighorn
Battle of Marston Moor
Battle of the Atlantic
Battle of the Boyne
Battle of the Bulge
Battle of the Nile
Battle of the Somme
Battle of Vimy Ridge
Battle of Wounded Knee
before one's very eyes
better dead than red
better red than dead
better safe than sorry
beyond one's wildest dreams
bitter pill to swallow
bounce an idea off
breath of fresh air
bright as a button
burned at the stake
called to the Bar
cherry on the cake
cuckoo in the nest
devil's in the detail
easier said than done
emerge from the ashes
famous for fifteen minutes
fiddle while Rome burns
firing on all cylinders
follow in one's footsteps
follow in one's steps
grease the palm of
handle with kid gloves
knight in shining armour
knight of the road
Leader of the House
League of Arab States

lesser of two evils
little bird told me
little love lost between
Little St Bernard Pass
little to choose between
living on borrowed time
Lloyd's Register of Shipping
loosen the purse strings
lowest of the low
Master of the Rolls
middle-of-the-road
monkey on one's back
mutton dressed as lamb
nature of the beast
needle in a haystack
object of the exercise
paddle one's own canoe
patter of tiny feet
pipped at the post
plough a lonely furrow
plough one's own furrow
preach to the converted
pretty as a picture
pretty kettle of fish
prince of the blood
Prince of Wales Island
profit and loss account
remain to be seen
riding for a fall
rushed off one's feet
school of hard knocks
silent as the grave
smooth one's ruffled feathers
sooner rather than later
splice the main brace
spread oneself too thin
strain at the leash
strike a blow against
strike a blow at
strike a blow for
strike a discordant note
strike a note of
strike the right note
strike the wrong note
stroke of good luck

sudden infant death syndrome
teeter on the brink
teeter on the edge
there's honour among thieves
there's safety in numbers
thrill of the chase
tricks of the trade
Valley of the Kings
weapon of mass destruction
weight off one's mind
wither on the vine
within an ace of
within an inch of
within a whisker of
Yeoman of the Guard

## 7-LETTER FIRST WORD

Admiral of the Fleet
against one's better judgement
beggars can't be choosers
believe it or not
benefit of the doubt
breathe down one's neck
breathe new life into
bulging at the seams
castles in the air
charity begins at home
citizen of the world
cracked up to be
feather in one's cap
feather one's own nest
Federal Republic of Germany
fifteen minutes of fame
filling in the sandwich
flavour of the month
fortune favours the brave
friends in high places
Friends of the Earth
hanging over one's head
harmony of the spheres
jumping up and down
Justice of the Peace
licence to print money
looking over one's shoulder

neither fish nor fowl
neither here nor there
nothing of the kind
nothing of the sort
nothing succeeds like success
parting of the ways
People's Republic of China
pushing up the daisies
quarter of an hour
receive one's just deserts
rewrite the record books
rolling in the aisles
savings and loan association
spanner in the works
Station of the Cross
suffice it to say
thereby hangs a tale
through the back door
through thick and thin
tighten the purse strings
tremble like a leaf
twinkle in one's eye
watched pot never boils
watches of the night
whistle in the dark
whistle in the wind
without batting an eye
without batting an eyelid
without fear or favour
without let or hindrance
wonders will never cease
wouldn't harm a fly
wouldn't hurt a fly

## 8-LETTER FIRST WORD

accident waiting to happen
bouncing off the walls
bursting at the seams
consider on its merits
cruising for a bruising
dialogue of the deaf
dispense with one's services
downhill all the way
European Court of Justice

grateful for small mercies
Minister of the Crown
practise what one preaches
princess of the blood
Provence-Alpes-Côte d'Azur
shoulder to cry on
skeleton at the feast
skeleton in the cupboard
standing on one's head
straight as a die
straight from the shoulder
strictly for the birds
stubborn as a mule
survival of the fittest
thankful for small mercies
Thousand and One Nights
tomorrow is another day
Victoria and Albert Museum

### 9-LETTER FIRST WORD

accessary after the fact
accessary before the fact
accessory after the fact

accessory before the fact
beginning of the end
curiosity killed the cat
different kettle of fish
exception proves the rule
Hashemite Kingdom of Jordan
Religious Society of Friends
snowball's chance in hell

### 10-LETTER FIRST WORD

Chancellor of the Exchequer
economical with the truth
frightened of one's shadow
Portuguese man-of-war

### 11-LETTER FIRST WORD

conspicuous by one's absence

### 12-LETTER FIRST WORD

Metropolitan Museum of Art

# 5 WORDS

### 1-LETTER FIRST WORD

I should be so lucky

### 2-LETTER FIRST WORD

as a matter of fact
as bald as a coot
as blind as a bat
as bright as a button
as brown as a berry
as clean as a whistle
as clear as a bell
as cool as a cucumber
as dead as a dodo
as dead as a doornail

as deaf as a post
as drunk as a lord
as drunk as a skunk
as dry as a bone
as fit as a fiddle
as fit as a flea
as flat as a pancake
as fresh as a daisy
as God is my witness
as good as one's word
as happy as a sandboy
as high as a kite
as light as a feather
as long as one's arm
as mad as a hatter
as nutty as a fruitcake

as old as the hills
as plain as a pikestaff
as poor as church mice
as pretty as a picture
as quick as a flash
as quiet as a lamb
as quiet as a mouse
as quiet as the grave
as rare as hen's teeth
as scarce as hen's teeth
as sick as a parrot
as silent as the grave
as sober as a judge
as sound as a bell
as straight as a die
as stubborn as a mule
as thick as a plank
as thin as a rake
as white as a sheet
at a rate of knots
at one's beck and call
be-all and end-all
be in on the act
be that as it may
by appointment to the Queen
by fair means or foul
by hook or by crook
go all round the houses
go down in the world
go down the wrong way
go from strength to strength
go off the deep end
go on one's merry way
go out like a light
go out of one's way
go out of the window
go to rack and ruin
go up in the world
he should be so lucky
he who hesitates is lost
if you'll excuse my French
if you'll pardon my French
in all one's born days
in a manner of speaking
in any shape or form

in front of one's eyes
in one's heart of hearts
in one's own good time
in one's own sweet time
in the fullness of time
in the lap of luxury
in the line of duty
in the nature of things
in the nick of time
in words of one syllable
is the Pope a Catholic
it takes two to tango
my heart bleeds for you
no news is good news
no rest for the wicked
no two ways about it
on a hiding to nothing
on the outside looking in
on the right side of
on the up and up
on the wrong side of
on top of the world
St Vincent and the Grenadines
to all intents and purposes
to whom it may concern
up hill and down dale
up to one's old tricks

### 3-LETTER FIRST WORD

add fuel to the fire
all in a day's work
all mouth and no trousers
all over bar the shouting
all roads lead to Rome
any port in a storm
bad penny always turns up
bad taste in the mouth
can hold a candle to
cut from the same cloth
cut off at the pass
die with one's boots on
err on the right side
err on the side of
far from the madding crowd

fat is in the fire
fly in the face of
for better or for worse
for the fun of it
for the hell of it
for the life of me
for the love of God
for the love of Mike
get a rise out of
get a word in edgeways
get down to brass tacks
get in on the act
get it in the neck
get it off one's chest
get no change out of
get the worst of it
get to the bottom of
hot on the heels of
how the other half lives
it's all Greek to me
lay it on the line
lay it on with a trowel
let it all hang out
let slip through one's fingers
mad as a March hare
new kid on the block
not a hope in hell
not by a long chalk
not by a long shot
not do things by halves
not for love or money
not give a tinker's curse
not give a tinker's damn
not have the foggiest idea
not hear the end of
not in one's right mind
not know where to look
not know where to turn
not long for this world
not much love lost between
not one's cup of tea
not to be sneezed at
not to be sniffed at
one good turn deserves another
one in the eye for

pot calling the kettle black
put a brave face on
put a sock in it
put ideas into one's head
put one's best foot forward
put one's foot in it
put one's house in order
put on one's thinking cap
put out of one's mind
put the lid on it
put two and two together
put up or shut up
put words into one's mouth
red in tooth and claw
red rag to a bull
rob Peter to pay Paul
rub salt into the wound
run before one can walk
run oneself into the ground
see the light of day
set one's house in order
set one's teeth on edge
set the wheels in motion
set the world on fire
she should be so lucky
sit up and take notice
sun is over the yardarm
too big for one's boots
two sheets to the wind
War of the Austrian Succession
War of the Spanish Succession
you ain't seen nothing yet
you bet your bottom dollar
you can't win them all
you could have fooled me
you reap what you sow
you should be so lucky

## 4-LETTER FIRST WORD

all's well that ends well
army marches on its stomach
back to the drawing board
ball is in your court
best thing since sliced bread

blow out of the water
blow up in one's face
bolt out of the blue
call a spade a spade
can't hold a candle to
chip off the old block
come apart at the seams
come back down to earth
come down in stair rods
come hell or high water
come out in the wash
come out of the woodwork
come out smelling of roses
come to a sticky end
come up in the world
come up smelling of roses
come up with the goods
dead from the neck up
don't know one is born
even a worm will turn
fall apart at the seams
fall flat on one's face
feel like a million dollars
fine feathers make fine birds
fine words butter no parsnips
give a wide berth to
give it one's best shot
give one's eye teeth for
give one's right arm for
give the devil his due
good wine needs no bush
grin like a Cheshire cat
hang one's head in shame
have a heart of gold
have a mountain to climb
have an axe to grind
have ants in one's pants
have a soft spot for
have bats in one's belfry
have bats in the belfry
have been around the block
have bigger fish to fry
have blood on one's hands
have eyes like a hawk
have had a good innings

have one over the eight
have one's guts for garters
have one's head screwed on
have one's wits about one
have one's work cut out
have other fish to fry
have seen it all before
have stars in one's eyes
head off at the pass
head over heels in love
jump out of one's skin
just what the doctor ordered
keep a tight rein on
keep a weather eye on
keep body and soul together
keep one's head above water
keep one's wits about one
keep up with the Joneses
knee-high to a grasshopper
life in the fast lane
like a dose of salts
like a duck to water
like a knife through butter
like a ton of bricks
like peas in a pod
like putty in one's hands
live out of a suitcase
live to fight another day
live to tell the tale
long arm of the law
look like a million dollars
look on the black side
look on the bright side
lose money hand over fist
make a day of it
make a dead set at
make a drama out of
make a fight of it
make a fool of oneself
make a name for oneself
make an ass of oneself
make an exhibition of oneself
make an honest woman of
make a night of it
make a pig of oneself

make a pig's ear of
make a run for it
make a spectacle of oneself
make head or tail of
make money hand over fist
make one's blood run cold
make one's life a misery
make up for lost time
many hands make light work
mind one's Ps and Qs
more power to your elbow
move in for the kill
neat as a new pin
nine times out of ten
once in a blue moon
one's best bib and tucker
ours not to reason why
pass the time of day
poor as a church mouse
pour oil on troubled waters
pull out all the stops
sail close to the wind
spit in the face of
stew in one's own juice
sure as eggs is eggs
take a dim view of
take a poor view of
take a rise out of
take it on the chin
take it or leave it
take leave of one's senses
take one's hat off to
take one's name in vain
take one's word for it
take the easy way out
take the stuffing out of
take time by the forelock
talk nineteen to the dozen
tell it like it is
tell that to the marines
that will be the day
thin end of the wedge
tied to one's apron strings
till death us do part
till the cows come home

turn one's nose up at
turn over a new leaf
turn over in one's grave
walk before one can run
what goes around comes around
what planet are you on
when one's ship comes in
when push comes to shove
when the balloon goes up
when the chips are down
with a fine-tooth comb
with a pinch of salt
with egg on one's face
work oneself into the ground
wrap oneself in the flag

## 5-LETTER FIRST WORD

blood is thicker than water
brick short of a load
bring back down to earth
bring down the curtain on
catch one's death of cold
chief cook and bottle-washer
clean as a new pin
close in for the kill
could hold a candle to
cross one's palm with silver
devil looks after his own
dirty end of the stick
early bird catches the worm
empty vessels make most noise
empty vessels make most sound
every dog has his day
every dog has its day
every man has his price
every trick in the book
fight like cat and dog
game's not worth the candle
here's mud in your eye
hoist by one's own petard
knock into a cocked hat
knock the stuffing out of
leave much to be desired
march to a different drummer

march to a different tune
nasty taste in the mouth
never hear the end of
never the twain shall meet
Order of the British Empire
other side of the coin
paint oneself into a corner
penny wise and pound foolish
pride comes before a fall
pride goes before a fall
rough edge of one's tongue
shape of things to come
shape up or ship out
shoot oneself in the foot
spend money hand over fist
sprat to catch a mackerel
stand on one's own feet
stand the test of time
stand up and be counted
there are no flies on
thick as two short planks
three sheets to the wind
throw caution to the wind
throw caution to the winds
throw good money after bad
throw in one's lot with
Uncle Tom Cobley and all
Union of Serbia and Montenegro
until death us do part
water off a duck's back
where the fancy takes one
where there's muck there's brass
where there's smoke there's fire
World Wide Fund for Nature
worth one's weight in gold
wrong side of the tracks

## 6-LETTER FIRST WORD

answer to the name of
beauty is only skin-deep
before you can say knife
before you could say knife
beware of Greeks bearing gifts

bitter taste in the mouth
bright-eyed and bushy-tailed
caught in a cleft stick
Charge of the Light Brigade
credit where credit is due
Empire State of the South
knight on a white charger
listen with half an ear
matter of life and death
oldest trick in the book
scales fall from one's eyes
scared out of one's wits
stitch in time saves nine
theirs not to reason why
there's no accounting for taste
there's one born every minute
unable to believe one's ears
unable to believe one's eyes
unable to hear oneself think

## 7-LETTER FIRST WORD

barking up the wrong tree
couldn't hold a candle to
dressed like a dog's dinner
honesty is the best policy
leopard can't change its spots
morning after the night before
nothing to write home about
rolling stone gathers no moss
shuffle off this mortal coil
warning shot across the bows
wouldn't be caught dead in
wouldn't be caught dead with
wouldn't be seen dead in
wouldn't be seen dead with
writing is on the wall

## 8-LETTER FIRST WORD

European Court of Human Rights
frighten the life out of
handsome is as handsome does

### 10-LETTER FIRST WORD

frightened out of one's wits
prevention is better than cure

### 11-LETTER FIRST WORD

Englishman's home is his castle

# 6 WORDS

### 2-LETTER FIRST WORD

as clean as a new pin
as mad as a March hare
as neat as a new pin
as poor as a church mouse
as sure as eggs is eggs
as thick as two short planks
at the bottom of the heap
at the drop of a hat
at the end of the day
at the top of the heap
be all things to all men
be all things to all people
by the seat of one's pants
by the skin of one's teeth
by the sweat of one's brow
go down like a lead balloon
go to hell in a handbasket
in the blink of an eye
in the cold light of day
in the heat of the moment
in the land of the living
in the lap of the gods
in the twinkling of an eye
in the wink of an eye
it never rains but it pours
no room to swing a cat
on a wing and a prayer
on the crest of a wave
on the edge of one's seat
on the horns of a dilemma
on the side of the angels
on the spur of the moment
on the tip of one's tongue

to be on the safe side
to cut a long story short
to make a long story short
up the creek without a paddle

### 3-LETTER FIRST WORD

add another string to one's bow
all fur coat and no knickers
all that glitters is not gold
big fish in a small pond
cat may look at a king
err on the side of caution
fed up to the back teeth
get a foot in the door
get in on the ground floor
get into the swing of things
get off on the right foot
get off on the wrong foot
get one's feet under the table
get one's knickers in a twist
get the bit between one's teeth
get the show on the road
has the cat got your tongue
hit the nail on the head
it's no skin off my nose
lay one's cards on the table
lay one's head on the block
not do a stroke of work
not take no for an answer
off the top of one's head
old enough to be one's father
old enough to be one's mother
one cannot live by bread alone
out of a clear blue sky

pen is mightier than the sword
put a gun to one's head
put a spoke in one's wheel
put one's cards on the table
put one's finger in the dyke
put one's foot in one's mouth
put one's hand in one's pocket
put one's head in a noose
put one's head on the block
put one's nose out of joint
put one's shoulder to the wheel
put the cart before the horse
put the cat among the pigeons
put the tin lid on it
see a man about a dog
see the error of one's ways
set the cat among the pigeons
tar people with the same brush
too many cooks spoil the broth
two can play at that game
two heads are better than one
two wrongs don't make a right
you can bet your bottom dollar

**4-LETTER FIRST WORD**

all's fair in love and war
beat a path to one's door
bite the hand that feeds one
boot is on the other foot
burn the candle at both ends
bury one's head in the sand
cast one's bread upon the waters
cost an arm and a leg
drag oneself up by one's bootstraps
draw a line in the sand
easy as falling off a log
from the bottom of one's heart
full of the joys of spring
give as good as one gets
have a bee in one's bonnet
have a bun in the oven
have a finger in every pie
have a foot in both camps
have a foot in the door

have a frog in one's throat
have a mind of one's own
have an ear to the ground
have another string to one's bow
have a plum in one's mouth
have a run for one's money
have a tiger by the tail
have a whale of a time
have a word in one's ear
have eyes bigger than one's belly
have eyes bigger than one's stomach
have gone out with the ark
have had a drop too much
have many irons in the fire
have many strings to one's bow
have one foot in the grave
have one's feet on the ground
have one's finger on the pulse
have one's fingers in the till
have one's hand in the till
have one's heart in one's mouth
have one's nose in a book
have other irons in the fire
have the bit between one's teeth
hide one's light under a bushel
hold a gun to one's head
home is where the heart is
honi soit qui mal y pense
iron fist in a velvet glove
jump in at the deep end
keep an ear to the ground
keep one's eye on the ball
keep one's feet on the ground
keep one's finger on the pulse
keep one's nose to the grindstone
keep one's side of the bargain
keep the show on the road
keep the wolf from the door
kill two birds with one stone
life and soul of the party
like a bat out of hell
like a bull at a gate
like a cat on hot bricks
like a dog with two tails
like a hot knife through butter

like a lamb to the slaughter
like a moth to the flame
like shooting fish in a barrel
like two peas in a pod
long and the short of it
make a clean breast of it
make hay while the sun shines
make one's hair stand on end
many happy returns of the day
pull oneself up by one's bootstraps
pull the wool over one's eyes
rule with a rod of iron
sell one's soul to the devil
sing from the same hymn sheet
sort the wheat from the chaff
take a load off one's feet
take a load off one's mind
take a trip down memory lane
take a walk down memory lane
take it into one's head to
take one's courage in both hands
take one's eye off the ball
take one's life in one's hands
take the bit between one's teeth
take the bull by the horns
take the load off one's feet
take the rough with the smooth
take with a grain of salt
take with a pinch of salt
trim one's sails to the wind
turn the knife in the wound
turn to ashes in one's mouth
wake up and smell the coffee
warm the cockles of one's heart
wash one's dirty linen in public
when all is said and done
wish is father to the thought
with one's back to the wall

with one's head in the clouds
with one's heart in one's boots
work one's fingers to the bone

### 5-LETTER FIRST WORD

beard the lion in his den
every cloud has a silver lining
faint heart never won fair lady
leave a lot to be desired
stand on one's own two feet
stand out like a sore thumb
start off on the right foot
start off on the wrong foot
stick out like a sore thumb
there will be hell to pay
throw one's hat into the ring

### 6-LETTER FIRST WORD

chance would be a fine thing
scrape the bottom of the barrel
square peg in a round hole
strike while the iron is hot
within an inch of one's life

### 7-LETTER FIRST WORD

brevity is the soul of wit
dressed up like a dog's dinner
variety is the spice of life
wouldn't say boo to a goose

### 8-LETTER FIRST WORD

separate the men from the boys